SOCIAL THEORY AND
SOCIAL PRACTICE

Social Theory and Social Practice

An Exploration of Experience

P FORD

Professor Emeritus
University of Southampton

SHANNON · IRELAND

SBN 7165 0500 2

Irish University Press Shannon Ireland
DUBLIN CORK BELFAST LONDON NEW YORK
Captain T M MacGlinchey Publisher

PRINTED IN THE REPUBLIC OF IRELAND

TO
G F

WORKS ON PARLIAMENTARY PAPERS

by Professor P and Mrs G Ford

1 Hansard's Catalogue and Breviate of Parliamentary Papers, 1696–1834

2 Select List of British Parliamentary Papers, 1833–1899

3 A Breviate of Parliamentary Papers, 1900–1916

4 A Breviate of Parliamentary Papers, 1917–1939

PREFACE

This book may be regarded as a sequel to the Breviates of Parliamentary Papers and arises partly out of the study of the hundreds of reports undertaken for those works. It is an exploration of our experience in efforts at conscious social planning, of the relationship between social theory and social practice. Such a study could be approached by discussion of the philosophical assumptions involved. An alternative adopted here is to see what happens to theories in the course of attempts to translate them into action. It studies several such attempts at 'social engineering', asks why some have been successful, why some have failed and why no attempts were made when circumstances seemed to call for them. Attention is concentrated on that process. For this reason economic and social theories in circulation when policies are being shaped are central to the argument, but it is not a technical history of either. It makes use of historical material, but it is not a continuous history and some matters which would loom large in one are not touched upon. Questions of administration and Party politics sometimes come into it, but they are not always the most important. Unless it were to consist of lightly supported generalisations, the study requires examination in some detail of the actual inter-play between fact-finding, the development of theories, their modification and education, and the invention of new institutions and practices. When appropriate the theory is followed from its first formulation through an examination of the evidence at inquiries to the conclusions finally drawn, and the testing of them in action. These details are, indeed, the stuff out of which conscious social guidance is made. The book is an exploration, and as in other explorations, it has occasionally been useful to have more than one look at a significant spot.

The first published statement of some of the themes in this book was in an article written amidst the distractions and fatigues of war. The ideas were developed a little further in the Introductions to the various Breviates, which were intended not only to give a lead to the understanding of their contents but as hints on what was to be undertaken. I hope that those who have written in friendly and encouraging terms about them will see in the book a part fulfilment of promises. For the approach to the endeavours to change the direction of British society in the years following 1945, the reader is referred for the present to the Introduction to the Breviate for 1940–54.

I am greatly indebted to my friend and colleague, Emeritus Professor W E Armstrong, for his careful and critical reading of the typescript. For the Index my special thanks are due to Miss D Marshallsay, Librarian of the Ford Collection, University of Southampton.

It is appropriate to take this opportunity to thank Mr J H Hansard for his interest in projects concerning Parliamentary Papers.

P FORD

SEPTEMBER 1968

NOTE

In the footnotes the Breviates of Parliamentary Papers are referred to by their volume numbers only, as follows:—

1900—16   Vol. I

1917—39   Vol. II

1940—54   Vol. III

CONTENTS

ix

Contents

PART III

A FIRST SOLUTION: 1906–1914

PART IV

PLANNING AND FAILURE: A POST-MORTEM ON RECONSTRUCTION 1914–1924

Contents

PART V

EPILOGUE—AND PROLOGUE

INTRODUCTION

I know not anything more pleasant, or more instructive than to compare experience with expectation, or to register from time to time the difference between idea and reality. It is by this kind of observation that we grow daily less liable to be disappointed

SAMUEL JOHNSON
Letter to Bennet Langton, June 28th, 1757

To speak on the most momentous and interesting topics in the company of intelligent friends is a thing that may be done with courage and safety; but to broach a theory while one is still a doubtful inquirer is a slippery course

PLATO

We are to-morrow's yesterday   MARY WEBB

In a modern dynamic society the decline of old and the rise of new industries, changes in the strength and balance of classes, new ideas on the value of the individual, on wrongdoing and on family and sex relationship, are continually disintegrating the old pattern of society, out-moding its machinery here and there, rendering some of its laws and sanctions harsh and inoperative. The changes may be connected with the wasting of some economic resource; they may be created by the application of a new technology or of new scientific discoveries or may arise from the attempt to develop a new ethical standard or to extend an existing one to a new field. To ensure its welfare, order and happiness society must respond with a continuous

I

process of integration. This response requires not only political and administrative, but intellectual effort. There may be periods in which the pace of change is accelerated, such as after great wars or in an upsurge of idealism, or in which a whole society may face a new situation requiring a fundamental choice, when the adjustments demanded are very great and the intellectual effort needed specially intense. It seems worth while to look at some of our past efforts, to ruminate on failures and scrutinise successes and so gather experience in society's endeavours to guide individuals' economic and other activity into a new design.

Conscious attempts to integrate public and private policies and to change the ends to be pursued imply, as Myrdal said,[1] a belief in reason as an independent force in history and in the freedom of choice by which man can change reality according to his own design. Rational attempts to plan, even piecemeal, pre-suppose the collection of the relevant facts, the formulation of the theory to interpret them and the invention of institutions and practices needed to make the plans successful. The plans themselves are conceived by their authors in a particular atmosphere. We have behind us, for example, two failures—in 1815 and 1918—and two successes, in 1906 and 1945. How far were these successes due to a happy coincidence of these elements, our endeavours misconceived or rendered abortive by the absence or weakness of some of them? Why did we slip in 1815? Or miss the opportunities in 1918? Was it lack of knowledge, defective theory, inadequate instruments or vacillating will? To aid us in answering such questions we have the advantage of a central core of information covering a century and a half, in the thousands of reports and volumes of evidence of Parliamentary and Government inquiries into precisely these problems of adjustment and adaptation as they arose. Though they have to be supplemented, they are contemporary records unique in range and depth, in which we can observe the thoughts, gropings, self-criticisms and sometimes flashes of imagination of a growingly free society trying to adapt itself to changes of its inward needs and outward circumstances.

In trying to understand the problems of an earlier generation as

[1]Gunner Myrdal, *Beyond the Welfare State* (1960), pp. 4, 15.

they saw them with the knowledge of their time there are some obvious traps. Looking back from the present it may be easy to see that the adoption of some policy was continuing or establishing a 'trend', while at the time its authors had no idea that they were at any point in a trend, nor indeed could have, without a knowledge of events which lay in the future. Later historians may be able to say that a new social principle was being established, yet its authors might not be conscious of it, but merely thinking how to handle an immediate difficulty. A whole series of acts may have common features which look like 'design', but in fact may just occur in the separate responses of different individuals and groups because the whole situation has given the problems a common twist. A bright idea which should have illumined a whole problem and shown the way to a solution may have been ignored because it was only a stray shot the significance of which was not appreciated even by its author or, like Ricardo's proposals for a secure and economical currency, may have to wait a century because the time was not ready for it.

We thus cross-examine history with particular questions in mind, and our use of its material is selective. For we are not seeking a full record of the events or the precise weight to be assigned to 'Party' calculations or class interests and pressures, but to gather experience in the processes of conscious social planning. Because of this limitation of our field of interest, we shall, indeed, be sometimes like Karshish, pickers-up of learning's crumbs. We may thereby become a little wiser; taking thought can sometimes add a cubit to our stature. If historians should be tempted to accuse us, as Mr Justice Shallow accused Falstaff, of having beaten his men, killed his deer and broken open his lodge, our answer must be, like Falstaff's: 'I have done all this. That is now answered.' But he went on to add, 'I have not kissed your keeper's daughter.' Though our questions are selective, we hope that in the answers due respect has been given to historical truth.

3

Part I

INADEQUATE DATA, INADEQUATE
THEORY, INADEQUATE INSTRUMENTS
1815—1830

Conflicts of interest are also conflicts of ideas
ALEXANDER MEIKLEJOHN

THAT WE MADE A POOR showing after 1815 is a commonplace; this was and remains a starting point for much broad social criticism and of the socialist attack on capitalism. The picture of the many depressing conditions and cruelties, painted with a broad brush by Arnold Toynbee and the Hammonds, has been filled in and somewhat altered by the work of later historians on new sources of information, such as business and prices records, so that we have to be more precise on which decade we are discussing and are a little clearer on whose standard of life was rising and whose was falling behind or dropping. But the main question remains: why at a time when adaptation to a new progressive technique was so important, were some of our political and social institutions so inflexible, so rigid? And this in spite of at least half a century of interest in invention of every kind, so vividly described by Witt Bowden in *Industrial Society in England towards the end of the Eighteenth Century.*

The features of the institutions of government at the time are familiar enough; the significant positions in Ministries, Parliament, Judiciary, Civil Service and Church were the preserve of a relatively small group or set of groups based on land ownership, the mass of the population being unable to penetrate it or participate in the task of ruling, even new powerful elements based on wealth acquired

4

first through trade and later through manufacturing finding it difficult to break into. The group was so close in common fundamental interests that a schoolboy doing his eighteenth-century political history often finds it difficult to remember which minister was Whig and which Tory, which was in or which was out, what difference this made, and feels certain only that Pitt was a great war minister, that North lost the American Colonies, that Walpole was efficient but corrupt, and that Fox made powerful speeches. This group of classes in the political offices, with vested interests in certain kinds of income and in certain kinds of ideas, had to adjust to a situation in which the very populations it was ruling were being redistributed in the country in a new way and in which rival sources of economic power were growing up outside it. We are here not concerned with the political struggles this caused, but with the reasoning on which it tried to handle the new problems.

I. OBSTACLES TO CONSTRUCTIVE THINKING

The classes which made public policy after the long wars with France had a complicated tangle of problems to analyse and decide upon. These included: the aftermath of war—demobilisation, cessation of war contracts, inflation; what was to be done about the new techniques of production, which required freedom of operation for full effectiveness in creating new industries, but destroyed or damaged existing ones; the change in the environment of the working population being drawn into factories where a new kind of discipline had to be discovered and imposed, and into massed living in urban conditions; finally, how the newly created wealth should be shared. Colquhoun's exhaustive statistical analysis—it became the text for intellectual and passionate discussion amongst economists and reformers—showed that in 1812 the labouring class and their families, some 44 per cent of the population, received only £45 to £48 per annum or 19 per cent of the national income. And it was clear that some groups in a strategic position or near to the new techniques were increasing their share, while others were losing ground relatively or absolutely.

5

In assessing what they made of it all, we have to avoid the pleasure of hindsight, of judging with knowledge of the great changes which were still to come and as we now see them in their full development. In 1815 these changes had still not gone so very far. Decision on policy had to be made in the light of the situation as it then was, and of their information about it. For their failure to distinguish clearly between the distresses arising from deflation or the cessation of war, and those due to long-run changes in the industrial structure we can scarcely now feel entitled to be so superciliously critical, since the generation in charge of policies after 1918 was at fault in a similar way. Then we have to allow for three elements in the problem, aside from our main theme, which affected their response. To begin with, industrialisation was then a novel experience and the difficulties which this process still encounters today, when knowledge is greater, give us a more lively understanding of what this meant. In an agricultural country where labour is not very mobile, the task of gathering together bodies of workers in suitable factory sites presents special difficulties: it was 'solved' in England by the use, near water power, of children and the young, in Russia after the 1917 revolution partly by the exercise of powers of compulsion and pressure, by the use of brigades of shock-workers and during one phase, of its industrial reserve army of political prisoners. Then the new factories required skilled artisans, managers and supervisors. The skills had to be developed and the men trained. Unskilled labourers had to be turned into a force of tunnellers and skilled navvies; millwrights had to be replaced by fitters, turners, pattern-makers. It was the first example of a problem that was to recur elsewhere. Thus the Indian *Industrial Commission* (1916–18), set up to examine the possibilities of industrial development, deplored India's dependence on imported technologists and engineers, the comparatively low efficiency of the plants which did not employ a high proportion of them, the almost complete absence of Indians in the ranks of foremen and supervisors, the lack both of Indians qualified for such positions and of provision for training them, as well as the low efficiency and unsteadiness of much Indian labour.[2]

[2]*Industrial Commission*, 1916–18, pp. 45, 99, 101–3, 151; 1919 Cmd. 51, xvii.

6

Russia after 1917 was in the same predicament. To increase the power of labour to produce wealth, said Lenin, would take years; it required the services of technical specialists, even foreign ones, at high salaries; even a scoundrel of deepest dye, if he had experience in organising production and distribution, must be learned from.[3]

In the same way the deplorable housing conditions of the working classes—a major part of the indictment of our handling of rapid urbanisation—were in part due to inexperience in providing for population growth at the current rate. The local authorities were small in size and resources, with no tradition of building other than of a few public institutions, and the response to the great demand came from private persons who, as they do now, looked around for available sites and fields and built on them, not perceiving at first what would happen if this process continued. The influx of Irish who crowded the houses, buildings not intended for use as houses and cellars of the north and of parts of London, created difficulties of a kind which the present immigration from the Commonwealth helps us to understand. (To meet a similar situation in 1880–1910 caused by the influx from east Europe the Royal Commission on *Alien Immigration,* 1903, recommended that in certain circumstances areas might be prohibited to alien immigrants.[4]) At a later date it was declared that large landlords would not touch these poor classes of crowded property, which was bought or built by the small shopkeeping class, who saved in that way. Sometimes the difficulty was land; as Hoskins has shown, over-crowding of houses on the site in parts of Nottingham occurred because land had not been enclosed and was not available for building.[5] But an inquiry a quarter of a century later showed what we had to learn.[6]

Expert witnesses—architects, surveyors and builders—who gave evidence before the Slaney Committee on the *Health of Towns,* 1840, were unanimous in condemning courts and back-to-back

[3] N Lenin, *Soviets at Work* (1919), pp. 15–17, 25; *Chief Task of Our Times* (1918), p. 12.
[4] *Alien Immigration,* R. Com. Rep., pp. 6, 24–5, 40, 42; 1903 Cd. 1741, ix.
[5] W G Hoskins, *The Making of the English Landscape* (1955), pp. 218–22.
[6] For example see the Report on the *Sanitary Condition of the Labouring Population,* illustrations and plans of old and new cottages following p. 66; H.L. 1842, xxvi.

houses, suggested desirable regulations on water, drainage, road width etc. and gave their experience in alternative ways of building.[7] But fears that a regulation to ensure that rows of houses should have a certain space back and front proportional to the height of the houses e.g. two-thirds, might by raising rents slightly have the effect of crowding people together even more, indicate that something more than planning regulations was involved. We did not then succeed—nor has any large agricultural country since apparently succeeded—in providing simultaneously from home sources sufficient capital both for the fixed equipment needed for rapid industrialisation and for housing a rapidly increasing population at an acceptable contemporary standard. We were still importing capital from Holland in the latter part of the eighteenth century and some of the profits of overseas trading e.g. in tobacco, and of the rising new manufactures, were turned back into industry rather than drawn out or paid out in wages for consumption. And Russia after 1917, without its pre-war sources of capital from foreign loans, gave priority to its industrial programmes and despite intense efforts, in much of its housing has had to work to a standard of persons per room we should not find acceptable here.

Next, there were a number of psychological hindrances to constructive thought on many subjects. The governing classes were in the main insulated[8] by their personal wealth from the 'lower orders' and the ills which afflicted them, and were able to combine an awareness of suffering of some kinds, as humanitarian movements regarding slavery and perhaps prisons show, with great insensitivity, even callousness, to sufferings of other kinds, for example, to the uncertainties of life in London, as vividly described by Mrs George; to the insane, as revealed by the Report on *Madhouses*,[9] to transportation, to public executions. The repeated failure to do anything for the chimney sweeping boys is perhaps a

[7]*Health of Towns,* Sel. Cttee., 1840 (384) xi. See especially the evidence of T Cubitt, G Smith and J Pennethorne.

[8]Geographical isolation may have a similar effect. Were the sufferings of the Tynesider and the people of South Wales in the 1930s as vividly realised as they would have been if Parliament had been sitting in the Tyneside or the Rhondda? See the comment of an outside observer, E M Almedingen, *Within the Harbour* (1956), p. 200.

[9]*Madhouses in England,* Sel. Cttee., 1814–15 (296) iv.

little less to be censured until a 'sweeping' machine had been invented[10] than the revolting flippancy with which some Peers spoke about Bills on the subject.[11] Or take the attitude to flogging in the Army. One would not expect practices in the Army to be as humane as in civil life, yet even so the attitude of Parliament was remarkable. The men were ill-clothed and ill-shod and their pay months in arrears—conditions which make men turbulent and desperate. Men could be sentenced to 1,500 lashes. Not until 1807 did the Commander-in-Chief make 1,000 the maximum and it was 5 years later that the powers of regimental courts were limited to inflicting 500 lashes. Yet when in 1808 Burdett asked for a return of the number of sentences and the number of lashes given at a time, he had the support of ten and seventeen Members respectively. And in 1815 a Bill for the limitation of flogging was negatived without a division.

A third trouble was the fright of the possessing classes at foreign revolutionary ideas and their determination to have none of them here. The French Edict of Fraternity 1792, calling on all nations to follow their example, the enormous circulation of Tom Paine's *Rights of Man* and of radical pamphlets and broadsheets,[12] the 3,000 daggers discovered in Birmingham, democratic organisations such as the Society for Constitutional Information, the Society of Friends of the People and the London Corresponding Society, their use of the terms and symbols of the French Revolution, the conviction that the societies did not intend to pursue the objective of annual Parliaments, but aimed at creating bodies which should supersede it[13] and that there was a traitorous conspiracy for the subversion of the established laws and constitution, the transportation of Muir, Palmer, Skirving and others, or the prosecution of Hunt, Cobbett, Carlile and the Society of Spenceans, the use of informers

[10]*On the Employment of Boys Sweeping Chimnies,* Sel. Cttee., 1817 (400) vi. See evidence of J Snow and app. 1, 2, *Climbing Boys* Report of Surveyor General on Experiments to Supersede . . . , 1819 (9), xvii.

[11]Gordon Strathearn and G B Cocks, *The People's Conscience* (1951), chap. iv.

[12]For an account of these see R K Webb, *The British Working Class Reader, 1790–1848* (1955), chap. ii.

[13]Committee of Secrecy on *Papers Belonging to the Society for Constitutional Information and the London Corresponding Society,* 1794, 8vo ed., 1st Rep., pp. 37–9; 2nd Rep., p. 90.

and spies[14] like Watt and Oliver, all gave rise to and indicate an emotional fear which lumped together violent reactions to economic distress and legitimate expressions of political unrest. It was not an atmosphere in which rational analysis of the problem of re-adjustment could be expected. Then through the post-war years, some of our statesmen were absorbed in foreign policy; so many international questions had to be settled and international congresses to be prepared for and attended from 1815 to 22. Their eyes were turned outwards, their interest was in what was going on in foreign capitals, but upon internal questions—quite apart from their entrenched class interests—they were often blankly ignorant. L G Hansard in his *Diary* (6 Mar. 1815) comments sharply that it was very indecorous of Lord Castlereagh to declare in favour of the Corn Laws on his first appearance after the Congress, and after having been away from the scene of transactions. Thus thought on reconstruction was limited and deflected.

2. LACK OF ESSENTIAL DATA

Reconstruction implies planning and inventing, but before one can undertake either, the facts must be known. Apart from the routine collection of figures relating to revenue and foreign trade, in 1815 the systematic collection of social facts as we now understand it was a newish idea. Government departments were not equipped for it. Even on matters with which Parliament had an obvious concern, such as trade policy, its inquiries were often prompted by, and took the form of committee hearings on petitions presented from outside bodies representing various trades, for example, the cotton trade, framework knitters, handloom weavers, Coventry watch-makers, etc. Some events which became characteristic of the new capitalism lay in the future. Occasions of bad trade were common enough, but in 1815 the crises of 1826[15] and 1836, which with later

[14]For a description of these methods in the 1830s and 1840s see F C Mather, *Public Order in the Age of the Chartists* (1958), chap. vi.

[15]For an interesting account of the succession of over-optimistic hopes and 'false dawns' which our lack of experience permitted after 1815, see M C Buer, 'Depressions after the Napoleonic Wars' in *Economica*, no. 2 (May 1921).

similar events contributed to the idea of recurrent trade cycles connected with capitalism, had not yet been experienced. Nor were we then properly equipped with the means of measuring such waves. Only over a century later were changes in fixed investment in building detected indirectly through variations in the price of bricks.[16] Index numbers of prices, production, etc. are an essential weapon for grasping these complicated movements, but this technique did not then exist. A number of writers who threw off hints or made primitive experiments can be traced, but it was not until Newmarch (1859) and *The Economist* (1869) began their series and until Jevons opened the theory of the subject, that index numbers took their place as a regular tool.

There were, of course, social observers who knew intimately the little bits of society in which they moved: as witness, Crabbe's poems, Jane Austen's shrewd observation of her limited circle, the Rev D Davies' *The Case of the Labourer in Husbandry* (1795). Individual physicians and surgeons whose professional duties gave them contact with the little-known world of the masses were amongst the most frequent and important witnesses in early Parliamentary inquiries. Eden's systematic and massive *State of the Poor* (1797), made considerable use of family budgets. Malthus' first *Essay on Population* (1794) contained no deep learning; the second edition, 1803, which was 'by comparison' a work of research, gave the evidence after the theory had been formulated. Not until three censuses had been taken—since the first, 1801, was incomplete—could the rate of growth and the regional redistribution of population be properly known. But official statistics were scattered through a great many Parliamentary Papers, so that to obtain a broad view a good deal of hunting was required; it was 1833 before a group which included Poulett Thomson, Porter, Bowring and McCulloch, was able to foster an attempt to draw them together in a large, rather ill-arranged and not very well printed volume edited by J Marshall.[17] The official *Statistical*

[16]H A Shannon, 'Bricks: A Trade Index, 1785 and 1849' in *Economica* (1934).

[17]J Marshall, *A Digest of all the Accounts Relating to the Population, Productions, Revenues . . . defused through more than 600 volumes of Journals, Reports and Papers . . . during the last 35 years* (1833).

Abstract did not appear until 1854, the Reports of the Factory
Inspectors and Poor Law Commissioners till 1834. The Manchester
Statistical Society, which commenced its active life with social
surveys,[18] did not hold its first meeting until 1833. And Engels'
case in the *Condition of the Working Classes in England* was based
largely on evidence available only after 1831, some of it not being
published until 1840. The policy-makers did not have in front of
them the mass of details collected with modern skills and the
understanding of the theoretical relations between them as are now
offered us by historians, such as Ashton. The trouble was that
whilst individual observers recorded separate bits of life, very few
seemed to have grasped what was going on as a whole. Eden's
researches, though undertaken out of benevolence and personal
curiosity, led him to emphasise economy and self-help rather than
positive State action. Patrick Colquhoun's great *Treatise on the
Wealth, Power and Resources of the British Empire*, published 1814,
with a second edition in 1815, was important for two reasons. The
work presented an estimate of national income and its distribution
between occupations and classes in a way which could not be
ignored. It seems to have been one of the books which Robert
Owen really consulted;[19] critics of the capitalist order were not slow
to seize upon it[20] and it was freely quoted in the famous radical
Black Book, 1820. This *'Map of Civil Society'*, as it was sometimes
called, was a substantial advance, yet without the aid of economic
theory developed more than a century later it could not be made the
foundation of social policy in the way such estimates have now
become. Perhaps, despite his crankiness, only Robert Owen at his
best sensed something of the full significance of the transformation
which was taking place. Cobbett understood it for the countryside,
but despite the wide circulation of his writings, left no school of
followers.

[18]T S Ashton, *Economic and Social Investigations in Manchester*, 1833–1933 (1934), chap.
ii and app. C. Poulett Thomson was said to have declared that there was no hope of the
Government's adopting an extensive scheme of collecting information throughout the
country (p. 16).

[19]R Podmore, *Robert Owen*, pp. 109, 256.

[20]John Gray, *A Lecture on Human Happiness* (1825; L.S.E. reprint, 1931), pp. 15–29.

3. INADEQUATE THEORY

To be of practical value the facts must be brought into relation with one another and interpreted in the light of an appropriate theory. The forces which were turning the England of Shakespeare, or shall we say of Wordsworth, into the England of Dickens were bound to produce a jostle of rival ideas seeking to control them. Apart from a few rather lone individuals, one group of whom something constructive could have been expected had little to say: the Church. It had become so much a part of the aristocratic system that when John Gray was calculating the effect of redistribution of the national income between the 'useful' and the 'useless' members of society, he placed the entire number of 'eminent' clergy amongst the useless.[21] Partly absorbed in the promotion of homely virtues— doubtless badly needed—out of contact with the new industry, it was inhibited by laziness and the pluralities and absenteeism pilloried in the *Black Book,* from presenting a troubled age with a social ethic. The challenge of rival secular and anti-clerical ideas was declined. On the other hand, the poets—Wordsworth, Coleridge, Southey (who read the evidence relating to children)— were repelled by the new commerical spirit, but they were not in the seats of political power.

Unless efforts were to be limited to easing the pinching shoe a bit here and there, if there were to be any 'design' or 'planning', some general notions were needed which would show the process as a whole, reveal the relations of the separate problems to one another. The great call from revolutionary France that all men were born free and equal, and that kings and priests must be removed, was one. The economists, the socialists and in due course the Benthamites, each tried to provide a theory of this kind. In Britain the most successful in this contest of ideas were the theories associated with the economists. But we have to ask whether we mean those of the writers to whom today we give this title, because

[21]Ibid., p. 17.

13

though initially concerned with specific problems, such as corn laws and currency, they developed a specialised technique of analysis which could be applied to other questions, or those of the politicians and the business men who sponsored legislation, and handled public policy. Despite the authority of Adam Smith's great work,[22] the subject as a recognised body of analytical principles was but newly developed, it had not yet become fully 'professionalised' and some of its principal exponents' work on it was an activity outside their everyday calling—business for Ricardo, journalism for James Mill, administration for J S Mill and McCulloch. But the speeches and debates show how many politicians had but the slightest and skimpiest acquaintance with the more closely-knit works of the economists and snatched at bits of ideas, vaguely expressed, floating around in the intellectual atmosphere of the time. There was increased dogmatism, a good deal of dilution and adulteration as ideas moved from the classical economists proper through the level of pamphlets and popular expositions to those who set the direction of legislation and even the larger number who just fell in with it. Economic principles turned into economic opinion. Or ought we to say that at this stage it was all economic opinion, that of the economists so called being only the most self-consciously logical part of it?

Room had to be found for the new techniques of production in an old society cumbered up with economic practices and administrative institutions irrelevant to the new processes. Adam Smith's unrestrained attack on the mercantile system, its laws and restraints, shaped much non-professional as well as later professional opinion. Both economists and the policy-making classes concluded that free contract, mobile capital, mobile labour, unimpeded trade and guidance by market price would ensure the maximum aggregate production and that capital and labour would find themselves in employments where their reward was greatest. This was, of course, a description of a society not as it was, but as it was becoming or could be made to become. Some of the decisive acts of policy—

---

[22]But note Wheatley's comment on Adam Smith: 'Though his work be more luminous on this subject than that of any other author, it has had no influence to effect an alteration in our policy.' *Currency and Commerce* (1803), p. iii.

the rejection of Whitbread's Minimum Wage Bills (1796–1800), the repeal of the wages and the apprenticeship clauses of the Statute of Artificers (1813, 1814), the passing of the Combination Acts (1799–1800)—occurred before the publication of Ricardo's *Principles* (1817), McCulloch's *Principles* (1825) or Mrs Marcet's popular *Conversations* (1816). But years had to pass before the goals were reached. (Sometimes, as in the case of agricultural enclosures, by greedy and harsh use of economic power and legal loopholes for which no excuse can be found.) In the meantime it was the task of classical economists, including the greatest of them, Ricardo—an economists' economist—whose difficult *Principles* large sections of which even the educated public would have found stiff going—to work out the relations of the various parts of the economic system to one another and to expose the principles on which the new economic order as a whole seemed to work. It was natural that able men interested in the world around them should be drawn particularly to examine the new forces of technology and enterprise which were transforming the economy under their eyes. Indeed, their writings were stimulated, perhaps primarily, by the practical problems of the corn laws, international trade, banking policy and population. Strides forward in analysis were made, and they developed the concepts of comparative costs, diminishing returns and the quantity theory of money. Though they were not always unanimous, their campaign was in the main successful—the corn laws were repealed, import duties reduced, the customs and navigation laws were put into more orderly shape, bank cash payments resumed, and to prevent the 'subsidies to population', the Poor Law reformed.

But the results of *laissez-faire* were not always beneficent. For the failure to foresee and take account of the ill-consequences, economists have been indicted on four counts—that they demanded unrestrained competition, attributed to their laws a sanctity they did not possess, ignored or were biased against the claims of the working classes and obstructed reform by a theory of population without sound foundation. First, that they advanced an uncompromising argument for unrestrained freedom of competition to the neglect of obvious social evils is, as Viner, MacGregor, Stigler and Robbins have shown,[23] easy to rebut. Not only is it fair to point out, as some contemporary socialist writers did, that Smith's great book was published in 1776 when, as a young student would say, the industrial revolution had scarcely begun, but he made a substantial list of cases where State intervention might be desirable. Ricardo, McCulloch and J S Mill wanted the taste for the comforts and conveniences of life to be widely diffused amongst the whole population. Bentham said that since they might lose their employment, workers would be right in objecting to machinery unless proper arrangements were made, whilst Torrens suggested a compensation fund to help retain those put out of work.

Yet we have not only to scrutinise their arguments in academic detachment a century and a half after their publication, noting the qualifications and nuances, but to ask how they struck contemporaries. Their emphasis and purpose was to put the case against mercantilist restrictions, and as their ideas spread, many of the qualifications and reservations (such as Adam Smith's about the tacit agreement of employers to keep down wages) were lost sight of and not taken into the body of opinion which determined policy. But this process of selection from the economists' writings was often biased by the class interests of the ruling groups: witness the contrast between the thorough-going way in which workers' wages were stripped of protection either of the law or of trade unions and thrown open to competition, and the opposition to the regulation of children's hours in factories. Then if in some of the more popular versions of classical doctrines and the lower levels of economic writing, as particular problems came up the answers generally turned out to be *laissez-faire*, what did they add up to but the assertion of harmony of economic interests? The writers were children of their time, living in a particular intellectual atmosphere. As Carl Becker has shown, in the eighteenth century, under the impact of Newtonian philosophy the notion that there were laws in the physical world was extended so that there were

[23] J Viner, 'Classical Economists and Laissez-faire' in *American Economic Review* (May 1949). D H MacGregor, *Economic Thought and Policy* (1949), p. 80. MacGregor notes (p. 39) that the term *laissez-faire* does not occur in Adam Smith, Ricardo, Malthus or Senior. L Robbins, *Theory in Economic Policy* (1952), pp. 22–9.

deemed to be laws which were the basis of government and laws of the economic world,[24] and it would at that time have been unthinkable that such economic 'laws' should not have been conducive to human happiness.[25] In his *Commentaries* (1765–69) Blackstone had argued that the Creator had so interwoven the laws of eternal justice with the happiness of the individual that the latter could not be attained but by observing the former; in consequence he had not prescribed a multitude of rules referring to the fitness and usefulness of things and actions, but had reduced the rules of obedience to one paternal precept, 'that every man should pursue his own free and substantial happiness'.[26] Whately, in his Oxford lectures, said that 'So man is in the same act doing one thing by choice for his own benefit, and another undesignedly under the guidance of Providence for the service of the community.'[27] It would be idle to pretend that such preconceptions did not, if unreflectingly, give a special flavour and imply a claim to a 'natural' or at least special authority for the principles set out by the more popular writers; and possibly even 'professional' economists were not entirely uninfluenced.[28] In this background of ideas, 'free competition' could not have the meaning of 'free-for-all-chaos' now often associated with it by monopolists and socialists who favour administered prices, but appeared a flexible process with orderly results.

Then whilst in the matters of great current importance to the economy with which the economists were as a group more closely

[24]Carl Becker, *The Declaration of Independence* (1922), chap. ii.

[25]On this the most influential of the Physiocrats, Quesnay, who opened the way to the study of economics as an independent science, was explicit. Natural law was comprised of physical law, 'the regulated course of physical events evidently the most advantageous to mankind', and moral law, the rule of every human action conforming to the physical order, 'evidently the most advantageous to mankind' and these were immutable and 'the best possible'. F *Quesnay et la Physiocratie* (1958), II, 740.

[26]William Blackstone, *Commentaries*, 9th ed. (1783), I, sect. 2.

[27]R Whately, *Introductory Lectures on Political Economy* (1831), p. 113.

[28]Hodgskin, a 'socialist economist', claiming that the laws which regulated the production of wealth formed part of the beneficial system of the natural universe, accused them of giving the same authority to social institutions and turned the tables by declaring the general poverty of the workers to be the result of the existing distribution of property in all its points a palpable violation of natural law. Thomas Hodgskin, *Popular Political Economy* (1827; reprint, 1962), pp. viii-ix, 264-8.

concerned, great advances in thinking were made, their theories were not well adapted to deal with contemporary questions relating to trades unions and socialism very much in the minds of intelligent workmen.[29] For they were more interested in the economic system as a going concern than in social dynamics or in the relation between developing technology, changes in the wealth and economic power of the various classes. Though Ricardo in the Preface to his *Principles* had said that the task of political economy was to determine what laws regulated the distribution of income between the capitalist, the landowner and the worker, in fact he stopped short at the first stage of the inquiry.[30] The power of the economic argument is well brought out in Stigler's analysis of Senior's Report on the Handloom Weavers. But the protests of the working classes through several decades, in pamphlets, machine-breaking riots and unions were the protests of hungry and suffering men. And to them the principles of the long run being developed by the economists, although becoming a permanent part of our technique of analysis, were not an immediate answer, and they might have replied in Keynes' later phrase, 'In the long run we are all dead.' This failure to solve the theoretical problems, or see their way through the practical difficulties, opened the way for remedies based on class interests and unanalysed prejudices. Advice to the workers to save and use friendly societies, was for most of them derisory. And what can be said of Mrs Marcet's comment on the Poor Laws: 'It is the idle and vicious who are alone losers by these regulations'?[31] Perhaps one may suspect that the harshness of the policymakers, mainly accounted for by the determination of the propertied class not to abate its privileges and the absence of any idea that the working class possessed more than a minimum of rights, was to some extent accentuated by the disposition we all have to push away from us painful situations we do not know how to handle. The impression one gets from witnesses describing to the Committee on *Mendicity and Vagrancy in the Metropolis*[32] the intolerable

[29]E Cannan, *Theories of Production and Distribution,* 3rd ed. (1922), chap. ix.
[30]Ibid., chap. vii, especially pp. 229–31; also *Economic Outlook* (1912), chap. vii.
[31]Jane Marcet, *Conversations on Political Economy,* 7th ed. (1839).
[32]1814–15 (473) iii.

conditions of want, misery, unemployment and vice, is that they did not know what to do about it. Against this background, J S Mill's comment that the new Poor Law, which ensured that no individual need perish from actual want, was 'something gained for humanity' possibly becomes more intelligible.[33]

Finally, the inhibiting fear of over-population grew as the influence of Malthus' first *Essay* and his theory of population spread rapidly outwards. He did, of course, demand attention from the public and set going the modern discussion. It is not necessary to engage in the easy sport of criticising Malthus' ratios—Ravenstone, though he slipped at the last step, got much nearer to the net reproduction rate—or of showing that the preventive checks Malthus introduced into his second edition, in operation eventually went to falsify his gloomy prophecies, nor of enlarging upon the confusion between short-run difficulties and long-run trends, or on the discoveries and inventions which continually postponed the date at which population pressure would become critical. The alarms swamped the socialists' protests that with education and emancipation women would be unwilling to have families of excessive size and that in any case increase of population, by widening the market and promoting invention, could be a source of industrial strength. And the contention of Torrens, Ricardo and McCulloch (and later J S Mill) that the raising of the natural wage, the psychological standard of comforts and conveniences below which people would not procreate, was the best security against a super-abundant population, was lost sight of in the lower levels of speeches and writings on public policy, which mostly assumed a broad, dogmatic Malthusianism. There was a population problem, but not quite what they thought it was. Though it is possible for a nation to cherish an illusion, it is unlikely that the theory would have gained such wide acceptance without some basis of fact to give it verisimilitude. The teeming overcrowded slums of St Giles and the Liverpool courts showed it at its worst. So intractable did it appear that many left it at that. And the condition of the Irish population

[33]The Poor Law Commissioners of 1834 were explicit on this point. 'Under the operation of this principle the assurance that no one need perish from want may be made more complete than at present.' 8vo ed., p. 227.

frightened them. Malthus and his followers thus tended to test every proposal for social amelioration solely by its possible effect on stimulating population. The Poor Law must be abolished, redundant population encouraged to emigrate.[34] His zeal even led him to dub a woman with ten children as a monopolist taking some other woman's share. What could be done for labourers, said McCulloch, was as dust in the balance compared with what could be done by themselves by limiting the size of their families. The theory was effective in building up public opinion for an attack on the Poor Law and such inducements to excessive families as it was held to offer.[35] But while drawing attention to an essential condition of improved welfare, its effect was also to inhibit constructive thought on other ways of tackling the social problem. For the intellectually lazy and the comfortable classes the theory provided an easy escape from uncomfortable questions.

Two writers are of interest in their reactions to these intellectual difficulties. Colquhoun asked why it was that with resources exceeding that of any other European country and with a rapid accumulation of capital, so great a volume of indigence existed that a ninth of the community were paupers and offenders living at the expense of a third of the remaining population.[36] He was no equalitarian, but the harsh phrase for which he had been so criticised, 'poverty is a necessary ingredient of society',[37] has been much misunderstood by those who have not read what he actually wrote nor paid adequate attention to the text surrounding his definition. His explanation is in fact followed by as exhaustive a list of the 'innocent' causes of indigence as was made a century later by the *Poor Law* Commission of 1905–09, including some which it made the subject of special treatment. The labourers, he

[34]His evidence before the Committee on *Emigration* appears to have been decisive. See 1826–27 (550) v, qq. 3186–3434.

[35]It is an interesting light on the way the Poor Law Enquiry was organised that whatever the views of its authors, the text of the 1834 Report makes little reference to 'population' and could have been written without that theory.

[36]Patrick Colquhoun, *Treatise on Indigence* (1806), pp. 19–20, 262.

[37]The point of the distinction between indigence and poverty is made plain in the Report of the Poor Law Commission, 1834, 8vo ed., p. 227, para. 5. See the comment on his official income, *Black Book* (1820), p. 29.

says, were exposed to many casualties from which the higher orders
were shielded and sometimes nothing could exceed the sufferings of
the useful class, upon which the strength, stamina and riches of the
country depended.[38] How could these workers be prevented from
falling into indigence? The obstacles to labour mobility which
permitted regional differences of wages, e.g. between north and
south, must be removed,[39] but no human wisdom could devise a
law which could perform the complicated task of regulating wages.
What was practicable was to hold out every encouragement to the
five great sources of industry, whose expansion would raise the
demand for labour and therefore wages.[40] Put in today's terms, for
improvement he relied on raising productivity through free competition. The results which Colquhoun hoped for he states in his
Power and Resources:[41] 'It is impossible to confer a greater blessing
upon a nation than by the adoption of practical arrangements which
will render the demand for labour somewhat more than equal
to the supply'—a near Beveridge definition of full employment.
'It is within the reach of possibility that this country, aided by
proper uniform direction of the national industry, might in the
course of a couple of centuries (or perhaps less) contain three
times its present population, and yet every man in the kingdom
be better fed and clothed than at present.'[42] By the end of the
century we had gone some way towards realising that confident
hope in the way he had envisaged, and it was accomplished by
greater production rather than by any substantial redistribution,
which had to wait until the twentieth century. The trouble was the
human cost of the process meanwhile.

The second, R A Slaney, was distinguished amongst M.P.s for
his ability and the strength of his sympathies for the working
classes.[43] The assiduity with which he studied the works of contemporary economists and Parliamentary and private inquiries into

[38]Colquhoun, pp. 10–12.
[39]In the Report on the Handloom Weavers, Senior pointed out that their difficulties
were accentuated by the obstacles to their entry into other trades.
[40]Colquhoun, pp. 278–80.
[41]Patrick Colquhoun, *Power and Resources*, 2nd ed., p. 426.
[42]Ibid., p. 5.
[43]Brentano's severe criticisms of Slaney have often been repeated without first
reading Slaney's books or speeches in the House.

social conditions is shown in his speeches in the House, his writings and in the range of detailed information in the reports (with their footnotes) of the Committees of which he was chairman. He is said to have himself drafted the Report of the Select Committee on the *Health of Towns*, 1840. 'It seems', this says, 'alike a matter of duty and policy in the legislature to take care that the industrious classes by whose hand the great riches derived from trade (cotton) are chiefly formed should be protected from evils such as has been described.'[44] There had been a great increase in the means of comforts and luxuries of the middle classes, as shown by the tax yield on male servants, horse carriages, etc., which greatly exceeded the corresponding advantages of the humbler portions of the community; the unskilled suffered many privations, and even those with higher wages were worse off than formerly, or if not worse off, in a low state which required improvement.[45] Discontent was due not so much to the Corn Laws or the limitation of the franchise as to more permanent causes, such as monopolies and unemployment through the introduction of machinery. 'The problem of the handloom weavers would occur in other industries.'[46] 'It is painful to contemplate in what appears to be an opulent, spirited and flourishing community, such a vast multitude of our poorer fellow subjects, the instruments by whose hands these riches were created, condemned through no fault of their own to the evils so justly complained of . . .'[47] On housing, town planning and education his proposals are clear and constructive and his efforts vigorous. For his fundamental difficulty we go to his *Essay on the Employment of the Poor*, 1822. After stressing the importance of an adequate working-class standard he starts characteristically with a calculation of the sum required to maintain a man, wife and three children on a minimum standard which allowed nothing for meat, tea, beer, illness, etc., of £30 2s od per annum and compared this with an income of wages for a man and wife, assuming full employment with no illness, of £28 12s od per annum[48]. Yet in the rest of the Essay,

[44]*Health of Towns,* Sel. Cttee. Rep., p. 11, 1840 (384) xi.
[45]Hansard, 3rd ser., xxxix (1837), col. 382, 383.
[46]Hansard, 3rd ser., li (1840), col. 1222, 1227.
[47]*Health of Towns,* Sel. Cttee. Rep., p. ix.
[48]*Essay on the Employment of the Poor,* 2nd ed. (1822), pp. 24–7.

22

in an intelligent and well-read search for remedies to bridge this gap, he is unable to get much beyond the usual negative ones— stop encouraging the over-supply of labour through the Poor Laws, employment cannot be increased by legislation, on balance machinery had increased the demand for labour. *In a plea . . . for the Working Classes,* written twenty-five years later, after a reasoned but moving review of the results of inquiries into their condition, he re-affirms that neither agricultural nor urban labourers had improved their position compared with that of the classes above them and that they did not have the fair share of increasing comforts to which they were entitled. A quarter of a century's efforts on their behalf led him to say that owing to the 'claims of politics measures for working-class welfare excited little interest in Parliament'. But again he concludes that since wages depended on the proportion between capital and population, there should be no government interference with investment nor government encouragement of population; so his remedies remained a vigorous attack on housing and the promotion of education, aided by a national three-man independent commission to devise measures for working-class welfare.

4. THE WORKERS AND SOCIALISTS: DISSIDENT THEORIES

To this intellectual situation the reaction of the working classes was a radical one. They were seething with critical ideas, reading pamphlets and books hostile to the new order, and experimenting with new communities, trade unions and the ideas of a general strike. 'Acutely critical of the actual and absurdly credulous of the ideal', socialist writers like Hall, Thompson and Gray attacked what the economists just assumed, the existing scheme of property rights and the separation of the producer from his instruments. They wanted a fundamental alteration in the existing system, and laid down many lines of thought on which socialist criticism has run ever since. Later scoffed at by Marx for utopianism, they were also largely ignored by professional economists because they were not interested in and contributed little to the technique of analysis. Of course they had something to say on technical matters—Hall on progressive taxation, Ravenstone and Thompson on population theory, Hodgskin on population and invention as dynamic factors in society and on the conflict between economic progress and static property laws. But for them the central problem was the contrast between the greatly increased productive power of society and the miseries of the working classes. Robert Owen argued (1821) that steam power and machinery had multiplied productive power twelve-fold, but placed the increase of wealth in the hands of a few.[49] The increase of productive power through steam and machinery 'in the last forty years', said J M Morgan in the *Revolt of the Bees,* had been computed to be equal to an additional supply of labour of 600 million men; instead of being made to increase prosperity it had been left unguided, so that on the contrary it depressed the value of labour and afflicted the country with misery.[50] With such figures in mind it was easy for him to poke fun at the Rev T Malthus' support for emigration as a remedy, by imagining a procession of political economists led by a gentleman in clerical garb holding a much altered MSS, going to Hungerford Steps on the orders of The Speaker, to emigrate to the empty spaces of America where they could take squaws and double their numbers every twenty-five years.[51] Gray, starting from firmer statistical ground by going through Colquhoun's table of the distribution of the national income between occupations and classes and deciding what proportion of each was 'useless', arrived at the conclusion that of the 17 million population nearly $5\frac{1}{2}$ million belonged to the 'useless' classes, who nevertheless received 48 per cent of the national income.[52] He thus inverted Davenant's view[53] that

---

[49]Robert Owen, *Report to the County of Lanark* (1821), p. 19.

[50]J Minter Morgan, *Revolt of the Bees,* 4th ed. (1850), pp. xiv–xv. I have not been able to trace the origin of this figure. Another estimate of 100 million was quoted by Slaney in his *Essay,* p. 75. Babbage gives numerous examples of increases of efficiency in the *Economy of Manufactures* (1832).

[51]Morgan, pp. 217–25.

[52]Gray, *Lecture on Human Happiness,* pp. 19–21.

[53]Davenant in his famous Schedule D of the yearly income and expenses of the various classes of the population, shows common seamen, labourers, out-servants, cottagers, paupers and common soldiers as having incomes smaller than their expenses and therefore decreasing the wealth of the country. *Balance of Trade* (1699), table facing p. 22.

the 'kept' classes were the poor unable to earn their subsistence and aided by the State or by private charity; on the contrary they were the unproductive, useless rich. As we have seen the economists' theory had not been pulled together in a form apt for this problem.

All this contributed several ideas which became a permanent part of socialist thinking. First, there was a heightened realisation of the existence of a working class. The fact was not new, nor its perception limited to socialist critics, for Ricardo based his analysis not on the activities of craftsmen buying materials and selling their products, but on labourers working for wages, and their numbers and income Colquhoun counted. The consciousness of class was probably due more to the silent growth of feelings of solidarity amongst workmen than to the socialist writers who helped to make them articulate and to drive home their significance. And while Ricardo had said that the interest of the landlord was opposed to that of every other class of the community, the socialists declared that it was the interests of the capitalists and landlords which were opposed to those of the working class, who failed to receive their proper share of the new productivity because the capitalist denied them the right to the full produce of their labour. The productivity which owners of circulating capital claimed was its result when 'advanced' for wages was in fact due to co-existent and co-operant labour (Hodgskin).[54] The flexible orderliness of the economic system which the economists asserted was the outcome of free competition was, on the contrary, rooted in disorder and accounted for the poverty and other ills from which the working class suffered. This would not be corrected, said Gray, unless it were brought within the control of a 'social system', in which 'a directing power took in hand the whole of our commerical affairs' and without which liberty and independence were impossible.[55] In one form or another these ideas were essential ingredients of the socialist view.

But pre-occupied with large ideas of social reconstruction and experiments, without that representation in Parliament which Lovett saw was essential, and faced with a class- and patronage-ridden civil

[54]Thomas Hodgskin, *Labour Defended against the Claims of Capital* (1825; reprint, 1922), pp. 38–52.
[55]*The Social System* (1831), pp. 231–2.

service which could not then be seen as what it ultimately became, an instrument by which great reforms could be made, the socialists were weak in immediate practical remedies. Spence's public ownership of land was unlikely to make progress in a society of voteless labourers ruled by landlords. Even William Benbow's proposed general strike—the 'Grand National Holiday'—was really a social protest having no specific practical objective. Many therefore fell back on Owenite co-operative communities which, utopian as they now seem, not only expressed ideals, but were then regarded as a direct, practical attack on the problem. But they were scarcely an answer appropriate to mass, mechanised industry. The Committee on the *Employment of the Poor in Ireland,* 1823, gave Owen a critical hearing because his obsession with equalitarian communities obscured his diagnosis: that a large part of the population was underemployed, that private capital would not find its way to Ireland owing to the disturbed state of the country and that a large Government expenditure for the development of industry was needed.[56] Since Senior, similarly impressed by Ireland's poverty and lack of capital, later also thought an extensive development programme preferable to creating a new Poor Law,[57] Owen deserves credit for an early diagnosis of it. Owenite and socialistic ideas gave the working classes a faith which for many survived practical failures, but blocked as they were from any use of Parliament, the instruments the workers created for themselves in an attempt to realise them proved too fragile. The failure of the Labour Exchanges, of the one big union, or to establish any permanently successful demonstration of a co-operative community which owned the instruments of production and in which the produce was distributed on some fair basis[58] meant that they obtained no direct control over the development of the new capitalism; they could only nibble into its defences at two points, by means of consumers' co-operation and 'business unionism' on the New Model.

---

[56]*Employment of the Poor in Ireland,* Mins. of ev., pp. 84, 156, 1823 (561) vi. Owen suggested a loan of £6 million at 3½ per cent.

[57]Marian Bowley, *Nassau Senior and Classical Economics* (1937), p. 247. But at another date he expressed the opposite view: Nassau Senior, *Industrial Efficiency and Social Economy* (1928), I, 195.

[58]But see W Pare's description on the Ralahine experiment in *Cooperative Agriculture in Ireland* (1870).

5. INADEQUATE ADMINISTRATIVE INSTRUMENTS

Finally, even had there been a full knowledge of the facts, and relevant and comprehensive social theory, it is doubtful how much could have been done without more efficient administrative machinery and practice. Adequate instruments of social control were not to hand. It was natural that when at the end of the century a modern civil service had been developed, people like the Fabians should think of using it, and equally natural that, considering what it was in 1815 when it was regarded by democrats as the machinery of oppression, it should not have entered people's minds that here was a potent instrument of positive as distinct from merely regulatory social guidance. One need not enlarge on the list of sinecures revealed by the various inquiries, including the thirty-six Reports to the Abbot Committee on *Finance* 1797–1803, during the long struggle to replace fees, gifts and gratuities by fixed salaries, even in the House of Commons' offices.[59] The amusing and satirical comments on the Civil List printed in the Radical *Black Book*,[60] 1820, are enlightening in what they imply as to the effect of all this on the Radicals. The Stationery Office, set up to get rid of abuses and to secure economy, had not succeeded in freeing itself from nepotism and other abuses even by 1833.[61] Even at the time of the Northcote-Trevelyan Report of 1853, years after the Napoleonic War had closed, the outlying offices of the Service were in practice at the disposal of the M.P.s for the constituencies and central appointments were largely influenced by their recommendations. In the Registrar's office, for example, one clerk was an insolvent debtor, another had defrauded the Bank of England, one was dismissed for inefficiency, the Deputy Registrar did not attend the office for fifteen months, and one clerk was so ill that he had to be given a room on his own, and even then died. Perhaps even more remarkable than such facts was the public reaction to them. Could

[59]*Luke Graves Hansard's Diary*, ed. Percy Ford and Grace Ford (1962), pp. xix–xxii.
[60]For example, see comments on Bathurst, Bentinck, Blockley, Canning, Cockburn, Eldon, Grafton.
[61]*Luke Graves Hansard's Diary*, p. xxx.

anything be more democratic than the appointment of civil servants by elected Members, said the *Morning Post*. The new scheme was an attempt to impose on the country a clever bureaucracy of the Austrian type, what we needed was not able men but honest men, said the *Daily News*. It was the later shock of failure during the Crimean War which helped these reforms through.[62]

In sum, an impasse had been reached. The policy-making classes in general assumed, with some reservations, that under the guidance of consumers' choices the new technique would work into a reasonable order. But had any group wished to embark on measures of social control, the administrative machine was not fit for the purpose. Working-class movements, denied access to it, and driven by a passionate desire to change the social order fundamentally, found that the instruments they had to invent for themselves broke under the strain of the problems they were devised to meet. Nor did there develop any widely accepted code of social justice.

6. ATTEMPTS TO BREAK THE IMPASSE: A NEW THEORY
WITH NEW INSTRUMENTS, A THEORY OUT OF ITS TIME,
AN ETHICAL THEORY

The working classes now passed into one of the most turbulent periods of their history, with Tory philanthropists, Anti-Corn Law Leaguers and Chartists competing for their support, working up their emotions and aiming at different objectives. There is no need to go over well-worked ground to note the legislative results of these pressures nor the way in which, in order to make room for humanitarian and medical insistence on limiting the factory hours of work of children and women, it was necessary to invent a modification of the doctrine of free contract so that these dependent groups could be granted legislative protection on the ground that they were not 'free'. But a glance at three efforts to break out of the intellectual, as distinct from the political impasse, by contrast brings out some

---

[62]*Civil Service Reform: Observations upon the Report by Sir C E Trevelyan . . . and Sir S H Northcote . . . with quotations from leading journals . . . by a Civil Subaltern* (1854). See the leaflets of the Administrative Reform Association.

weaknesses which had led to the failures of the preceding years. One was in a large measure successful, one had no immediate practical result, one had little permanence in practice but more in inspiration. The first, the work of the Benthamites, offered a partial solution. It rested on a new theory, limited its objectives and involved new instruments. It ran alongside this tangle of social and political movements, but did not get its driving power from and was in some matters opposed by these popular campaigns. Nor did some of the leaders have the common touch necessary to run them. But an unusual convergence of circumstances led it to success. Starting with a realistic view of the motives that moved men, the Benthamites did some hard, fresh thinking in the fields in which other movements were weak—on the machinery of government and on the principles and practices of administration—and succeeded in uniting theory with inventiveness. Though their theory had been worked out earlier, it was after 1832 that their influence on public policy— Municipal Corporations, the Poor Law, the Board of Health, etc. was most dramatic. The ideas of economists had influenced policy by their slow diffusion in various versions, precise or crude. By contrast, that of the Benthamites was more direct and in some ways more organised; put sharply, they were a group with a theory and a method. While this and their name perhaps suggests a more unanimous, cohesive and organised group than they were, they had much in common. In his *Autobiography* J S Mill claimed that Bentham's influence was exercised through his writings; and despite his difficult style in his later years, their vast learning and acute judgement account for their influence in the circle of experts and educated readers. While the spread of his thought was due to the Parliamentary work and writing of brilliant men like Romilly, Molesworth, Brougham, Charles Buller, Grote (all M.P.s), James Mill, J S Mill, Austin the jurist, the task of turning theory into practice was done by very able men such as Chadwick and Southwood Smith who, though perhaps not as brilliant as the more prominent figures, were engaged in public official work. The group thus had its lawyers, philosophers, M.P.s like Joseph Hume, political wire-pullers like Place, and a journal in which they could express their views, the *Westminster Review*.

They had a clear theory of politics which both had a cutting edge when applied to a whole range of existing institutions and provided a basis for the invention of new ones. It was based, not on Burke's idea that political institutions were the repositories of ripe wisdom to be added to only by slow accretions, nor on the indefeasible rights of Tom Paine nor on the innate goodness of men, like that of Robert Owen (who in 1836 advertised the date of the coming millennium), but on a simple, if over-rational view of the actual motives which they thought moved men. They set out to be scientific observers: legislation should be the outcome of systematic investigation, and their favourite device was the Royal Commission of Enquiry, with volumes of evidence and a report with specific recommendations. And Chapter IV of the Report on the *Sanitary Condition of the Labouring Classes* with its attendant maps, shows how far they had advanced beyond reliance on the 'traditional' hearings of evidence into methods of scientific social investigation.

Armed with a theory and a method, their approach to current problems had two sides. First, despite the great range of matters in which their influence was decisive, from the point of view of the socialist critics their attack was on a limited front. They made no direct attack on the central problem of the distribution of wealth as it was envisaged by the socialist commentators on Colquhoun's table. They believed in freedom of enterprise and the competitive process. Since every man was the best judge of his own interests, he should be allowed to make his own decisions on his economic and private affairs. They disliked the regulation of wages, the restrictions on trade and shipping: for though State interventions were called for to make the competitive process effective, or where spontaneous exertions of individuals did not do all that was required or imperilled the subsistence of all, the 'leading principle' (McCulloch) or the 'axiom of politics' (Colquhoun) was that individual activities in agriculture, manufactures and commerce should not be obstructed. But secondly, they mounted a large-scale attack on the atrocious environmental conditions of working-class life in factories, housing, water supply, poor relief, and did it by inventing for special purposes the administrative instruments which had been lacking. They hammered out some of the machinery needed for the efficiency of the new order—the registrar, the government inspector, the centrally approved salaried officer, the device of the central government Orders, etc. Bentham envisaged a unified central and local machine of government: a logical and comprehensive list of central departments, set out in his constitutional code, should replace the odd, untidy assortment we then possessed. To replace the congeries of ill-sorted and corrupt corporations, open and select vestries, improvement commissioners and Quarter Sessions, he proposed a unified local authority exercising all the functions of its area and in its organisation mirroring that of the central authority, to which it should be bound by the passing of information, by supervision and inspection. And the bodies were to be elected and representatives chosen on a franchise, not much larger than that of 1832 according to James Mill, or by manhood suffrage according to others, or even including women, as suggested by J S Mill. To remedy the current bureaucratic procedures Bentham made a number of prescriptions for salutary administrative practice: 'give no extra reward without proportional extra service, proved by evidence not less than that required to prove delinquency with a view to punishment'; 'keep the appointment of agents in the hands of those for whose happiness they exist'; 'minimise the quantity of money the agent has at his disposal, minimise the number of hands through which it passes on its way to the hand by which it is finally received in payment'.

The transition from theory to practice involved some compromises and inconsistencies. J S Mill made some modifications in the theory, while Chadwick had to adapt it to the practical tasks of administration. It was seventy years before the plan of the central departments was something like Bentham's proposals. He had wanted a unified local authority for all purposes; they actually set up *ad hoc* authorities for specific functions, boards of guardians, boards of health, highway boards, which later created administrative confusion. Bentham himself scorned 'many-headed boards'. But perhaps in view of the entrenched interests in the unreformed civil service, the only way their end could be achieved was to create new central departments with relevant local boards and with administrative procedures on the pattern they desired. The local bodies were to be representative of local democracies, but they found themselves bullied by Chadwick, who hated bodies which would not accept his theories, nor drive at his pace. He once said to Playfair, who argued that local authorities should be encouraged to show independence and initiative, 'Sir, the devil was expelled from heaven for objecting to centralisation.' Some far-sighted proposals were lost sight of or defeated; such as buttressing manufacturing districts against commercial distress by providing a 'mixture of employment' or balanced industries, as we now say; prohibiting children from entering factories even for the six hours a day unless they could show a qualified teacher's certificate that they had attended school three hours a day in the previous week (defeated in the Lords); the Poor Law Act left out some of the more humane suggestions and lost ground not recovered until after 1909. Sometimes, as in the case of the Report on *Municipal Corporations*,[63] there was a risk that the remedies derived from theory rather than from the evidence. More important, there was an internal dichotomy in their thinking which would not reveal itself in practice till later; the individual was to be given freedom of enterprise and contract, but the very process of investigation sometimes led to conclusions which involved large-scale interference with that freedom.

The other two movements of opinion had little or modest immediate practical influence, and represented bids for a place in the scheme of thought which should control the new order. Though they fall outside the period of failure and even after the peak of the Benthamites' constructive work, nevertheless it is worth while straying a little to glance at them because their limited effect at the time showed their inappropriateness to the circumstances and emphasised deficiencies which had to be filled in if they were to become effective. One, Marxism, though greatly influenced by English socialist writings and based in considerable measure on the study of English conditions, was alien in origin. The other, Christian Socialism, though not uninfluenced by Continental writings (Fourierism) was very English.

Marxism was expressly devised to help the worker to understand

---

[63]See *Municipal Corporations*, R. Com., F Palgrave's *Protest*, 1835 (135) xl.

his position in society and to provide a plan of proletarian tactics. It assumed, as in a general way did the economists and the Bethamites, that human motives were rational, and concerned with individual calculations of interest and advantage. But it parted from them in that whereas while in the economists' reasoning under *laissez-faire* this led to maximised production, and in that of the Benthamites to the creation of special institutions and codes, with the Marxists it led to the workers perceiving common interests and to the class struggle and to revolution. Engels published his *Condition of the Working Class in England* in 1844, the *Communist Manifesto* was published in London in 1848 and Marx came to London finally in 1849. One has to realise how close they were in time to many stirring events in the history of the working class, which had been through twenty-five years of turbulence in thought and action. They would find many active leaders and rank and file workers who had either read the critical literature which the movements had produced or to whom its ideas had filtered down, and who in one way or another had taken part in aggressive, anti-capitalist action. Bray's *Labour's Wrongs and Labour's Remedy* was but ten years old, while Pare's edition of Thompson's *Distribution of Wealth* and the fourth edition of J Minter Morgan's *Revolt of the Bees* were not issued until a year after Marx's arrival. A young worker who had heard Hodgskin's lectures at the Mechanics' Institute, later published as *Popular Political Economy* (1827), or who had read Gray's *Lectures on Human Happiness* (1825) would still be only in his forties. Though not then active in any significant working-class movement, Owen still had nine years of propaganda work in front of him, and Lovett another twenty. Notions of the economic interpretation of history, that laws were but the reflection of basic property relations between rich and poor, of the opposition of class interests and a socialistic rendering of the labour theory of value were here already. So were discussions on tactics. There were many whose experience went back to the repeal of the Combination Acts in 1824–25, who had participated in Owen's co-operative efforts and the labour exchanges, in the rise and collapse of the Grand National Consolidated, and in the rise and failure of Chartism. Chartist dissensions on whether at elections they should support radicals who promised to back the Charter and to vote against undemocratic legislation, or to support the Tories rather than the Radicals who might be 'worse than the Tories', or to take a line independent of both the old plutocratic parties; debates on whether strikes should be used to support political demands or confined to wage questions—discussions repeated with vigour in speeches and leaflets in the years 1917–19—must have been fresh in the workers' minds then because they had taken place only eight years earlier. They had tried 'political action', 'direct action' and frontal attack through Owenite communities. Yet, though these theories were thus apparently ripe for that systematisation which Marx and Engels expounded, the immediate influence of the two— though they gained some followers—on legislation and practice was nil, and on most of contemporary English working-class thinking, limited.[64]

That for a quarter of a century from the time of their arrival the English economy was expanding and was, to use Adam Smith's words, in that progressive state of society in which the condition of the labouring poor, of the great body of the people, is most happy and comfortable, is no doubt part of the explanation. Though the gains were unevenly distributed between different groups of workers,[65] the feel of the period was different, so that in that sense the appeal of the *Communist Manifesto* would be less immediate, less relevant. But there were checks in the upward trend, it would take time for this more optimistic and resilient mood to be diffused, and as the much later surveys by Booth and Rowntree showed, there was

[64]This is not altered by the fact that the existence of active little groups can be traced. Those who have participated in minority movements will know how filled with meetings, committees, conferences, etc. the life of such a group can be, and how favourable the scene can appear when viewed through its eyes, while in fact it is at the time politically insignificant. Even in a sympathetic historical study of such a group, it may be difficult to avoid a similar misapprehension, especially if it is an early stage in the development of ideas or an organisation which became important later. Note Hyndman's assessment: '. . . it is safe to say that in the autumn of 1880 the principles of what is today the greatest, and indeed the only growing international party in the world had made no serious impression on this side of the Channel. . . . It is not too much to say that the whole movement was dead as far as Great Britain was concerned. The socialist conceptions of the old chartists, which Marx systematised, coordinated and put on a scientific basis, had died down and nothing had arisen to take their place; the very names of the leaders were forgotten. Even the few convinced socialists then in England did not all know one another.' *The Record of an Adventurous Life* (1911), p. 224.

[65]For a recent summary of a discussion about this, see A J Taylor, 'Progress and Poverty in Britain, 1780–1850: A Re-appraisal' in *History* (1960), 15–31.

plenty of poverty, bad housing and malnutrition left. Under-employment must have been substantial, though they did not possess, nor
do we now possess, any effective means of measuring what the
extent of it was. This explanation is thus not completely sufficient,
and for what is left out we look to the theory and the circumstances
surrounding its exposition.

Engels came to England in 1842 to work in a firm in which his
father had shares, and published his book in 1844, when he was aged
twenty-four. On any showing this was a most astonishing performance, the more so because he was a foreigner. There was, indeed,
from the 1830s onwards a considerable volume of criticism, British
and foreign, on the conditions of British factory operatives and
miners, much of it, including that by Engels, relying in the main on
the evidence taken before Select Committees and Royal Commissions
from 1832 onwards—bodies manned, one has to remember, by
members of the gentry and middle classes—on the employment of
children in factories and mines, on the Poor Law, on the sanitary
conditions of the labouring population and on the health of towns.
His book was notable for two reasons. Unlike some other studies
which dealt with more limited fields, it brought together in a single
book material covering the whole field. Its great merit was that he
set out fully the many depressing and ominous facts about the
industrial and social conditions which some of the more orthodox
writers—Senior must be excepted—content to dwell in the realms
of principles, failed to face up to or even, judging by their writings,
to weigh seriously. If he highlighted some of the grimmer incidents
described in the evidence, he may be excused; most of them were
facts and did take place. That he sometimes sharpened his quotations
a bit was natural for a young man in a hurry, who was not writing
history but a tract using historical evidence. These, defects in an
historian, would rather have aided its acceptance as a tract. We may
well ask why at the time it had so little influence.[66]

First, the book was published in German. In spite of the fact that
it contained a dedication and an appeal to the English working class
in English, no English translation appeared before 1887 and that

[66]See the introduction by W H Chalenor and W O Henderson to their edition of
Engels' book (1958).

was in America. Copies may have come here, but according to Engels' Preface to the 1892 edition, it 'was never extensively circulated on this side of the Atlantic'. It is difficult to find any evidence that extracts or quotations from it were published in England before the full English translations appeared. Seeing that he had made enough contacts with workers to be allowed to write articles for Owen's *New Moral World,* this situation is remarkable. Was there no demand for it? Secondly, the evidence given to Committees and Commissions on which he drew so heavily, was given in the thirties and used by him in 1844. It had been gathered 'from above' in the Benthamite spirit during the decade as part of a wide-fronted attack on working-class conditions and had been followed by legislation. Comparison of what was done with what remained to be done shows these steps as tiny enough, but they made an important change in the sense that the walls had been breached. Engels had been in England only twenty-one months and perhaps could not have been expected to see the direction of movement.

Finally, keen and industrious observer though he was, so short a stay set limits to his knowledge. It is not belittling Engels' achievement to conclude that Laski, in his introduction to the centenary edition of the *Communist Manifesto,* overlooked this limitation to Engels' work and in typical Laskian phrase exaggerated his 'knowledge of the trade union and Chartist movements from the inside', and of the English trade union movements 'in massive detail'. For it is possible to know a subject in 'massive detail' and yet to miss the essential spirit. In his conclusion Engels confidently prophesied that there would be an English revolution, that popular feeling would reach an intensity greater than that which animated the French workers in 1793, and that the war of the poor against the rich would be the most bloodthirsty the world had ever seen. Engels' own explanation in his Preface to the 1892 English edition that some of this was due to his youth, and his list of the events and State intervention which had postponed the revolution is not fully convincing. It was a misreading of the English situation and it sprang less from the facts than from the theoretical conceptions by which they were interpreted. He was not the last to detect a 'revolutionary situation' where none existed; Laski himself was moved to say something near it in various passages in *Democracy in Crisis* (1933) and *Reflections on the Revolution of Our Time* (1943).

The *Communist Manifesto,* like Engels' book, made little impression on contemporary general English working-class thinking. Written by Marx after a draft by Engels, it was published in 1848 on behalf of a small group of revolutionaries, some exiles, assembled in London. It also was in German. Its appeal was made not just to English, but to all workers, though the context of its argument was European. At the outset the *Manifesto* says that it is to be published, amongst other languages, in English and a translation appeared in parts of Harney's Journal, the *Red Republican* in 1850. Apparently there was no further version in English (and that published in America) till 1871–72, copies of which may have reached this country and a revised translation by Moore in 1888.[67] The group, perhaps a little isolated by language and mental habit from those around them, does not seem to have been very large, nor despite Engels' comings and goings and endeavours to gather support, were its English working-class connections enough at this stage to make it anything but small in the working-class landscape. Harney and Ernest Jones were active. Lovett and Thomas Cooper are said to have given their 'support' to an educational association, but judging by their respective biographies, this seems to have made little impression on them. The support of Applegarth, who was able, generous and farsighted, for the International Working Men's Association, could scarcely have included much sympathy with their theoretical doctrines, if his evidence before the Commission on Trade Unions is any guide.

There were, of course, personal factors. Marx, whose ability, knowledge and sincerity about workers' emancipation was recognised by those who met him, with Engels developed a habit of purging those who did not accept their doctrine and their leadership.[68] Harrison Riley, who had been associated with him in the

[67] H M Hyndman says that in the 1880s 'at most a few ill-printed copies of the famous *Communist Manifesto* of 1847 by Marx and Engels done in English could be found by searching for them in the most advanced revolutionary circles.' *The Record of an Adventurous Life,* p. 224.

[68] In this connection, note the querulous tone of some of Engels' and Marx's references to Ernest Jones. J Saville, *Ernest Jones* (1952), app. I. This aspect of Marx's political quarrels is rather mercilessly recorded by L Schwartzschild, *The Red Prussian,* especially chaps. xi–xiii. Hyndman, p. 282.

37

International, 'never esteemed his heart at a high rate', thought he had a powerful head, but regarded him as a 'poor executive officer'.[69] Hyndman, who admired Marx, neither liked Engels nor trusted him.[70] Perhaps the group exhibited some of those psychological traits to be detected in exiled groups and Governments after Hitler and after 1939. But again, another obstacle was their theory. Despite their denunciation of utopianism, there is a millennialist quality in their writing. For both the revolution seemed just round the corner and just as Engels was led to misjudge the English situation, so Marx over-estimated the probability of revolution in Germany. At that time Marx had little personal knowledge of the English working-class movement and must have derived his impressions mainly from Engels. The contemptuous reference to Owen's experiments as 'pocket editions of the new Jerusalem' was not likely to win support of many of the Owenites, who continued to respect him even in failure. But the English working class were by that time experienced and mature in the class struggle, perhaps more experienced and mature than their mentors. For the *Manifesto* was published when Engels was twenty-eight and Marx only thirty. But an active English workman of thirty at the date of the repeal of the Combination Laws and now only fifty-four, would already have had practical experience of twenty-four years of class struggle. To be told after their immense efforts over a quarter of a century that the ends of the communists (with which many of them would have sympathised) could be obtained only by 'the forcible overthrow of existing social conditions', that 'the first step in the revolution of the working class was to raise the proletariat to the position of the ruling class', of what practical help could it be? Instead, when so many varied efforts had in existing circumstances come to nothing, slowly and painfully the stronger groups began to forge new instruments of a different kind to establish their position in the new order. The Rochdale pioneers in 1844 started the co-operative store movement, which aimed at replacing capitalism in limited fields, while after the formation of the Amalgamated Society of Engineers in 1851 the

[69]H W Lee and E Archbold, *Social Democracy in Britain* (1935), p. 38.
[70]Hyndman, p. 279.

'New Model' trade unions set out to ensure that the gains of capitalism were shared at least with the organised craftsmen. To these were added the spread of non-conformist chapels and the training they gave in self-government. Out of the fusion of these ideas in forty years there grew an effective liberal-labour philosophy.

While, therefore, Marx's products at this time had a limited number of enthusiastic purchasers, on the mass market they made a much smaller impression. Though he became deeply read in the writings of the classical economists, his interest and perhaps that of the early English socialists was in the development of capitalist society and its internal tensions rather than in the daily workings of the market. As these critics had not at the time absorbed into their thinking more of the technique of analysis of the classical economists, their immediate practical proposals were sometimes a little detached from contemporary realities. But the long-run negative effects of this were no less important. The two works of Engels and Marx did little to correct this deficiency, for though the beginnings of later ideas can be found in them, Marx did not—for English readers—add to his theory of social development his more specifically economic arguments till the issue of *Das Kapital* twenty years later (English translation 1867). The two streams of economic thought, classical and socialist, thus flowed separately, the socialist one in some obscurity. It was long before they came together in a way which could affect State policy on the acute problems of the new society. In the meantime these were left to the stronger currents of thought derived from classical economics and those which branched from it.

The third effort, Christian Socialism, as an organised movement also began as Chartism was defeated. The small group of Anglican clergy and laymen—Maurice, Kingsley, Ludlow, Tom Hughes, Vansittart Neale and others—rebelled against the acquiescence by the Church in the contemporary approval of competitive industrialism, as contrary to the social implications of their religious faith. They were not influenced by collectivism or by Marx's scientific socialism, nor did they accept its view of human motive; the heart might be deceitful above all things and desperately wicked, but it could be redeemed. They were shocked not by poverty alone, but

39

by the fact that it shut men out of a wider life, and most of all by the absence of moral values in industry, by the neglect of the problem of the relation of man to his work, by his divorce from ownership of his instruments which compelled him to accept the wage system. In its brief but vigorous life it established two things: that Christian moral values had to be restored to industry, and that Christian middle-class men, clerical and lay, were and should be involved in the conditions and struggles of the workers. Its one permanent success was the foundation of the Working Men's College in 1854. Despite immense efforts and much sacrifice its chief economic experiment, workers' co-operative productive societies, failed. But it started a current of thinking which, occasionally less evident, occasionally surging up strongly, has remained a distinctive tributary to English social thought ever since.

Part II

OLD THEORIES, NEW PROBLEMS: THE SEARCH FOR A NEW THEORY 1880–1895

'Mr Carlyle, again, had true vision of the changes that were sweeping an unconscious nation away from the bonds and principles of the past into an unknown future. But he had no efficient instruments for controlling or guiding the process'

JOHN MORLEY, *Life of Cobden*, 1881

1. ECONOMICS IN THE SEVENTIES

A prevailing economic or political doctrine may lose its force because actual social life is being lived on quite different assumptions, as in the 'Cotton South', where the equalitarian doctrine of the American Founding Fathers was faced with an economy expanding on the basis of slavery,[1] or it may be slowly eroded by new facts which it is increasingly inadequate to explain. Adjustment is more difficult when the theory has apparently been confirmed by past experience. By 1870 it seemed clear that free enterprise and trade were the means whereby all classes could be lifted to a higher material standard. The economic progress which had generated an atmosphere in which the theories of Marx and Engels were unable to live a prosperous life was, to those in positions with powers of economic and political decision, practical proof that the first presumption of economic policy should be natural liberty. Provided that some of the rougher inequalities of bargaining power, such as between children and

[1] W E Dodd, *The Cotton South* (1921).

41

employers, were corrected, and trade unions permitted on certain conditions, the economic system could be thought of as self-regulating. There were inquiries into the civil service, railways, sanitary laws, safety in mines, education, trade unions and the labour contract. The last two made the worker more secure in defending his standard of life, while compulsory education in due course helped him to improve it by widening his fields of possible employment. And the provision for labour protection which, as Dicey points out, began in order to prevent the ill-treatment of children in factories and by the end of the century gave a shop girl a legal right to a seat, became so extensive that Morley was led to say that 'in the country where socialism had been less talked about than in any other country in Europe, its principles have been most extensively applied'.[2] With these provisos, the speculative principles of these lay versions of political economy having thus been apparently confirmed by practical success, little more seemed to be required than to keep the machine running in accordance with received principles. In this sense, English political economy was enjoying immense prestige.

A little has to be taken off the remarks of the various non-professional and political speakers at the famous dinner of the Political Economy Club held to celebrate the centenary of the *Wealth of Nations,* for they were no doubt influenced by the occasion, but they showed which way the wind was blowing in high political circles. Jevons had now formulated the principle of diminishing marginal utility, and the whole subject was at the beginning of a development which was to put it on a more logical basis, and make it a more powerful instrument. Yet Mr Lowe did not feel sanguine that there was a very large field left for political economy or that there would be any large or startling development in it. 'The controversies which we now have in political economy, although they afford exercise for the logical faculties, are not of the same thrilling importance as those of earlier days; the great work has been done.' Gladstone said that 'there was not much remaining to be done in the sphere of direct legislation'. Newmarch was hopeful that there would be a large negative development of political economy which would reduce

[2]*Life of Cobden* (1908), p. 326.

the functions of Government to a smaller and smaller compass, and he complained that the Government was setting up one lot of inspectors after another.[3] Political economy, once regarded as a set of rules which should be followed if economic activity were to yield its maximum results, and dynamic when used to cut away mercantilist obstacles, was thus in some risk of being regarded as static, a defence against new forms of State intervention. It is not surprising that in one of his essays Bagehot should conclude that notwithstanding these triumphs, political economy 'lies rather dead in the public mind. Not only does it not excite the same interest as formerly but there is not exactly the same confidence in it.' 'Young men either do not study it, or do not feel that it comes home to them.' He also said that 'many young men, even serious men, especially those educated abroad, had not studied its best writers and have but vague views upon it'.[4]

2. PROTESTS IN THE EIGHTIES: FINDING A NEW ETHIC

This bald description of a prevalent mode of thought leaves out of account the nuances and ignores the dissidents. There was, of course, the continued tradition of Tory and upper-class philanthropy, of which Shaftesbury's Society for the Improvement of the Poor (1844), Burdett-Coutts' buildings in Bethnal Green (1856) and Peabody's housing trust (1862) were an expression. At one time, says Hyndman, there was a 'boom in slumming'. Though after the fading away of Chartism the force of the early English revolutionary socialist writers seemed to have spent itself and they had no native successors, there was a sharpened interest in actual social observation and criticism from varied emotional and ethical sources. By the eighties these had transformed the intellectual scene. Dickens' novels were a heavy onslaught, Carlyle's revulsion from unfettered capitalism was welcomed by some individualist radicals,[5] though

[3] W S Jevons, *Principles of Economics* (1905), pp. 188–192.
[4] Walter Bagehot, *Economic Studies* (1880), p. 73.
[5] John Morley on Carlyle in *Miscellanies* (1888), I, 136–7.

working-class ones, such as G J Holyoake were not deceived into overlooking his authoritarianism.[6] J S Mill's immense influence on the economic teaching in this country not only lasted through a couple of generations of professional economists but his book, especially in the one-volume edition, was widely read by the middle-class individualists and by working-class radicals attracted by his radicalism and later his socialism, long after the time when the 'professionals' had moved beyond many of his theoretical notions. In 1856 came Mayhew's *London Labour and London Life*, in 1857 the Social Science Association, which in its Papers showed much interest in housing and sanitation. Interest in art led Ruskin from a famous Chapter VI in *Stones in Venice* on 'the Nature of Gothic', which related architecture to the conditions of work and life, on to attacks on classical political economy in *Unto this Last* (1862) for failing to emphasise human welfare and on to the curious periodical for workers, *Fors Clavigera* (1871–74). The Christian Socialist Movement was urging that the idea of 'the kingdom of God' had some relevance to human society. An opposite current, radical secular positivism, led Frederic Harrison, Crompton and others to place their legal and professional skills at the disposal of trade unions.[7] All these con-tributed to a varied pattern of ideas, at once critical and idealistic. They helped to wear away the intellectual and emotional resistance of the ruling groups to new ideas of social responsibility and to stimulate and diffuse a concern for the social results of the economic system, to enliven the social conscience.

By about 1883–84 the vigour and pertinence of the criticisms reached a new high level. In 1883 Francis Peek, a member of the London School Board, published *Social Wreckage*, a criticism of the laws and their inequalities as they affected the poor. Much was religious in origin. General Booth's Salvation Army had gone to the slums with street corner evangelism and rudimentary social work. Cardinal Manning's care of the Roman Catholic masses, particularly the immigrants of Irish stock in the big cities, seaports and some agricultural areas, led him to support the Agricultural

---

[6] G J Holyoake, *Sixty Years of an Agitator's Life* (1906), I, 191.

[7] Six Christian Socialists and Positivists joined in a letter to *The Times* supporting the building unions in the trade dispute. Webb, *History of Trade Unionism* (1906), p. 229.

Labourers' Union and write the *Dignity and Rights of Labour* (1874). The London Congregationalists, through Preston and Mearns, startled the public with a harrowing if exaggerated[8] story of housing conditions in the *Bitter Cry of Outcast London* (1883), which was followed by similar studies in other towns. The Anglican Samuel Barnett, as a result of his work in his Whitechapel parish formulated the idea of the University Settlement in which university men would share learning and local activity on the basis of equality. Certainly the list of residents who later became distinguished in social affairs, Llewellyn Smith, Aves, Mallon, Tawney, Beveridge, showed how much one 'side' gained. Then the Oxford Anglicans in *Lux Mundi*, ed. Gore (1889), in setting out the implications of their faith argued that from a Christian standpoint every transaction between man and man was personal and therefore ethical, that the most significant fact of our time was the transition from political to ethical economics, that the Church was not committed to any particular form of property, and that our problem was now to supersede the technical by the personal.[9] Edward Carpenter in *England's Ideal* (1883) and *Towards Democracy* (1883) so widely read by working-class intellectuals and his 'Labour Chant', *England Arise* (1888) habitually sung at labour meetings till 1919, continued the ethical strain which had been so permanent a part of English socialism. In contrast, Hyndman, moving from radicalism to doubts about the whole economic system after reading a French translation of *Das Kapital*, became the channel through which Continental Marxism, based on the class struggle, passed into fresh life in England: his *Historical Basis of Socialism* (1883) put the case in a form likely to be understood by Englishmen. This point is relevant, for in Morris, who left the Liberal Party in 1880, the artistic revolt allied itself to economic socialism: in *How I Became a Socialist*[10] he confessed that the economics of Marx gave him 'agonies of confusion of the brain' (as it has done many Englishmen ever since), but that it was the historical portions which

---

[8]See Ben Tillett's comment on a 'hysterical journalism', though he recognised its service, willy-nilly, in the dockers' cause. *Memories and Recollections* (1931), p. 92. In a slip he attributed the authorship of *Bitter Cry* to Arnold White.

[9]*Lux Mundi*, ed. Gore, 3rd ed., pp. 393–5.

[10]Reprinted in *William Morris*, ed. G D H Cole (1944), pp. 655–9.

interested him. Mill's teaching on rent had prepared the way for the great working-class welcome for Henry George's *Progress and Poverty* and single tax on rents (1880). And the Fabian Society was founded in 1884. And though Toynbee had had active contacts with trade unionists—Broadhurst secured him a listener's seat in the Trade Union Congress in 1877—his famous lectures on the *Industrial Revolution* which were for so long the standard picture of those events, were not actually published till 1884.[11]

Such were the ideals circulating amongst the dissident intelligentsia. What did they accomplish? First, the confidence in the doctrines of *laissez-faire* with which the phase opened, had been eroded. 'Perhaps there never has been a time within the last half century', wrote Llewellyn Smith, 'when political economy has been regarded with such widespread feeling of distrust as it is at the present day . . . when its methods have been so greatly impugned and its conclusions so generally discredited.[12] The social question . . . whose solution was once declared by Bastiat to lie simply in the word Liberty, confronts us today as ominously as ever.'

Secondly, although many of the literary critics were, as we now say, of the upper, if not ruling class, in the sense that they went to the same schools and universities as those with high political office they were not—a critical intelligentsia rarely is—in the seats of political and economic power, shaping policy. The passage of

[11]Mrs Webb in a brilliantly written passage in her *My Apprenticeship,* citing the rather too-often quoted words of the sensitive Arnold Toynbee, somewhat over-played her hand in her attribution of the interest of the intelligent wealthier class to a collective or class sense of sin; and in this she has been followed a little incautiously by a number of other writers. But a reading of the pamphlet containing his two lectures on George's *Progress and Poverty* (1883) showed that they were delivered extempore in conditions of extreme physical weakness, that he did not see the proofs and was unable to revise the reports (Prefatory Note), that owing to physical exhaustion he had to curtail the second (p. 50, et seq.) including the portion in which the passage occurred, and that his audience consisted of two classes, one of which was apparently impatient, wanting revolution (p. 53). It may represent his view, but not many of us would wish to have too much built on the precision of our words used or reported in such circumstances. A sense of sin may imply a sense of guilt, but the idea that righteousness alone exalteth a nation may be outward looking, objective and even imply denunciation, a very different emotional attitude. There were clearly critics to whom these descriptions, rather than Mrs Webb's, would be appropriate. But Mrs Webb may possibly have been influenced by her own personal history. *My Apprenticeship* (1926), pp. 62–3, 179–83.

[12]H Llewellyn Smith, *Economics of Socialism* (1887), pp. 2–3.

ideas to those concerned with government takes time, is often hindered by the opposition of vested ideological as well as political interests, ignorance of some vital aspect, or lack of means of application. Although some of these movements loom large in the history of socialist thought, at the time they were politically small: Hyndman's hoped-for mass party never amounted to more than 10,000, and the Fabians were professedly tiny.

Thirdly, there surged up from below varied ideas from men quite outside the university and school club—the trade union leaders. We are not here concerned with the famous junta who fought for the legal status of unions and equality of the labour contract, but with younger generations, of Thomas Burt, Henry Broadhurst, Ben Tillett, Tom Mann, whose impressive autobiographies record the way their ideas were shaped. Broadhurst shook off an unloved schooling at the age of twelve to start his roving stonemason's life.[13] Burt began his thirteen- to fourteen-hour day as a pit boy at the age of ten, Tillett was working at the age of six and had little schooling to speak of. For these it was union experience which was formative, for Broadhurst almost wholly so. Burt had such books as could be picked up in a pit village from friends and the secondhand shop—Cassell's Self-Educator, penny copies of Shakespeare's plays and Wordsworth's poems, and later drew inspiration from *Unto this Last*.[14] To Ben Tillett, absorbed in his hard labourer's life and bitter struggle to organise casual dockers, 'the literature of revolt'[15] came later.

It would be a mistake to accept without caution Mrs Webb's sweeping claim that no section of the manual workers were 'secreting the poison of socialism' as Asquith called it, that it was not from the sweated workers, skilled unions or slum dwellers, but from the ranks of men of wealth that ideas of State intervention were to come again, and that the earlier critical ideas survived only in a few old men in their anecdotage.[16] Ideas do not cease to exist when they are not

[13]Henry Broadhurst, *Henry Broadhurst, MP: the Story of his Life from the Stonemason's Bench to the Treasury Bench* (1901), chaps. i, ii, esp. pp. 4, 40–1.
[14]Thomas Burt, *An Autobiography* (1924), chap. ix.
[15]Ben Tillett, *Memories and Reflections* (1931), p. 77.
[16]Beatrice Webb, *My Apprenticeship*, pp. 178–9.

47

obviously visible, or because people meet in small groups, do not write and have no formal organisation. In places the oral radical tradition was strong and important, and was fertile ground.[17] But Mrs Webb underestimated it because she was not born in that tradition, but in an extremely wealthy one[18] and because her early work was with London casual labour, partly Irish immigrants and with sweated workers, partly alien, and therefore without it. Work in the provinces might well have modified her assessment. The union branches and districts had much more autonomy in many matters than they have today, and it is significant that it was to these and not to the head offices that the Royal Commission on *Depression of Trade* sent out its many circulars for information on unemployment, and the Royal Commission on *Labour* its elaborate questionnaire on strikes and union organisation.[19] Although their replies were answers to specific questions, a careful study of them suggests that men in the branches can scarcely have failed to talk about wider issues or to have formed part of the readership of the then radical *Reynolds* and *Leeds Mercury* newspapers.[20]

As the magnitude of the social problem and the entanglement of poverty, overcrowding, irregular employment, drunkenness and crime was uncovered, social workers in the field, reformers, missioners, magistrates and guardians became confused and often a little hopeless.[21] Philanthropists and reformers were alike discouraged.[22] And Charles Booth, presenting his first results, told the Royal Statistical Society in 1887 that 'it is the sense of helplessness that tries everyone. The wage earners are helpless to regulate and obtain

[17]For example, Philip Snowden, *Autobiography* (1934), I, 18, 19. See also E P Thompson's 'Homage to Tom Maguire' in *Essays in Labour History* (1960), pp. 276–80, 291–2. It should not be overlooked that sometimes the reading workers bought books by common subscription, read them together in local pubs and stored them there.

[18]R Meinertzhagen, *The Diary of a Black Sheep* (1964).

[19]See *Labour*, R. Com.; 1892, C. 6795–vii, viii, vol. xxxv, pt. iii; C. 6795–ix, vol. xxvi, pt. iv. *Depression of Trade and Industry*, R. Com. 2nd Rep., app. pt. ii; 1886, C. 4715–i, xxii.

[20]See, for example, replies to the R. Com. on *Depression of Trade* by the Edinburgh Trades Council, the Tobacco Strippers Mutual Assn., the Scottish Typographical Assn., Ardrossan Branch. pp. 96, 97, 98.

[21]Helen Bosanquet, *Social Work in London,* 1896–1912, pp. 17–18.

[22]Smith, *Economics of Socialism,* pp. 2, 3.

the value of their work; the manufacturers and dealers can work only within the limits of competition, and the rich are helpless to relieve want without stimulating the source; the legislature is helpless because the limits of successful interference by change of law are closely circumscribed.'[23]

3. GATHERING THE FACTS: THE GREAT INVESTIGATIONS AND THE PUZZLES OF THEORY

Such was the climate of opinion in 1885. But at this point, as a result of the frustrations of individual, voluntary and local effort, matters which had caused so much uneasiness—the level of wages of the poorly paid, housing and the maintenance of employment—were raised to the level of urgent national policy. The State machinery of inquiry was set to work again with renewed energy and on a generous scale. Private investigations were made on a magnitude and with a penetration which had few precedents. What is of interest to us here is not the evils they described, vivid as the accounts of them sometimes were, but the way those dealing with national policy tried to think their way out from accepted views to new principles suitable for grappling with them.

i. *The great depression*

The problem widest in scope was 'the Great Depression'. Though at its appointment there were some awkward political cross-currents,[24] the inquiry by the Royal Commission, 1885–86 showed how difficult it was for people to understand large economic changes going on around them; and there was a sharp difference between popular and expert opinion. Giffen, the first witness, in oral evidence made a distinction between depression as a feeling in the minds of business people and the actual depression of business.[25] As Beales

---

[23] *Journal of the Royal Statistical Society* (1887), 376.

[24] For example, see Broadhurst on 'labour' members of the Commission in his *Henry Broadhurst*, pp. 159–61.

[25] Robert Giffen, oral evidence, qq. 88–9.

has pointed out, debates in Parliament, speeches, discussions amongst economists and the testimony of witness after witness in oral evidence leave no doubt that many sections of business men were pretty solid in their complaints that there was one. On the other hand, two great contemporary experts, Giffen the statistician and Marshall the economist, were of a different mind. Giffen said that while there was a general impression that the depression was unprecedented in duration, the facts were entirely the other way: it was singularly light in its effects on industry and wages.[26] Marshall's view was that though there was a depression of prices, interest and profits, this was quite consistent with the condition of prosperity.[27] Some historians have doubted whether in fact there was much of a general depression to inquire into.

The Commission's work has to be viewed first in the light of knowledge then open to it. The Commissioners themselves were rather bemused by the conflict between two sorts of evidence. The extensive oral evidence, answers to some 15,000 questions to witnesses concerned particularly with 4 groups of industries, coal and iron, shipping, the textile trades and agriculture, which they regarded as representative or typical, but which we now see were exceptionally vulnerable, led them to conclude that the condition of trade could fairly be described as 'depressed', by which was meant 'a diminution and in some cases absence of profit', and 'diminished employment' (Final Rep. para. 27). It had started about 1875 and with the exception of a short period of prosperity, continued up to the time the Commission was sitting. But the written evidence from Giffen, on behalf of the Board of Trade, and Algernon West for the Board of Inland Revenue, to the sceptical surprise of some Commissioners, seemed to point to the opposite conclusion, for the chief statistical series—except those for agriculture—imports, exports, shipping cleared, railway traffic, all showed increases per head, though at varying rates. And even where there was a fall in value, as in pig iron production and manufactured exports, this was due to

[26]Giffen, *Essays in Finance* (1880), p. 118. See also Viscount Goschen's *Essays and Addresses on Economic Questions* (1905), p. 3.

[27]Alfred Marshall, oral evidence before the Gold and Silver Commission, qq. 9823–25; C. 5512–i, xlv. Also in *Official Papers* (1926), pp. 98–9.

price changes, for quantities had increased. Income and profits assessed to tax, save in particular cases, e.g. from mines and iron works, had increased even per head. Production had increased faster than population (Final Rep. para. 34). The Majority were unable to come to any clear conclusions (para. 92–3) or to make any 'but few definite recommendations' (para. 94). A strong Minority led by Lord Dunraven thought their view too optimistic. Its Report went over the same ground with rather more self-consistency, but dared to challenge the sacred doctrine of free trade by recommending a tariff of 10 to 15 per cent on all manufactured imports to off-set foreign competitors' advantages arising not from 'natural causes' but from bounties, subsidies and protective tariffs. One Commissioner in this, as in other inquiries of which he was a member, put it down to private ownership of land.

What was the reason for this rather tame result of a great inquiry? First, the Commission excluded any detailed examination of the fall in the value of money, the relation of gold and silver, as needing a separate inquiry. Secondly, as both the Majority (para. 35) and the Minority (para. 43) Reports complained, there were few statistics of production, measures of unemployment were limited to skilled trade unions' figures of out-of-work members, and of the unskilled nothing was certainly known beyond what could be guessed from statistics of pauperism. Some of the essential factual basis of cycle analysis was thus wanting. They were unable to define 'depression' clearly or to measure it; and long waves had not been heard of.

The Minority Report thought that the existence of depression was established, because in the cotton industry employment had not increased proportionately to the growth of population (para. 49)— as if it would in an advancing economy with industries becoming more varied (para. 49). But relevant cycle theory was lacking as well. The members of the Commission were men in the middle, active years of life in public and industrial affairs: what ideas on political economy would they have been armed with had they studied it in their early years or even had time to keep pace with ideas set out in the currently approved books? The two chief reports, speaking of the evidence on the fall of profits, repeat the old doctrine of the tendency of profits to a minimum in advancing countries (paras. 51, 59, 60) and refer to general over-production (paras. 51, 61, 62), another long-standing item of discussion. These were scarcely of use for the particular diagnosis in hand. In the standard books these recurrent difficulties were often thought of as 'crises' (frequently referred to as 'panics') connected with the banking system[28] and relegated to books on that subject, e.g. Gilbart's *History and Principles of Banking* (ed. 1882) or to use the phrase of a much later writer, regarded as the childish ailments of capitalism. In spite, therefore, of the charges made by Marx and Engels that these recurrent depressions were inherent in the system, and of the early sketches by the speakers at the Manchester Statistical Society, e.g. by Langton in 1857 and John Mills in 1856,[29] and of papers by Jevons in 1875 and 1878, at the British Association, a platform which then ensured excellent publicity, the problem and task of analysing the trade cycle had not really been brought into the body of principles.[30] Giffen refers to the periodical depressions at tolerably regular intervals as alternations having their roots in human nature (1877), while Marshall said that times of spasmodic inflation have always sown the seeds of coming disasters—a point not brought prominently to the front again until Wesley Mitchell declared that 'prosperity breeds depression' (1916). The current expositions of political economy, to which they might have turned for guidance—Fawcett's *Principles* (1883), Cairnes' *Leading Principles* (1879), Sidgwick's *Principles* (1883) and A and M Marshall's *Economics of Industry* (1879)—had little to say about it. Jevons was a notable exception. His attempts to determine the periodicity of cycles and to relate them to physical causes (through sun spots to harvest variations, which were 'triggers' which might set off a collapse) were unlikely to be regarded by business men as of immediate practical value.[31] But in a little shilling primer on *Political Economy* (1878)

[28]See the statement in the Majority Report of the Labour Commission (1894), para. 213, which is in advance of anything in the *Depression of Trade* report.

[29]Ashton, *Economic and Social Investigations in Manchester*, pp. 71, 74.

[30]C Juglar's *Crises Commerciales* (1862; 1st English ed., 1916) is not mentioned in these works. Marshall's *Principles* (1890 ed.), *Industry and Trade* (1919) and *Money, Credit and Commerce* (1923) do not refer to it.

[31]Letters to John Mills in *Letters and Journal of W Stanley Jevons,* ed. Harriet Jevons (1886), pp. 378–83. William Stanley Jevons, *State in Relation to Labour* (1866), p. 97.

intended for younger people, he gives a clear description of the succession of events in typical cycles, the place of credit and expectations of business men, argues that prosperous trade was sure to be followed by bad trade, that their causes were not well understood, but that the time to start a new factory was when trade was bad. The little book went through 5 editions by 1887, and sold 99,000 copies. One witness, James Mawdsley, secretary to the Operative Cotton Spinners, regarded the events as one of the ordinary trade depressions, perhaps complicated by special circumstances which would pass away in due time.[32] But the Commission did not follow this clue to ask in what respects it was different and in what respects it was similar to previous depressions. Dunraven's group, on the contrary, thought that in the main the depression was due to permanent causes (para. 27). It is not surprising that the Commission had little influence on policy except a negative one of warding off attacks on free trade.

The difficulty which the Commission had in reaching more positive conclusions is understandable, for modern historians, economists and statisticians who have made the period their happy hunting ground, though armed with more information, more sophisticated techniques and refined theories, have still not yet brought finality to the discussion either.[33] It is agreed that the protracted 'depression', though there were ups and downs within it, lasted beyond 1886, that it was not confined to this country, and that a factor of primary importance was the secular fall of prices. For this the explanations are varied: that its origin was monetary, the price level falling, according to Cassel,[34] because the relative gold supply (the percentage by which its annual growth differed from the 'normal' increase of 2.8 per cent per annum) fell throughout the period. But this could not be true because of the lack of connection between gold stocks and changes in the quantity of money in

---

[32]qq. 5128, 5129. Hargreaves, Secretary of the Over Darwen District of the union, took the same view: 2nd Rep., app. ii, pp. 72; 1886, C. 4715-i, xxii.

[33]See an excellent review on the state of knowledge on the subject by A E Mussen, 'The Great Depression, 1873-96; a Re-appraisal' in *Journal of Economic History*, pp. 199-228, and 'British Industrial Growth during the Great Depression' in *Economic History Review* (1962-63). Also R Coppock, 'Causes of the Great Depression', *Manchester School* (1961), pp. 203-30.

[34]G Cassel, *Theory of Social Economy* (1923 trans.), pp. 441-9 and charts pp. 440, 448.

E

the hands of the public (Phelps Brown and Ozga). Yet did not gold have something to do with the behaviour of prices in the gold-using nineteenth century? (Robertson). Alternatively, the price fall was due to changes on the supply side—the fall of transport costs resulting from mechanical transport increased the supply of primary products, yet it accounted for only part of the fall in costs (Coppock). When industrial production grows more slowly than the output of primary products, the latter fall in price and this fall spreads itself via final prices, etc. to the general price level (Phelps Brown and Ozga). There was no decrease in actual production, but a slower rate of growth (Hoffmann). There was little significant increase in unemployment amongst skilled workers (Rostov), yet there may have been some increase in the insecurity of jobs (Robertson). There was a lower rate of capital accumulation (Paul Douglas), and a check to exports because we were no longer the world's only workshop (Musson) and had reached our climacteric in iron production per head (Eckel).[35] Some of these difficulties were due to the absence of data, such as statistics of production, wages and employment of unskilled workers, not available to the Commission then and now beyond recall. And the Great Depression was a 'number of things'; but 'cycle theory' was not developed enough to give either expert or Commissioners a grip on the problem. For this reason Mrs Webb's description of the Commission as a 'humiliating failure' must, in the sense she intended it, be rejected.[36] For the Webbs' own thinking was focussed on the problems of the ownership and organisation of industry and there is little evidence even in their later writings that they understood the nature of trade cycle phenomena or the theory required for their analysis; a deficiency they but shared, of course, with contemporaries.

ii. *The housing of the working classes*

If there were uncomfortable doubts about the capacity of the system of free enterprise to provide economic stability, there were also

[35]E Eckel, *Coal, Iron and War* (1921), pp. 15, 16.

[36]Beatrice Webb, 'The Failure of the Labour Commission' in *Nineteenth Century*, XXXVI (1894), 21.

disconcerting questions as to why the conditions of large sections
of the workers were so unsatisfactory. The inquiries into housing,
sweating, labour relations were intended to find some of the answers.
It would perhaps be appropriate to apply to the nineteenth-century
housing reformer Wolfram von Eschenbach's description of
Parzival as 'a brave man slowly wise'. The difficulties facing attempts
to house the workers in the first half of the nineteenth century have
already been mentioned; the rapid growth of the population by
birth rate, influx and immigration in places like Liverpool, leading
to mass overcrowding in existing houses; speculative new building
under pressure of demand, in ignorance or disregard of the elements
of drainage, water supply, refuse removal; the difficulty of raising
capital for a large-scale mechanical revolution and housing the
working population at the same time; and the lack of available land
in some areas. Set against this were the efforts of some employers,
e.g. Samuel Oldknow and Salt, to provide improved cottages for
their workers; and some of the new houses, now demolished as
unsanitary, were then better than the existing ones. Certainly the
difficulties did not remain for want of Parliamentary effort to get at
the facts, not only by a single great inquest, like *Depression of Trade*
or *Sweating,* but by persistent inquiry: papers by Kay and Southwood
Smith in the fourth and fifth annual Reports of the Poor Law
Commission; Farr's *Analysis of the Causes of Death* in the Registrar
General's first annual report (1839); the *Health of Towns* Committee,
1840 (Slaney); Chadwick's great report on the *Sanitary Condition of
the Labouring Population* (1842); the Royal Commissions on the *State
of Large Towns and Populous Districts* (1844, 1845) (Duke of Buccleugh)
and the *Health of the Metropolis* (1847–48). These all dealt with the
dilapidation of the older houses, the problems of water supply,
drainage, which did not seem so important in rural conditions from
which England was emerging, until their association with epidemic
diseases—witness the cholera outbreaks, Chadwick's maps showing
street distribution of cholera and other diseases in Leeds and
Bethnal Green,[37] and the fear of Bermondsey fever mists—drove
the inquiries along. On the whole the problem of housing was

[37]See *Sanitary Condition of the Labouring Population* (1842), maps facing p. 160. On
London, Jephson, *Sanitary Evolution of London* (1907), gives a vivid account.

looked at rather as one of sanitation and regulation, than of the provision of houses.

But soon there was a check even to this activity, the instruments for carrying them out being woefully inadequate. Partly owing to its experimental and progressive character, the law resulting was confused, frequently unknown, difficult to understand and often optional. In complete disregard of the Benthamite principle of a unified local authority, each group of Acts designated a new authority for their particular purposes, and there was a great variety and want of coincidence in their particular areas. Many duties were seldom discharged. Codification of the law, a single health authority for all health purposes in every area, each with a qualified medical officer able to carry out the law and to spread knowledge amongst the population of the significance of the restrictions imposed upon them, and a supervisory central authority combining all the medical and sanitary powers scattered amongst the Departments, were the remedies proposed by the Royal Sanitary Commission, 1871[38] some of which were carried out by the Act of 1872, though weaknesses remained and the administrative confusion and lack of democracy in the Vestries was not tackled until 1888 and 1889.

There had been much to learn in medicine, sanitary engineering and administration, but as the policy began to move slowly from regulation towards the supply of house-room there were difficulties of a different order. There is no need to repeat the sorry and tragic story of the housing conditions of the poor. The clergy protested. The *Bitter Cry of Outcast London* (1883)[39] (Preston), *The Homes of the Bristol Poor* (Rev E A Fuller) stirred public opinion, whilst skilled journalists such as G R Sims, in *How the Poor Live* (1883), highlighted some bad quarters. Witness after witness before committee and commission gave ample and moving evidence. Public-spirited people invested funds at modest rates of interest in societies in London, Bristol, Newcastle and other places, to provide tenement accommodation or 'industrial dwellings' at modest rents thought to be within

---

[38]*The Sanitary Laws*, R. Com. 2nd Rep.; 1871, C. 281, xxxv.
[39]But see Mearns' admissions, *Housing of the Working Classes*, R. Com., vol. ii, Mins. of ev., qq. 5556–86; 1884–85, C. 4402–i, xxx, and Tillett's critical comment in *Memories and Reflections*, p. 92.

the reach of the working class. But as the *Unhealthy Areas* Committee confessed much later,[40] the task proved so complicated and difficult that there was no one panacea, all the legal powers had to be used and methods adapted to difficult circumstances. The problem had to be broken down into its parts, its various components distinguished and fresh principles evolved for settling the boundary between individual and social obligation, on the right of the State to purchase compulsorily, on compensation, on its claims to improved values. Some of these grew out of the experience—often bitter—of local authorities and philanthropic bodies and in the end took the State to the roots of the social question. The Select Committee on *Artisans' and Labourers' Dwellings Improvement*, 1882, and the great Commission, 1884-85, on the *Housing of the Working Classes* set out to gather up and assess the experience of voluntary and public efforts. What this had been is shown by the citations below (pp. 57-61) all from the evidence before the Commission, except that given by the Rev Samuel Barnett to the Select Committee (qq. 3020, 3223, etc.)

First, there was the difference between a town like Birmingham, with a considerable population of artisans in cottages, and London or Bristol, with masses of unskilled, unorganised casual labourers in tenements. A preliminary effort to check the most obvious overcrowding, that of persons per room in old houses used as tenements, was made by the Sanitary Act, 1866 (Sect. 35), which authorised the local authority to register and inspect them and to fix the maximum number of persons who might occupy a house or part of a house occupied by members of more than one family. But the powers were not widely used, often forgotten and presented obvious difficulties. The Medical Officer for Hackney, for example, admitted that enforcement of the regulations had simply moved those dislodged to other parts of London, where their wages might not be big enough to enable them to get better accommodation (qq. 9558-65), and overcrowding was sometimes added to by dislodgement of the population by public improvements (Mearns, qq. 9493-98; Sims, qq. 5611-6; Williams, q. 5929). Until there was alternative

---

[40]*Unhealthy Areas*, Cttee. Final Rep., non-Parl., 1921, p. 16.

house room, clearly this power did not go beyond the fringe of the problem.

The overcrowding of houses on the site and dilapidated houses were provided for by the Torrens' Acts, 1869–79, and the Cross Acts, 1875–79. These introduced new principles of State action. The former concerned individual houses and small groups of bad houses, and assumed that houses unfit for human habitation ought not to be so used, and if not improvable, where necessary in the public interest should be closed or demolished. Their principle was that the responsibility for maintaining a house in good condition rested upon the owner, and if he failed to do so the law was justified in stepping in. (The original Bill provided that the local authority could rebuild, but this power was struck out and not re-instated till 1879.) The Cross Acts, 1875–79, on the other hand, provided machinery for dealing with large unhealthy areas which, because of overcrowding and bad arrangement of houses on the site, could be dealt with only by complete clearance and reconstruction. But this meant giving local authorities large powers of compulsory purchase and of turning people out of their homes, and imposing on the authorities, or on other promoters of clearance schemes a new obligation, that of housing at least as many persons as were displaced.

The operations under these Acts show how many were the ramifications of the problem. The Metropolitan Board of Works purchased clearance areas of forty-two acres, nine acres of which were given up to new streets. Before clearance 20,335 persons occupied 5,555 separate holdings; in pursuance of their obligations, new accommodation provided for 22,753 persons. Yet few of the displaced persons had returned and the 'loss' over and above income was about £1,500,000. In one case accommodation was offered in near-by Peabody dwellings, but few accepted.[41] To what was this fantastic result due? First, in the uncleared areas a large proportion of the inhabitants were casual labourers, hawkers and others of low and irregular incomes who occupied only one room. Of the 5,555 separate holdings, 3,349 were of one room only, 1,483 of two rooms and 723 of three rooms or more. The new accommoda-

---

[41]*Artisans' and Labourers' Dwellings Improvement*, Sel. Cttee. Rep., p. v, 1882 (235) vii. See Barnett's evidence, q. 3220.

tion of 6,206 separate holdings provided only 1,535 of one room, 3,849 of two rooms and 822 of three rooms or more. It was this drop in the number of one-room holdings which was significant.[42] In this and in other schemes the original population had moved on to create another slum elsewhere and the new inhabitants were better-paid workers. Similarly, in the Boundary Street scheme completed by the L.C.C., amongst the 2,300 adults, there were no bricklayers, plumbers or carpenters, most being unskilled or irregular workers occupying one room only. But in the new accommodation of 1,069 tenements, there were only 15 single rooms and 542 of two rooms. It is not surprising that only eleven of the original inhabitants returned.

The rents were too high. Even the Peabody dwellings did not reach the lowest level of the population for whom life was a perpetual struggle (Young, qq. 6061–2, Nichols, qq. 9246–7). The average rent for a single room in a Peabody building was 2s 1¼d or in Whitechapel 2s 9d (Barnett, q. 3023). But the earnings of costers and hawkers were ten shillings to twelve shillings per week, of casual dockers in a week of full work eighteen shillings (Sims, q. 5755). Even at these low rates it was estimated that 88 per cent were paying more than one-fifth of their wages in rent. In Bristol the proportion was one-third. Octavia Hill agreed that one-fifth was the maximum which could be afforded (q. 8993), though she thought they could pay three shillings for one large and one very small room. These rents could not be evaded by moving away, since the workers had to live near their work or the chance of work—a docker for a possible call, a married woman to be near the giver-out of work. Then they needed the cheap evening markets, traders who gave credit in bad weeks, etc. Even the cheap workmen's rail fares would not solve the problem where nearness to work was important, especially if there were subsidiary earners, or unless they were low enough not to raise the total of rent plus fare higher than the old rent. Shaftesbury complained that overcrowding had become worse, and that the one-room system was spreading. Barnett, Sims and Octavia Hill said that a great part of the population in the areas

[42] J J Clark, *The Housing Problem* (1920), p. 228.

they knew lived one family per room (q. 5782). But all three declared that one-family rooms were needed. This realistic assessment shocked some members of the Commission, who asked, if children were to continue to be brought up in a one family per room system, how were we to get improved health and standards? (qq. 9171-2). 'I am certain that you must get single rooms into which you put these people as a first step' (Barnett q. 3223). Improvements in habits and health and in accommodation must and can be made to go hand in hand (Hill qq. 9172, 8936). Miss Hill agreed that her system did envisage the continuance of the one-room system for large numbers of the poorest class in the populous areas (q. 9171) but very great immediate improvements could be made for the modest rents she charged (*Nineteenth Century*, XIV, 929).

The Commission was thus face to face with the teeming population of low-paid and often irregularly employed labourers. If it were useless to try and insist on a standard of rooms per family which they could not attain, what was the solution? Something could be done to reduce costs by simpler accommodation, giving them what was really essential (Hill, qq. 8552-8833) and it could easily be designed so that a family with one large room could later add a very small one (Hill, *Nineteenth Century*, XIV, 1883, 930). Should rents be subsidised? George Shipton, secretary of the London Trades Council, agreed that the labouring and poorly paid workers, as distinct from artisans, could not pay for expensive arrangements; they should be provided with assisted dwellings inferior in size and appearance, but containing the essentials for health and efficiency, let at a loss if necessary (qq. 12,861-2). To F G Barnett, a Bristol guardian and solicitor to the local Industrial Dwellings Company, the only solution was to fix rents having regard to wages, provide house room at these rents, and for the State or locality to make up any difference out of rates or taxes (qq. 7139-40, 7181-2). But rents below market rates were rejected by Hill on the grounds that they would just become a rate in aid of wages of which employers would take advantage, and that wages would fall, a contention which had point when the prospective tenants were a mass of unskilled competing labourers tied to an area (qq. 8996-7). Sims, however, said that this could not happen to the many self-employed (qq. 5740–3). Chamberlain would reduce costs as much as possible, but would not let below competitive rents (qq. 12,614–5). Government loans at specially low rates were urged by many witnesses and the Commissioners, but others thought that this would check individual builders whose efforts had sometimes been paralysed by the housing trusts in this way (Hill, qq. 8874–8; Goschen, Cross, reservations to Report pp. 64–5).

A major cause of the high cost of accommodation was the high cost of land and the scale of compensation. Could these be reduced? In the case referred to above, the location of the site gave it a high value for commercial purposes—three times the price at which it was sold to fulfil the re-housing requirements, for use for working-class houses. The re-housing requirements in these conditions meant that the estimated difference between cost and recoupment was £560,000.[43] The 1882 Committee therefore recommended that the requirement to re-house on or near the site should, for the Metropolitan Board of Works, be reduced to one-half or to two-thirds and for the City of London to one-half the number dispossessed, leaving the rest to be provided for in other districts where travelling facilities made it convenient.[44] Further, the Act had provided for compensation at 'fair market value'. What is fair market value? Should it be the value as between a willing buyer and a willing seller in the open market, or a willing buyer and an unwilling or indifferent seller? (Chamberlain, qq. 12,413; 12,493–4). A decision that all the interests in the property had to be valued at the same time meant that short tenancies which could have been allowed to run out had to be bought at once at inflated prices, and allowance made for loss of trade profits in small shops, which were often exaggerated. 'We paid £300,000 or £400,000 more than the property would have fetched if sold as private property' (Chamberlain qq. 12,385; 12,408–9). There was to be no compensation for compulsion, but in practice in England and Wales 10 per cent was added, partly for the cost of re-investment. In addition the complicated procedure so raised costs that often local authorities added to their price part of the seller's costs.

[43] *Artisans' and Labourers' Dwellings Improvement,* Sel. Cttee. Rep., p. v, 1882 (235) vii.
[44] Ibid., p. ix.

It was clear that financial burdens of this kind were frightening local authorities off schemes for clearance and reconstruction. The difference between the price paid for sites with a commercial value and their value for re-housing thus became an obvious target for criticism. Mill's ideas on rent and on landlords who grew rich in their sleep without working, without sacrificing, without risking, had percolated down into the thoughts of artisans who had never read his book, and the followers of Henry George, who had toured the country in 1882, in a vigorous campaign, were expounding the doctrine that socially created land values should be taken by the State. From all this little practical result followed. The search for a solution brought out two more limited possibilities—betterment and recoupment. The owners of property surrounding an unhealthy area might well obtain from the clearance and reconstruction a particular rise in value or betterment over and above that of the community generally. To share in this betterment the public had a claim because it was due to the specific onerous effort and expenditure by the local authorities; they could not be expected to bear all the burdens while others went off with the financial benefits. It was thus less on theoretical than on the narrower grounds of hard finance that the public case was based.

These two principles had to make their way against practical difficulties. The Public Health Act, 1875, had empowered local authorities to charge the cost of supplying a deficiency in sanitary accommodation as a private improvement, but this had to be the exact expenses of ameliorating that property. But by the Artisans' Dwellings Act, 1879, the purchase price could take account of the consequential increase of value caused by demolishing obstructive buildings of other property of the same owner; a provision widened in 1882 to cover the property of different owners. Although on the general principle the Royal Commission was indecisive, the provisions were embodied in the *Housing of the Working Classes Act,* 1890 (para. 8). But a London County Council scheme for widening parts of the Strand which provided that a large area marked on the map should be a betterment area and that an arbitrator should apportion the betterment, not to exceed half the cost, between the buildings on it, aroused great hostility both because the boundary of the betterment area was not easy to draw and because the task of apportionment was regarded as technically impossible.[45] The Halsbury Select Committee agreed that the principle of betterment was equitable, though eminent valuers differed on whether it was possible to pronounce with certainty that such an effect had been produced. Some argued alternatively, any improved value should be obtained by recoupment, that is, by the purchase and resale at an enhanced value. But the procedure of compulsory purchase was so complicated that in the Strand case the L.C.C. thought recoupment too expensive a method. Though H L Cripps told the Halsbury Committee that in no single case had recoupment proved other than an extravagant operation (qq. 343–4, 351)[46] the Committee was not convinced, since it had never been tried in circumstances calculated to make it successful. The purchase of trade interests required was inevitably attended by wasteful and extravagant expenditure. And recoupment would involve a departure from a long-established principle that lands bought compulsorily must be restricted to those actually required for the undertaking. (It is worth noting that the Scott Committee of 1918, which looked once more into the law and practice involved in compulsory purchase of land for public purposes, adhered to this principle, for it rejected any general power of recoupment save in such cases as fringe land for street widening, on the ground that local authorities should not become speculators in land not required for their undertakings.)[47]

The experience of these two methods—'Torrens' for individual and small groups of houses and 'Cross' for large unhealthy areas—raised a third possibility: what should be the power of local authorities to build houses not just for re-housing persons displaced by clearance, but because they were needed to add to a deficient total supply? This was less complicated, but more far reaching. The difficulties of rent and management, as well as the apathy or hostility of undemocratic bodies, were enough to explain why the *Labouring*

---

[45]*London Streets (Strand Improvement) Bill,* Sel. Cttee. Rep., 1890 (239) xv. See also Schuster in *Dictionary of Political Economy* (1901), I, on 'Betterment'. He favoured recoupment.

[46]*Town Improvements (Betterment),* Sel. Cttee., H.L. 1894 (292) xv.

[47]*The Acquisition and Valuation of Land for Public Purposes,* 2nd Rep., pp. 21–2; 1918, Cd. 9229, xi.

Classes' Lodging Houses Act, 1851, which enabled local authorities to borrow on the security of the rates in order to build lodging houses, remained a dead letter.[48] The Royal Commission, though directed to inquire into the housing of the working classes, was moved by the evidence to give most of its attention to the 'housing of the poor' and it did not really investigate the question whether it was possible for private enterprise to build houses for ordinary workers at a price they could pay, in the sense in which this was interpreted after the First World War. Octavia Hill was certain that accommodation for artisans could be made to pay. According to Chamberlain, Birmingham relied on private enterprise for building, the supply was adequate in quality and quantity and had increased faster than population. The 1881 census had shown—though the Commission's report did not mention it—that over the country as a whole the vacancies were about 8 per cent. The Commission took the view, however, that the State should lend for building working-class houses at the lowest rate possible without loss to the Treasury (Rep., pp. 38–40) and that building and borrowing powers given by Shaftesbury's Act should be exercised by the Metropolitan Board of Works for the whole of London. But Goschen, Stanley and S Morley, felt that since it was on private enterprise that the public must in the main rely for the supply of houses, it was impossible to give large powers of building to local authorities and at the same time expect that private capital would flow into the trade if at any moment it might be faced with large-scale municipal competition. 'The question whether we are to look to private enterprise for the future supply of working-class dwellings or are to invoke the action of public authorities seems to us the most important '(Rep., pp. 64, 65). At the time municipal building was such a tiny fraction of the total that this must have seemed mere defensive pedantry. Looking ahead to the years after 1918 it was prophetic. Their question was in effect answered by the *Housing of the Working Classes Act,* 1890, Pt. III. This permitted appropriate local authorities to provide houses for the working class if needed, and not merely as part of slum clearance schemes; they could do the building

---

[48]*Housing of the Working Classes.* R. Com. Rep., p. 46; 1884–85, C. 4402, xxx.

themselves or arrange for private enterprise or semi-philanthropic bodies to do it. They had powers of compulsory purchase. They could get capital at low rates through the Public Works Loan Commission or by borrowing on the security of the rates. This development was really significant, for we were then apparently the only country to try to increase the supply of working-class houses, not simply by making it easier for private builders, but by the State itself providing them. A new course had been set which eventually led to the situation Goschen and his colleagues had envisaged: the State was to become the chief provider and owner of working-class houses.

Some matters were left unsolved. Site values were left untaxed and unrated,[49] technical difficulties restricted the operation of better-ment, recoupment was rejected, and despite the evils caused by 'house knackers' who dealt in the fag ends of leases, the only proposal for leasehold enfranchisement was that where demand was adequate local authorities might buy up leases and sell to occupiers.[50] Then the level of rents to be charged for 'council houses' presented difficulties of principle. If they were competitive, private building might be discouraged; if unremunerative, the tenants would be given an unfair advantage over their fellows, if subsidised out of the rates —except in the special case of the very poor—the tenants as a group were favoured at the expense of the rates. These questions had to be thought over again after the First World War had given the whole problem a new magnitude. But the effort had brought to light many of the main components of the housing problem, all of which were relevant to policy in later periods, though different relative values were assigned to them from time to time. It led to the formu-lation of new principles, which, it is arguable, were a more significant break from *laissez-faire* than other more quoted examples, e.g. the Factory Acts. And they were the outcome less of 'outside' theory than of the painful efforts of local authorities urged forward by housing reformers moved by compassion.

---

[49]*Town Holdings. Taxation of Ground Rents and Improvements,* Sel. Cttee. Rep., 1892 (214) xviii.
[50]*Town Holdings,* Sel. Cttee., 1889 (251) xv. Sidney Webb regarded leasehold enfran-chisement as a reactionary proposal which had no place in the modern socialist programme. *Fabian Essays,* p. 36.

iii. *Sweating*

The third great inquiry was the Lords' Committee on *The Sweating System* (Ch. Lord Dunraven). In this case the exercise of the members of their right to make inquiries themselves by oral examination of witnesses which proved so blunt an instrument in the case of the Trade Depression and Labour Commissions, was well adapted to its purpose. For the Committee was brought face to face with the suffering victims of this unknown, grim industrial underworld, and that much of the evidence was repetitive was perhaps an advantage. For the Committee was able to grasp what the evils meant in personal terms and expressed their admiration of the courage of the sufferers and the absence of any desire to excite pity by exaggeration. The Committee found that the evils 'could hardly be exaggerated', that earnings of the lowest class of workers were barely sufficient to maintain existence, hours of labour such as to make life one of almost ceaseless toil and sanitary conditions injurious both to the workers and the public. But when it came to practical steps the complexities of the problem involved the Committee in difficulties. Prohibit sub-contracting? But sweating occurred also where there was no sub-contracting. Prohibit alien immigration?—but it occurred where there was no immigration. Prohibit outwork?—but this would be hard on the hundreds of married and single women who added to meagre family wages during intervals in the housework to which they were tied. Well-considered trade unions would help, but how could these half-starved scattered workers pay union subscriptions? The Committee regarded as the chief cause the gathering together in towns of a helpless community, an excessive supply of unskilled labour with a low standard of life,—conditions which could supply an unscrupulous employer with workers helplessly dependent on him.[51]

[51]Fawcett had argued (1870) that population had increased by a tenth in one decade, that if this continued any advantage from the improvements in production would be gradually absorbed in the support of mere numbers, that the extra number competed for employment as able-bodied labourers and every trade was overcrowded. But a hearing of the evidence alone would have led the Committee to this conclusion. A modern economist, E H Phelps Brown, leaving aside Fawcett's Malthusian worries about food supply, has pointed out that with population increasing at that rate, a check to demand would mean more applicants for work than vacancies, so that the worker got the worst of the wage bargain. *The Growth of British Industrial Relations* (1959), esp. pp. xvi, 100.

They suggested for immediate action increased enforcement of sanitary legislation, lists of outworkers, registers of owners of workshops, prohibiting girls and women from doing certain types of heavy work in chain-making, and thought good might come of well-considered combination amongst the workers. The scandal of sweating on Government and other public contracts should be ended by taking precautions to ensure fair and reasonable terms to the workers. Only practical experience could determine how this could best be done. But the House of Commons' Fair Wages Resolution set as the principle the payment of wages generally accepted as current for a competent workman in the trade. According to circumstances this might have some reference to, and in time did come to mean trade union negotiated rates. They did not say, as did the later Labour Commission, that some of the evils might be removed by 'natural forces', but that in the circumstances prohibition of home work could be arbitrary and could not be enforced. Unable to see their way out, they said that when legislation had reached the limit to which it was effective, real improvement must depend on the increased sense of responsibility of the employer and of public opinion which the exposure of the evils should bring about. That it was not only the general presumption at that date against State wage-fixing which inhibited them from suggesting a legal minimum wage in such conditions—the Labour Minority of the Labour Commission did not either—can be seen from the fact that thirteen years later the Royal Commission on *Alien Immigration* found that large numbers of immigrants were still pouring into the same trades, doing work which the English population were not willing to do, in poor industrial conditions. It was twenty years before the Committee on *Home Work* (1908) felt clear enough to recommend experimental wage-fixing by industry or to say that parasitic industries should not continue. Even they argued that the actual prohibition of home work was not then advisable.

iv. *Industrial disputes: the Labour Commission*

The difficulties which overtook the Labour Commission 1891–94 were of a different kind. The setting was two-fold. First, a series of large-scale and alarming strikes, partly by established, partly by new militant unions of unskilled and general labourers, a vigorous campaign for an eight-hour day, demonstrations by the unemployed with William Morris participating and an Anglican parson, Stewart Headlam, leading past St Paul's the funeral procession of a killed demonstrator. Secondly, the inquiries had drawn aside the veil which had obscured the appalling housing conditions, the long hours, unsanitary conditions and derisory pay of sweated workers. Judged by the quality of its members and the number of reports and papers it issued, it was one of the most high-powered, large-scale and productive Commissions ever appointed. High hopes were entertained of it.

It examined nearly 600 witnesses, asked nearly 100,000 questions and armed itself with the services of a number of young graduates, mostly women, who made a precis of each witness's evidence and plentiful indexes. It sent out questionnaires to a large number of trade unions, great and small, took oral evidence from many of their representatives and occasionally from a representative of a group of unorganised workers sent to state their particular case. The secretary, Geoffrey Drage, with immense industry and skill prepared summaries, occupying 350 pages of double columns, of the evidence from all sources on the principal subjects of inquiry presented to each of the three trade group committees and to the Commission sitting as a whole. There were seventy-six pages of similar summaries on women's employment and an array of appendices, including an agreed summary of Sidney Webb's writings on socialism up to that date.[52] Embedded in its sixty-seven separately numbered Papers[53] is a mass of information on labour conditions and organisation, some of it to be found nowhere else in such detail.[54] Yet *The Times* gave its Report but limited notice, the *Economist* wrote it off as a disappointment, whilst Mrs Webb poured bitter scorn on the Commission for

---

[52]App. lxxiii; 1893–94, C. 7063–iiia, xxxix, pt. i.

[53]The mass of papers and their special numbering make reference to them difficult. They are set out in full in the *Select List of British Parliamentary Papers, 1833–1899*, ed. P and G Ford, pp. 72–3. This gives a clear idea of the organisation of the inquiry and of its proceedings.

[54]Despite the impression given by Mrs Webb. See footnote following.

the clumsiness of its methods and the futility of its conclusions.[55] In assessing its place in the effort to understand and bring under control the changing relations of employers and employed it is therefore necessary to distinguish between short-run controversies and long-run influence.

Mrs Webb, in a harsh judgement prompted a little by drawing-room gossip she felt to be hostile, declared the Commission to be a gigantic fraud, made up of a knot of dialecticians (amongst whom she included A Marshall) who puzzled workmen with economic conundrums, plus a carefully picked parcel of variegated labour men, while the rest were landlords and capitalists.[56] On the contrary, a Royal Commission on this subject had to have men representative of different interests and approaches.[57] Few Commissions compare with it in individual knowledge and experience, the current standing of its members and the eminence to which they ultimately attained. Amongst the industrialists were the founders of Harland and Wolff and of the White Star Line, of a great coal-mining concern and David Dale, a north-eastern iron-master whose forebears had a connection with Robert Owen and who pioneered a north-eastern conciliation board. The trade union representatives included men of the right, like Thomas Burt and of the left, like Tom Mann. Amongst the politicians were Hicks-Beach, who became the Chancellor of the Exchequer, Gerald Balfour, who held several Cabinet offices and John Gorst, a 'liberal' Tory. Then there were Collings, who was one of the founders of the Agricultural Labourer's Union and Samuel Plimsoll. Standing outside these interests were Pollock, eminent in law, and Alfred Marshall.

The trouble was not in the quality of the personnel. It lay partly

[55]Beatrice Webb in *Nineteenth Century*, XXXVI, 2–22. But see Geoffrey Drage's caustic rebuttal, 'Mrs Webb's Attack on the Labour Commission' in *Nineteenth Century*, XXXVI (1894), 456–67. For another contemporary defence see L L Price, *Economic Science and Practice* (1896), chap. vii. It is interesting that a more charitable account of it was given by Tom Mann, who signed the Minority Report. *Tom Mann's Memoirs* (1923), pp. 98–102.

[56]Beatrice Webb, *Our Partnership,* pp. 40–2, and *Methods of Social Study,* pp. 141–6. But see Marshall's statement on how workmen giving evidence should be questioned. *Aged Poor,* R. Com. Mins. of ev., qq. 10, 199–202; 1895, C. 7684-i, xiv.

[57]Drage, who was in a position to know, says that on certain matters the evidence led some members to alter their preconceived opinions. *Nineteenth Century*, XXXVI, 459.

F

in its interpetation of its terms of reference—questions affecting the relations between employers and employed, the combinations of employers and employed and the conditions of labour which have been raised in the recent disputes,[58] and whether any evils could be remedied by legislation. These the Commission interpreted[59] in a precise way and specifically excluded the consideration of the 'social question', 'the fundamental causes of wealth and poverty, and other questions not bearing directly on trade disputes.' Disputes are primarily about wages and conditions, not about general social conditions, so that the Commission's decision is understandable. But the exclusion of the background of unrest had unfortunate effects on some of its conclusions. The Minority, in a report drafted by Sidney Webb (though not a member of the Commission), would have none of these limitations: the fundamental cause of disputes was the unsatisfactory position of the working classes in society, and disputes would remain until by the extension of collective ownership and administration of industry this was remedied.

The Commission was hampered by lack of information on some matters and far too much on others. Like the Commission on *Depression of Trade,* it complained of the absence of reliable statistics essential to the problem, on man-power, wages, conditions of industry, housing, etc., that the Board of Trade had no permanent staff able to collect them, and recommended that steps should be taken to build one up. It attempted to fill the gap by a massive use of the method of oral evidence and returns imposed upon it by Parliamentary tradition. Comprehensiveness was in the air: Booth set out to make his survey cover all working-class families in London. Mrs Webb, fresh from having with Sidney completed their *History of Trade Unionism* a month before the Commission presented its Final Report, severely criticised it for the reliance it placed upon oral evidence, for spending too much time in getting witnesses' opinions on the pros and cons of piece-work, over-time, the eight-hour day, etc.[60] while making little use of direct factual investigation by skilled

[58]Final Rep., p. 3; 1894, C. 7421, xxxv.

[59]Ibid., p. 8.

[60]See L L Price's defence of the Commission in *Economic Science and Practice,* pp. 147-9. To assess what exaggeration there was, if any, in Mrs Webb's accusations of the

researchers. Colour was lent to this impression by the way in which the Majority Report set out its arguments in a cool, detached way without any attempt to reflect the contemporary violence of feeling and action in the labour world it was studying or to drive it home by full citation of or guidance on what was significant in the mass of evidence out of which it was supposed to grow. Its review of the evidence, though intended to be an integral part of the Report, is relegated, as Part II, to a separate volume, and in fact consists of Drage's summaries.[61] These do in fact contain a mass of solid information.

For the Majority the main problem was that of preventing disputes. In addition to the extensive oral evidence, the Commission had received a large number of detailed returns from trade unions on the number, causes and duration of disputes, the loss of wages, the amounts paid out in dispute pay, and their result.[62] The Majority discussion is quite straightforward. It told a public, alarmed by the scale of contemporary disputes, that the loss of wages due to strikes was less than 1 per cent of the total annual wages bill, and surprised *The Times* by concluding that despite obstinate strikes and

---

dialectical bludgeoning of working-class witnesses and the resentment it caused, so vigorously made in 'The Failure of the Labour Commission' and in extracts from her diary in *Our Partnership*, would require close reading of the evidence of every one of them. The leaders of the established or bigger unions, though sometimes using language different from their questioners, seemed well able to take care of themselves. Wifely loyalty may have added some acidity to Mrs Webb's comments, for Sidney himself did not show up very well in part of his evidence. The record of his first day's evidence and of the beginning of the second bears marks of some tactful suppression by the secretary. Keen examination of his opinions was to be expected from Commissioners of that calibre, but there may have been some friction because he had obviously studied it more deeply than some of his questioners. It was indiscreet to step off his own ground to cross swords with Marshall on what the classical economists had said about State intervention, since Marshall pointed out that Adam Smith made fifty first-class exceptions to the general principle of natural liberty (q. 4076, vol. xxxix, pt. i, C. 7063–i). It was illustrative of the Commission's difficulties that the discussion between these two masters of their subject should have added nothing of value to the knowledge either of industrial relations or of collectivism.

[61]The Minority agreed that the task of summarising had been intelligently and impartially performed. But only a reader of considerable industry and competence would be able to work through the 350 pages of summaries and say with confidence—especially in the absence of abundant quotations or of reference to it in the Report—whether the weight of it always led to the Majority's conclusions.

[62]See the appropriate pages showing unions' replies to questions in 1892, C. 6795–vii, C. 6795–viii, xxxvi, pt. iii; C. 6795–ix, xxxvi, pt. iv.

the increased scale of some of them, their frequency was diminishing, and that increased organisation on both sides tended to make relations more, not less harmonious. Strong organisation on both sides made it possible for them to see that the agreements they made were carried out. Its proposals, therefore, did not provide either a magical immediate remedy or a long-term plan for a new industrial order, but relied on a steady development of bargaining between responsible organised bodies. Voluntary experiments in conciliation and arbitration were increasingly successful, and any attempts to set up statutory boards or to make the awards of voluntary boards legally enforceable would undo the progress made. The Board of Trade should be empowered to inquire into disputes, to promote the formation of voluntary boards, to offer its services in conciliation and if both sides wished, to name arbitrators to whom matters could be voluntarily referred for awards having moral, but not legal force.

The collectivists' road to industrial peace through the nationalisation of the major means of production, they rejected in terms which seemed arid and theoretical in the eighteen-nineties, but which have more point in the nineteen-sixties; the workman would still have to struggle for what he would consider the due remuneration of his labours, although the struggle would be with a different opponent and conducted by different methods. It might lead to new conflicts arising between workman and the community or between different classes of the community.[63] Nor were they very confident on the outcome of attempts to remove the sources of industrial conflict either by creating an identity of interest between employer and employed in the same undertaking through profit sharing and co-partnership, or by replacing employers altogether by workers' co-operative production.

The case put forward for workers' co-operative production specially called for attention because some authoritative economists whose books were in wide circulation at the time, believing that a rigid wage fund blocked any other way, saw in it the one means of promoting industrial peace. Thus Fawcett[64] had argued that

[63] Majority Rep., para. 366.
[64] H Fawcett, *Manual of Political Economy* (1883), pp. 248-9.

strikes were inseparable from the economic system as long as the relationships between employer and employed were those of buyer and seller, since one party could always refuse the price offered by the other, so that conciliation and arbitration were not a completely sufficient remedy. Strikes could be effectively remedied by removing the antagonisms of interest, and this required co-partnership and producers' co-operation. J E Cairnes, in *Leading Principles* (1874)[65] by a more rigid line of reasoning stated in even sharper terms the narrow limits to wages; unions could not raise wages in general, though they could improve the position of some workers at the expense of others and by a sound knowledge of trade conditions take advantage of temporarily favourable circumstances. So long as the worker depended only on the produce of his day's work, co-operation offered the sole means of escape from his condition of mere hand-to-mouth living. The Majority Report does not go into these theories—although Webb referred to them in his statement of evidence—but decided on grounds of practical experience that these enterprises had little chance of success except in simple industries or where there was a special clientele. But Fawcett and Cairnes were becoming the old guard. For the critical attitude of economists to unions engendered by rigid versions of the wage fund had already been softened by the attacks on the doctrine itself by Longe (1866), Leslie (1868), Thornton (1868), by the reverberation of Mill's famous recantation (1868), by Walker (1872–74), Sidgwick (1883) and Thompson (1892). Both George Howell and Thomas Burt had followed the development.[66] And Marshall had recently (1890) issued the first volume of his famous *Principles,* which set out what became the authoritative statement of English wage theory. The way was no longer blocked. Even the Lords' Committee on *Sweating* had gone so far as to favour for sweated workers 'well-ordered combinations'.

These undramatic conclusions, pallid as they were beside the sweeping demands of the collectivist Minority, nevertheless from the

---

[65] J E Cairnes, *Leading Principles of Political Economy* (1883), pt. ii, chaps. iii, iv and pp. 282–3, 289.

[66] Thomas Burt, *Autobiography* (1924), chap. xiv. George Howell, *Conflicts of Capital and Labour* (1878), chap. iv.

unions' point of view had one major, if negative virtue: they were an authoritative vindication of what in a broad way was the unions' policy and continued to be up to 1919—and a defeat of any hostile demand for a curb on them. If, therefore, the Commission had been a 'State trial of the leaders of trade union opinion', as Mrs Webb declared it to be,[67] they had certainly come well out of it.

There was one vital omission. They did not say how these advantages were to be secured for the mass of unskilled, unorganised workers whose conditions Ben Tillett has so vividly described[68] and among whom unrest and disputes figured so largely in the next twenty-five years. They pointed out the difficulties in organising them (paras. 76–8), that because they have no monopoly of special skill their entry to their occupations was uncontrolled, and employers could easily replace them, so that disputes often took a bitter, even violent turn (paras. 94–5) and sympathetic strikes were called. Their organisations tended to be unstable and were unlikely to resort to a tribunal for the settlement of disputes on existing contracts (para. 296). Yet it is difficult to see how the voluntary conciliation machinery on which the Majority relied could extend if one side remained unorganised. The practical minded left-wing Tory, John Gorst, in a dissenting Report argued that as the highly organised trades which had this successful joint machinery were outnumbered by the unorganised by six to one, most of whom it was impossible to organise, these should be given similar advantages by establishing public boards empowered to make binding awards in disputes over existing wage contracts and to mediate in other disputes. The Majority were obviously conscious of the problem of surplus labour in individual trades (paras. 233–41). It would have been possible for them to say outright, as the Lords' Committee on *Sweating* came near to saying earlier,[69] that in this teeming unskilled population, many protective and restrictive measures would be broken down by the incoming stream of competing labour from its high birth rate. Instead they were relying on their view that the deplorably large residuum of the population led wretchedly poor

---

[67]*Nineteenth Century*, XXXVI, 18.
[68]Tillett, *Memories and Recollections*.
[69]See above, p. 66.

lives, but by absorption of part of it into higher levels of labour was diminishing in numbers relatively, and perhaps absolutely (paras. 57–8).

Their final comment is remarkable: 'Many of the evils to which our attention has been called are such as cannot be remedied by legislation, but we may look forward with confidence to their gradual amendment by natural forces now in operation, which tend to substitute a state of industrial peace for one of division and conflict.'[70] And they thought that the course of events was tending to a settled and pacific period in which, in industries so organised, there would be, if not an identification of interests at least a clearer perception of the principles which must regulate the division of the proceeds. Alfred Marshall as well as Burt and Collings, signed this. We do not have the materials enabling us to say exactly what part Marshall played in shaping the Report, but its phrasing had been foreshadowed in A and M Marshall's *Economics of Industry* (1879) which declared that in their work arbitrators must conform to nature and not set up arrangements widely different from those which would naturally be brought about, for if they did they would conflict with natural forces and their work would be destroyed (p. 215). One advantage of boards of conciliation was that trusted workmen could obtain information on the condition of their trade and its 'hidden workings' (p. 217). Two years before the Commission reported, however, J A Hobson had pointed out that 'the identity of interest which is based on general consideration that capital and labour were both required in the conduct of a given business is no effective guarantee against a genuine clash of interests between the actual forms of capital and labourers engaged at a given time in that particular business'.[71] Viewed as a generalisation about the trend in the practice of collective bargaining, the Majority's conclusions had some validity, but as a forecast were much damaged in the next twenty years by the massive disputes needed to establish and secure bargaining recognition of the growing unions of unskilled, unorganised workers, and later by the widening of the aims of unions

[70]Majority Rep., para. 363.

[71]J A Hobson, *Problem of Poverty* (1892), p. 227.

beyond the contents of the wage packet to the ownership and control of industry.[72]

By contrast the wider sweep of the Minority Report, signed by four (Abraham, Austin, Mawdsley and Tom Mann) but not all of the labour members, as well as the circumstances in which it was produced, gave it a much more dramatic quality. It is clear from its last minute production, that it was intended less to convince the Majority members, than to serve as a 'plausible and practical manifesto of labour reforms which would quickly be circulating up and down the country in every workmen's club and trade union meeting'.[73] Though it made free use of the evidence presented to the Commission to strengthen its case, it cannot be said that this was really derived from it.[74] Its punch and cogency came from a coherent theory which had already been worked out in other circumstances and in relation to other experience.[75] Starting from its insistence that disputes came from the unsatisfactory position of the working classes in society and that strikes and disputes were symptomatic of healthy and promising discontent with social conditions, it set out the standard, contemporary socialist case for the public ownership of industries and extended collective action. It proposed, first, to deal with sweated trades by extending the Factory Acts, so that home work was discouraged and transferred to premises under proper regulations; secondly, a legal eight-hour day, flexible in its application to different industries; thirdly, to extend the field of public

[72]The Marxists preaching the inevitability of the class struggle—Hyndman gave evidence before the Commission—were still a small if vocal group, and the most popular propaganda was that of Henry George in *Progress and Poverty* (1880), but he focussed attacks less on the capitalist than on the landlord.

[73]B Webb, *Nineteenth Century*, XXXVI, 22.

[74]Mrs Webb openly declares this and that the reforms proposed could have been written without any Commission. Ibid., 8.

[75]Some of the early experiments in municipalisation were undertaken not because of any socialist theory of the desirability of State ownership as such, but because, e.g. private tramways, gas and water meant that the local authority lost full control of its own streets, because they feared monopolistic prices, poor quality of gas, etc. Tom Mann's practical proposals for improving the situation in the London docks, which deserved consideration on their merits, were preceded by a disquisition on State and municipal ownership in general, nationalisation of railways, etc. as if they sprang from and were a desirable illustration of socialist theory, instead of being, as they were, positive suggestions for dealing with a difficult problem. See the summary of Sidney Webb's writings included as an appendix to the evidence taken by the Commission as a whole. App. lxxii; 1894, C. 7063–iiia, xxxix, pt. i.

industry under trade union conditions as a means of ameliorating unemployment due to seasonal variations and recurrent depressions. On the more specific problems of disputes they did not have very much to say: they wished to see the voluntary extension of joint boards to make awards, not legally binding, on the interpretation of existing agreements. In disputes on new agreements, the Board of Trade should be empowered to make and publicly report on full inquiry (including the inspection of accounts) into all material facts.

In one respect this group's thinking, like that of the Commission on *Trade Depression,* was affected by lack of theory. The argument (put forward also by Sidney Webb in his oral evidence) that extended municipalisation had made steadier employment possible, though having point regarding regular as distinct from mere casual engagements, really put the cart before the horse: the successful municipalisation of tramways, water works, etc. was easy just because they were in their nature industries of stable employment. To cite the stability of employment in the Post Office and Cooperative Wholesale Society, as examples of methods for ameliorating trade depressions, not only showed lack of contact even with such knowledge as there was of trade cycles—which admittedly some of the formal books seemed to share—but must have given rise to private derisory astonishment from the founders of a great firm of shipbuilders and of a great shipping line so subject to the blasts of depressions, who were members of the Commission. Equally so must their view (carried over from successful municipal trading) that every extension of the area of public administration almost necessarily results in an increase in the area of constant as compared with irregular employment (pp. 141–2). In their proposals for sweated trades they, like the Majority members and the Dunraven Committee, relied on strict sanitary measures to force the home trades into well-regulated factories. Three years later, in 1902, it was still the view of the Webbs as set out in *Industrial Democracy,* that as trade unionism could not put down industrial parasitism by sectional industrial action, a national minimum wage (not yet put forward by any section of trade unionists)[76] was the way out, though it would

[76]Sidney Webb and Beatrice Webb, *Industrial Democracy* (1902), pp. 766–75.

have to be low. The solution eventually adopted in 1909 for fixing rates for each trade had not yet been arrived at.

The Majority report marks a much more important stage in our thinking on industrial relations than its prosaic qualities suggest, for it confirmed and helped to make permanent what was already becoming characteristic of British industrial relations: direct negotiations between well-organised voluntary associations, the State intervening only if necessary to smooth the process or to help in special difficulties. The two labour men who signed it, Burt and Collings, thus correctly perceived the direction in which the future of British trade unions lay. To the progressive employers, such as Mundella, it must have seemed the next logical step to more ordered industrial relations. The Commission had taken some trouble to examine alternative methods used in other countries,[77] but although their reluctance to try new methods may have been due partly to insular conservatism, there must have been an element of deliberate choice. Nevertheless, this policy left striking gaps in our arrangements. What was to happen if disputes extended beyond local or regional cases where the effects were in the main limited to the employers and workers involved, to nation-wide strikes or lock-outs, in coal mining and transport, for example, affecting drastically employment in the whole economy? If employers were not organised or while unionism amongst the unorganised was growing, but reached only a half-way house and agreements were difficult for either side to enforce? Or if workers again became conscious about 'democracy in the workshop'? It was just at these points that the pressure of industrial strife of 1906–14 imposed strains on the machinery for which it was not fully prepared.

To this story a footnote may be added. Although the Commission roused great interest by its call on so large a number of witnesses from many industries and movements and numerous requests for information from so many bodies, perhaps because of its affirmation of the traditional position of the unions the Report fell out of notice and for many years its masses of material were neglected by historians. In the meantime, as a long-run contribution to the public

---

[77]e.g. Final Rep., paras. 261, 315, and app. v.

understanding of the labour problem, it had less influence than the private work of the Webbs in their *History of Trade Unionism*[78] (produced at the same time) (1894) and *Industrial Democracy*[79] a few years later, although these were written from a definite point of view and had weaknesses which have since become evident.

v. *Poverty: private inquiries. Booth, Rowntree*

Various investigators had endeavoured to get at the position of the working classes by estimating their income as a group and per head. In 1867 Leone Levi[80] had calculated that they received about half the national income, while Dudley Baxter,[81] allowing for short time, in 1868 arrived at 40 per cent. Levi fully understood that the incomes of the poorer section were substantially below the average, but the figures of savings in building societies, of progress of co-operative societies, etc., which he quoted and Giffen used (1884)[82] to measure the progress of the working classes were more relevant to the better-off amongst them. It was the standard of the worst paid which was not easy to get at. The condition of this depressed class was the main concern of those two great private investigators, Charles Booth and Seebohm Rowntree. It is no small tribute to their work that their findings have not only become part of the stock-in-trade of the social historian, but also a main dish in the menu for young social workers. What was their contribution to the urge for and the processes of social control? However much moved by human sympathy, both approached the problem scientifically in the sense that they asked quantitative questions and set out to get answers unaffected by personal preconceptions; and in contrast to the Benthamites, Marxists and some classical economists, did not move from a body

[78]See the warm review in the *Economic Journal* by Edgeworth, reprinted in *Collected Papers*, III, 47–50, although he thought their general ideas contained 'an element of hypothesis'. *Econ. Jn.*, VIII (1892), 64 et seq.

[79]See L L Price's warm, though not uncritical review. *Econ. Jn.* (1897), 64–75.

[80]Leone Levi, *Wages and Earnings of the Working Classes* (1867), pp. xlv–xlvi.

[81]Dudley Baxter, *R. Stat. Soc. Jn.* (1868).

[82]Robert Giffen, *Progress of the Working Classes in the Last Half Century* (1884). But he lamented that there was a residue still unimproved, though it was smaller in proportion (p. 20).

of fixed principles towards the facts, but rather worked in the reverse direction. Booth wanted to find out what were the facts behind the journalists' somewhat sensational accounts. Both found that the census results and other official information were not capable of yielding the information they wanted. Booth had a disagreement with Hyndman on what proportion of the population were in poverty. Rowntree wondered if Booth's first results about London would be applicable to provincial towns. They were not the first to do this kind of thing: Southwood Smith had tried to relate social class to housing and various diseases in Bethnal Green, Colquhoun had tried, a little *a priori* perhaps, to separate personal from social causes of poverty. But their work was an immense leap forward in three respects. First, they enlarged our vision by breaking away from the ideas natural to social workers, clergy and others having the task of handling individuals with all their quirks, that distress was due to personal failings, by asking how much derived from the character and variations of employment and defects of social organisation. They investigated, as Beveridge later put it, not the poor, but poverty. This general change of attitude, which they helped largely to bring about, was fundamental. Secondly, they decided that the facts could be discovered only by a house-to-house survey of the whole working-class population of the areas, and thus initiated survey methods on the most massive scale. Thirdly, they tried to give a precise quantitative meaning of the word 'poverty', and to apply it uniformly over the populations they were concerned with.

Poverty is not destitution or pauperism, but implies some kind of minimum standard widely understood, even though there may be some differences of view on where the boundary line should be drawn. Booth's personal knowledge led him to such a standard. Rowntree tried to make it more than a base line for measurement and to endow it with a little more significance for policy by defining it as the minimum necessary for purely physical efficiency, including a minimum food standard worked out in calories related to age, sex and character of work. He endeavoured to bring some settlement to a long-standing controversy by distinguishing between—and measuring—poverty due to insufficiency of income and that due not to insufficiency of income but to its use for other purposes, wasteful, extravagant or useful. Such 'secondary' poverty is difficult to measure and it is not always clear to what extent Booth included it in his estimates. Nevertheless the two standards appear to have been near enough to be on speaking terms and to be thought of together. This technique which, had it been available, would have made it possible for Colquhoun to give a numerical assessment to his list of twenty-nine innocent (mainly industrial) causes of indigence and to his similar list of 'culpable' causes, enabled Booth to do so for poverty arising from unemployment, from habit or from circumstances,[83] and Rowntree for that arising from death, illness and old age of the chief earner, from unemployment or irregularity of employment, from large families and from low wages for regular work.[84] Further, the use of Rowntree's distinction between primary and secondary poverty, despite its difficulties, had made it plain not only that the wages of the unskilled were below the sum needed to keep a family of moderate size at merely physical efficiency, but that for many others above the poverty line, any expenditure on tram fares, postage, church or union or sick club contributions, children's toys and even a funeral could be met only by limiting diet, thus pushing them below the line:[85] the spending habits of the poor were thus seen in a better perspective. A revolution had thus been made in the diagnosis of poverty, and accurate diagnosis is a condition of effective treatment.

The development of methods since then has shown what was scientifically unnecessary or weak in their work. The immense labour needed to cover the whole population can be reduced by sampling methods, but even had these been ready, the results would not at the time have made the impact on the public or produced the conviction their startling figures actually did. There was an element of personal assessment by Booth's investigators, but they were knowledgeable, he was careful, and though this may have led to some lack of uniformity in detail, it probably made little difference to the broad results. Then granted the structure of society, the amount of poverty is what one makes it by definition. The line can be drawn

[83]Charles Booth, *Labour and Life of the People* (1889), pp. 146–9.
[84]Seebohm Rowntree, *Poverty* (1902), pp. 119–20.
[85]Ibid., pp. 133–4.

'high' or 'low' as one likes. There is an element of convention in the content of any 'poverty line', in the level of house room (rent), clothing one allows for the purpose, and even the same number of calories can be provided in an expensive or inexpensive way. For the purpose of determining whether poverty has increased or decreased over moderate periods of time, the 'poverty line' is simply a 'poverty datum line'[86] and many later surveys have been based on Booth's and Rowntree's standards for that reason.[87] But these first surveys were meant to throw light on contemporary social policy, and Booth's instincts were sound when he elected to work from what was ordinarily regarded as poverty—(though Leone Levi, who knew a good deal about wages, thought the standard had been drawn too high)—and so were Rowntree's in choosing a meagre standard based on a worse-than-workhouse diet, and which assumed that all family income was pooled, which it was not and could not be. The wicked could not cavil at it.[88]

Though they are now so familiar, it is still easy to under-estimate the immense impression, even intellectually explosive effect of those results. Examination of the conditions of two whole populations by new methods had shown that approximately the same large proportion (London 30.7 per cent), (York 27.8 per cent) were in poverty and this seemed to sum up in one figure the gloomy evidence of the great public inquiries into social conditions and to confirm the worst fears. Its haunting presence was felt in all contemporary discussions, it found its way into speeches, pamphlets, denunciations, investigations and sermons, and it became the one figure which those reflecting on social matters could remember. Booth's results for London gave the first shock, Rowntree's the second by showing that provincial populations were likely to be in little better condition. At the same time they established how much of the poverty was due not to individuals' personal failings, but to defects of social and industrial organisation outside their control, that an unskilled labourer's wages were insufficient to keep him above the line, and

---

[86]P Ford, *Work and Wealth in a Modern Port* (1934), pp. 113–17.

[87]For a summary of these see *New Survey of London Life and Labour* (1934), VI, chap. v.

[88]See Charles Stewart Loch's criticism of both in the Report on *Physical Deterioration*, app. iii; 1904, Cd. 2175, xxxii.

that he would pass through a 'poverty cycle' falling below in child-
hood, in the middle years when his family was dependent and again
in old age.

Booth's undertaking did not end there. Having demonstrated
that much poverty was traceable to conditions of work and employment he passed on to investigate London's industries (five vols.) and
then religious influences (seven vols.) Neither project had the same
explosive effect as the study of poverty. While the work on industries
contained many penetrating studies by Aves, Schloss, Mary Collet—
and we can include those of Beatrice Webb and Llewellyn Smith—
it was not organised to tie up with the poverty survey to become
one piece with it.[89] Different systems of classification were used:
though one which brought them together would have added labour
which probably not even Booth could have carried. But the evidence
did not move him towards the solutions proposed by collectivists.
The seven volumes on religious influences were an imaginative
endeavour to analyse the various denominations' influence on and
reaction to the social situation, the relation of their numbers and
methods to the various social classes. Some of this was not new.
The congregations of the little democratically run Bethels and
Churches of the Baptists, Methodists and Congregationalists, standing in physical as well as spiritual rivalry with the village and town
Established Churches, knew that their income and social levels, doctrines and even political allegiances were different from those of the
Establishment and from one another's. It is a subject on which it is
very easy for journalists, parsons, and sociologists to make generalisations which are shallow and often inaccurate, and it was typical of
Booth that he should try to get at the facts by hard, detailed, personal
research. He made an outside, objective assessment of the quality
of the various Churches' activities and brought out very sharply
the aloofness of the mass of London's population from any formal
or even direct influence by any religious communion. But the
massive record of his work was too overwhelming in bulk and
detail for the public to take it in or for it to exercise the influence his
labours deserved. A scrutiny of the abstract of the volumes on

[89]See T S Simey's account in *Charles Booth* (1960).

83

religious influences, given in the final volume of his whole project, and of the apt comment even in the summaries, shows where his mind was moving and what might have come of the materials he had gathered.[90] His attitude of cool assessment differed in temper from the zeal of those who were now exploring the social implications of their theology, in which he was not particularly interested, so that his work gave no evidence, except negatively, on how far these ideas were beginning to stir the local religious bodies, or had growing points in them. Yet it was the new social ethic to which these fresh theological ideas contributed, which later provided some of the drive to remedy conditions he had revealed. Not only were the objectives of these two projects such that they could not be summed up in a single dramatic statistical figure, but two groups of reformers, collectivists and religious, who might have been taken up with them, though they used his material, appeared to have felt some disappointment.

What was the practical outcome of all these investigations? In contrast to their scale, in the short run, meagre; in the long run immense. Ideas of this kind, once launched, to survive have to be carried along by the contemporary social and political currents. Booth seems not to have realised the full force of his results, and viewed in the light of subsequent history, when it came to their practical application, it could be argued that he lost his way. For the dock workers he suggested decasualisation by means of a register of permanent dockers, call stands and a supplementary list to cope with seasonal and other fluctuations, but he was always conscious of what this would mean and the opposition it would and did arouse from the 'excluded surplus'. As remedies for sweating he rejected emigration, protective tariffs, the exclusion of immigrants and the suppression of home work, and he wanted employers and workplaces to be registered so that hours and sanitary regulations could be enforced, but rested his hopes on the prospect of improvement through a gradual raising of the standard of life, aided by combination.[91] For those in poverty through vice, idleness or reckless child-breeding he had not much sympathy. But his analysis of

[90]*Life and Labour of the People in London,* final vol., pt. i, 333–428.
[91]*Life and Labour,* I, 496–8.

its non-personal causes arising from the economic and social order, expanded and developed by later workers, led on logically to and became the factual basis of the great campaigns for those extensions of State intervention and of social services which ended in the Welfare State. These conclusions he did not draw. Perhaps, despite his scientific detachment, his individualistic preconceptions, strengthened by his business success, resisted these practical applications. Intellectually he had parted company from the radical left and the collectivists, though it was their political strength which later embodied in legislation the conclusions which flowed from his work. Alternatively, there are examples enough in great research undertakings to make it very plausible, as Simey suggests, that the immense labour of the later projects so filled his thoughts and absorbed his energies that he was never able to reflect upon it adequately. But that is not the whole story. We have only to think of the high birth rate, the influx of children from London's unskilled workers which dismayed the Committee on Sweating and contemporary social workers, and to remember our own doubts on the best policy for some undeveloped countries where an uncontrolled increase of population eats up all the external aid and leaves standards much as they were, to realise that things looked more difficult then than they do now when the fall in the natural increase has made effective collective action more simple.[92] For his Class C (irregular employment and improvident habits) Booth thought it was not enough to pick out the deserving and admonish the rest—'to raise this class we need some larger plan'—and his Class D (poor regular minimum) could be 'helped only by a movement which shall succeed in raising the whole standard of life'.[93] Perhaps he was not so misguided after all. For as Bowley's two studies *Livelihood and Poverty* (1915) and *Has Poverty Diminished?* (1925) showed, it was precisely by that gradual rise in the wages of the unskilled which he had relied

[92]For England and Wales as a whole, the index of the fertility rate (live births per 1,000 married women aged 15 to 49) fell from 100 in 1870–72 to 88 in 1880–82, remained at 88 until 1890–92 and then fell to 62 in 1910–12. D V Glass, *Population* (1940), p. 5. Booth's first volume on East London was published in 1889.

[93]*Life and Labour*, I, 596–7.

G

upon, and by a fall in the size of families[94] that the fall in the numbers below the poverty line to the latter date had occurred. The major exception to his cautious attitude was provision for the aged, whose plight had long engaged his sympathy. His proposals for a universal old age pension of five shillings at the age of sixty-five was received with bitter opposition by some, including the Charity Organisation Society, but was supported by others in a vigorous campaign, in which he took part. He did not, however, live to see it in operation, for the proposals became involved in political storms, conflicts of values, calculations of expediency and for a time were lost in the distractions of the Boer War.

4. TENTATIVE APPROACHES TO NEW PRINCIPLES

Yet great as the impact of these new inquiries were, they did not resolve all the intellectual difficulties which helped to inhibit immediate action upon them: how to provide for greater social responsibility without weakening the fundamentally individualistic motives which still ruled economic life, especially when the institutions created by the working class—mutual insurance and collecting societies and trade unions—sometimes opposed the necessary measures. There was some fumbling to find new principles. Three examples illustrate these struggles of opinion. They concern difficulties, some of which bore most acutely on the lower-paid worker, which either could not be avoided at all or were often quite outside personal control: onset of old age, industrial accidents and involuntary unemployment. What is of interest is the reasoning which delayed the final decisions on these questions.

i. *Old Age Pensions*

Even before Booth had driven home his case for old age pensions there had been a good deal of thinking about it. On its ethical

[94]In 1913 he still felt that the conditions of employment in both organised and unorganised industries had responded to influences common to the whole field of industry. *Industrial Unrest and Trade Union Policy* (1913), p. 8.

aspects Ruskin, in the 1862 Preface to *Unto This Last,* had declared that the aged should be provided with comfort and home, and that when misfortune had been separated from guilt, this would be honourable instead of disgraceful to the receiver. A labourer served the country with his spade just as a man in the middle rank served it with his sword or pen, and it would be as natural for him to take his pension from the parish as for a man of higher rank to take his pension from his country. This plea for what was to become the public attitude half a century later is of interest, because the qualification, 'when misfortune had been separated from guilt,' was the difficulty which bedevilled constructive discussion right up to the Act of 1908.

Those who argued that the poor should make provision for themselves assumed two things: that there were suitable savings institutions for the purpose and that wages were high enough to permit savings. For a large part of the population neither assumption was true. Gladstone had vigorously rejected the first when introducing his scheme of Government annuities (1864), pointing out the high expense ratio of companies and societies, that many were small, local and ignorantly managed, that hundreds collapsed and that there were abuses and even fraud. But few annuities were bought, partly because they were not publicised, partly because the problem of ability to pay still remained. Two ways out of the difficulty were proposed: compulsory insurance with or without State aid, and non-contributory State pensions. For thirty years public discussion, sometimes bitter and even acrimonious, raged round these alternatives.

The first, proposed by Canon Blackley, was a scheme of compulsory insurance which combined personal thrift with security. Young men between eighteen and twenty-one when their wage was at its maximum and before their responsibilities were too great, were to pay £10 over a period to a State guaranteed fund. This would provide a pension of four shillings a week at seventy and the scheme would be self-supporting. But it was not clear that the lowest paid worker could afford it, women's wages were lower, their earning life shorter and they could not participate. It was not a fatal objection that such a reform should be partial in scope at the onset:

so were the later health and unemployment insurance schemes. But it would be years before any considerable proportion of the old would benefit. And proposals for general insurance had to make their way against the vested interests of companies and the collecting societies who strongly objected to any scheme which would 'make the thrifty pay for the thriftless'. Faced with this opposition, the Select Committee of 1885 decided that further development of public opinion must be awaited before any scheme of general insurance could be recommended. But many who supported contributory insurance—even Marshall—did not realise the weakness and abuses of the companies and societies.

The alternative course had been suggested by the Rev R Hookham in 1879. Since it was impossible for labourers with low wages to save enough to provide for old age, and even stringent present sacrifice would not save them from later dependency as paupers, he therefore proposed a universal old age pension irrespective of income, which would not have that taint of pauperism since all could draw it[95] and would not discourage the thrift which would provide extra comfort.

Although the Charity Organisation Society and Octavia Hill, opposing anything which would apparently weaken this spirit of self-help, thought that the ill-condition of the aged poor had been exaggerated, the facts were not substantially in dispute. Booth had made them plain in his early surveys and in an admirably clear 'Conclusion' to his rather forbidding statistical book on the *Aged Poor* (1894). In following the reasoning of subsequent public inquiries it is instructive to pay regard to the directions they were given and their methods of investigation. The Aberdare Commission (1895) reported that none of the schemes they examined could be recommended; amongst these was Chamberlain's proposal for a State-aided contributory scheme of three categories, including one for friendly society members, each of which would be encouraged by having the pension increased by the State. But so many members had already publicly committed themselves, that it would have been interesting to have overheard what went on in the Committee room,

[95]It is amusing to note that one of the lines of objection was that there would still be a taint of pauperism because the rich would not bother to draw it.

for there were no less than a dozen dissenting memoranda. Two groups, one including Brassey and Joseph Arch and the other including Booth and Chamberlain, said that the Report did not go far enough or as far as the evidence warranted. The second group also said that the evidence was over-weighted by that from official sources and did not proportionately represent popular sentiment, and that no actuarial evidence had been taken. Both groups proposed a small expert body to work out a scheme. Broadhurst declared that for the ordinary unskilled labourer wise fore-thought meant providing food, clothing and shelter for his family, union subscriptions, etc., and that this required thirty shillings a week. As large classes of workers received lower wages than this he saw no prospect of raising them sufficiently to make saving for old age possible, and he came outright for a State pension of five shillings at sixty-five.

The small expert body, duly set up with Rothschild as chairman, was directed to examine schemes to encourage the industrial population, by State aid or otherwise, to make provision for old age. It held that this direction ruled out schemes based on compulsory insurance, because compulsion went beyond encouragement, schemes of universal general pensions, because these would not have been provided by the recipients, schemes confined to members of friendly societies who were only part of the industrial population and those requiring no contribution from the pensioner. And State aid could not be justified unless it were limited to individuals whose circumstances had made it impossible for them to save—a rule which could not be enforced by looking at the past history of savings and therefore implied a qualifying income. But State aid for those with a qualifying income meant that the poorer were helping the better off. Having thus slammed every door, it is small wonder that they did not recommend any of the 100 schemes presented to them. With principles of this sort in mind, they need scarcely have bothered to look at any of them. Spencer Walpole attacked this conclusion in a trenchant dissenting note, in which the opposition of companies and societies with 60 per cent expense ratios was not spared. But the campaign which Booth's proposals and participation had initiated was now in full swing. The 'undeserving' poor were much in mind and in 1899 the House, still haunted by the spectre of working-class thriftlessness,[96] appointed a Select Committee (Chairman, Chaplin) to consider the best means of improving the conditions of the 'aged deserving poor'. As various proposals had come to naught because it was thought they would include the dissolute and unthrifty, the Committee took evidence, including some from the Charity Commission, which had practical experience, on how far it was possible to discriminate between the deserving and the undeserving. Universal pensions they regarded as ruled out by their terms of reference, compulsory contributions because these would delay the start of pensions for many years, but savings should not be discouraged. They therefore proposed pensions at sixty-five, but attached a number of fancy conditions. Conviction and punishment with penal servitude or imprisonment without the option of a fine, poor relief at any time in the previous twenty years and income above ten shillings should be disqualifications. And officers should be satisfied that the recipient had tried to make provision. To those with less than the qualifying income there was to be better out-relief.

ii. *From employers' liability to workmen's compensation*

The discussion on employers' liability and workmen's compensation was prompted by the increase in the number of accidents as mechanisation in industry and transport proceeded. Whatever the virtues of the common law principle that the employer was liable for accidents caused by his own fault or that of his servants working under his instructions, they were outmoded by the growth in the size of the firms and in the numbers they employed. For it was less easy to prove negligence by an employer in a big firm, more remote from actual operations, than in a tiny one; and by the doctrine of common employment he was not liable for injuries caused to a workman by the fault of a fellow-workman of the same grade, so that in this respect the area in which the injured man had redress

[96]When one remembers the wealth and display of extravagance of many of the upper classes, including politicians, at the time, this attitude was an affront to decency.

contracted. Then the workman might jeopardise his claim by contributory negligence even if the machine he was using were defective; employers might 'contract out' by special bargains; bringing an action might mean dismissal. In practice, therefore, in return for his wages the workman virtually accepted liability for accidents and all this involved for himself and his family. The two obvious requirements were to encourage safety precautions and to compensate the workman and his family for the losses, which might be severe or even calamitous. Gorst argued (1880) that some simple general principle should be laid down to cover the rights of all citizens, whether workmen or servants, in factories or outdoors, in public, trade or private employment, Chamberlian (1893) that there should be compensation for all injuries sustained in the ordinary course of employment not caused by the workman's own act or default. These would clearly involve some form of compulsory general insurance by the employer. But these considerations were lost sight of in a swirl of cross-currents and even opposition where support might have been expected—from trade unions whose members would have benefited. It was not right, it was said, to make an employer liable not only for the safety of his works but for injuries caused by the negligence of another person, his employee; the relations between employer and workmen should be left to individual bargaining and workmen should make their own provision—although many insurance societies were small and the position even of the large ones sometimes precarious. The cost of compensation would eventually come out of wages; or it would raise costs; compulsory insurance would mean that good employers would be paying for bad ones. For many years trade unions were determinedly hostile to compulsory insurance because they wanted to force the individual employer to take precautions by pinning down on him the financial responsibility. Their case was safety, not compensation. The Employers' Liability Act, 1880,[97] established the principle of responsibility though in an inadequate fashion, the employer's liabilities being limited to accidents arising from defects in works or plant, negligence of fellow servants following rules or instructions, who were superintending or whom the workmen had to obey.

[97]For a contemporary view, see the *Economist*, 17 July 1880, 820–1.

But it did not apply to seamen or household servants, damages were lump-sum payments with a maximum of three years earnings, and insurance was voluntary, so that the problem of the uninsured or insolvent employer was not dealt with; and in practice many workmen got nothing. There was no general fund which would relieve employers of liability, other than payment of premiums, and give workmen and their dependents full security. Some insurance companies and lawyers had bad records for bullying claimants to accept lump-sum settlements. It was not until 1897 that the Workmen's Compensation Act adopted Chamberlain's principle and tried to get rid of litigation on whether the employer or workman was at fault by providing that compensation should be payable for injuries arising in and/or out of the course of employment, that it should be based on earnings up to one-half. It was still not compulsory for employers to insure, though there was a great growth of this type of insurance. And it was 1900 before persons in private employment were covered.

iii *Unemployment*

The third example concerns unemployment, knowledge about it and the practical ways of providing for the unemployed. Policy could scarcely be formulated without a factual basis and this was wanting. Scanty statistical data and unemployed demonstrations were not enough to build upon. The Commission on *Depression of Trade* had floundered because the statistics then available were limited to unemployment reported by trade unions (usually on the basis of benefit paid) when these contained only a fraction of the working population and the most skilled portion at that; of the rest, the unorganised, little was known. The *Labour Commission* lamented that the total numbers employed even in the skilled trades were not known. Following the formation of the Labour Department of the Board of Trade, promoted by Mundella, and the appointment of Llewellyn Smith as its head in 1893, in some respects a great stride forward was made.[98] At the time of the Committee on

[98]See Memo on the *Labour Department of the Board of Trade* for its organisation and programme of work, 1893–94 (194) lxxxii.

Distress from Want of Employment (1895–96) the factual basis remained limited. The ten-yearly census gave the numbers occupied, not the numbers employed, and included self-employed, dealers, etc. The Labour Department had to rely on the unions' returns and such information as it could get from its local 'labour correspondents'. As the total number of employed persons and therefore the percentage in each trade organised were not known, it was impossible to use the unions' figures of employed members to estimate the total number of persons unemployed, either in trade or in the country as a whole. And there was no information about women, boys and girls not in organised bodies. So that in 1895 there was the fantastic spectacle of Keir Hardie trying to fill the gap by a private census conducted through local committees composed of delegates from trade unions, socialist organisations, I.L.P. branches, clergy, etc. He did arrive at a figure of 1¾ millions, but his answers to the Committee show how dubious and fragile it was.[99] No improvement in this matter was possible until there was a national system of labour exchanges and registration for insurance benefit, but these were many years ahead.

But in analysis there was great advance. Llewellyn Smith's evidence and his endeavours to bring precision into the discussion by his charts, breaking down the total volume of recorded unemployment from 1887–94 into seasonal and cyclical variations separately, seasonal and cyclical variations for separate trades,[100] and demonstrating that even in good years there was apparently an irreducible minimum of 2 per cent of unemployment,[101] brought us straight into the modern world of unemployment analysis. Similarly, there was a better grip on trade cycle behaviour. As we have seen, the Commission on *Depression of Trade* had no understanding of it. The *Labour Commission* had argued that these cycles were connected 'in some way' with the state of commercial credit and with changes in the willingness of business men to embark on new ventures, and

[99]*Distress from Want of Employment*, Sel. Cttee. 1st Rep., Mins. of ev., qq. 767, 897, 703–36, 1895 (111) viii.
[100]*Distress from Want of Employment*, Sel. Cttee. 3rd Rep., Mins. of ev. facing pp. 52, 54, 56, 1895 (365) ix.
[101]Ibid., qq. 4588–89, 5018–19.

depended on business conditions throughout the world, so that Great Britain and particular industries were peculiarly sensitive to them.[102] Not everyone had got as far as this. Even Booth told the Committee that 'expansion and contraction succeed each other by natural law',[103] that depressions might be inevitable and come in regular cycles. Llewellyn Smith, on the other hand, said that there was enough experience to make it likely, 'though it could never be certain', that whatever happened before could happen again, that three, four or five years of good trade would be followed by bad trade, but that we had not at present sufficient data to be able to fix the length of the cycles though they used to be ten years and are now getting shorter.[104] Seasonal variations affected the distribution of work over time, not its total volume, fluctuations due to process changes were bad for the individual because he lost the value of his skill, but cyclical variations were worse for the country as a whole—the last assessment being important because the later Poor Law Commission took a different view. We had been set on a more scientific approach to the problem and how good a start it was can be seen by the extension of the series backwards and forwards in the Board of Trade Memoranda in *British and Foreign Trade*, 1904,[105] and by comparing it with Beveridge's later analysis of 1908.

But there was much less progress in the art of aiding the unemployed by agencies outside the Poor Law, and neither in dealing with the difficulties of the winter of 1894–95 on which immediate report was asked, nor on the permanent problem, had the Committee on *Distress from Want of Employment* much to offer. As to the former, Keir Hardie had proposed assistance by a grant of £100,000 to match equally local sums raised from public and voluntary sources, only to be reminded by John Burns[106] of the difficulties that might arise if adjacent areas were unequally aided and that amateurs coming in to give relief outside the work of experienced Guardians' officers would make matters worse. More significant in

[102]Majority Rep., para. 213.
[103]*Distress from Want of Employment,* 3rd Rep., Mins. of ev., q. 10,515, 1895 (365) ix.
[104]Ibid., qq. 4748–49, 4836–40.
[105]1905; Cd. 2337, lxxxiv, pp. 79–126.
[106]q. 982, 1st Rep., 1895 (111) viii.

the long run was Hardie's suggestion that if adequate relief were not given the unemployed should apply *en masse* for poor relief, so that their numbers would break down the system and create a crisis[107]—as in effect they did in Poplar, West Ham and certain other places in 1926–28—and his claim, asserted also by George Lansbury, that it was the duty of the State to provide work or maintenance,[108] thus foreshadowing later Right to Work Bills. But since periods of distress would recur, more permanent arrangements were needed to help prudent artisans and others who had made every endeavour to maintain their independence and yet were thrown out of work through no fault of their own, without compelling them to resort to the Poor Law with its stigma, harsh conditions and loss of the right to vote. Chamberlain's famous circular of 1888,[109] directed to local authorities and not the Guardians, had aimed at encouraging them to provide work outside the Poor Law for precisely these classes of men. This not only implied a recognition by the State of its responsibility for the unemployed, but officially started us on that course of combating unemployment through public relief works which continued, with so many frustrations and disappointments and on which we had so much to learn, right up to the depression of the nineteen-thirties. For the work was not to involve any stigma, as did the Guardians' test work; it was to be such that all could do it whatever their previous occupation, it was not to compete with that of other labourers in employment nor to hinder men from resuming their normal trade.

Though to a radical trying to find his way to a practical solution these restrictive conditions must at the time have seemed sensible enough, and a reasonable defence could be made for each of them, together they so limited the room for manoeuvre that they gave rise to difficulties which haunted the policy for a long time. The further condition that pay should be at less than the standard rates, lest men should be encouraged to look on it as a permanent job, had to be dropped because the trade unions feared the undercutting of normal work, as was the proposal that the Guardians should

[107]Ibid., q. 744.
[108]Ibid., q. 819; qq. 10,454–56, 3rd Rep., 1895 (365) ix.
[109]Local Government Board, 16th Ann. Rep., app. A, no. 6; 1886–87, C. 5131, xxxvi.

select the men, since many borough engineers preferred themselves to choose the men for the job in hand. As it turned out the casual worker was attracted to the work as just another job, the standard of work was very low, the cost extremely high and in due course there was much more disturbing fundamental doubt: if the work were useful and would at some time have been undertaken anyway, was it not forestalling ordinary work by permanent employees? In view of these difficulties the Committee on *Distress from Want of Employment* finally reported that they did not find it possible to devise any scheme involving the compulsory provision of work for all applicants. The best ways of dealing with the unemployed were still experimental and these efforts should be continued.[110] Nevertheless, even ten years later the Government could think of nothing better than the Unemployed Workmen Act, 1905, which formalised and extended the arrangements and created outside the Poor Law permanent local Distress Committees to provide temporary work for the *élite* of the unemployed, as Balfour called them, to run labour exchanges, etc. So that there were in effect two systems of unemployed relief running alongside. Though Keir Hardie gave some support to the Bill because it accepted public responsibility for the unemployed, neither the trade unions nor the Labour M.P.s were much more positively constructive, for in various ways, including their Right to Work Bills, they merely asked for more of the same thing. And although one cannot be precise, in the difficulties after the Boer War there must have been several hundred thousand unemployed men not on relief works and with little or no resources to fall back on. A little earlier Herbert Gladstone had suggested a national survey to determine what improvements could be undertaken with State initiative.

Proposals for a system of Labour Exchanges took some time to make their way. Reviewing the experiences of experimental labour registries started by local and voluntary effort, the *Labour Commission* thought that not much could be expected of them, since they were of little use to unskilled men and were of least help when the need was greatest, in time of general depression when jobs were

---

[110]*Distress from Want of Employment*, Sel. Cttee. Rep., p. xv, 1896 (321) ix.

scarce all the way round.[111] But as Llewellyn Smith replied to a similar objection, even in bad times not all trades were equally depressed at the same time, and in any case exchanges would help an out-of-work man to find a suitable place.[112] The trade unions, whilst not offering organised opposition, still feared that, as the exchanges would be helping even non-unionists in the way in which they helped their own members, they might be used to undercut wages or break strikes, and the members might lose a relative advantage of membership. The Distress Committees were empowered to, and some did take over or start exchanges, but there was still inadequate recognition that the essential condition of success was that there should be a nation-wide system of exchanges.[113]

Outside the circles called upon to influence policy, there was, however, a dissentient voice, that of J A Hobson. Attempts to measure unemployment more precisely, and to prescribe remedies for it, revealed the bewildering variety of circumstances in different industries which put men out of work and there was some confused discussion on how it should be defined. Booth, as a result of his East London studies, had in effect argued that in trades run on casual labour, as in the docks, where there was not enough work for all who tried to earn their livelihood in them and all had but a few days work a week, the 'true' measure was the 'superfluity', the excess above the numbers needed if they were manned by a full-time staff only. Extending this idea to the building trades, were the numbers required in the summer over and above those needed in the winter, so that the total volume of work undertaken in the year would be decreased if they were not available, to be regarded as 'unemployed' in the winter, or simply as part of the industry's staff whose higher summer earnings made up for the lower winter ones? Were those needed in the shipbuilding industry during the boom

[111]Majority Rep., para. 243. See footnote below.

[112]*Distress from Want of Employment*, 3rd Rep., qq. 4862–72, 1895 (365) ix.

[113]But see Rev W Tozer's intelligent evidence on the Ipswich Labour Bureau, which he formed, qq. 1032, 1061. Also his comments on travelling expenses for men going to jobs, qq. 1031, 1054. Ibid., Rep. ev., 1896 (221) ix. *Labour* Commission, Mins. of ev., Commission sitting as a whole, qq. 6173–6306; 1893–94, C. 7062–i, xxxiv, pt. i.

years and not employed in depression a 'necessary margin' 'belonging' to it, without whom the volume of production and employment
over the years could not be maintained? Repelled by these ideas,
Hobson defined unemployment as involuntary leisure, attacked it
as economic and social waste, and thought that even palliatives
which apparently increased employment were futile unless they led
to a redistribution of consuming power and increased aggregate
consumption. This heterodox view, put forward in 1896[114] and
developed in later writings, was rejected at the time and later by
experts in the field, e.g. Beveridge in 1909. As far as official circles
were concerned, his was a voice crying in the wilderness, but the
gospel it preached made an obvious appeal to and penetrated the
thinking of trade unionists, and in due course was taken note of by
the unorthodox orthodox, such as Keynes. But that lay in the future.

5. DELAY IN PRACTICAL RESULTS:
IMPERFECTIONS OF ADMINISTRATION AND
TRANSITIONAL POLITICS

What had been accomplished? What omitted? In the short period
of fifteen years or so, 1880–94/5, there had been a remarkably active
re-appraisal of the economic and social system. Idealism and social
criticism from the most varied sources—clerical, anti-clerical, theological, secular, artistic and economic—reached a new peak and was
subjecting it to ethical tests. The range and vigour of both public
and private inquiry led to an immense advance in our knowledge
and in the techniques of investigation. In some fields, as in the
housing of the working classes, there was a substantial development
in the arts of reform embodied in legislation, though not much in
practice; in the case of sweating no lack of ethical standards, but a
confession that perhaps the complexities of the problem were such
that it could not be handled with the knowledge and administrative
apparatus available; in old age pensions, a growing realisation that
the problem was not one of discriminating between 'deserving A

[114] J A Hobson, *The Problem of the Unemployed* (1896).

and undeserving B', but of a want of confidence, perhaps courage in coming to a decision; in unemployment, still a lack of factual knowledge and very inadequate trade cycle theory, but the beginnings of a grip on it; in the field of labour relations, a conclusion that the most effective solution lay in negotiations through stable, responsible trade unions. In all these studies one very intractable problem emerged: the condition of the mass of unskilled, unorganised labour. In a remarkably balanced and full book written near the end of the period, *Problems of Poverty* (1892), J A Hobson concluded: 'The great problem of poverty thus resides in the condition of the low skilled workman. To live industrially under the new order he must organise. He cannot organise because he is so poor, so ignorant, so weak. Here is a great dilemma, of which whoever shall have found the key will have done much to solve the problem of poverty.' Some experienced investigators, e.g. Booth and the Majority of the *Labour Commission,* felt that at any rate until inflow of numbers through the birth rate began to decline, we should have to rely largely on 'the forces making for the general rise of standards'.

Not only were there hesitations of theory, but the administrative and political instruments were not fully ready for the new tasks. In the seventies, the point at which this stage of inquiry begins, it was an impossible machine to work with; in housing and sanitary regulation, for example, it was actually obstructive; there had been superimposed on the existing confusion of authorities three special *ad hoc* authorities for vital services—the poor law guardians, the local sanitary boards and the school boards. But in 1883 there still remained (amongst other bodies) 2,051 school boards, 649 unions, 1,583 urban and rural sanitary districts, 424 highway districts and 5,064 highway parishes. And the franchise was narrow. Taken as a whole the arrangements were neither efficient, sensitive to new needs nor responsive to popular demand.[115] By 1888 county councils were

---

[115]For example: 'Nine-tenths of the population in an English country parish have at this moment less share in local Government than belonged to all classes of freemen for centuries before and for centuries after the Norman Conquest.' See G Broderick, 'Local Government in England' in *Local Government and Taxation in the United Kingdom* (1882), p. 52.

established, in 1894 urban, rural districts and parish councils, and some unification had taken place, though there was still more to do. And the widening of the franchise gave more drive and a greater sense of urgency. In central government, partly because of their membership of an upper social class, their education, their appointment by patronage and nomination, and because the duties they were called upon to perform by a State largely non-interventionist, did not require it, in the fifties and sixties few civil servants other than those with special tasks, such as factory, mine or Poor Law inspectors, had any close acquaintance with working-class conditions. No less important therefore were the steps taken to improve the competence of the Civil Service following the Northcote-Trevelyan, Playfair and Ridley inquiries, by a closer definition of the duties of various grades and by opening them step by step to recruits selected by competitive tests. It would, of course, be a misreading of history to think of the dates on which these changes were made as heralding a corresponding transformation of the Service. They did open appointments to some new social groups, which had been excluded by the processes of nomination, but some years had to elapse before those selected by more exacting tests began to form a noticeable proportion of the Service, and certainly before they rose to posts of senior responsibility and were able to participate in policy-making. The effects were significantly less in this period when they were made than later for the work which, as it turned out, lay before them.[116]

At this point the political parties were in a too unsettled, transitional condition to be effective instruments for the new social tasks. As the economy grows, the changes in the balance of industries not only raise new problems of party policy, but mean shifts in the internal balance of power, and the rise of new groups with new economic interests and new ideals, which have to be accommodated in the party organisations and counsels. And these have to be sorted out whilst the old political battles have not yet been won and the older, declining groups are still fighting them and crying slogans which are ceasing to attract. Sometimes the old battle concerns

[116]The significance of these changes is dealt with on p. 119.

valuable items in an unfulfilled programme which ought to have been carried earlier, but have got left over to a time when to the public they seem a little stale, *manqué* simply because others have become of greater interest. Then there is the play of personal ambition and conflict. The Liberal Party, whose dependence first on the middle-class, and then on the working-class votes might have prompted action, was an amalgam of Peelites, Whigs, Cobdenites and radicals, and there was an obvious strain between its traditions of individualism and free enterprise and the radical demand for more State action, e.g. Chamberlain's *Radical Programme*. Too much emphasis either way might mean a shedding of personnel and loss of votes. The extensions of the franchise not only brought up the demands of the English urban workers for more attention to social conditions and of rural workers for a solution of the land question, but also the claims of the new Irish voters for Home Rule. With the intrusion of Parnell's solid block of Irish M.P.s determined to obstruct until they got it, the Home Rule problem could not be avoided. Though Gladstone was sensitive to trends of opinion, it was not clear that he had much understanding of social problems arising out of a process of development, and in the end Home Rule became an obsession which pushed aside other interests.[117] The Party was torn asunder by the controversies about it and the Boer War, and lost its most vigorous radical exponent, Chamberlain, while Dilke lost his place and influence owing to the circumstances surrounding his divorce, and Mundella his by an administrative slip. These losses occurred when it was necessary for the Party to reformulate its doctrine in the light of the new social tasks. Out of office, it did not regain it for nineteen years. Labour men were already trying to gather the working-class votes. And although it was having some doubts on agricultural tariffs, in the main Conservative policy also was based on individual enterprise. Then part of the working class was caught in the imperialism of the time: the music-hall songs show the popular leanings. Intellectual and political energies, as well as the resources, were thus drawn off to cope with the matters which aroused so much passion.

---

[117]See Bob Smillie's impressions at an interview. *My Life for Labour* (1924), p. 264.

H

In view of the intellectual difficulties and ambiguity of political attitudes it is not surprising that the meagre practical results of these years of intense investigation contrast sharply with the almost dramatic way in which action followed investigation after the Reform Act of 1832. Then the reformers were able to act with great speed. The Reports on the *Employment of Children in Factories,* on the *Employment of Children in Mines and Manufactories* and on the *Poor Laws,* had each been followed by legislation within about a year and the Reports on *The Health of Towns* and on *The State of Large Towns and Populous Districts* within four years. The problems of the eighties and nineties were in themselves more difficult that those of imposing regulatory controls and restrictions—though some of these had to ride storms enough—since they went to the heart of the economic system. Before the fruits of all the work could be gathered, there was more to be done. The resolution of these difficulties depended not only on the adjustments of powers and influence within the parties, but also on the development of new doctrines which would enable them, whilst settling some of the old battles, to provide for the growing new interests and ideals. There were new principles of social action to find, new administrative instruments to be made; in the meantime, the miseries of the poor went unrelieved. Nevertheless, society was 'groaning in pain and in travail', trying to draw it all together and to find that more complete knowledge and clearer vision which should lead to a juster society. The endeavour to accomplish this synthesis came after 1906.

Part III

A FIRST SOLUTION: 1906–1914

'Tis not too late to seek a newer world

TENNYSON

So on our heels a fresh perfection treads,
A power more strong in beauty, born of us
And fated to excel us

KEATS

The creature Man will fight for an idea like
a hero

GEORGE BERNARD SHAW

I. A CHANGE OF TONE

The tone of the years 1906–14 is in sharp contrast to that of the twenty years or so which preceded them. The intellectual inhibitions and political difficulties which had hindered the understanding of our social problems were broken through, the range and sweep of reforming legislation representing a first solution. In many fields of fundamental public policy there was a searching out of facts and fresh constructive thinking. The reports of inquiries not only have a new ring of confidence, a sense of purpose and resolution, but exhibit a great change of point of view and a capacity to find solutions where earlier none had been found. The difference between the Final Report of the Dunraven Committee on *Sweating* (1890), sympathetic though it was, and that of the Committee on *Home Work* (1908), measures the distance thought had travelled. This

103

change was wrought by a convergence both of ideas and of social and political movements.

In sorting some of them out one has to avoid slipping into the notion that the great reforms of the period were simply the outcome of 'social imperatives', as if a social or national situation were bound to produce appropriate responses. But these are the result of individuals' and groups' aspirations, calculations and passions and both may lose their way through the opposition of vested interests, the stubbornness of entrenched ideas or just lack of knowledge. We are not relieved of the task of studying the reasoning behind different choices of policy. Nor do the clashes of the party battalions alone explain the way in which problems are approached, the kinds of evidence demanded, why some arguments are regarded as cogent or the ethical values by which they are judged. Sometimes the ideas which active policy-makers just picked up from those in circulation at the time—or even earlier, in their intellectually formative years[1]—contributed to form their judgement on what were or what were not acceptable solutions. We must therefore turn to the intellectual history of the time. Just as an unsolved moral problem does not 'lie still in the mind', but to aid its solution draws to itself ideas and emotions from varied sources, so by its insistence the unsolved social problem called upon a wide range of ideas and aspirations from which to work out a new synthesis able to cope with it. Some had their origin in the ferment of the late eighties and nineties, others were very new, the different currents of critical thinking—ethical, theological, economic—expanding, crossing or merging to produce a broad stream of general notions which inspired or secured the acquiescence of various groups in the new reforming policy.

i. *Greater awareness of poverty*

First, there was a heightened awareness of the suffering, deprivation and uncertainty endured by a substantial part of the working

---

[1] John Morley set out explicitly those which contributed to his pattern of thought in *Recollections* (1917), I, chaps. ii–iv. See also autobiographies of Labour leaders, e.g. Burt, *Autobiography*, chaps. ix, xi; Smillie, *My Life for Labour*, pp. 50–3.

population. C F G Masterman in *The Condition of England* (1909) described English society, marked by public penury and private ostentation, as an unpremeditated, successful plutocracy to which the life of the working population was an unknown world. The inquiries of Booth and Rowntree and the public inquiries on *Sweating* and the *Aged Poor* were followed by private studies which showed what life was like on *Round About a Pound a Week* (Mrs Reeves, 1913), *Across the Bridges* (Paterson, 1911), *At the Works* (Lady Bell, 1907) and Robert Tressall (Robert Nooman) the socialist housepainter recorded with realism and humour the life of his mates in *The Ragged Trousered Philanthropist* (1914).[2] All this activity did more than provide the facts on which policy should be based: it revealed the social consequences of individuals' economic acts, and by so doing led to the extension of moral standards to include them.

ii. *More statistical knowledge*

It was characteristic of the period that by the aid of fresh statistical techniques an official endeavour should be made to establish the precise quantitative facts by large-scale statistical investigations into the trade of Great Britain and her competitors, the resources of the Dominions, wages and earnings, trends in public health. Thus, in 1908 by a collection of sample working-class family budgets, rents and wages, and the use of weighting, was officially introduced a measurement of cost of living in large towns traced back to 1880, the changes in which have played so large a part in English wage bargaining and social policies. A notable attempt was made in five great reports to determine the working-class cost of living as compared with that in Germany, France, Belgium and the United States. To get round the difficulty that an Englishman has different habits and modes of living from his compeers in similar occupations and buys different things at different prices, an ingenious calculation was made of what it would cost him in wages if he migrated to these countries, and how much a German, Frenchman or Belgian

[2]Lenin's impression of the working class in London in 1902 can be found in N Krupskaya, *Memories of Lenin* (1942), pp. 49–51.

would need to keep their standard in this country.[3] The information on standard rates of wages and hours gathered after the Labour Commission's complaint on the lack of information was only half the story: what was relevant was not only wages but earnings, not only average earnings but the proportion of workers in the higher, middle and lower earnings brackets; this was supplied in medians and quartiles for eight industrial groups.[4] And the rhythmical variations of the labour market were tested by trade union statistics. Similarly, there was improvement in health statistics, Arthur Newsholme, L.G.B. Medical Officer, being a technical leader in this field.[5] For good measure much of this wealth of new material was gathered into two special, if bulky, volumes.[6]

It was not only actual deprivation—for since 1880 the national income had grown faster than population, and most classes, including much of the working class, were sharing the advance in standards[7]—but the contrast between wealth and poverty of which both reformers and workers became more acutely conscious. But if there were not an even greater rate of increase at the top end of the scale—the income from overseas investments now reached about 8 to 10 per cent of the national income[8]—the absolute increase was enough to permit a great increase in the conspicuous consumption of the wealthy. Although this may have been in some degree restrained by English social tradition, there was plenty of it. It showed itself in a mixture of the vulgar extravagances of Edwardian days, from which the circles of the Court were not immune, with the evidences of the older forms of wealth in the great house parties referred to by Margot Asquith, the great staff

---

[3]*Cost of Living*, German, French, Belgian and American Towns Reps.; 1908, Cd. 4032, cviii; 1909, Cd. 4512, xci; 1910, Cd. 5065, xcv; 1911, Cd. 5609, lxxxviii.

[4]For a list of these see *Breviate of Parliamentary Papers*, I, 216–17.

[5]Arthur Newsholme, *Vital Statistics* (1889). This went through successive revised editions.

[6]*British and Foreign Trade and Industrial Conditions*, 2nd ser., Bd. of Trade; 1905, Cd. 2337, lxxxiv. *Public Health and Social Conditions*, Local Gov. Bd.; 1909, Cd. 4671, ciii.

[7]A L Bowley, *The Change in the Distribution of the National Income, 1880–1913* (1920), pp. 21–2.

[8]Ibid., p. 25. H Feis, *Europe the World's Banker* (1930), p. 16. Bowley and Stamp, *The National Income in 1924* (1927), p. 113.

at Belvoir Castle mentioned by Lady Duff Cooper, the Meinertz-hagen's servants at Mottisfont Abbey coping with fires in twenty rooms every day, and the activities of a more cultivated kind in the social competition in providing the musical performances described by Sitwell in *Great Morning*.

All this existed side by side with a distribution of income, according to estimates of Chiozza Money, published in 1905[9] which meant that while out of a total national income of £1,710 million, 1¼ million persons took £585 million, 3¼ million persons took £245 million, the remaining 38 million persons received £880 million. Probably one in seventeen of the population had some contact with the Poor Law,[10] and the infant mortality rate amongst the poorest part of the population, unskilled labourers, was twice that in wealthier classes.[11] As compared with the similar measurement made earlier by Colquhoun, this was issued in a setting of much wider social protest, in which not only the victims of the new industrial system took part, but persons and groups from all ranks of society. The book went through a number of editions: the questions asked and suggested were obvious; how much and by what means could some of the surplus of the wealthy be transferred to the poor?

It was not until the conclusion of the First World War that Bowley,[12] after an analysis of the various sources of income open to attack by taxation, better wages and improved services, concluded that the amount which could be transferred to the lower incomes would have barely sufficed, without an increase in productivity, to bring up the wage of the adult men and women to much above Rowntree's 'human needs' standard. The calculation had its difficulties since, as Bowley pointed out,[13] a large-scale redistribution would change monetary demands and prices and therefore react on incomes, and so make the final numerical result different; but this was as far as it was then possible to go.

[9]L G Chiozza Money, *Riches and Poverty*.
[10]Ibid., p. 318.
[11]Registrar General's Rep. for 1911. Also W A Brend, *Health and the State* (1917), pp. 81–7.
[12]A L Bowley, *The Division of the Product of Industry* (1919), pp. 49–58.
[13]Bowley, *Change in the Distribution of the National Income*, p. 21.

2. SOCIAL CRITICISM: THE FORMULATION OF
NEW STANDARDS AND PRINCIPLES

The great range of social criticism established the connection between these social evils and existing social institutions. Some of it was formally economic and political, some ethical, some literary and even artistic. This fresh way of looking at things not only produced a greater willingness to accept social experiments, but gave rise to dreams of a social order based on new principles, lent drive and passion to social movements and produced a willingness to search for approaches to it in legislation. It was the jostling of these new ideas, at once critical and imaginative, their crossing and interweaving, which produced a pattern of social thought distinctive, if not unique. Common to these varieties of view was the condemnation of the guidance of economic life by unrestrained individualism and the conviction that grave social evils had their sources not in personal failings, but in imperfect institutions.

i. *Socialistic criticism*

Socialist criticism showed these characteristics. Despite Marx's and Engels' long stay in England, Marxism had made but modest impact on English workers. Popularised in England by Hyndman, the idea that evils were inherent in the system was in some measure acceptable, but the further contention that it would be superseded only through the class struggle and some cataclysmic process was not. In its early phases, the Social Democratic Federation was cool to trade unionism, its exclusive dogmatism[14] proved uncongenial in a country with a long history of religious and social dissent and to groups of workers, like miners, who were class conscious in the sense that William Lovett was class conscious, having a distinctively working-class point of view, but were not socialists. Though the object of its propaganda was to detach workers from their allegiance

---

[14]In *The Evolution of Revolution* (1920) Hyndman criticised the Bolsheviks for starting the revolution in Russia, an agricultural country, whereas according to theory it should come first in an advanced industrial one.

to capitalism it was always small in membership—10,000 at its height—and was laughed at by Bernard Shaw for fighting elections which revealed that the massive support it claimed was in fact infinitesimal. But it remained an active group faithful to its creed.[15]

The appeal of Robert Blatchford and Keir Hardie was different. Hardie had a mystical strain, Blatchford was anti-clerical if not anti-Christian. Neither were scholars like Marx, but workmen. With Hardie, largely self-taught, the original inspiration was drawn from Carlyle, Ruskin and Henry George. Blatchford, in simple, vigorous prose a workman could understand, in *Merrie England* (1894),[16] *Britain for the British* (1902), both of which had an enormous circulation, declared that Britain did not belong to the British, but only to a few of them, who employed and exploited the rest, so that the few were rich and the many poor. The remedy was socialism. This gospel was carried to town and village by his famous *Clarion* vans manned by volunteers, and by *Clarion* cycling clubs, whose vigour, cameraderie and songs were so much a part of this phase of socialist propaganda. Hardie's plea, equally simple and reinforced by a strong ethical strain, made a really deep impression on the working class and it was to his determination, aided by others, such as Glasier, in whose thinking the ethical element was no less strong, that the formation of a working-class labour party independent of other parties was due.[17] But neither Hardie not Blatchford made any original contribution to thought.

The founding members of the Fabian Society (1884) were mostly

[15]It is unnecessary to go into details of the split in the Marxists on the question of trade unions, the formation of Connolly's Socialist Labour Party (1903) with its declaration that the workshop was the battlefield and 100 per cent industrial unions the weapon, the breakaway Socialist Party of Great Britain, the transformation of the S.D.F. to the Social Democratic Party, or the formation of the British Socialist Party, or to decide how much there is in Murphy's view in *Preparing for Power,* that the doctrinal self-isolation from the masses was a deviation from the Marxist analysis. These vigorous controversies over Marxist theology all contributed to create an atmosphere favourable to experiment.

[16]By 1908 total sales of various versions in Britain, Europe and the U.S.A. were said to have reached two million. Twenty thousand copies of the 1908 ed. were ordered before formal publication.

[17]Estimates of the I.L.P. membership vary according to the accounting basis—central dues paid or 'local members', but 10,000 in 1895, 20,000 in 1906 and 33,000 in 1913 give a fair indication.

untouched by and not very interested in Marx, who had neither indicated a method nor devised any machinery for managing the transition to the new order. Many of the members were or had been civil servants, who naturally thought not of starting little socialist communities or of catastrophic changes, but of using for the purpose the administrative machinery already applied to labour protection. It was 'civil servants' socialism.[18] It was equally natural that persons living in the country's financial centre should, in the famous Fabian *Essays on Socialism* (1889) and numerous Fabian tracts—Nos. 5 and 7 particularly—all of which had wide and continued circulation,[19] extend Henry George's notion of taking for social purposes the income from monopolised land to include unearned incomes from monopolistic advantages and properties of every kind. And when industrial units became so large that their problems became administrative, they were to be taken over by the State. All this demanded an expert, democratically controlled civil service, local as well as central. Its appeal was to the intellectuals, and not middle-class ones only. But there was a deeper reason: as Pease put it, the *Essays* offered a great release from the dogmatic exclusiveness and not always comprehensible Marxism of the S.D.F. and Socialist League.[20] The actual membership was always small— 2,600 in 1909.[21] An important dynamic concept developed from the work of two of its members, the Webbs. In *Industrial Democracy*[22] they had concluded that since the competition of the unemployed and under-employed labour prevented effective sectional pressure by trade unions for minimum standard rates adequate to stamp out industrial parasitism—that is, the failure of employers to pay wages adequate to cover the cost of minimum needs, which had therefore

[18]E R Pease, *History of the Fabian Society* (1925), p. 63.

[19]By 1908, 30,000 copies of the *Essays* had been sold (Pease, pp. 89–90). Up to and including 1914, 176 Tracts were issued.

[20]Shaw adds that while he and other Fabians were constantly speaking for the S.D.F. and Socialist League, 'Hyndman, Morris, Helen Taylor and the other S.D.F.-ers and Leaguers were too old for us; they were between forty and fifty when we were between twenty and thirty.' Pease, p. 62n.

[21]Pease, pp. 101, 185.

[22]S and B Webb, *Industrial Democracy* (1897), pp. 749–83. Pease, p. 185n; earlier figures, p. 101.

to be borne by others—a national minimum should be prescribed by law. In due course this idea expanded beyond its original limits in two ways: the minimum should not be restricted to food, clothing and shelter, but comprise all the elements of civilised life; and if this could not be attained through wages, it should be provided by positive State action.

A little later there was a change in mood amongst younger socialists: it was not only better wages, but control over their conditions of work which men wanted—self-government in industry, Guild Socialism. And a critical attitude to collectivism was expressed in a brilliant and bitter cartoon by Will Dyson which prefaces Cole's *World of Labour* (1913), but then the First World War was upon us. Other critics rebelled against both the actual tyranny of capitalism and the possible tyranny of State Socialism. G K Chesterton in *What's Wrong with the World?* (1910), *Manalive* (1912) and *Napoleon of Notting Hill* (1904), and H Belloc in the *Servile State* (1912) and the novel *Mr Clutterbuck's Election* (1900), formally and in fancy argued that a man's freedom should be guaranteed by a wide distribution of property, which neither capitalism nor socialism permitted, and wanted equally freedom from bureaucracy of either type.[23]

ii. *Literary criticism*

Novelists, playwrights and art critics joined in the attacks on the existing social institutions and conventional standards: Shaw in his plays (and *Prefaces*), Galsworthy in *Strife* (1909), *Justice* (1910), *Man of Property* (1906), *Country House* (1907). H G Wells, with his mercurial temperament and responsiveness to the mood of the public and the questions passing through its mind, was less consistent than Shaw. But from *Kipps* (1905) and *This Misery of Boots* (1905) (a Fabian Tract) he went on to sketch a *Modern Utopia* (1905) in which a more rational and humane society was led by an

---

[23]On one occasion, shocked by the proposal of a local authority that to deal with the verminous condition of some slum children, it would be necessary to cut off the girls' hair, there was a typical Chestertonian outburst: 'Why take away the children's hair, why not take away the slums?'

élite samurai, to a broad statement of socialist ideals in *New Worlds for Old* (1908), both of which had an immense appeal not limited to the younger, livelier generations, followed by the *History of Mr Polly* (1910). Works of art, wrote R L Stevenson, mould by contact, we drink them up like water, and are bettered we know not how. If the criticism of the littérateurs were more free ranging, it was not less a solvent because its argument was neither statistical nor logical, but aesthetic and emotional, or because it reached so many who would never look at or even see a Fabian tract. It contributed no less to a general loosening of inherited social ideas and to more open-mindedness on new ones.

iii. *Theological and ethical criticism*

In the same way streams of thought from various religious sources converged to produce and strengthen the ethical quality in political thinking, a desire to see individual activity in harmony with the social good. The religious bodies turned their attention to the problems of 'social righteousness'. One main stream, the Anglican, beginning partly as a protest against social conditions which rendered the proper development of spiritual life an impossibility, drew from theological concepts the conclusion, as Gore did in *The Incarnation of the Son of God* (1891), that commercial and social selfishness were antagonistic to the spirit of Christ. A veritable shelf-full of books and sermons went on to claim that the Church must not draw within itself, nor surrender or allow itself to be excluded from any department of human relations (Bussell, Scott Holland, William Temple). Attracted by the idealistic side of socialism some, like Scott Holland, acclaimed Wells' *New Worlds for Old*,[24] and Gore wrote *Christianity and Socialism* (1908). It was not always clear whether socialism was regarded as Christianity in practice, whether the task was to Christianise socialism or to socialise Christianity, or whether some did not wander off into an

[24]Henry Scott Holland, *A Bundle of Memories* (1915), esp. pp. 171, 179–83. Note William Temple's comment: 'Yet the thing that really lives with me is Scott Holland's extraordinary oration on the power of Christ to regenerate society.' F A Iremonger, *William Temple* (1948), p. 125.

humanitarianism having little theological content. The formal organisations always had a small and modest membership, the Guild of St Matthew, 400, the Christian Social Union, 6,000,[25] the Church Socialist League, 1,200, but many of those active went on to bishoprics and other offices of great influence. The two greatest were yet to come. William Temple, who early had exclaimed that the choice was between socialism and heresy, that the Church must set forth in teaching and practice the relation of Christian faith and life to the labour movement, denounced the competition, as in the docks, of men for the right to work which was the right to live. Throughout his life he elaborated with clarity and conviction the application of Christian principles, at its end expressing his view in *Christianity and the Social Order* (1942). The other was a layman, R H Tawney, whose historical learning and prose style in the *Sickness of an Acquisitive Society* (1920), requiring the subordination of economic activity to social purpose, had so much influence on the working-class intellectuals.

A further and very different source was the application of modern historical, archaeological and linguistic methods of study to Old Testament literature. These traced through a sorting out of the basic Jahvist, Elohist and Priestly documents, the development of Hebrew religion from primitive forms to the moral revolution preached by the prophets, e.g. Amos and Hosea, who demanded justice and mercy rather than sacrifice and were concerned with public and social, as well as private morality. Opened in the period of 'ferment' with the *Prophets of Israel* (1882) and the *Religion of the Semites* (1889) by W Robertson Smith, who lost his Chair through unorthodoxy, the discussion was carried on into this period through technical theological works as well as wider versions for students, such as Duff's *Old Testament Theology* (1891, 1900) and *Hints on Old Testament Theology* (1908) published in the *Christian Commonwealth*, Addis' *Hebrew Religion* (1906), and in commentaries for the layman, and joined the stream of popular social criticism to give sanction to claims for social justice in Rauschenbusch's *Christianity and the Social Crisis* (1912).

[25]Compare with the Fabians' 2,600.

It was typical of the way these currents merged that the Fabian Society should publish two tracts by a great Non-conformist, Dr Clifford, on *Socialism and the Churches* (No. 139, 1908), and *Socialism and the Teaching of Christ* (No. 78, 1897), and by two high churchmen, Stewart Headlam on *Christian Socialism* (No. 42, 1892), and Percy Dearmer on *Socialism and Christianity* (No. 133, 1907). And in a remarkable volume on *Property; its Rights and Duties* (1913) a number of leading scholars in sociology, theology and philosophy (Hobhouse, Rashdall, Lindsay, A J Carlyle, Wood, Scott Holland, Bartlet) directed attention to the fact that the Church had always regarded the right to property as conditional on the social good and not as a means of power over others.

By contrast there were the Non-conformist undogmatic Adult Schools, founded by local leadership, democratically organised, with dominantly working-class membership.[26] Fostered by members of the Society of Friends, they aimed at intensifying the social spirit by bringing men together for free study of the deeper problems of life in relation to the ideals set forth in the Gospels. Declining to recognise any sharp division between religious and social or secular studies, not only Biblical, but general cultural studies—literary, historical, social—were pursued. Undenominational, they attracted many not concerned with formal church-going, including a share of agnostics. These conditions, including the atmosphere of free discussion and participation, made them a natural home for some intellectual workers. Their growth was therefore remarkable and significant. In 1906 there were 1,400 schools with 95,000 members, in 1909 1,800 schools with 112,000 members and an average attendance of between 50 and 60 per cent. The interest in social questions implicit in their purpose, though its strength varied considerably from group to group, became steadily more conscious. Though they had no religious or political dogmas, to anyone acquainted with the rank and file of the radical and labour movements their influence was definite, unmistakable: it was the emphasis on the ethical aspects of social questions. Their *Fellowship Hymn Book* gave prominent place to a number of hymns popular with

[26]See Reports of the Adult School Union, and of the Cttee. on *Adult Education,* Final Rep., pp. 211–14; 1919, Cmd. 321, xxviii.

the members—concerning democracy, brotherhood, social justice and the ideal city. For example, 'When wilt thou save the people?'; 'The Golden city with wrong banished from its borders'; Carpenter's 'England Arise', 'God send us Men, His lofty precepts to translate, until the laws of Christ become the laws and habits of the State'; 'These things shall be a loftier race . . . with flame of freedom in their souls and light of knowledge in their eyes'. The peak was reached in 1910, after which many drifted into the I.L.P. with its more definite point of view, and to the more intensive studies organised by the developing Workers' Educational Association (10,000 in 1914), but there were still 90,000 remaining in the Adult Schools when the war broke out. As its members took their place in other democratic organisations, spilling over into the I.L.P., radical and labour parties, they took with them the ethical quality— and even the hymns named—which so marked the English Labour Movement at that time.

The 'Labour Churches'—perhaps that of Southgate was the most important—were few in number and despite their sincerity, significant of a trend rather than an influence. Trevor and Wicksteed, who were originally concerned, were trying to find a 'home' for those who found the Churches unreal and their activities irrelevant and were seeking a non-religious ethic. Into them moved disappointed non-conformists, people from the 'ethical movement' and sceptics. Similarly, the Socialist Sunday Schools often associated with them,[27] the sincerity and the liveliness of the children, and their own set of 'commandments' (e.g. 'Be courteous to all, bow down to none'), were a part of a lively, but impermanent life.

English radical socialism of the time, if such a term could be applied to it, was thus a curious compound of the class consciousness of many trade unionists who were not socialist, Ruskin, the Bible, the administrator's hatred of waste and injustices, gas and

[27]See *The Socialist Sunday School Hymn Book* (1910), comp. by the National Council of British Socialist Sunday School Unions. There was also an I.L.P. *Song Book* published by the *Worker* at Huddersfield, which studiously avoided any trace of religious sentiment. It was re-published as *Labour's Song Book*. It was not uncommon in provincial I.L.P. meetings at that time, for a little pile of the red-covered song books to be placed on a chair inside the room to be handed to members as they came in—just as in an orthodox mission hall.

water socialism and claims to the national ownership of some of the major means of production. How odd it seemed to a continental outsider is clear from Trotsky's complete astonishment when with Lenin and Krupskaya, he visited what he called a 'Social Democratic meeting in a church' (Southgate) the meeting sang the hymn 'When wilt thou save the people, not thrones and crowns, but men', which he remembered as 'Lord Almighty, let there be no more kings or rich men'. Lenin's comment was that the revolutionary and socialist elements amongst the English proletariat were prevented by religion, etc. from breaking through.[28] But of course it *was* the English breakthrough.

iv. *New turns in economic theory*

Fourthly, the spread of scientific economic studies, though not primarily concerned with ethical questions, worked in the same direction. As far back as 1880 in *Elementary Political Economy* and later in *Wealth* (1914), Cannan had broken with the traditional arrangement of exposition in order to answer directly the questions then in people's minds—what determined the material welfare of groups and persons—and found that the greatest cause of inequality between individuals was the inheritance of property and the cost of training for the better-paid occupations, and suggested[29] that the principle of diminishing utility of income indicated that the inequality of income might be an evil in itself and that distribution according to need might give a better result. Sidgwick, in the famous Book III of his *Principles of Political Economy* (1883), had already argued that complete *laissez-faire* was not to be taken as a political ideal, that as applied to labour it left room for serious inequalities, that a more equal distribution of wealth tended *prima facie* to increase happiness, and that there was a large class of cases in which private interests could not be relied upon as a stimulus to

[28]Leon Trotsky, *My Life* (1930), pp. 127–8.

[29]This argument was later questioned on the ground that marginal utility of income to different persons cannot be compared or added, and that there was 'no bridge from the individual to the group'. But J E Meade re-instated it in *Economic Analysis and Policy* (1936). p. 210.

socially useful services. At this point the great figure of Alfred Marshall came on the scene, importing an humane spirit[30] and developing the marginal analysis in his *Principles* (1890) which, although its influence in England was nearly all pervasive, was perhaps less important than the race of economists that he stimulated and trained. Pigou, applying and developing the Marshallian technique in *Work and Wealth* (1913)[31] and later in more developed form in *Economics of Welfare* (1921), found circumstances in which the statutory limitation of the hours of work, minimum wages in certain trades, restraints on diminishing returns industries and stimulus to increasing returns industries, and an increase in the share and stability of the national income received by the poorer classes, had sound economic reasoning behind them. This great book expresses perhaps more than any other the change which professional economic thinking had undergone and the way in which it and social idealism were moving in the same direction. Thus the views of the professional economists and those of the critics, socialists and others, which had so diverged in part of the nineteenth century, came together in this area of common ground.

v. *The development of a new synthesis*

Fifthly, this play of ideas enabled the radicals of the Liberal Party to undertake the reconstruction of its approach and doctrines

[30]The following quotations from 'The Social Possibilities of Economic Chivalry' in *Economic Journal* (1907) illustrate this. 'There has been similar, but less complete convergence as to social ideals and the ultimate aim of economic effort' (p. 8). 'But there still remains a vast expenditure which contributes very little to social progress, and which does not confer any large and solid benefits on the spenders beyond the honour, the position and the influence which it brings in society. Now there is a general agreement amongst thoughtful people, and especially amongst the economists, that if society could award the honour, the position and the influence by methods less blind and wasteful; and if it could at the same time maintain all that stimulus which the free enterprise of the strongest business man derives from the present position, then the resources set free would open out to the masses of the people new possibilities of a higher life and of larger and more varied intellectual activities' (p. 9). 'The amount of socially wasteful private expenditure . . . some put as high as four or five hundred millions a year. . . . But it is sufficient for the present that there is a margin of at least two hundred millions which might be directed to social uses, without causing any great distress to those from whom it was taken' (p. 10). 'Economists generally desire increased intensification of State activity for amelioration . . .' (p. 17).

[31]For the importance attached to this book, see Alleyn Young's review, *Quarterly Journal of Economics*, XXVII (1913), 672–86.

I

needful if it were not to be lost in *ad hoc,* pragmatic attempts to deal with the problems as they arose, without the aid of clear principles to give its policies purpose and direction. J A Hobson in the *Crisis of Liberalism* (1909) and the *Industrial System* (1909)[32] concluded that the belief that poverty would eventually be abolished by steady, slow economic progress in free conditions was inadequate at a time when the intelligent use of technical progress would make it unnecessary to wait, and that a new and more positive role must be given to the State. One of its duties, Hobhouse argued in *Liberalism* (1911), was to guarantee to each individual a share of the common stock, while 'the living wage' and 'the right to work' were valid property rights. Economic justice implied that to each function, whether of work or enterprise, must be rendered the amount needed to sustain that function and to ensure its adequate growth, that the surplus above this could be taken for social purposes, that inherited wealth had less claim to recognition than acquired wealth, and that socially-created wealth should belong to the community. Access to land was vital both for urban housing and the regeneration of agriculture and the countryside.

vi. *Intermingling and diffusion of new ideals*

Sixthly, in this exciting period new ideas poured into the different groups of society from all quarters and intermingled. Some originated within the ranks of the workers, reaching them direct in simple pamphlets, also working upwards, while others were diluted and simplified as they percolated downwards.[33] In the areas where Methodism was strong, it was no uncommon thing for a miner to be a chairman of his local union lodge, a member of the co-operative society management committee and a lay preacher, or to have on his little book-shelf a Bible and a commentary on it, a social history,

[32]This book had a very large readership among the workers' classes, e.g. in the Workers' Educational Association. In *Free Thought in the Social Sciences* (1926), pt. ii, chaps. ii, iii, Hobson objected to some of Pigou's reasoning.

[33]For more active working-class students there were the classes of the Workers' Educational Association and the Plebs League, which was Marxist and partisan. For the details of the numerical strength of these and other bodies, see *Adult Education,* Cttee. Final Rep., app. i, pt. i; 1919, Cmd. 321, xxviii.

Hobson's *Industrial System* and some socialist pamphlets. At the mass level, the process was helped by the decline of illiteracy—the 200 out of every 1,000 men who in 1870 signed the marriage register with a mark had fallen in 1907 to 14[34]—the rise of the popular press, an enormous output of political leaflets,[35] periodicals as varied as the *Clarion* and the *Christian Commonwealth*, and aided by those newspaper rooms in public libraries which so impressed Lenin.[36] It was thus that workmen, middle-class radicals, intellectuals, reforming parsons and ministers of religion and progressive employers were able to give drive and support to the changes of 1906–14.

This great surge of ideas had two important consequences. First, it was from them that the English political, or should we say, social process selected some for immediate implementation, or ignored others; secondly, whatever the numerical calculations of political parties, the great social changes from 1906–14 were urged forward by a disinterested zeal for reform which had no precedent in English history.

3. IDEALS INTO PRACTICE: NEW INSTRUMENTS

i. *The administrative instrument: a new competence in the Civil Service*

It was out of this exciting clash of ideas and their application to the problems on which we had been brooding so long that our first large modern experiment in social control emerged. But they could be embodied in social institutions and practice only by the aid of responsive administrative and political agents. It was fortunate that there were—for a time—convergent currents in these areas also.

The civil servant, the local medical officer, the education officer had become dynamic elements in society led, irrespective of their

---

[34]*Public Health and Social Conditions;* 1909, Cd. 4671, ciii, chart 2, following p. 104.

[35]Some assessment of the volume of it is needed. For the Fabian output, see A M McBriar, *Fabian Socialists and English Politics* (1962), p. 170; Pease, *History of the Fabian Society,* app. iv.

[36]Krupskaya, *Memories of Lenin,* p. 51.

political philosophies, to enter new fields, apply new knowledge, to think out how to deal with new problems arising within their own fields of responsibility. They contributed not only out of the public eye in their own official work, but as members of official committees, as responsible for initiating inquiries or as expert witnesses.

Why did the civil service come to play such a role at this time and not earlier? To answer these two questions, its efficiency and achievements in 1906–14 have to be set against the obstacles which prevented their earlier attainment. The kind of civil service required simply to keep the ring in a *laissez-faire* competitive economy was one thing—though in the Irish famine and in war, as the Crimean disasters showed, its incompetence could be appalling—and its organisation and knowledge before it could take on more positive economic and social functions, were another. Staffed by patronage, in 1849 it had been condemned by Sir Charles Trevelyan, then Permanent Secretary to the Treasury, as over-staffed in numbers, inactive and incompetent. It was in fact all that the radical and socialist critics had declared it to be. There must have been, and indeed the peculiarities of the English social structure ensured that there were, a number of able men in it—at different times and levels the names of Farr, Horner, Chadwick and Giffen occur—for it to have carried administration through half a century of unprecedented social change without disaster. The first necessary step was to ensure that only properly qualified persons were appointed, the second to grade the work and to relate the tests to the kinds of duties to be performed not only initially on entry, but later in life. The third, to go beyond testing the competence of those nominated from the circles on whom the benefits of patronage were bestowed to opening the way for talents which lay outside it. But the influence of changes takes time to show itself; it may be ten or even twenty years before the new recruits reach positions of responsibility, decision and participation in policy-making; and they may not leave the service for thirty or forty years. Though at each stage of civil service reform there were important advances of principle, the attainment of these objectives took forty years, and now began to show their full significance. The Northcote-Trevelyan proposals (1853) that patronage should be abolished and recruits admitted by competitive examinations conducted by an independent body had been whittled down to requiring from nominees, for junior posts only, a certificate of qualification, and in all cases power of appointment remained with the political heads of departments. Even so, in the years 1855–59 for over 8,000 of the 10,000 appointments to which the order applied only one candidate had been nominated and of nearly 2,500 rejected candidates nearly 2,000 failed to pass the educational test.

Though this system of qualifying examinations and irresponsible nominations was in 1860, for junior examinations, replaced with a more effective system of limited competition between nominated candidates ('at least three for each vacancy') who had previously passed a qualifying test, and in 1870 for certain classes a competitive test became obligatory, at that time the higher administrative officers were still recruited partly by promotion, partly by appointment from outside sources, usually without examination. Even in the higher second class only twenty men had been subject to a competitive test on entry, the rest having been appointed earlier by patronage or limited competition. The Playfair Commission of 1874–75 stressed the importance of division of labour between the administrative class, which should be chosen from within by merit, a Higher division for men who would otherwise go into the open professions, and a Lower clerical division, and the need of a relevant test for each. But the Order in Council which followed did not mention either the administrative or the Higher division. The next attempt by the Ridley Commission was not made till 1886–90, i.e. within the period of active social inquiries and only partly successful thinking. The Higher division, it found, was too large, the line between it and the Lower having been drawn too low. It therefore recommended that a limited number of men of the same standard of liberal education as those entering the open professions should be recruited by higher examination to fill important posts direct and should be trained for selection to fill the highest posts. Both these changes were much more than a replacement of nomination by selection from the same social class on tests of competence; the positions hitherto the preserve of the members of the ruling class and those to whom they gave their support, were now open to recruits from new, larger social groups whose parents could afford to send them to the schools and universities attended by some of the older groups. The tests thus implied an education to which only limited classes had access and that the service was in layers like the English class system.[37] But a new stream of ability had been tapped. And the ethic of these new groups included a sense of duty and freedom from personal corruption unique at the time: qualities which, whatever the other defects, became a distinguishing mark of British Home and Colonial administration.

Thus by the end of the century the service was not only drawing in boys from the newly developing (Secondary) schools at the Second Division level, able to cope with the new tasks which were to be thrust upon them, but it was beginning to receive a refreshing new stream of vigour and ability into the administrative grades. In the period, say 1890–95 to 1906–12, these included Llewellyn Smith,[38] in due course involved in unemployment insurance. Amongst the many entering in this phase and seconded from various departments to assist in the establishment of national health insurance and who later went on to distinguished careers were Braithwaite, Warren Fisher, Ernest Gowers from Inland Revenue, John Bradbury from the Treasury, John Anderson, Arthur Salter, Wilfred Greene, Henry Bunbury, G M Young, C Schuster and Alexander Gray from other departments; these not only brought new ability, but shared the new awareness of the strains and disorders of industrial society. Llewellyn Smith and Miss Collet had had their sympathies and understanding enlarged

[37]The Northcote-Trevelyan reforms have been criticised for creating an upper civil service class detached from the realities of the outside world and blocking the way to recruitment by promotion from the lower ranks. The service was already a class-ridden system but untested for competence. As the facts given above show, the lower ranks also needed appropriate tests. Appointment from outside? But at that time and for long, business was personal, and posts were filled by sons, relatives, etc. of their owners. If therefore patronage was to be eliminated and competence tested, the reformers had to take the educational system as they found it. At the time, where were the English universities outside Oxford and Cambridge? It is worth while noting that in 1914 both Majority and Minority of the MacDonnell Commission expressly said that they had to fit their proposals into the educational system, school-leaving age, etc. as it existed. Both recommended increased opportunities for passage from the primary school to the universities. 1914, Cd. 7338, xvi, pp. 101, 149.

[38]For an appraisal of Llewellyn Smith's work, see the obituary notice by Beveridge, *Econ. Jn.* (March 1946), 143–7.

by work on Booth Surveys, Beveridge, Braithwaite, Wise by residence at Toynbee Hall.

There were also the experts in a more technical sense, not only in the central and developing local government services, but in independent professional life. Llewellyn Smith and Beveridge were certainly that in their own right. It was no accident that many of the great official investigations into labour conditions were undertaken during Llewellyn Smith's tenure of office, that Dr Arthur Newsholme who, whilst Medical Officer at Brighton, was an important witness before the Poor Law Commission, became Chief M.O.H. to the Local Government Board and was the author of official reports on *Infant and Child Mortality,* that James Kerr, 'the first school doctor', of the London School Board and L.C.C., W L MacKenzie, Medical Officer to the Scottish Local Government Board, George Newman, Medical Officer of Finsbury and later Chief Medical Officer, Local Government Board, author of *Infant Mortality* (1906), and A H Hogarth, County Medical Officer for Buckinghamshire and assistant medical officer to the L.C.C., author of *Medical Inspection of Schools* (1909), should have been so active in working out and impressing on the public mind, the social as well as the strictly medical implications of their problems and solutions.[39] Similar things could be said of other fields, e.g. education. Their contribution was not, however, limited to their expertise on particular topics, for the pace and great range of new legislation all involved an immense amount of work in planning, drafting and implementation, which had to be carried by a relatively small number of permanent servants. Even by 1914 the total number of officers of the administrative class for all departments was only about 450.[40] It was a contribution not to be underrated.

These events were a decisive turn; they were the reverse of what the Marxist analysis had implied. Marx had no occasion to love Continental bureaucracy, which had made him feel its tyrannous authority more than once, but his study of the French revolutionary

[39]The bibliography in Hogarth's book, pp. 298–302, indicates the range of the relevant professional writings in this period. It is worth noting that the preface to the book was written at Toynbee Hall.

[40]*Civil Service,* R. Com. 4th Rep., para. 39; 1914, Cd. 7338, xvi.

uprisings had apparently led him to the conclusion that the workers should not take over, but must break up the bureaucratic machine and see that workers themselves did the work of administration.[41] Whether Marx's temperament would ever have permitted him to guess the extent to which liberalisation and changes in the manning of the service would release creative energies is perhaps uncertain— he was, we are told, a poor executive officer.[42] But Lenin in *State and Revolution*[43] (1918, English trans. 1919), in a gloss on Marx's re-affirmation of his conclusion in a letter to Kugelmann (12 April 1871), said that while in 1871 England was still the pattern of a purely capitalist country in large measure without a bureaucracy and a revolution could be imagined without the destruction of the available, ready machinery, by 1918 it had degenerated so that this would now be necessary—a comment made after one of its most successful periods of creative work, in which the foundations of the Welfare State were laid.

ii. *The political instrument: the revived Liberal Party*

Political parties have mental lives of their own so that social ideals, as they pass through them into practice, are filtered and modified, added to, sometimes with incongruous ingredients. The great reforms did not come, as might be expected today, from a political party with an authoritative set of principles and prepared plans for their translation into practice. There were such groups, e.g. the I.L.P., the S.D.F. and, if they had been interested in fighting elections, the Fabians. But these were small. On the contrary, the vehicle by which these ideas found their way into practice was the Liberal Party which, following the Home Rule and Boer War splits, had been in intellectual and political confusion. It was drawn together and its creative energies released by the General Election of 1906. For this was fought, not on the measures of social reform for which the Ministry is now remembered, but on the issue presented to it by the Conservative Government, its traditional principle

[41]Karl Marx, *Eighteenth Brumaire of Louis Napoleon*, Eng. trans. (1913), pp. 141–2.
[42]Lee and Archbold, *Social Democracy in Britain*, p. 38.
[43]N Lenin, *The State and Revolution*, Eng. trans. (1919), pp. 39, 40.

of Free Trade. This was one on which the quarrelling factions—the Liberal Imperialists, the Pro-Boers, Radicals, and old Whigs—could unite: the 'Free Breakfast Table', copiously depicted on coloured posters, made their election campaign easy. With its mass meetings, poster campaigns on unprecedented scale, the Tariff Reform League and the Free Trade Union throwing masses of figures at voters even at street corner meetings, leaflets and even propaganda stage plays on tariffs and Free Trade, for those who passed through it the excitement and emotions stirred exceeded that of the most exciting elections since. And the question happened to be one on which Labour candidates could take the same stand. The Conservatives were overwhelmed, the Liberals returned with a majority over all parties and freed from dependence on Irish Nationalist members. The huge Liberal majority included not only great radicals such as Lloyd George, and vigorous collectivists, but extreme free traders and Hilaire Belloc, who was not only anti-landlord, but anti-capitalist, anti-collectivist and even anti-Parliamentarian. There was therefore some intellectual settling down to do and some jostling of ideas within the Party and the Cabinet itself, especially as apart from an unhappy interlude, they had not held office for so long. For these reasons, the off-duty gossip, some said to be anti-reform, in which Ministers early engaged at the Webbs' and which Beatrice Webb recorded in her Diaries, was trivia of little practical importance.[44]

There was no pre-existent plan of the 'welfare state': it was made as they went along. The electorate had not been presented with one, but simply with a list of some particular reforms, some of the 'historic' measures which laid its foundations not even being mentioned in the electoral battle. Indeed, a few critics urged that an electoral victory on the Free Trade issue—after all, an expression of free enterprise—ought not to be used for such measures so tinged with socialism and not put to the public vote.

The intellectual pressures were exercised within the Government and the Party, but the movement from theory to practice was not

---

[44]B Webb, *Our Partnership*. See various entries under Ministers' names. Such gossip is not new in political parties engaged in breaking fresh ground. See the revelations of personal differences, despite the successful programme of reform, in the memoirs of Attlee, Morrison, Dalton and in Leslie Hunter's controversial *Brighton Pier* (1959).

guided by one or two leading intellectuals having well-thought-out social philosophies, such as Attlee had when he presided over the second experiment after 1945. The two most brilliant and lively radicals, Lloyd George and Churchill, were sympathetic, responsive and imaginative, but no one would have claimed them as formal political thinkers as that term is usually understood. They were pragmatic, experimental, drawing general and some particular ideas from the intellectual climate in which they worked. But there is a large gap between affirmations of social ideals and the practical details of administration in quite new fields, such as social insurance and wage regulation, needed to give them effect. The way was open both for unofficial advice and for the initiative so conspicuously displayed by the civil service at this time. It was one mark of the ability of Lloyd George and Churchill that they were both capable, in their different ways, of making good use of the experts.

The tariff issue settled, the way was open for pressure by the radicals. And in this they were favoured by the composition of the House, which had a fresh look. In *My Mission to London* the German ambassador, Lichnowsky, in an apt comment recorded that the British gentlemen of both Parties had the same education, went to the same colleges and universities, had the same recreations and habits of life and though they did not consort together in times of political tensions, were members of the same society.[45] The Liberal Ministers of 1906 were, like their Conservative predecessors, comparatively wealthy men, Lloyd George being a bit outside the group. The appointment of John Burns, as he himself did not fail to proclaim, was something of a novelty. Nevertheless, there was clearly a large group in sympathy with the swirl of ideals of the time, of which the long list of major and minor reforms introduced by the less prominent radical ministers is evidence. The rank and file of the House now contained many more representatives of groups on which the Liberal Party had always depended; the number of Nonconformists now exceeded the total number of Tory members, there were fewer dependent on inherited landed and rentier wealth and more getting their income from current business and professional

---

[45]Prince Lichnowsky, *Heading for an Abyss* (1928), pp. 66–7.

earnings. But it was still true that as Members were not then paid, no workman could become an M.P. unless he held office or was otherwise supported by a working-class organisation,[46] as a small group were. Working-class voters were therefore apt to vote for Liberal and Radical candidates, whose success depended on them. Finally, victory had been obtained partly by an electoral pact quietly negotiated by Herbert Gladstone for the Liberals and Ramsay MacDonald for the Labour Representation Committee,[47] by which each engaged—not without local protests and refusals[48]—to persuade local parties not to oppose the other's candidate. Working-class candidates had already been elected as Liberals (Lib-Labs) and Gladstone was alive to the possibilities of a drift of working-class votes from the Party and of its capture by Chamberlain. For both there were advantages at the time since, if there were Liberal M.P.s partly dependent on Labour votes, there were also Labour members partly dependent on Liberal votes. And it implied a significant overlap of ideas on immediate measures.[49]

The swings of popular support during the eight years, the increasing independence of the local Liberal Associations, the permeation of the Gladstone and Radical Workmen's Clubs by advanced radicals and socialists, do not here concern us, but one must ask how far the political machinery contributed to the pause in the process of social reform after 1911. Whether or not the radical programme could or should have been carried further by the Liberal Government's use of its enormous majority, is not as simple as J A Hobson and Hamilton Fyfe suggested. Perhaps in the long run the transfer of working-class votes to the Labour Party which in the

[46]When Henry Broadhurst entered Parliament, as Secretary of the Parliamentary Committee of Trade Union Congress he had a salary of £150 out of which he paid for clerical assistance. For years of his life at Westminster all his clothes were made at home by his wife. *Henry Broadhurst,* pp. 101–2.

[47]The negotiations are clearly described by P P Poirier in *The Advent of the Labour Party* (1958), chaps. x-xi.

[48]For example, Smillie, *My Life for Labour,* p. 98.

[49]In the outcome, though the Labour group maintained its independence there was, and after the 1910 elections had to be, a good deal of co-operation in the House. Keir Hardie wrote to Lord Tweedmouth that had Campbell-Bannerman been twenty years younger he might have come over to the socialists. Poirier, p. 193. See Smillie's favourable impression of C-B in *My Life for Labour,* pp. 264–6.

end made another Liberal Government impossible could not have
been avoided. At the time, attempts to clear out of the way the
many 'old' problems—plural voting, the liquor trade, religious
differences in education—which elbowed their way forward to claim
Parliamentary time in competition with the politically 'new' ones
of unemployment, etc. were frustrated by the Lords' veto and
time was wasted which could have been more profitably used on the
social measures so impatiently demanded. But despite the enthu-
siasms aroused by Lloyd George's vigorous attacks on landed
wealth ('a Duke costs twice as much as a Dreadnought and is much
more terrible'), the Liberal land song ('God gave the land to the
people'), and the anti-Peer cartoons, e.g. caricaturing the Tory
'Peers' Shilling Defence Fund' as a row of coroneted and out-at-
elbow Peers with collecting boxes, like the processions of the
unemployed then taking place, after the Lords' veto and Budget
elections of 1910 the Liberals alone were no longer the dominant
party in the House. Either because of the experience of the trade
recession of 1908 or of the re-introduction of the Home Rule issue
to which many English voters had become indifferent or remained
hostile, or because of the conversion of many constituencies in the
south and south-east to tariff reform, or because the country was
not sound on the Lords' question, they lost a hundred seats and
could carry their measures only with the support of the Labour
group, also diminished in numbers, and the toleration of the Irish
Nationalists. There must have been some defection of working-
class votes.[50] Is it always certain that when the working-class electorate votes right, it is because the left is not left enough? In not
one of the twenty-six seats in which Labour candidates opposed a
Liberal, did the Labour candidate win.

After the Insurance Act of 1911, not only was Parliament pre-
occupied with debates on the preparation for imminent war, but
legislative time was again wasted by the Lords' insistence on the

[50]This was not the only occasion when enfranchised workers had voted against
Governments which tried to benefit them, for they treated both Gladstone and Disraeli
in the same way, and in 1930 many of the unemployed voted against the Labour Party
trying to protect their dole, presumably in fear of losing most of it. See Arthur Henderson's comment to Malcolm Muggeridge, *New Statesman*, 13 Aug. 1965, 215, col. 2.

powers of delay which the Parliament Act had given them to reject or mangle Bills before they automatically became law without their consent, and this in a period when the interest of many workers, in England at any rate, was shifting to industrial questions and 'industrial action' through trade unions. It is often overlooked that the explosive Government of Ireland Act did not become law until after the First World War had broken out. It is a comment on the skill with which the problems of management of the Party and of the political situation so created were handled, that some of the great reforms associated with their name, e.g. health, and unemployment insurance, were carried after the Party had lost its own dominant majority in the House.

iii. *Before 1906 election. The experts' contribution. The Report on Physical Deterioration*

The first breakthrough to new conceptions of social policy was made on two fronts, one narrow—the health of school children—and the other broad—the physical condition of the nation. And though humanitarian impulses played their part, the spearhead was official and expert opinion. On the first, a gale of fresh air was let in to our conceptions of elementary education by the Royal Commission on *Physical Training (Scotland)* (1903).[51] Not only did the witnesses include many schoolmasters, inspectors of schools, etc., but a vital and indeed decisive part of its argument was based on an investigation made for it by Professor Hay, of Aberdeen University, and Dr W L MacKenzie, M.O.H., Edinburgh, into the comparative physical condition of 100 boys and 100 girls in 3 groups of schools in Aberdeen and Edinburgh. It condemned the long confinement of school children in the atmosphere and surroundings of the classroom, and recommended not only the extension of physical exercise and organised games as well as the provision of facilities for them, but notably the systematic inspection of school children, the appointment of medical and sanitary experts to the inspecting staff, and the

[51]Rep., paras. 104–148; 1903, Cd. 1507, xxx.

encouragement of voluntary arrangements for feeding under-nourished children.

The second was the work of the Inter-Departmental Committee on *Physical Deterioration* (1904),[52] which was an early and vigorous example of the part to be played by expert opinion. It had been alleged that the high percentage of rejection of recruits for the Army showed that certain classes of the population showed signs of physical deterioration; the Committee was to inquire into the extent of and the means of diminishing it. Appointed in 1903, thus a couple of years before the advent of the new Liberal administration, its seven members were high departmental officers: the Clerk to the Council, the Board of Education's Inspector of Physical Training, the Inspector of Reformatory and Industrial Schools, the Inspector of Marine Recruits, the Head of the General Register Office and two administrative civil servants from the English and Scottish Education Departments. There were no 'political' or 'public figure' members. Part of their terms of reference required and, indeed, enjoined them to consult medical opinion, but other parts were more general and the evidence ranged over a wide field of environmental and home conditions not technically medical. The witnesses included not only representatives of the Colleges of Physicians and Surgeons, but the central and local government medical officers, factory and sanitary inspectors, as well as Booth and Rowntree. There was a notable absence of witnesses from political propagandist or pressure groups.[53] The Committee and witnesses were experienced and informed, and the reading of the evidence shows not only that there was much less of the useless material often found in evidence before Commissions, but a real inter-change of ideas between experts and often a movement of opinion.[54] One incident showed the advantage of this sort of inquiry. The Committee had been forming the view that there had been insufficiently energetic supervision of, and pressure by the Local Government Board on laggard local authorities because it had been too much absorbed in

[52]1904, Cd. 2175, xxxii.

[53]See list of witnesses in the Report, pp. iii-v.

[54]The various references to the work of the Committee in A W Fitzroy's *Memoirs* suggest that it worked very efficiently.

routine work. The Board's witnesses denied this, but the Committee, all experienced administrators, in their Report, showed that they did not accept this denial.[55] Unhampered by political considerations, they were free to make whatever suggestions their expertise suggested, a large number of them foreshadowing later developments in social legislation.[56] Amongst a long list eventually carried out were: local authorities should notify a date after which overcrowding in excess of a fixed standard of persons would not be allowed (Housing Act, 1935); should preserve open spaces in areas contiguous with other towns and in process of urbanisation (green belts), and provide open spaces in some proportion to the population (town planning practice). The ordinary householder should be made aware of his responsibilities in regard to domestic smoke pollution (smoke-free zones). There should be systematic medical inspection of all school children, arrangements made by municipal and voluntary effort to feed habitually underfed children, recommendations followed by a further Committee of 1906 and the Acts of 1906 and 1907. Following the radical findings of the Royal Commission on *Physical Training (Scotland)* (1903) there should be better provision for organised games and physical training. There should be an organised medical service in factories.

iv. *After the election: a convergence of forces*

The sweeping reforms of 1906–14 were thus brought about by an unusual conjunction of forces by no means always found working together—a wide variety of opinion at once critical and constructive, an insistence on new ethical standards in social matters, the increase of knowledge and theoretical advance, the creation of a bureaucracy, at once sympathetic and dynamic, able to devise new institutions and practices needed for their operation, and the resolution of the deadlock in one of the great political parties. From the canvassing

---

[55]Rep., para. 124, and Lithiby's evidence, qq. 13,687–699, show a number of difficulties in administration.

[56]The form of the printed Report, with its marginal notes and attribution to witnesses, makes it possible to track down the discussions with them out of which some of the suggestions came.

of ideas, bit by bit a coherent set of proposals took shape, though they were not all equally developed. The design which emerged was three-fold. First, social: the establishment of guaranteed minima in old age, sickness, wage earning and unemployment; secondly, economic: State intervention to improve productivity; thirdly, financial: finding new sources of taxation to provide money for the new services which should also be in line with the egalitarian trend of the programme.

The inter-play of forces can be seen if we look at the separate problems as they presented themselves when they entered the stage of becoming questions of State policy, at the available knowledge about them, and at the choices considered and made. The relative contributions of the expert, the economic theorist, the practical politician and the noisy malcontent varied from case to case. Sometimes a new political courage revealed that what had been regarded as a difficulty was no difficulty at all. Sometimes the important thinking was that of the civil servant, as in health and unemployment insurance, or of the medical expert, as in mental defficiency, or of independent investigators, as on small holdings. In other matters the way out was proffered by Commissions and Committees, as on income tax, home work, shipping rings and canals.

One inquiry into 'the social question' stands out from all others in scope and importance. A new element was injected by the massive researches, set out in fifty-three separate Papers, and the principles enunciated by the Royal Commission on the *Poor Laws and Relief of Distress* (1909).[57] It is one of our greatest seminal inquiries, with an influence extending far beyond immediate legislation. For instead of considering, as earlier inquiries had done, unemployment, ill-health, the aged poor, as isolated problems, as its title implies it examined them as connected parts of a whole field of distress. Both the Majority and Minority Report, influenced by the contemporary developments in the social sciences, set a new standard in approach, in the use of expert investigators and in gathering up the results of independent economic and social studies. On some vital matters they arrived at similar conclusions, though by different routes. The

[57]Final Rep.; 1909, Cd. 4499, xxxvii. For full list and references of its Papers see *Breviate*, I, 448–51.

immense appeal of the Minority Report to a whole generation was
due to the hope it offered of sweeping away the evils which had
plagued the social conscience for so long, while its thinking on the
organisation of the labour market and the prevention of distress was
particularly welcome to collectivists of all kinds, because for the
first time their principles were applied consistently not only to this
or that particular problem, but to the whole question of the poor in
society and the function of Government in relation to them. It
correctly detected and based its proposals on the position of the
experts and their dynamic function in the society of the future. What
contribution did these intense intellectual efforts make in bringing
the baffling problems to a point of solution? Once launched, their
ideas had to take their place and compete with rivals for the determination of social policy, and their fate depended partly on their
own sea-worthiness. After such efforts had been made to reach them,
why and how were some conclusions accepted, others modified, rejected or even ignored? Was it because in the analysis something
vital had been overlooked? For in considering the planning process,
one has to ask why some proposed solutions are rejected or fall by
the wayside.

4. THEORIES IN ACTION: THE INVENTION OF NEW INSTITUTIONS. THE CONTRIBUTION OF THEORISTS, EXPERTS AND MINISTERS—I

i. *Old age pensions*

A decision at last. In contrast to the difficulties of dealing with
sweated trades and unemployment, the solution of the problem of
old age pensions, which had been inquired into so often and canvassed for so long, was easy. For it required no expert knowledge,
save in estimating numbers and cost; there were no technical difficulties and there was no risk that men might come on the funds
voluntarily, as in unemployment insurance through lack of effort,
for as we get old whether we will or not, the test is objective. All
that was needed was a shift of viewpoint and courage to face the
costs. Though the Chaplin Committee, 1899, had advanced beyond

133

K

the Royal Commission of 1895, it cannot be said that it displayed either very effectively.

Instructed to think about the 'deserving poor' it spent a lot of time trying to find out how to discriminate between the sheep and the goats. Its conclusions made the eye of the needle small enough to keep out anyone with the slightest of reproach for thriftlessness. The income from all sources was not to exceed ten shillings a week—a proposal later criticised as discouraging thrift. The applicant must not have received poor relief (other than medical) for the twenty years preceding, unless in circumstances wholly exceptional in character, so that even minor and infrequent relief would disqualify. He must prove industry and the provident exercise of reasonable prudence by some definite mode of thrift (e.g. through a friendly society, etc.) All this for the poor struggling on low incomes to keep out of the workhouse! And there must have been no convictions for a serious offence in the previous twenty years. In weighing up vice and virtue the Committee doubtless had an eye on their cost, but nobody knew how many people of pensionable age these rules would exclude and therefore what the cost would be, either immediately or in the future.

The Hamilton Departmental Committee, 1900, set the task of estimating what the effect of these restrictions would be, on the basis of a house-to-house sample inquiry concluded that with pensions at 65 the proportions disqualified would be, on the crime test, 2 per cent, on the income limit, 37 per cent, for the receipt of poor relief in the previous twenty years, 27 per cent, while 10 per cent of the remainder would be ruled out on the thrift test. Less than one-third of the persons aged sixty-five plus would receive pensions. But owing to the increasing length of life the cost would probably rise from £10 million in 1900 to £12½ million in 1911 and over £15½ million in 1921. Raising the pensionable age to seventy would reduce the cost by about two-fifths to £6 million, £7½ million and £9½ million respectively. As the debates show, it was these figures of cost and their prospective growth at which Parliament boggled. Another Select Committee with the long history of inquiries in mind, in 1903 concluded plaintively that nothing was to be gained by more investigation, since 'all the materials available for the purpose of enabling Parliament to arrive at a decision had been exhausted by the numerous inquiries'; only experiment could carry matters further.

After 1906 the change in both point of view and courage brought the decision. There were still some voices from the past. Austin Chamberlain and Balfour both expressed a preference for a contributory scheme, although it had been shown repeatedly that this would postpone pensions for many years. Lever, in a private member's Bill, proposed to meet the situation by pensions in stages at seventy-five, seventy, sixty-five. But Asquith, speaking in 1907 on future policy, ruled out any contributory scheme, said that pensions must be disassociated from the Poor Law, that the problem was cost and that progress must be tentative. Universal pensions at seventy, which the Labour group and some radicals had wanted, were passed by, since the cost of granting them would have been twice as much as pensions on the Chaplin scheme at sixty-five. In the end,[58] raising the pensionable age to 70, which would reduce the number of claimants by 300,000, was exchanged for an amelioration of the disqualifying clauses which unamended would have excluded about half a million. The poor relief disqualification was not to be its receipt at any time in the previous twenty years, but its current receipt; the means limit was twelve shillings not ten shillings, and the thrift test was narrowed and made more specific; proving 'industriousness' was altered to 'habitually failing to work according to ability, opportunity and need'. In the final Commons division on the Bill some Conservatives voted for, and some against, but most abstained. And one Rip van Winkle in the House of Lords thought that the Act would be a mortal blow to the Empire. On the other hand, the Labour pacifist left, e.g. Philip Snowden, drew a scornful comparison between armaments expenditure and the miserable five shillings a week at seventy.[59] For the five shillings was one-quarter to one-third the agricultural labourer's wage, one-fifth to one-sixth the general labourer's wage; and for general labourers, after the age of sixty, unemployment increased and earnings definitely fell. But the many moving scenes when the

[58]Old Age Pensions Act, 1908, sects. 2, 3.
[59]Philip Snowden, *Autobiography*, I, 189–91.

pensioners collected their first payments showed how much even this sum meant to them. War, however, was not very far round the corner. Nevertheless, in the light of the financial obligations of the time, the Act of 1908 was a most significant step, more significant than the critics of the inadequacy of the payment perhaps realised. For by 1911–12 cost of pensions had risen to the equivalent of half the cost of the Army or two-thirds the entire central expenditure on educating the children. In 1911 nearly 30 per 1,000 of the population were over 70 and in 1912 three-fifths of these were old age pensioners. Between 1900–13 the numbers of paupers over 70 dropped by 75 per cent.[60]

Perhaps it was as well for the immediate passage of the Bill that the significance of a vital point of demography—the effect of the increasing length of life on the numbers and proportion of the population of pensionable age, estimated for a short period by the Hamilton Committee—was not fully realised. Even Beveridge's plain warning in 1942[61] did not make people understand the full force of it or that it would eventually become a dominant factor in the finance of the social services. The Webbs themselves, though they might have adhered to their recommendations on other grounds seemed not to have grasped it fully, for in the Minority Report they recommended that as soon as possible the pensionable age should be reduced to sixty-five or even sixty, nor had they noticed that the effect of their own proposed health reforms by lengthening life might eventually make this particular problem more difficult.[62] And in 1907 the T.U.C. had also demanded pensions at sixty.

[60]It is perhaps important to realise what difference old age pensions made to the whole pensions scene. Though it must have been difficult to get all the facts, the L.G.B. Memo (1907, Cd. 3618, lxviii) indicates that outside a limited range of employments it was pretty bare. They estimated that there were about 250,000 having pensions of some sort; 153,000 being men in military, naval and police services where early retirement was necessary, some 48,000 in civil and local government offices, and teachers, most of the rest receiving friendly society or trade union payments.

[61]W H Beveridge, *Social Insurance and Allied Services*, p. 91; 1942–43, Cmd. 6404, vi.

[62]*Poor Laws*, Minority Rep. pt. i, chap. vii (D, i, and E) in 8vo ed. pp. 273–4, 285. They were thinking in terms of the past. The Memos on *Public Health and Social Conditions*, 1909, p. 9, table 4, show surprisingly little change between 1851 and 1901 in the proportion of persons over seventy. Chiozza Money was clear about this: *Riches and Poverty*, p. 276. For an analogous point see also *Health Insurance*, where Duncan and

ii *Labour policy*

(*a*) *Minimum wages in sweated trades.* The problem of the sweated trades to which no answer had so far been found was brought rapidly to a solution partly by the revival of political courage. Though at first overshadowed by the distractions of wars and Irish politics, the interest aroused by the revelations of the eighties and nineties, kept lively by Dilke, Gertrude Tuckwell, Clementina Black, Mary Macarthur, Mrs MacDonald, Margaret Irwin and Church workers,[63] eventually rose to a peak after 1906, and ended in a vigorous campaign and a dramatic exhibition, sponsored by the *Daily News*, of sweated goods marked with both their prices and the wage received for making them. To compassion was added a sharp note of indignation. The question became one not only of social and moral, but political urgency, and legislators were nerved to take risks they would not have done ten years earlier.

Secondly, a way was found out of the practical dilemma. What was this? As we have seen, though the Dunraven Committee was later criticised for complacency because of the timidity of its recommendations, e.g. on conditions in the chain-making industry, their fundamental difficulty was that in London sweating was but part and an expression of the far larger problem of the conditions, aggravated by a high birth rate and foreign immigration, of the mass of poor, unskilled, unorganised and perhaps unorganisable workers, willing to snatch at any chance of an income. But they declined to prohibit outwork, as this would be arbitrary and oppressive. They had reason to, for as the evidence, e.g. before the Housing Commission had shown, the households of many male casual labourers were in fact kept going by the earnings of their wives,[64] who, with widows, deserted wives, wives with husbands ill, etc. and without the protection of the social insurance system, were glad to take work home

---

Gray argue that unless directed primarily to removing the causes of ill-health, health expenditure might occasion further expenditure on health. R. Com. Rep., p. 294; 1926, Cmd. 2596, xiv.

[63]*Home Work*, Cttee. Mins. of ev., C Dilke, q. 4001, 1908 (246) viii.

[64]Still true for some in 1916. See H A Mess, *Casual Labour in the Docks* (1916), pp. 49–51.

even for a pittance, to do in such time as they had available. Nor were the Majority, the collectivist Minority of the Labour Commission, 1894, or even the Committee on *Home Work*, 1908, able to take any other line.

As Dilke, who was active all through the campaign, confessed in evidence before the Whittaker Committee on *Home Work*, 'at this time we were not united on the remedy we proposed for sweating'.[65] In 1890 immigrant shoe finishers in London went on strike to be taken into factories.[66] The Amalgamated Society of Tailors wanted to make factory work compulsory.[67] But this was a dead end. Thereafter two lines of policy were proposed. First, a series of Bills introduced annually from 1900 and sponsored by the 'labour group', proposed in effect a system of licensing, that workplaces in dwelling-houses should be registered, and that no employer was to give out work to any outworker who did not possess a certificate, granted after an inspection of the premises. At first limited in application to clothing, fur-pulling, furniture, etc., as a result of further routing round by the group, the scope of the Bill was extended to many other trades—steel cables, chains, anchors, locks, keys (1905), umbrellas, feather sorting, sacks, nets, tents, paper bags and boxes, stuffed toys, etc. (1907). This would have involved the inspection of the home of every home worker every six months and was rejected by the *Home Work* Committee as impracticable.

The alternative came from Dilke, whose 1898 Bill for setting up wages boards was introduced annually substantially unchanged.[68] These proposed (1) the fixing of minimum wages, not by an outside body, but by the industries themselves through wages boards containing equal numbers of employers' and workers' representatives. (2) That the boards should have wide discretion in fixing the time- and piece-rates. Clause 5 gave them power to calculate the minimum rates either by time -or piece-work, but so as to give the employer the option of paying by either, except that in the case of outworkers

---

[65]*Home Work*, Cttee. Mins. of ev., q. 3923, 1908 (246) viii.

[66]*The Times*, 31 Mar. 1890, 6d; all issues 1–8 April.

[67]*Home Work*, q. 3923.

[68]*Sweated Industries Bill*, 1907 (27) iv; 1908 (2) v; 1909 (6) v. The last was withdrawn on the introduction by the Government of the *Trade Boards Bill*.

a piece-rate must be fixed. (3) That as the scheme was experimental, it should be limited at first to the apparel-making trades. Australasian experiments in wage regulation had made a great impression, but Aves' report and evidence had shown that because the numbers involved were relatively small and the demand for women's labour high, this was not relevant to English outworkers. (4) It could be later extended to other sweated industries, i.e. those in which out-workers were largely employed and in which remuneration was low. But, as Booth had pointed out, sweating could not be defined by the type of industrial organisation, but only by its results.[69] The Act of 1909 took this point and gave the Board of Trade power to set up Wages Boards 'when the rate of wages prevailing in any branch of the trade is exceptionally low compared with other employments'. Section I (2).

In effect, it was the Dilke policy which the Committee on *Home Work* recommended. Instead of prescribing, as some participants in the 'Living Wage' campaign had suggested, a specific minimum of money wage, the Act of 1909 set out to reproduce for these un-organised workers the bargaining strength of unionised workers by requiring wages boards to contain equal numbers of employers' and workers' representatives. In the initial stages the Board of Trade, by calling meetings, etc., actively promoted the election by un-organised workers of their representatives,[70] who were often officers of unions having few or no members in the industry, but who were experienced in negotiation. The sweated workers were thus, as it were, to bargain collectively by proxy. Secondly, though it was the intent that the 'unduly low' wages should be raised, again following the pattern of union bargaining, the Act left the Boards free to arrive at whatever wages they thought fit, named no specific mini-mum sums and gave the Boards no guidance on what these should be or on what principles they should be based, e.g. whether they should be 'living wages', 'fair wages' or 'what the traffic could bear'. These had to be worked out by the Boards themselves. In practice

[69]*Life and Labour*, I, 486.

[70]For example, R H Tawney, *Minimum Wage in the Chainmaking Trade* (1914), pp. 28–30.

they moved cautiously from existing rates to a varied mixture of all three principles.[71]

There remained two other difficulties to solve, one economic and technical, the other moral. Would it be possible to fix minimum piece-rates for every variation of every detail of every article and pattern in trades subject to fashion changes? On this, the evidence of G R Askwith, already building up his great reputation in industrial conciliation, was decisive.[72] Yes, he said, citing the sixty-page list of tailors and other lists of piece-rates with which he had been concerned; one could begin with a minimum time-rate and steadily build up piece-rates from that. The Committee on *Home Work* therefore reversed the detail of the Dilke plan by which Boards could fix a minimum time-rate or piece-rate but must fix a piece-rate for outworkers, by recommending—and they attached the highest importance to it—that the Boards must fix a minimum time-rate and in due course minimum piece-rates for home workers, but that any piece-rate, whether fixed by the Board or not, must be such as to yield an average worker not less than the equivalent time-rate.[73] This would make it possible to prevent employers from evading them by continual changes of design. This is in fact what the Act of 1909 did. Sections 4, 8.

Secondly, there was the moral issue. Restriction on the number of foreign, largely Jewish, immigrants from oppressive conditions abroad, who were still arriving and by accepting low pay driving women out of some trades,[74] had been rejected by the Commission on *Alien Immigration* of 1903. Could wages be raised without restricting the imports of competing foreign goods? But the Free Trade election had settled that issue, and the Committee argued that we should not try to compete with low wages abroad by low wages here, but by efficiency and if necessary by diverting labour and capital to more suitable channels.[75] And what if improved rates

[71]For a good account see E Burns, *Wages and the State* (1926), pt. ii.

[72]*Home Work*, Cttee. Mins. of ev., qq. 3936, 3934, 1907 (290) vi.

[73]*Home Work*, Sel. Cttee. Rep., para. 49, 1908 (246) viii.

[74]*Home Work*, Sel. Cttee. Mins. of ev., q. 4144, 1907 (290) vi.

[75]*Home Work*, Sel. Cttee. Rep., para. 51, 1908 (246) viii.

meant that the trades could not be carried on? If, said the Committee, in a noteworthy phrase, the trade will not yield an income at least adequate for the necessaries of life to average industrial workers engaged in it, it was a parasite industry and it was contrary to the general well being that it should continue.[76] This was not an answer which policy-makers could have given ten years earlier, but in this assertion of new ethical standards there was a ring of confidence that the industries were flexible enough to ensure that this drastic contingency would not arise.[77] In this they proved to be correct, save in one case, dress-making. This was so widespread, especially in the south-west, that at first the Act could not be enforced, and when it was, it accelerated the death of that form of work, already doomed by competition of the machines producing ready-made garments.

(*b*) *Minimum wages in a unionised trade. The Coal Mines* (*Minimum Wage*) *Act,* 1912. Though, like the Trade Boards Act, embodying the principle of a minimum wage, the Coal Mines (Minimum Wage) Act, 1912, was very different in the ideas and processes which brought it on to the Statute Book and in its results. It did not arise from and had no connection with the campaign which led the State to accept responsibility for protecting and fixing minimum wages for the specially ill-paid, unorganised workers. On the contrary the miners were strongly organised, able to stage a massive strike. The Act was State intervention to put a floor to the wages negotiated by two well-organised bargaining groups; this was new. And it therefore required a different kind of justification. Nor, though the miners did indeed strike to obtain from the owners an individual minimum wage, did they originally come out for a minimum fixed by the State. The Act was an isolated *ad hoc* measure, passed by the Government to end a deadlock in collective bargaining. In this sense it was an historical accident.

Of course there had been discussions in the miners' unions about the proper basis for their wages, e.g. that they should not depend,

[76]Ibid., para. 38. The proceedings of the Committee showed that this was signed without dissent.

[77]See Burns, *Wages and the State,* pp. 297–404.

as did the general minimum addition to their basic wages, on the price of coal, and protests—not without reason[78]—on the low standards of many of the miners; but the Act had its origin in the practical difficulties of piece-rates for 'abnormal places' in which, owing to varied geological and working conditions, the agreed rates would not yield a man a normal or adequate wage. There was sometimes bitter bargaining—and in South Wales a long lock-out over the 'consideration' to be paid for such work. Fruitless and frustrating negotiations led the miners to merge it into a national demand for an individual minimum for every man and boy working underground. The miners then proceeded to give it definite meaning (1) by drawing up a list of minimum piece-rates for each district and, to make the issue clear, by dropping any demand for an advance and setting the rates as near as possible to the prevailing rates; (2) to protect poorly paid day-wage workers, by including a minimum of five shillings a shift for men and two shillings a shift for boys. Since most, perhaps two-thirds or more, of the men were getting more than this wage and would get nothing from it, the strike really was a generous effort on behalf of the more poorly paid men.

There were thus two issues: the principle of the individual minimum and the specific minimum rates. The Government, fearing the damage to the economy which a nation-wide strike would involve, accepted that there were cases where the underground workers could not earn a reasonable minimum through circumstances over which they had not control, and decided that the power to earn such wages should be secured by district conferences of owners and miners, Government representatives being given power to decide outstanding points if complete settlements were not reached within a reasonable time. Sixty-five per cent of the owners were induced to accept these proposals, but those in South Wales, Scotland and Northumberland rejected them. Asquith agreed that, if necessary, they would be coerced by legislation. But the miners refused to move from their position. Asquith, whilst willing to coerce the minority of owners to accept the principle of a minimum, was not willing, especially in view of the complication of district

[78]Smillie, *My Life for Labour*. See his references to his own standards of life.

wage calculations,[79] to coerce them also into accepting specifically named rates they had had no part in negotiating. In the hope of breaking the deadlock, the Government nevertheless went ahead with a Bill incorporating their own proposals, but not including any specific rates.

The reaction of labour was two-fold. First, it was clear that the Bill raised, formally at least, a third issue, the English tradition that wage settlements should be freely negotiated between the unions and employers without outside interference. Suspicious of, if not hostile to compulsory arbitration, the labour spokesmen regretted the necessity for the Bill, demanded that it should not be a precedent or be extended to other industries, and that it should be temporary in character—conditions which were accepted.[80] Secondly, Mr Edwards, the miners' leader, pointed out that the miners did not ask for the Bill, and now pushed for the inclusion of the district rates and the five shillings and two shillings minimum. In a moving speech he said that these low-paid men wanted to know how much they would take home at the end of the week, and that it would be reasonable.[81] Although later they said that they would accept the insertion of the five shillings and two shillings clause only, and the settling of district rates with the help of a neutral chairman if necessary, they would not agree to his acting as a formal arbiter. But the Government would not agree to the insertion of any specific figure. Politically the settlement had been made more difficult to handle by the publicity given to a pamphlet, *The Miners' Next Step*, issued by a small group of South Wales syndicalists, which advocated the 'irritation' strike and the reduction of output to one-half in order to reduce the value at which the mines could be taken over. Both the miners' unions and the Government had to defend themselves against criticisms that they were yielding to syndicalist pressure.

[79]Asquith's critical references to the complications of miners' wage calculations foreshadowed Mr Baldwin's famous outburst in 1926 over the anachronistic methods. Snowden seemed on reflection to have appreciated the difficulty of including the rates. P Snowden, *The Living Wage* (1912), pp. 126–7.

[80]Snowden, op. cit., pp. 125–8. J Ramsay MacDonald, *Parl. Debates,* 19 Mar. 1912, Coal Mines (Minimum Wage) Act, clause 6.

[81]E Edwards. *Parl. Debates,* 19 Mar. 1912, col. 2097; also Brace, col. 2119.

The result of these cross-currents was not completely satisfactory. In spite of its containing the principle of a legal minimum wage, the Labour members voted against it on the third reading because it contained no specific figures. And while in the miners' ballot the largest district, South Wales, voted for a return to work, there was not a majority for continuing the strike by the two-thirds majority the Executive deemed required. The bitter bargaining was therefore transferred to the district conferences, some of which did not award the five shillings and two shillings,[82] nor, the miners alleged, did the chairman always take full account, as Clause 2 (1) of the Act required, of the prevailing district rates. Although the establishment of a statutory minimum for organised adult workers was a remarkable gain in principle, whereas the Trades Board gave the workers a new sense of hope, the Coal Mines (Minimum Wage) Act left some miners disillusioned and resentful.[83]

(*c*) *Labour disputes*. The problem of industrial unrest and labour disputes which the *Labour Commission* had investigated so comprehensively and had reported on in 1894 came up again only a dozen years later, both as a sharp question on what the legal rights of the trade unions should be, and in the form of a storm of strikes on a nation-wide scale which certainly most of the Commissioners had never really envisaged and which put the policy the Majority had adopted to a severe test. If we were to rely upon the behaviour of large voluntary bodies on both sides, what were to be the rules of the game?

The ways in which economic pressure might be exercised by trade unions came up with the Trade Disputes Bills. It is not necessary to go into all the legal ins and outs of the familiar story, viewed simply as another stage in the emancipation of trade unions, of the Taff Vale judgement and the Trade Disputes Act, 1906, which set out to reverse it. But the legal doctrines surrounding the Act, as developed in Court judgements both in trade union and commercial

[82]In the House Asquith had said that he thought the figures reasonable.

[83]H S Jevons in *British Coal Trade* (1915) gives a clear account of the 'abnormal places' problem (chap. xix) and particularly of the difficulties of the Act in operation (chap. xxii). See also R Page Arnot, *The Miners* (1952), II, chap. iv.

cases, expressed and helped to build up a point of view on the activities of organised economic groups of far-reaching importance. Before 1875 the attacks on trade unions had been under the Criminal Law; after the Acts of 1871 and 1875 this method was not possible. In the meantime, many unions had grown in strength, stability and financial resources, and this opened out the possibility that they could be made to pay damages. Strikes could cause a firm to lose thousands of pounds, and not only did they interfere with its right to conduct its trade freely, but the unions were combinations of persons agreeing to take steps to injure. How did this look to the trade unionist? A single employer could lock out and inflict loss on many, perhaps hundreds of employees, but the Trade Union Acts had, he understood, tried to level up the conditions of economic power by making the funds of trade combinations of workmen immune from legal attack on account of trade disputes. The award of £23,000 against the Amalgamated Society of Railway Servants was therefore a shock because it seemed to endanger the power the union had hitherto possessed of exerting economic pressure. The resentment it caused was not mollified by the argument of the Majority of the Royal Commission on *Trade Disputes*[84] that although in practice the unions had enjoyed immunity, they never had been nor were intended to be completely immune legally. (Majority Report, paras. 13–31.)

What were the practical questions as seen by the union and its officers? If in an industry where notice of termination of employment was provided for or customary, a union officer induced workmen to break their contract and strike without notice, e.g. for a rise of pay or to make an employer dismiss a non-unionist without notice, he had committed a tort against the employer in the one case and against the non-unionist in the other, and was therefore at common law liable. And there was some risk that unions might be showered with actions because of some indiscretion of an ill-informed branch officer, especially as at that date in different unions varying degrees of power, sometimes complete power, of declaring strikes lay with branches, although the strike pay might come from

---

[84]*Trade Disputes and Trade Combinations,* R. Com.; 1906, Cd. 2825, lvi.

the central funds. But even if in these two cases no notice of termination of employment was customary, though the union officer might
not be liable the union itself in certain circumstances might be. For
it was a common law right of every man to use his capital and labour
as he willed, but a combination of men in a union might prevent
this, for the whole purpose of its activity might be to cause an employer loss in order to get him to accept certain terms. But ordinary
economic pressure can sometimes become so great as to be coercion,
and the Courts have usually endeavoured to protect from coercion.
Where is the line between legitimate economic pressure and economic coercion to be drawn? In the *Mogul Steamship Co.* v. *MacGregor*
(see p. 199) the Court had decided that the action of a group to
prevent undercutting by ruining a rival and driving him out of the
trade was a legitimate pursuit of their economic interests. But in
Quinn v. *Leathem* a trade union, admittedly acting drastically to
damage an employer over the dismissal of a non-unionist, was not
deemed to be simply pursuing a legitimate trade interest. And despite
certain circumstances—and the opinion of two legal members of
the Royal Commission—it is now widely agreed that the commercial combine and the trade union received very unequal treatment.

   To deal with this situation and the vigorous protests it aroused,
there was the Royal Commission, a number of Bills promoted by
Labour M.P.s[85] and a Government Bill.[86] One solution proposed
was immediately swept aside. The Majority of the Royal Commission
made a suggestion that harked back to a proposal made by some
members of the *Labour Commission* (and which also, better than they
knew, looked forward to practices to develop in Scandinavia thirty
years later), that unions and employers' associations should be empowered if they wished to make binding agreements with one
another, and to this end the benefit fund of trade unions should be
separated from other funds and protected. The unions gave this a
chilly reception and for a second time this course was rejected. In
the outcome, the Government Bill was based on other chief recommendations of the Majority of the Commission, which included
Sidney Webb. These were:—(1) an individual should not be liable

[85]Bills 5 and 32, 1906.
[86]Bill 134, 1906.

for any tortious act committed in contemplation or furtherance of a
trade dispute on the ground solely that it induced some other person
to break a contract or interfere with the trade of another person or
his right to dispose of his capital and labour as he wills (Rec. 4,
Trade Disputes Act, Section 3). (2) An act done in pursuit of an agreement or combination of two persons or more, if done in contemplation or furtherance of a trade dispute, should not be actionable
unless it were actionable if committed without such agreement or
combination (Rec. 9, *Trade Disputes Act*, Section 1). (3) The Bill as
introduced provided that the funds of a union should not be liable
for tortious acts done in contemplation or furtherance of a trade
dispute unless they were done by a committee in charge of the dispute or persons acting under its instructions, nor for any act committed by a person which was unauthorised or immediately and
expressly disavowed (Rec. 6, Bill 134, Section 4). While this protected the union from liability for mistakes by branch officers, it did
not give their funds complete immunity. The Majority of the Commission had argued vigorously (paras. 32, 33) that a trade union
which could inflict heavy damage should not be permanently
licensed to cause loss to others without redress. But that is what the
Bill as amended (apparently after an interview Keir Hardie had with
Campbell-Bannerman)[87] actually did: Section 4 now prohibited all
actions for tort against trade unions.

There remained the question of what was legitimate economic
pressure and what was illegitimate coercion. On this the development of effective opinion has to be traced in the decisions of the
Courts. Its trend is best seen by jumping ahead to two legal cases
outside the period. In 1924 in *Reynolds* v. *The Shipping Federation* it
was decided that an agreement between the National Union of Seamen and the Federation to operate a rigid closed shop, men being
recruited through a joint office, which deprived a member of a rebel
union of the means of earning his livelihood in the trade, was a
justifiable agreement designed to advance the interests of the employers and employees and was not primarily aimed at inflicting loss

[87]This seems to have been the personal decision of Campbell-Bannerman. The lawyers
in the Cabinet did not like it. For the confusion it caused in the Government's ranks,
see the Debate, 155 H.C. Deb. 4s, 25 April 1906, cols. 1482–1543.

on the individual. In 1942, in the Harris Tweed case, the Courts refused to rule against an embargo imposed by dockers in Stornaway on the import of mainland-spun yarns by small-island weavers and designed to protect the island spinners against undercutting, so that they could pay higher wages to employees who were members of the same union. This was regarded as a justifiable defence of their interests and as providing a better basis for collective bargaining. These decisions and the doctrines by which they were supported, meant that not only could it be legitimate for unions to use their power against rival unions and to make arrangements with commercial firms which enabled them to share the spoils of monopoly, but that with the growth of large business combines and trade unions, the Courts were beginning to think of their problem less in terms of trying to preserve individual freedom of contract and more of regulating the activities and relations between the organised groups which were becoming the parties. Was the rule now becoming *laissez-faire*, not for individuals but for groups?

Next, there was the general question of industrial unrest and the settlement of disputes which arose from it. The theories and policies which had been developed to deal with them did not prove very serviceable, and the Ministry which had such striking achievements in the fields of sweated trades and unemployment ran into great difficulties for which they were not well prepared. For the unrest took not only well-understood, but also new forms. A number of circumstances gave it a special complexion.

(1) In 1906 three-quarters or more of the workers did not bargain collectively but individually, taking jobs at local market rates, some of which were 'customary', others possibly influenced by the presence of a strong union in some neighbouring industry. Those in trade unions probably numbered about two millions—many in small unions—and those in unions represented at Trade Union Congress a little over one and a half millions, a figure but 6 per cent larger than the peak in 1890.

(2) The two millions were concentrated in relatively few industries, most of them being in coal mining, textiles, iron and steel, engineering, building and transport—and a quarter were in craft unions. Both in industry and in geographical regions there were great desert

148

areas with little effective unionism to speak of. The pace of unrest, of strikes and lock-outs, was set by three groups, coal mining, railways and port work, with engineering coming into the picture as well. On the whole in the other areas, though not free from disputes, when unrest occurred it was not such as to cause a crisis in State policy.

(3) The long period of decline and stagnation in union membership between 1890 and 1900 was replaced by rapid growth, the increase between 1900 and 1913 being 760,000 or 50 per cent. The growth was partly the 'filling out' of unions in industries which had been only partially organised, partly amongst those unorganised and unskilled workers for whom the *Labour Commission* had no remedy. These were not all workers at once unorganised, unskilled, casual and low-paid, though some were. They included casually engaged dockers, carters often following one firm, general labourers who moved from industry to industry and employer to employer as job opportunities occurred, whilst others were in regular employment in municipal transport and works, with a relatively good wage. But many of them were obviously more open to blacklegging than craftsmen's unions.

(4) As unions swarmed out to occupy new fields, they often trod on one another's toes, each being apt to put a fence round the works they had organised, not only against non-unionists but against members of other unions. And there was a good deal of 'poaching'. These were not disputes between craft unions on the boundary lines between work which should be done by different types of skill, but between unions on which should have the right to organise, the 'bargaining rights' in particular workplaces.[88]

(5) Often employers were badly or only partly organised. If the union made an agreement with such an employers' association, thinking they had established terms 'for the trade', how were they to deal with non-federated employers who did not observe them? Was the union entitled to break its agreement and call out even its members working for employers who observed them, to protect men not getting the terms? This occurred e.g. with the London

---

[88]This was not new. Much earlier there had been difficulty between Tillett's Dockers' union and Throne's Gas Workers' union.

L

Carters.[89] But this could happen in industries where bargaining was already established, as in the north-east shipyards in 1908, when many unions accepted a modified wage-cut but some did not, and after a four-months strike the employers locked out all of them in their area.

(6) Sometimes the new unions had little or no experience in wage negotiation or in devising or working union constitutions. Troubles arose when the employers and unions met only when one or the other had presented a demand for an immediate cut or acceptance of a principle and expected an immediate answer, as the north-east shipbuilders did in 1907 and the railwaymen did with a twenty-four-hour notice of a national strike in 1911. Often the wage agreements were very sketchy and limited affairs which stated only a few simple things—rates, hours, etc.—but said nothing about the effect on valued workshop or local practices and customs upon which they had to be superimposed. (For example, in London docks.[90]) When the long-standing demand of the miners for a legal eight-hour day was embodied in legislation—after a Departmental Committee had concluded that output would not be proportionately reduced—its application to the varied conditions of individual pits wrought such havoc with local working customs that there were many strikes immediately, as well as by the Northumberland and Durham miners, who had never liked it. Then there were many experiments in constitution making. Where should the power to call or terminate a strike reside—in a members' ballot, a branch vote, a convened conference or in the executive? What powers should be given to the union's negotiators to accept compromises? What was the position of the executive if the rank and file threw over the settlement arrived at, as the Amalgamated Engineers did three times between February and August before finally accepting only by a narrow majority, or when the miners' ballots over the five shillings and two shillings minimum showed a balance of votes in favour of going back in the strongest areas, but

[89]*Industrial Agreements,* Industrial Council Mins. of ev., 5 March, qq. 96–117, 179, 238, 250; 1913, Cd. 6953, xxviii.

[90]Ibid., Mins. of ev., H Orbell, qq. 373–82; in coal mines, qq. 15,918, 15,934–35, 15,985–87, 15,991–94.

against going back in the country as a whole, though not by the two-thirds majority which, by a disputed interpretation of a rule, the executive declared to be necessary?

(7) The unions involved in some of these disputes could be fairly easily blacklegged. The law—and the *Labour Commission*—had sought to protect an individual or a minority of workmen who did not wish to come out on strike with their fellows, from interference other than peaceful persuasion and from finding the entrance to their workplace beset by numbers of men in a threatening manner. They were thinking of men in the same employ and normally working alongside one another. But suppose the employers organised the importation of blacklegs from outside the area, as the South Wales railways did at the time of the Taff Vale dispute. What was to be done if an agency arose, such as Collison's National Free Labour Association, which set out to provide blacklegs whenever required?[91] The most highly organised strike-breaking agency was the Shipping Federation, which not only imposed on crews the 'Federation ticket' without which they would not be taken on, but used depot ships, out of reach of Havelock Wilson's Seamen's and Sailors' Union's pickets on shore, from which crews were filled up.[92] Did the right of employers to choose men and the men's freedom to work specified by the *Labour Commission* include such arrangements? When, for the first time, nation-wide or large-scale stoppages occurred on the railways and in coal mining and in the ports, damaging the country's economy as a whole, could the State stand aside? Had the other workers and the country also rights which should be looked after? Ought it to give protection to any men willing to work freight trains? Or to guard any willing to move meat vans from the docks in order to feed the population? At this point the policy of 'no State intervention' broke down. When, in

[91]Collison, who had been very active in organising London busmen, was started on his course because, having got involved in a dispute with his union—those with experience on how these situations arise might feel that whatever may be said about his later record, there may have been something to be said on his side at this point—after leaving the union found that he could not get work in the docks because he had no union ticket. W Collison, *The Apostle of Free Labour* (1913), chaps. vi, vii.

[92]For the Federation's own statement on this practice, see *Trade Disputes and Trade Combinations,* R. Com. Mins. of ev., qq. 5396–403; 1906, Cd. 2826, lvi.

accordance with theory, police and/or troops were used to protect freedom so interpreted or to safeguard essential supplies, fighting, rioting and even shooting took place as in South Wales, and in Rotherhithe.

All these difficulties cropped up in one form and another in the industrial storms of these years. For a century the essential struggle had been to establish the right of workers to form unions and make collective bargains, so that the assertion of the *Labour Commission*[93] that industrial relations should in the main be left to voluntary responsible organisations was healthy and in line with tradition. The 'Failure of the Labour Commission', to use the title of Mrs Webb's critical article, was not, as she alleged, simply that the Majority had paid no attention to the social background of unrest, but that neither the Majority nor the collectivist Minority had envisaged these difficulties or gave any guidance on how they should be tackled, even though they lay only a dozen to twenty years ahead. The one course it had emphasised, embodied in the *Conciliation Act*, 1896, was that the Board of Trade should be empowered to inquire into disputes, to encourage the formation of registered conciliation boards, to take steps to bring disputing parties together, and to set up on the application of either workers or employers a conciliation board, and on the application of both to appoint an arbitrator who should issue an award, though this was not to be binding on either side. For a time a large number of boards were set up which, as the Board of Trade Reports show, settled many disputes, though not of a major kind. And the arrangements gave opportunities of which that great conciliator, G R Askwith, took full advantage. But they provided no help in some of the great disputes because the boards did not exist in the industries concerned and could not until both sides were sufficiently organised. These conditions did not hold on the railways, in the docks or amongst the enormous number of London's carting firms and carters. And as unions grew stronger, many preferred direct negotiations.

The gaps turned out to be serious. In 1906 we were almost alone

[93] *Labour Commission*, Majority Rep., paras. 331–4.

amongst the great countries in having no special provision to deal with stoppages in vital public utility services. The Commission had made no recommendations which would have led unions and employers to replace the sketchy and limited agreements, which often had no clause about revision and left room for so much friction, by anything more detailed or specific as the 'labour contract' became in America; or to get rid of strikes for union recognition or the troubles between unions over bargaining rights by providing that employers must deal with any union which its workers decided by democratic vote should represent them, as did the later Wagner Act of America. The Commission's general view excluded the line of policy adopted by New Zealand in its Compulsory Arbitration Act, 1894, which gave power to registered societies to take disputes to a Board of Conciliation whose award, if accepted, had the force of law, or if not accepted, to a court whose decision was binding; strikes and lock-outs after reference to the board or during the currency of the award being punishable offences. English labour opinion was divided on compulsory arbitration. On the political side, Snowden thought strikes futile,[94] Webb that they were a method of private warfare which inflicted loss on third parties and carried with them no presumption that the result would be to remove the injurious conditions of employment.[95] This lack of guidance on principles had two results. First, that unions and employers had to work out their own private solutions of these difficulties, by reasonableness derived from experience and by burning their fingers and, in a period when neither side was fully organised, to arrive by painful effort at a mutually acceptable code of industrial conduct. But in this matter the trade union movement as a whole was not in a position to give much help. In contrast to Germany, where the unions had been set going deliberately in well-thought-out industrial groups and there was a strong central body,[96] in England they had grown up spontaneously and were not willing to yield any of their autonomy to Trade Union Con-

---

[94]Snowden, *Living Wage,* chaps. xviii, ix.

[95]*Trade Disputes and Trade Combinations,* R. Com. Rep., p. 18; 1906, Cd. 2825, lvi.

[96]S W Sanders, *Trade Unionism in Germany* (1916).

A First Solution

gress. The limited functions of its chief committee, the Parliamentary Committee, were implied by its name: it exercised no authority in the industrial affairs of the unions. When the T.U.C. was pressed by its more belligerent members to take a more active part in these matters, the demand was met by founding (1899) a separate body, the General Federation of Trade Unions, which should help the unions as a whole by creating and managing a common strike insurance fund to aid unions in disputes. This it had to do with care, and it gained useful experience, but a number of big unions did not join; it was given little authority. Thus there was no central body able to speak effectively on the techniques of industrial diplomacy. Secondly, since they had no standing powers of coercing either side, in great industrial disputes with which they were faced, Ministers just had to improvise. It fell primarily to Lloyd George and Churchill, in turns President of the Board of Trade, to play a large part in these improvisations.

In the difficulties of the north-east shipbuilder's wage-cut Churchill brought the parties together and secured an acceptance for the cut at the price of 'permanent machinery' for negotiations. But neither Lloyd George nor he were able to bring about a termination of the strike by the engineers, who returned beaten after seven months. When in 1907 the several railway companies, who had always settled the wages of their own men independently, refused three times to meet the Amalgamated Society of Railway Servants who had launched an 'all grades' movement for a national agreement, the union voted for a strike. This raised the whole issue: it was a vital national service. Lloyd George had to threaten the companies with legislation making conciliation arrangements compulsory in order to get them to agree—they still refused to meet the union and sat in another room—that each company would set up boards of conciliation for each section, with provision for a central board and finally an arbiter. But in the early stages they were not compelled to do what they had always refused to do, negotiate with a union officer not in the employment of the company. In 1911 resentment at the lack of recognition of the union and at the delays and difficulties which the companies made in implementing the scheme led the union to give twenty-four hours' notice of a national strike.[97] The men declined to budge despite Asquith's appeal and warning, a Commission was appointed to investigate the scheme's operation,[98] and Lloyd George again by bullying got the companies to send two representatives to meet the unions, and the men returned to work. The union demanded and the companies still rejected recognition and the Commission's report was an ambivalent affair; the 'companies could not be expected to permit intervention between themselves and their men on questions of management and discipline', but more friendly collaboration would be useful, and each side should be free to choose its own secretary. The companies later refused to meet the men to discuss amendments to the report, and only when the Commons passed a unanimous resolution that the parties should meet did they do so and agree that a union officer might accompany the men in deputations. The Shipping Federation sent a vessel to London with blacklegs to unload cargo, but Churchill got it stopped below port. We have seen, in the miners' strike over the minimum, intense efforts to secure agreement and in the three weeks' strike, the Government had to introduce a Minimum Wage Bill not knowing whether the miners would accept it. The London transport workers, dockers and carters came out again in 1912 on a number of questions, mainly recognition. But the new Port of London Authority was unyielding, rejected the Government's proposal for joint conciliation boards, and despite the Commons' resolution refused to accept any conditions before the men returned. And they used blacklegs. Again, the Government had no standing powers of coercion.

In the meantime the exploration for alternative methods went on. The Canadian Industrial Disputes Investigation Act, 1907 provided that if in mines, railways, shipping and public utilities, a proposed change in the terms of labour contract proved unacceptable, there must be a compulsory 'cooling off' standstill of thirty days during which there might be no strike or lock-out,

[97]For the union's reasons for this, see *Industrial Agreements,* Industrial Council Mins. of ev., q. 13,554.

[98]*Railway Conciliation and Arbitration Scheme of* 1907, R. Com. Rep.; 1911, Cd. 5922, xxix, Mins. of ev.; 1912–13, Cd. 6014, xlv. See J H Thomas's account, *Industrial Agreements,* Mins. of ev., qq. 13,543–558.

whilst the dispute was investigated and an award made. The award was not legally binding. In his report on it,[99] G R Askwith named as its attractions that it did not interfere with the unions' or employers' associations nor prohibit finally any strike or lock-out. But English unions feared that the delay period could be used by the employers to accumulate resources to defeat a strike and the model did not then prove acceptable in England. So the idea was put into cold storage and not taken out again for further scrutiny until the end of the First World War. The next step (1911) was to set up a National Industrial Council of thirteen experienced employers and thirteen experienced trade unionists, with Askwith as chairman. It could deal with disputes in any industry and in any part of the country and recommended terms of settlement. It was like an enlarged conciliation board. But it was too big, too remote, and there was never a chance of success. After the industrial confusion of 1912 it did make a big investigation into the problem of making and enforcing industrial agreements. The report[100] was sensible enough, for it set out the difficulties of making agreements unless each side had a well-defined authority, of knowing beforehand the exact wishes of the parties. The Majority were in favour of making collective agreements enforceable at law, opinion was divided on whether arrangements should be made to inflict monetary penalties for breach of them or for assisting persons who broke them. The parties to an agreement should be able to apply to the Board of Trade to determine, after inquiry, whether it should be extended to and made obligatory on firms and men not members of the signatory associations. But the success of industrial agreements, it claimed, was really due to the recognition by both sides of the moral obligations involved. It came therefore to no striking recommendations for positive action. But the long hearings of evidence must have helped to educate both sides. The report was really a statement of the best current practice. It was not signed until July, 1913, and in a year the whole situation was changed by the outbreak of war.

[99]*Industrial Disputes Investigation Act of Canada, 1907,* Rep. G R Askwith; 1912–13, Cd. 6603, xlvii.
[100]*Industrial Agreements,* Industrial Council Rep. Mins. of ev.; 1913, Cd. 6952, xxviii. On all the difficulties in this period of unionisation, the evidence of the members of the docks, railways and miners' unions is very informative.

(d) Unemployment: labour exchanges and insurance. Between 1900 and 1910 there was a greatly increased awareness of and a change in the public attitude to unemployment and the condition of the unemployed. The factual investigations and social criticism had been doing their work, while the distressing processions of the unemployed, with their collecting boxes, and the emergency soup kitchens of 1908 highlighted their condition. What was the way out? The Labour group's successive 'Right to Work or Maintenance Bills' expressed vigorously the moral claims of the unemployed, but it added little to constructive thought. In affirmation of the principle, their Bills of 1906, 1907 and 1908[101] though varied in detail, were in substance the same. It was to be the duty of local authorities to register unemployed persons, and within six weeks to provide work for them at standard rates or in default, maintenance for them and their dependants. The Local Government Board was to draw up schemes of work of national utility for employment of such persons, and if unemployment exceeded 4 per cent in any area, or in periods of exceptional distress, was to put them into operation out of national funds. The Bills gave little guidance—which later proved an essential condition of any unemployment scheme—on when a man should be deemed unemployed. For though ethically humane, intellectually the proposals were no advance: they were little more than old public relief works on a larger scale. The Labour Members, in close contact with those out of work and driven by a sense of the urgency and the scale of unemployment, were right to press the matter home, and they were impatient—as were many Liberals equally concerned and no less committed electorally—when the years 1906, 1907 and 1908 passed and nothing was done. Why should the Government wait for the Report of the Commission on the *Poor Laws* 'appointed by its opponents'?

The Government's dilemma was that though the delays were weakening its electoral support as the unemployed grew tired of waiting, it could scarcely undertake to create work at standard rates for any large unknown number of the unemployed who cared to register. In the long run, as far as arriving at constructive measures

[101]Unemployed Workmen Bill, 1907 (273) iv; 1908 (5) v; 1909 (9) v.

was concerned, the Government's decision to hold its hand was right.[102] One has only to read Beveridge's masterly analysis given in evidence to the Commission[103] to feel in a different intellectual world of constructive ideas. Even on the specific point of the Bills, Bowley carried the discussion further by showing that if public bodies could hold back or accelerate their works and wages bills between the good and slack years of a decade to the extent of $1\frac{1}{2}$ per cent of the annual wage bill, the demand for labour would be regularised without using relief works specifically directed to the unemployed, with all the difficult problems of selection they involved. For the works would be carried out under ordinary commercial contracts at standard rates, and it would not matter whether they used unemployed men or not, or if the men came from other work. When therefore the Commission's Reports were published, Ramsay MacDonald's earlier impatient declaration (1908) that the Local Government Board already had all the necessary facts was seen to be beside the mark. It is a matter for reflection how it came about that the two streams of thinking could have flowed along separately, and that the Labour group's Bills should have been apparently untouched by the new dynamic thinking on a problem they had so much at heart.

The new material for understanding the problem, of which Llewellyn Smith's evidence before the 1895 Committee was the early example, came from Beveridge's evidence and later the masterly *Unemployment, a Problem of Industry* (1909), from the Majority and Minority Reports of the Commission on the *Poor Laws* (especially the latter, produced by the Webbs), the Memoranda of the Commissioners' special investigations, Steel-Maitland, Miss Squire, Jackson and Pringle, and Llewellyn Smith's paper on *Unemployment Insurance* read to the British Association in 1910.[104] What was the problem of unemployment as they saw it? It was

---

[102]See Asquith's statement, *Parl. Debates,* 4th ser., CLXXXVI (1908), cols. 85–8.

[103]*Poor Laws and Relief of Distress,* R. Com. Mins. of ev., W H Beveridge (14–15 Oct, 1907), q. 77,831, statement, sect. 2; A L Bowley (10 Dec. 1907), q. 88,192, statement. sects. 7–9; 1910, Cd. 5066, xlviii.

[104]Extracts printed as Paper 97. *Unemployment Insurance,* R. Com. Mins. of ev., pp. 1299–1363; 1931–32, non-Parl., Min. of Labour.

not, as it still is to those who passed through it in the inter-war years, the searing experiences of world-wide depression, nor the collapse of great industries. Though the existence and danger of trade cycles was recognised 'as a distinct problem',[105] it was not the feature of unemployment which dominated the minds of the Commissioners on the *Poor Laws*. There had been no crisis of the magnitude of 1873; from 1895 the economy was in a period of rapid growth, and the crises which occurred seemed to be getting weaker, the waves of boom and depression gentler. True, the crisis of 1907 was sharp and the subsequent unemployment deep, though fairly short-lived. But from 1910 we were building up into a boom. Then there was still no properly worked-out theory of trade cycles; they were thought to be due to causes, some traceable, some obscure, which would certainly continue to operate for a long time.[106] (e.g. Beveridge, *Unemployment,* 1909, p. 67: Nicholson, *Elements of Economics,* 1909, pp. 309–10). Professor Chapman told the Commission that their intensity was decreasing, that their causes were psychological and that as they recurred, employers would learn to take appropriate steps.[107] (It was not until 1913—four years after the Report and two years after the 1911 Insurance Act—that Wesley Mitchell had shown that depression was bred in prosperity, or Hawtrey had emphasised in *Good and Bad Trade* the importance of monetary causes of fluctuations.) Nor, though unemployment as a result of changes in technology and demand was recognised, did 'structural unemployment', as we now call it, in the sense of large contractions of great staple industries, as in cotton and coal during the inter-war years, loom large in their minds: these two industries were still part of the world's economy. Even had they regarded these features as the most important, they were not theoretically or practically equipped to deal with either. What dominated the minds of the Commission—and the concern for it

[105]Majority Rep., pt. vi, chap. i, para. 166.

[106]J A Hobson's Underconsumption Theory has already been mentioned (p. 97). Set out in *Problems of the Unemployed* (1896), it was repeated in this period in the new edition, 1906, and in *Industrial System* in 1909. But it found little support among economists, e.g. Beveridge, *Unemployment* (1909), chap. iv.

[107]*Poor Laws,* R. Com. Mins. of ev., qq. 84,791(d), 84,792–93. This same view was expressed by Chapman and Hallsworth, *Unemployment* (1909).

animates their vigorous pages of analysis and constructive proposals
—was not mass unemployment, but under-employment,[108] the
chronic over-supply of casual labour in relation to local demand.
Though we have now no means of recalling the full statistical facts,
our experience of underdeveloped economies, side-lights in
Dickens's novels and some of the evidence before the Dilke Commission on *Housing*, 1884–85, suggest that it may have been serious
for decades. There is no doubt that the increase of the port and
urban distributive trades, which used much casually employed
labour, had been adding to it. Both Majority and Minority regarded
it as a *new*, serious and growing evil.[109] The former did not feel
able to say exactly what proportion casual bore to total unemployment, while the latter thought that two-thirds of all able-bodied
pauperism came from that under-employed class. These chronically
under-employed included not only those in seasonal trades, but
men in discontinuous employment, as in the building trades,
moving from job to job, employer to employer, most of the
personnel having weeks out of work each year, casual labourers
such as dockers, wharf labourers, market porters and the fringe
about skilled trades. Beveridge drove home with great force the way
in which separate enterprises gathered round them little pools of
reserve, unemployed labour. And a major contributing element was
the wasteful misuse of boy labour in blind alley jobs as van boys,
messengers, and their discharge from school into the labour market
with no vocational preparation at all for permanent work.

These facts led to conclusions on which the informed, including
the Majority and Minority Commissioners, were practically
unanimous. Two were negative. It was useless to try to drive a man
to work on the 1834 deterrent principles if there were no work he
could get. That was dead. Secondly, public relief works were misguided, had failed in their object and should be stopped. It followed
from their analysis that their positive recommendations, those of

[108]The authors of the Toynbee Hall analysis of the Reports used the following words:
'The enquiries of the Commission . . . have proved conclusively the existence of a much
more serious state of affairs than mere cyclical fluctuations of employment.' *New Poor
Law or No Poor Law* (1909), pp. 120–1.

[109]Majority Rep., pt. vi, para. 167; Minority Rep., pt. ii, chap. iv (C, vi); in 8vo ed.,
pp. 596.

the Minority particularly, were concentrated on improving the organisation of the labour market by a nation-wide system of labour exchanges, by promoting decasualisation of labour, including making employers pay an employment termination tax (Majority), by creating a Ministry of Labour with the positive duty of organising the labour market and dovetailing seasonal employment (Minority) and minimising the use of child labour by organised vocational advice, raising the school-leaving age and more practical instruction. Demand for labour should be regularised (which did not mean maintaining a high level of employment by monetary means), by a better timing of local authorities' works (Minority). The Majority, however, would not accept any proposal deliberately to make irregular the authorities' regular work on which regular men might be employed, but thought that they should make an endeavour to carry out their irregular work in the slack years. But neither the Majority nor the Minority dealt with the practical difficulties in which the authorities would be involved in trying to hold back work for some bad period at an uncertain date ahead, nor did they ask whether if additions to the demands for labour in the slack years stimulated enterprise, decreasing it in the other years would have the reverse effect. Finally, it was paramount that arrangements should be made for unemployment insurance, especially for the unorganised and unskilled, and for the insurance fund to be built up 'ready for the depression that must come in due course' (1913 Cd. 6965, para. 269).

How did these plans fare?

(*a*) *Labour Exchanges*. Six months before the Royal Commission reported, the Minister, Mr Winston Churchill, who had some knowledge of how it was thinking,[110] had obtained the assent of the Cabinet to the establishment of labour exchanges,[111] and at the same time had asked his civil service advisors, led by Sir H L Smith, to prepare possible schemes of unemployment insurance. To organise the first he called in W H Beveridge. The Labour Exchanges

[110]See the various entries from Mrs Webb's diaries in *Our Partnership*, especially the 1908 conference at the Board of Trade, pp. 416–19.

[111]See account in the 1930 ed. of Beveridge's *Unemployment*, pt. ii, pp. 262–6.

Act (1909) simply empowered the Government to establish and maintain exchanges: the rest was left to the Minister and his advisors, and this enabled them to cut through the difficulties. Churchill took the bold course, absorbed or closed existing exchanges and established a national system, and within 18 months there were 150 of them, with staffs selected on new principles. The trade union fears that they might be used to undercut wage rates or to blackleg strikes were met by regulations that no men should be penalised for refusing to accept a vacancy at less than recognised rates and that any applicant should be told if a strike or lock-out existed.[112] And following the practice of the Rev Tozer in his Ipswich Exchange,[113] the exchanges were empowered to pay the fares of a man going to a job obtained through them. The work of the exchanges was not only humane, since they reduced the weary tramping, hawking one's labour in search of a job, but by speeding up the contact of employer and applicant, they reduced the volume of interstitial unemployment.

(*b*) *Unemployment Insurance.* In unemployment insurance also the Minister and his advisors went further than the Royal Commission, and indeed had to think their way through difficulties which might otherwise have proved fatal. Unemployment was a risk which individual savings could not meet because a man's losses might be heavy and no one could be certain on whom unemployment would fall; provision for it was beyond the means of those most affected and had to be collective. At the time Lloyd George claimed that only 1,700,000 had been able to make provision through the unions for even rudimentary unemployment benefits.[114] Both the Majority and the Minority had proposed unemployment insurance—the former indeed regarded it as paramount for unorganised and unskilled workers—but both rejected compulsion: the Majority because the State would have to compel three-quarters of the working classes to join organisations and would therefore have to

[112]Labour Exchanges Act, 1909, sect. 2 (2).

[113]See above, p. 97n. 109.

[114]The incomes of casual labourers were 'so small and precarious that they could not pay a subscription to a club or tontine'. Mins. of ev., q. 35,432; Minority Rep., p. 1149n (8vo ed., p. 594n).

fix contributions and administer the scheme, and because voluntary bodies would oppose it, the Minority because it could be applied only to workers in regular and not to those in irregular employment. Since many trade unions gave members out-of-work benefit, provision should take the form of encouraging this by giving trade unions who offered it State financial aid (Majority) equal to one-half the sums paid in benefit (Minority). And the Majority, rejecting any general scheme, suggested insurance by separate industries.

These affirmations of principle, important though they were, contributed very little to the solution of the practical problems involved. This had to be provided by the Minister and his advisors; and they had to reverse or go beyond some of the recommendations. First, how would a subsidy to unions, whose members were already able to obtain benefit, assist the unorganised? And clearly if it were paramount that these should be brought in, compulsion would be necessary. A man must not be able to come in and out of the scheme as he thought fit, but must stay in for his working life. This, now so much a part of our working lives, was a breakthrough into new territory requiring political and administrative courage; for at the time nowhere had compulsion been tried on any scale with significant success. Then how could one prevent the insurance fund from being drained by those less regularly employed, by the man too wedded to his existing job, type or place of work or living, by the men not personally energetic enough to seek and hold individual jobs, by the loafer? When was a man involuntarily unemployed? Unless these questions could be adequately answered, the bewilderment and fears which had inhibited thought for so long could not be swept away. Professor Chapman[115] and many others thought that unemployment was a non-insurable risk. Success at this point was therefore critical.

Some remarkable constructive thinking worked out solutions, many of which have now become part of everyday working life. First, Llewellyn Smith's charts on the variations of unemployment and Beveridge's further work—one has to remind oneself how limited were the data then available—had shown that in a number

[115]*Poor Laws,* R. Com. Mins. of ev., qq. 84,793 (43), 84,872–78.

A First Solution

of clearly marked trades the influence of cyclical, seasonal and other changes beyond the control of any individual workman was more important in determining the volume of employment than his personal characteristics. In these trades—building, construction, shipbuilding, engineering, ironfounding and vehicle building—insurance was actuarially possible in the sense that a reasonable scale of contributions could provide reasonable benefits of sufficient duration to cover ordinary unemployment in them.[116] It was therefore decided to start the experiment at first in these trades only. But it was not insurance by industry, each with separate rates of contributions and benefits, for this would complicate and discourage industrial mobility.[117] Contributions and benefit were therefore uniform within the scheme. And if the less well-paid were to participate, the worker's contribution had to be low, and correspondingly the benefit was not a replacement of the whole or some percentage of wages, but a limited uniform amount to help meet necessities as a first line of defence.

Secondly, tests had to be applied to the individual applicant. Genuine unemployment could be tested by the exchange offering a job. He could be penalised for a period for refusing suitable employment, leaving voluntarily without just cause and for discharge for industrial misconduct.[118] On these points there was to be right of appeal to a local Court of Referees, composed of a legal chairman and representatives of employers and workers, with a final appeal to an independent, permanent Umpire. In practice a most interesting case-law was built up. And a one-in-five rule limited benefit to one week for every five contributions. Further, in the hope that the unions would help to protect the funds by keeping an eye on bad risks, it was arranged that, on condition that they added a certain proportion of benefit out of their own funds in return for a subsidy of one-sixth of the amount so spent, members could draw statutory

[116]H Llewellyn Smith's Paper before the British Association, 1910. Extract, Paper 97, *Unemployment Insurance*, R. Com. Mins. of ev., p. 1302, col. 2; 1931, non-Parl.

[117]Ibid., p. 1310.

[118]National Insurance Act, 1911, sects. 86, 87. These conditions, together with the rights of appeal, have remained part of the insurance system ever since.

benefit from the union's office instead of the exchange. But it seems that this particular hope was not fully realised.[119]

The Act also established a fresh principle in financing a social service. Elementary education was free, the Old Age Pensions Act, 1908, in substance made pensions a State grant, subject to qualifying conditions, without previous contributions from industry. Unemployment—and health—insurances were financed not only by the State and the worker's contributions but also from industry through the employer's contribution. These two social services were thus started off on very different financial courses.

Insurance was a far call from 'work or maintenance' but gained support from solid trade unionists, if not from the more advanced socialists,[120] because it was in line with their practice and would replace hated contact with the Poor Law relieving officer by benefits obtained as a statutory right. There were still millions of workers outside the scheme, but it was remarkable for its dynamic quality, for what it held in store for the future. As it became established and its advantages perceived, there were bound to be demands for its extension to more industries, more classes of workers, for higher benefits. The gates had been opened and in due course the whole employed population would pass through them.

iii. *Health policy*

The continuing growth of medical and scientific knowledge was bound to raise the whole question of how this should be brought to bear on the whole population, and what part should be played by the State and its officers in the process. It was already evident that the work of the local and central medical officers of health, involved as it was in that problem, was essentially dynamic. But much depended on the willingness of the public to accept new habits and restraints and to provide the necessary means for its extension at a

[119]H Llewellyn Smith, Paper 96, para. 2, *Unemployment Insurance,* R. Com. Mins. of ev., p. 1289; 1931, non-Parl.

[120]The Webbs, of course, were committed to their own proposals, but E C Fairchild, a Marxist, was in favour of State insurance, with equal contributions by the employer, the worker and the State. *Poor Laws,* R. Com., 1909, Mins. of ev., app. xxiv, 23; 1910, Cd. 5066, xlviii.

M

time when scientific progress and rising standards of medical and surgical practice were making it more costly,[121] and on the readiness of professional groups and voluntary organisations to adjust themselves to changing medical and social demands. In this period work pushed out into fresh fields in which the inter-play of these different pressures led to varied, and from the point of the application of medical knowledge, uneven results.

(*a*) *Health insurance*. Here it is convenient to depart a little from chronology to look first at the Health Insurance Scheme since this was, with unemployment insurance, part of a single project embodied in one Act, and financed by contributions from the individual, the State and the employer. It was also a field in which the hardest battles were fought. In its establishment, the relative roles of formal inquiry, minister and civil servants, were different from those in the preparation of the Unemployment Insurance Scheme. Whereas in the latter the civil servants had to go beyond the Royal Commission's somewhat tentative principles, in setting up national health insurance its proposals were just 'passed by'. What eventually emerged aptly illustrates a remark made by its chief author, Lloyd George, in another connection—'Every one who has been engaged in any kind of reform knows how difficult it is to make way through the inextricable tangle of an old society like our own.'

The problem of ill-health had three sides. First, scientific—how to ensure that the full knowledge of medicine and science should be made available to the entire population through a proper distribution of doctors, consultants and institutions; second, social—how the poor were to be given access to treatment for which they were unable to pay or to pay enough; third, economic—how to provide against the loss of wages, etc., which the wage earner's illness would entail. It was characteristic of the period that an exhaustive searching out of the facts, set out in *Public Health and Social Conditions* (1909)[122] and in the Reports of the Commission on the *Poor Laws*, gave the legislators more than ample material to work on. The first, while

---

[121]See *Public Health and Social Conditions*, pp. 59-60; 1909, Cd. 4671, ciii.
[122]Cd. 4671, charts facing p. 16.

showing the steady fall of the death rate from the seventies and the successful attack on some infectious diseases, e.g. scarlet fever, brought out the obstinate persistence of a high infant death rate[123] still running at 120 per 1,000 births, and comparative mortality rates of dock labourers, costermongers and general labourers three and four times greater than those of clergymen, with the condition of general labourers apparently actually deteriorating. One-half the total cost of pauperism arose from sickness. Some of the reasons for this disastrous state of affairs were exposed by the Royal Commission. The 1834 deterrent principle was to have applied to medical, especially outdoor medical relief, and although there had been improvements the atmosphere of deterrence hung about all Poor Law medical work. Some guardians had practically abolished outdoor medical relief, others gave it more freely. In the majority of unions the sick were still housed in the general mixed workhouse, many of the infirmaries being grim bastilles for the sick, with untrained paupers as nurses. There were free dispensaries, provident dispensaries, doctor's private clubs with low fees, poor medical attention and bad debts, and some 3 million members of friendly societies, some of which were strong and others barely solvent, having contracts with 'club' doctors at rates per head which doctors protested were too low to permit anything but the most rudimentary treatment. The voluntary hospitals, with admission based on subscribers' letters, were geographically distributed in a haphazard manner and some unions had tried to fill the gap by developing modernised infirmaries. There was no co-ordination or general policy for the medical service of any kind. All this was driven home by the reports with great force. The doctors and the Commission declared that the dispensaries and hospitals were abused by the people who could afford to pay for treatment, though neither of them seemed to have inquired what these people could do in areas where facilities were inadequate. In total, it was a very unsatisfactory result for a great expenditure of public and private money.

What were the solutions offered? The Majority Report, starting

---

[123]See also Newsholme's Report on *Infant and Child Mortality;* 1910, Cd. 5263, xxxix.

from two principles of curative treatment and encouragement of thrift, argued that all the scientific methods for prevention and cure which were reasonably accessible to persons of average means should be available to the poor on payment according to means and to the very poor without payment. They proposed to transfer the Guardians' health functions and infirmaries and other institutions to the new Public Assistance Authority (County and County Boroughs) and to re-organise medical assistance on a provident basis, local medical assistance committees being charged with this duty, while those not members of a provident society would be assessed by the Public Assistance Committee through its relieving officer, now to be termed Public Assistance Officer. The Minority would have none of this. The aim, they said, must be prevention in the widest sense, treatment should be what was medically necessary irrespective of a patient's economic condition. If cases were handed over to the Public Assistance Committee they would be thought of primarily in terms of destitution and not prevention or cure. All health functions and institutions of the Guardians should be transferred to the public health authority and all public health services unified under its control. A Registrar with proper rules would charge and recover when appropriate. Arthur Newsholme, in his evidence, wanted prevention, the earliest recognition and treatment of disease before serious symptoms appeared, by giving every man the right to call for free diagnosis, treatment and provision of medicines. To this end all the Poor Law institutions and services should be transferred to and unified with other health services by the local health authority.[124] Dr McVail, on the other hand, rejected the idea of a free service supported by taxation and wanted a voluntary provident scheme with contributions possibly deducted from wages, and aided by the State; compulsion he regarded as impracticable in England.[125] But Ireland was already moving towards the State medical service. All poor persons—and a large proportion of the working class were held to be such—were entitled to the services of a dispensary doctor, and since there was normally only one

[124]*Poor Laws,* R. Com. Mins. of ev., qq. 92,617–644, 92,726–756, 92,807–810, Statement, pp. 160–4; 1910, Cd. 5062, xlix.
[125]J C McVail, Report on *Medical Relief,* app. vol. xiv, pp. 157–62; 1909, Cd. 4573, xlii.

doctor in a district they were unlikely to pay several pence per week for what they were already having for nothing. The Vice-Regal Commission of 1906[126] had already recommended that all hospitals and institutions should be taken out of the Poor Law and run by a State-salaried medical service. With a remarkable obscurantism and lack of understanding of developments natural in Irish conditions, the Majority Commissioners rejected this proposal and in their passion for provident schemes proposed for Ireland its English principles—namely, to transfer Poor Law hospitals and dispensaries to the Public Assistance Authority. In the meantime in England the doctors, discontented with their contract terms with friendly societies, with the competition of free dispensaries and provident dispensaries without a wage limit, and fearing that the Commission might propose a salaried service or not insist on free choice of doctor, were working out a scheme for medical service run by the profession.

It is only against the background of these varied suggestions that the real significance of the choice or rather the series of choices of policy actually made can be understood. In the outcome, despite the authoritative inquiries which preceded them, none of them was adopted—perhaps it would be accurate to say that they were 'passed by'. The policy did not derive from the Commission's report, nor from any preceding committee of civil servants, nor from departmental initiative. It was a result of a purely personal decision by Lloyd George, whose sympathies were aroused, especially after a visit to Germany, and who in 1908, before the Commission had reported, had asked a young civil servant, Braithwaite, to consider schemes of health insurance. From that moment Lloyd George had set in motion policy-making forces which took a direction of their own. Though he must have had some idea of what was going on in the Commission and had an interview with the Webbs most entertainingly described by Braithwaite,[127] in which they criticised his ideas with some lack of tact, there seems

[126]*Poor Laws*, R. Com. Mins. of ev., qq. 92,617–644, 92,726–756, 92,807; also *Breviate*, I, 414. *Extension of Medical Benefit . . . to Ireland*, Cttee. Rep.; 1913, Cd. 6963, xxxvii; *Breviate*, I, 415.

[127]W J Braithwaite, *Lloyd George's Ambulance Wagon* (1950), pp. 115–17.

no evidence that he had studied the Commission's report.[128] Thereafter were drawn into the work more and more able civil servants, energetic and touchy, both because they were exceptional and working under strain, being driven and driving themselves. As the scheme evolved from this process, it cut across many of the cherished principles on which other proposals had been made. It was to be general, covering employed manual workers and other workers earning not more than £160 per annum;[129] it was to be compulsory, and despite the socialist left, it was to be contributory; it was not purely provident, for employers also were to contribute, and there was to be State aid, not deterrence. Yet the position of the friendly societies was to be safeguarded. It was an immense undertaking, involving 13 million to 15 million persons for all of whom separate accounts had to be kept with the hand methods of the time. There was no precedent and no machinery. Braithwaite's Memoirs give a vivid picture of the way in which the successive choices were made by Lloyd George and his advisors. Should a new bureaucracy be set up, as with the labour exchanges? Could the post office, already handling savings banks, be used? As friendly and collecting societies were already dealing with about one-third of those to be covered, could they handle it? As the scheme was to be compulsory each society would have to be approved for solvency and be democratically controlled; would the State have to guarantee benefits? Some societies were highly selective and would not accept bad risks—how were these to be provided for? Compulsion would bring in older men with a higher sickness rate, making higher claims for cash benefits, yet who so far would have made no contributions to help pay for it—how was this gap to be bridged? Unless the principle of paying annual benefits out of annual contributions were adopted,

---

[128]The story, associated with John Burns, then President of the Local Government Board, that the scheme was arranged to 'dish the Webbs' and repeated by Beatrice Webb, Margaret Cole and others, is too trivial an explanation. Burns was hostile, but Mrs Webb was prone to think of 'moves' both for and against their schemes. The series of events set in train just passed these by. The Webbs later admitted this; see *Our Partnership*, p. 478n. But Lloyd George was too adept a politician not to be ready to use anything which might help him in his struggle.

[129]National Insurance Act, 1911, sect. i, and 1st schedule, pt. ii (g). This limitation sprang from the doctors' opposition to including those who could afford to pay.

contributions must begin early (aged sixteen) and the State must provide funds for a period until the position became more balanced. The problems seemed endless.

At first welcomed, the proposals aroused violent opposition in many quarters. The friendly societies, many of long standing, feared the effect of a rival scheme of insurance on existing members and—as the years proved, rightly—on the recruitment of new members. A large proportion of their members were Liberal voters and at that date their total membership exceeded that of the trade unions. Non-political, they could nevertheless be formidable politically. The demand of commercial insurance companies to be admitted to the scheme, though they had no experience in this field, proved impossible to resist since there was no guessing what their thousands of agents might say, were perhaps already whispering, in the millions of households they visited. The doctors were thwarted in their hopes for a scheme run by the profession, while the friendly societies did not want to hand over their control of doctors, by whose certificates their funds might be drained. The socialist left ran a campaign of opposition to any contributory scheme.[130] Lloyd George with courage and imagination, by a mixture of mass appeal, persuasion, giving the House an occasional free vote, setting up an Insurance Commission with unheard of delegated powers, and hard bargaining, sometimes paying a high price for agreement, defeated his enemies. The opposition of the medical profession, continued to the last moment, collapsed.

Although, therefore, the Poor Law Commission's Reports helped to build up knowledge, that millions of workers obtained medical help and cash sickness payments as a statutory right and that the machinery for doing it lasted for a third of a century and some of its principles longer, was a personal achievement of Lloyd George, aided by a brilliant team of civil servants. One Liberal wit said at the time that the Act had been placed on the Statute book by a Minority of one! And the measure of Lloyd George's achievement may be gauged by the forecast in the Minority Report: 'any attempt to *enforce* on the people of this country—whether for supplementary

[130]Pease, *History of the Fabian Society*, pp. 224–5. Snowden, *Autobiography*, I, 228–9.

pensions, provision for sickness or invalidity—a system of direct personal weekly contributions must in our judgement in face of so powerful a phalanx as the combined Friendly Societies, Trade Unions and Industrial Insurance Companies, fighting in defence of their own business, prove politically disastrous'.[131]

There are two new questions—did this particular process of policy-making give the best immediate answer in the light of the knowledge available at the time? Did it give the best long-term answer, and if not, were the defects due to inadequate knowledge or to the process by which the policy was shaped? The Majority's provident scheme was against the whole upsurge of the time. The socialist opposition campaign for the Minority proposals was a failure; and while Lloyd George's declaration that the workers would obtain ninepence for fourpence implied a remarkable theory of the incidence of the employer's and the State contributions, it seems clear from the problems and storms aroused by the Budget of 1909 that the sharp increase of taxes which would have been required without them might have been difficult to carry. On the other hand, Lloyd George was not able to get his local health committees[132] on which he set some store and his attempt at fixing social responsibility by the excessive sickness clause,[133] which would enable the Insurance Commission to recover from slum property owners, negligent local authorities and bad employers the cost of excessive sickness due to their default, was impossible to implement because it was not a matter subject to precise legal proof. Nevertheless, Lloyd George had a more acute sense of what the public would accept than his critics either on the right or the left.

The long-term appraisal of this brilliant work of improvisation was less favourable. First, administration through approved societies, which had helped to make compulsion acceptable, was costly and wasteful, some towns having many over-lapping societies each looking after a modest number of members, while as members moved,

---

[131]Minority Rep., pt. i, chap. vii, D(vi), 8vo ed., p. 276. How they underestimated his political skill!

[132]Newsholme regarded their replacement by the Local Insurance Committees as a great blunder. It was due to the doctors' opposition. Op. cit., p. 36. See also Brend, *Health and the State*, pp. 222–4.

[133]Sect. 63.

localised societies found themselves with members scattered in tiny clusters over wide areas. Worst of all, the differences in the test for admission meant that strong societies had surpluses which they could use for additional benefits, whilst weak ones could add little, and contributors could not understand why a compulsory uniform contribution should produce different scales of benefits. And the insurance companies were a strong vested interest. The system became difficult to uproot. In 1926, the Royal Commission on Health Insurance agreed about these weaknesses and that the system prevented the unification of services. The Majority, which included Anderson and Gray, both of whom as civil servants had participated in creating the scheme, still felt that they must be retained for the administration of cash benefits, but the Minority was quite clear that the arrangement should be ended. But this was not done until 1948.

The medical arrangements left much to be desired. True, a large part of the working population had access to a panel doctor as of right, and in that sense were brought or could place themselves under medical supervision. This was a vital step. But the standard of medical care was low. By 1917 criticism had become pungent. As Dr Brend, in *Health and the State* (1917), and Sir Arthur Newsholme objected (1917), there were no rights to specialist or hospital treatment; this had not been drawn into the scheme. If we look back on it we may ask whether, if both could not be provided, it would have been better to start not with the general practitioner service, some of which the patients could have obtained for themselves with some pretty severe scraping, but with the specialist hospital and other expensive services which were otherwise completely out of their reach. Or is the question meaningful only if there is already a minimum of general practitioners' service? Or did the scheme confirm the English idea that medical care means a bottle of physic? So was started a problem of policy still with us and the health services were thus divided between the public services, the doctor and his panel patients, and the hospital. Newsholme, in his Annual Report of 1917–18, a document of great power and importance which foreshadowed the National Health Service, still as far away as 1948, pointed out the losses from the failure to undertake the unification of services which he had proposed in his evidence in 1909.[134] In 1919 he argued that an essential condition was that medical care should be separated completely and free from the limits of insurance against economic loss.[135] Brend attributes the failure to the fact that those concerned in shaping the scheme had no experience of medical questions and did not seek advice on them,[136] Newsholme to the fact that the Act was conceived ill-advisedly, had too short a period of gestation, and suffered from premature and forced delivery.[137]

(*b*) *Health of children*. In shaping policy on the health of children, the medical officers, either themselves taking the initiative, or aided by or aiding voluntary effort, had a much less obstructed influence. It was a subject which called out sympathy without stirring up conflicts of group interest. (1) Infant mortality in 1906–09 was still running at over 100 per 1,000 live births, maternal mortality at 5.0 per 1,000, but the complacency with which the loss of infants and mothers was accepted as natural could not be shaken until more was learnt of the causes and that they were preventible. Knowledge already accumulated was added to by Dr George Newman[138] (M.O.H. Finsbury), Dr Arthur Newsholme (M.O.H. Brighton and later M.O., L.G.B.) and Dr Mary Scharlieb. Dr. Newsholme in particular pointed out that the mortality rate was not just 'selective', or in plain terms did not just weed out the weak babies, but was a sensitive index of social and industrial conditions, being largely influenced by industrial urbanisation, overcrowding of houses on the site, overcrowding per room and the 'insanitary barbarism' of the rural areas, and that the adverse causes which killed some damaged others, and continued to operate adversely on the survivors up to the age of five.[139] The conditions could be dealt

[134]pp. x-xx; 1918, Cd. 9169, xi. See also his *Public Health and Insurance* (1920), pp. 32, 60, 95–6, 109.

[135]Ibid., pp. 68, 112.

[136]Brend, *Health and the State*, p. 263.

[137]Arthur Newsholme, *Public Health and Insurance*, p. 36.

[138]George Newman, *Infant Mortality* (1906). Note the sub-title, *A Social Problem*.

[139]Newsholme, *Infant and Child Mortality*. Supp. to 39th Ann. Rep. L.G.B.; 1910, Cd. 5263, xxxix. See summary, pp. 74–8 and Dr Yule's statistical app. on selectivity.

with by appropriate social action.[140] He was led to criticise with some vigour the view, 'comfortable for the well-to-do person to adopt', that maternal ignorance of the working-class mother was the chief factor. There was no reason to assume that she was more ignorant than the better-off ones—she at least did more breast feeding—but her lack of knowledge was more dangerous because it was associated with social helplessness, unfavourable environment and lack of medical advice which others had.[141]

(2) The feeding of ill-nourished children had grown up spontaneously by voluntary effort in 'ragged schools' and poor, public elementary schools, and had been recommended by the Royal Commission on *Physical Training (Scotland)*, though with a proviso that it should not be at the expense of the State. The medical evidence before the Committee on *Physical Deterioration* favoured it, W L Mackenzie and that able and liberal Tory, Sir J Gorst, both arguing that to submit ill-nourished children to the strains of school might be harmful. But despite some public agitation there was a lag in political and some official opinion. The effort of the L.G.B. to deal with it through the Poor Law by the *Relief (School Children) Order*, 1905, which enabled Guardians to relieve the children of an able-bodied man without offering him either the workhouse or test work, was largely ignored, while the Committee on the *Medical Inspection and Feeding of School Children* (1905) was still asked to report on what could be done without cost to the State. The Select Committee on the *Education (Provision of Meals) Bill*, 1906, took a turn for the better. But it started from the view that the evils, though real, were limited in extent and spasmodic in period of occurrence. It is not surprising therefore, that it placed first reliance on voluntary agencies, which it was felt might collapse if the feeding of school children were made a statutory duty. Nevertheless it advanced to accepting that the service should be run not by the Poor Law but by the education authorities, and that when voluntary resources were insufficient, rates might be called on up to $\frac{1}{2}$d in the pound. Parents should be made to pay where possible. That the powers were

[140]See his comments on areas guilty of neglect; op. cit., pp. 77, 83–109.

[141]Newsholme, Rep. on *Child Mortality at Ages 0–5*, pp. 64–6; 1917, Cd. 8496, xvi.

optional meant that by 1910 only rather over one-third of the authorities were using them; there were difficulties in picking and choosing the children if their parents did not pay and without aid of systematic inspection; the menu varied from the good to the ignorant, for the study of nutrition had not gone far or spread widely. And by somewhat severe logic it was ruled that school children should not be fed when not at school but on holiday. But by 1914 social investigators had already concluded that as long as social conditions existed as they were, school meals should be offered to all children without inquiring into parents' means, in holidays as well as term, and that the menu should be devised in consultation with the School M.O.H.[142]

(3) The drive for systematic inspection of school children was overwhelmingly medical. The Education Acts had already involved the sorting out of epileptic and other handicapped children and those with infectious and other diseases, and some of our knowledge arose simply from the school attendance officers' inquiries into why children were not at school. Though Dr Kerr at Bradford had been able to take a wider view of his task, the amount which hard-pressed school medical officers were able to do beyond their specific duties was limited, the authorities' views were narrow and it was all spasmodic, unorganised and without clear central guidance. The popular campaign which high-lighted certain aspects of the problem —brain-fag, underfeeding, infectious diseases, etc.—no doubt helped, but these were not the real issues. This was that experience had shown that there was a very large amount of remediable physical defect which if not attended to might grow worse, that much of it was unrecognised by parents or teachers, and could be discovered only by systematic medical attention of all school children. This was made compulsory on all education authorities in 1907.[143]

(*c*) *Mental deficiency.* Whereas in the other reforms social ideals and expert advice on the whole ran alongside and reinforced one another, the storms in which the *Mental Deficiency Act,* 1913, was born were stirred up because the legislation for which a body of

[142]M E Bulkley, *The Feeding of School Children* (1914), chap. vii.
[143]Education (Administrative Provisions) Act, 1907.

independent expert opinion was pressing in some ways ran contrary to the whole assumptions on which the social programme rested. These were that the poverty, unemployment, ill-health and even delinquency of the lowest income groups were largely due to economic and social conditions which no ordinary person could on his own breakthrough. The *Mental Deficiency Act,* by contrast, assumed that for a certain proportion of the population (about $4\frac{1}{2}$ per 1,000)[144] these evils were the results rather than the cause, which was inherited, irremediable and sometimes uneducable mental defect, and that there was some risk that the proportion of mentally deficient persons in the population might increase. Both known social facts and biological theory prompted the Act. The social workers of the time testified to the immense drain on the health, resources and happiness of families caused by the presence in the home of an imbecile child; there were feebleminded children who could make no progress at school and who later could not compete easily in the labour market, suffered unemployment, neglect and drifted into delinquency. The Royal Commission on the *Poor Laws* had called attention to the 'ins and outs'—feebleminded girls who came into the workhouse to have illegitimate babies, only to get out and return later for the same reason. There was, of course, compassion from both sides. They were often exploited and cruelly treated, and such children were often dubbed by their fellows as attending a 'silly school'. Both the Royal Commission on the *Care and Control of the Feebleminded* (1908) and the Memorandum to the first Bill (134)[145] declared that their claim to aid was primarily that they were suffering from mental incapacity and not that they were poor, destitute or criminals. But at this point the unanimity between idealists and the eugenists ceased. For the eugenists— Galton had founded the Eugenics research fellowship only in 1904 —argued that these traits were inherited, that the people concerned were less sexually restrained than normal people, and that because of their high fertility they were a source of race degeneracy and should be prevented from producing children in their own image.

[144]Of whom about 45 per cent were in need of supervision, etc.
[145]1912–13, Bill 134, Bill 213, iii.

But the cruder versions and wider claims of the eugenists' proposals were that with proper selective human breeding, delinquency and other social problems could be greatly reduced, the lack of success of the lowest strata of society being partly due to their being inferior biological stocks,[146] and that by the differential birth rate society was being 'recruited from the bottom'. Social reformers assumed that changes due to improved social conditions were 'handed on', but studies by Pearson and Elderton suggested that they had little influence on the intelligence of children. To the social reformers all this was hard doctrine. For they thought, as Pigou put it, that 'bad social environments also produce children'.

We know now that the early eugenists' views on the processes of heredity were far too simple, that the results of scientific human breeding would be uncertain and slow, that their studies of 'degenerate families', e.g. the Jukes, were fallacious, and that the qualities which made a man of value to society are derived from nurture as well as inheritance. Nevertheless, if it were difficult to pick out those human qualities which should or should not be preserved, it was simpler to apply the principles to the much narrower problem of mental deficiency, about which there were established social and biological facts. For the Royal Commission felt able to define four groups in which the brain was undeveloped at birth or early age and would remain undeveloped throughout life: idiots, imbeciles, feebleminded and moral imbeciles. The possible courses of policy were oversight, certification and segregation.[147] Following the Royal Commission's recommendations, the Home Office Bill gave powers of certification and supervision and compulsory detention of these groups for their own welfare and that of others. But it aroused a storm of protest partly, no doubt, directed against some of the vigorous and extreme eugenic anti-democratic propaganda which supported it,[148] partly because it

[146]E Schuster, *Eugenics* (1912). But note a dissentient voice in Leonard T Hobhouse, *Social Evolution and Political Theory* (1911), chap. iii, 'The Value and Limitation of Eugenics'.

[147]*Care and Control of the Feebleminded*, R. Com. See *Breviate*, I, 292–4.

[148]H.C. Debates, 5th ser., LIII (28 May 1913), cols. 242–8. See also speeches by Atherley-Jones and Booth, and Wedgwood's speech on the *Feebleminded Persons (Control) Bill*, 5th ser., XXXVIII (May 1912), cols. 1466–78.

suggested that in some cases social conditions seemed of less consequence as causes of social evils than irremediable inherited defect.
There were criticisms in the *Manchester Guardian* and the *Daily
Citizen*; Belloc in the *Eye Witness* called it an outrage on individual
liberty, J Wedgwood, in the House, in effect denounced it as a
class measure in that besides keeping 100,000 in permanent incarcera-
tion, it would permit anyone with a friend in an institution to
obtain his release on condition that he assumed responsibility for
the patient, a privilege which could be exercised only by those with
enough money to do it.

During the debates in the House and the Standing Committees
on the frequently revised Bills, the chief practical points of contention were three. First, what were to be the conditions of 'trial' of
the defective person who might be sentenced to 'detention' for a
long period, and even prohibited from marrying, what the nature
of the evidence required for securing 'conviction'? One unsuccessful Bill provided for a single medical certificate, but eventually the
procedure decided upon was the presentation of a petition to a
magistrate, either by a parent or guardian, or the duly authorised
officer of the local authority, and two medical certificates. And the
justice's order was in the first place to be for a year only, renewed
for another year, and thereafter for five years.

Secondly, who were the mentally deficient? The Royal Commission's four categories, incorporated in Clause (1) of the Acts, were,
of course, grades, rather than clear-cut categories and were dependent not on lay, but medical assessment. It was indeed the difficulty
of turning sets of criteria derived from scientific research into precise legal phrases, coupled with the serious personal consequences
which might follow, which caused so much controversy. For
example, in the Committee stage of the Bills, amendments and
counter-amendments varied the description of the 'feebleminded'
from persons 'incapable through mental defect from birth or an
early age of competing on equal terms with their fellows and or
managing their affairs with normal prudence', to 'persons capable
of earning their living under suitable supervision, but incapable by
reason of defect of mind of managing themselves and their affairs
with sufficient prudence to maintain an independent existence'. Nor

was the House willing to have the power of detention either at the request of parent or guardian or authorised public officer applied to any of these groups ('and no others', one Bill said)[149] unless in addition to the defect there were other circumstances making it desirable—that they were found neglected, abandoned, wandering about without visible means of support, cruelly treated, or were habitual drunkards or found guilty of crime and liable to be ordered to an approved school and so on (Clause 2). The provision in one Bill that the defectives to whom the Act would apply should include those 'in whose case it was desirable in the interests of the country that they should be deprived of the opportunity of having children' was struck out.[150]

iv. *The Poor Law—the residual problem*

It was in the field of the Poor Law generally that, in spite of its great efforts, the Commission was the least effective, in which the disagreements of the Majority and Minority were at their greatest, and in which both the proposals on which they were agreed and those they presented as alternatives came to naught. For the explanation one has to take another look at certain aspects of the familiar story of the inquiry.

First, was the membership of the Commission geared in the hope of producing a given result? It seems that the L.G.B.'s permanent officers were hoping that the Commission would help in abolishing elected bodies, the Boards of Guardians. Mrs Webb, and Mrs Cole following her, suggests that the Balfour Government succeeded in 'bringing together a body whose report would, in all essentials, stand by the principles of 1834'. The mixed motives which determine whom shall be appointed to a Commission often lie in obscurity; only, as in this case, a report of all the conversations between the Minister and his advisors and the minutes which passed between them would give us the real light. One can scarcely criticise the Commission because its members already knew something about the subject, as nearly all of them did; and if Loch and Octavia Hill were already committed to some general views—in their case to the

[149]Bill 213, clause 17.
[150]Bill 213, clause 17 (I) (e).

Victorian virtue of thrift—so were Beatrice Webb and Lansbury. Booth's view was hardening but his prestige and knowledge of social investigation were very great. Perhaps too many of them were very senior people, whose experience of the Poor Law may have made it difficult for them to see it from the outside and who, though sharing the new concern with the social question, had not been caught up by the fresher ways of thinking about it. As the Committee on *Physical Deterioration* showed, civil servants left on their own to deal with a problem not involving any single department could do a first-rate job, but the inclusion with members of the public of four high officers of the Local Government Boards of England, Ireland and Scotland on a body which was to examine the efficiency of administration and policy within their departmental field was, in spite of their special knowledge, questionable. In the outcome, as we have seen, on matters in which there was no exclusive Poor Law responsibility, e.g. labour exchanges and unemployment insurance, both official and independent members did move out to wider views.

Secondly, there were differences of approach. As the Chairman, Lord Hamilton[151] wrote, there was much in common between the two Reports on matters of substance. The revolutionary proposal that the time-honoured bodies, the Boards of Guardians, should be abolished was backed by both, the Majority declaring severely that the system of direct election for this special purpose had not prevented deception, dishonest contracting and conspiracy to defraud the ratepayers, nor provided representatives of proper quality. Both wanted counties and county boroughs to be the units of administration, both condemned the general mixed workhouse, the lack of classification, the inadequacy and lack of outdoor relief, etc. But his comment that both Reports were explicit in condemning a system of mere deterrence and in urging that in the new processes of treatment relief should be accompanied by a conscious attempt to remove the causes of distress,[152] concealed fundamental differences. To the

---

[151]*Poor Law Scotland;* 1909, Cd. 4922, xxxvii, p. 383.

[152]At the end even Beatrice Webb realised that she had been too sweeping in her attitude to the Majority Report, that they had come a long way from deterrence and that she had misread the situation. *Our Partnership,* p. 426 (entry for 27 Feb. 1909).

181

Majority the various types of cases—the infirm, able-bodied, sick, widows, etc.—had one common characteristic, they were applicants for State assistance who should be helped back to independence. They should therefore all be looked after by new statutory Public Assistance Committees of the county and county boroughs, aided by close working with co-ordinated voluntary charitable agencies, which should be represented upon them. To the Minority the most important features of these categories were those that distinguished them. They should not be treated by a general destitution authority, but the Poor Law should be broken up and each class dealt with by the authority dealing with their basic problem—the children by the education authority, the sick by the health authority and so on. And they set out new principles of relief: prevention—the State should step in at an early stage; compulsion—for just as the State had a right to compel in the case of infectious disease, it had equally the right to insist in the interests of the recipient and the community that a man following a course of life which would run him down economically into a state of dependence should follow its guidance; universal provision—the services must be offered to all who required them and not to applicants only; charge and recovery—those who could afford to pay should be assessed according to proper rules (scales, as we now call them) by a special officer.

But thirdly, in this branch of the problem the contributions of the department and the civil servants were different from those made in formulating either unemployment or health insurance. For they and the Minister were hostile to the 'Minority principles'. Of its permanent officers one, Dr Downes, a member of the Commission, in a most obscurantist memorandum of dissent[153] declared his disagreement not only with the Minority's proposals, but those of the Majority as well. From the five days' evidence by J S Davy, the L.G.B.'s official witness, some grim statements of the need for deterrence can be extracted. Yet to understand what he was talking about one must carry one's mind back to conditions as he saw them. If one remembers the mass of chronically under-employed having to

[153]*Poor Laws and Relief of Distress*, R. Com. Majority Rep., pp. 671–6; 1909, Cd. 4499, xxxvii. 8vo ed., Maj. Rep., II. 279–86.

snatch at any sort of income, the lax administration he saw during his weekly attendances at Guardians' meetings, his belief that women's trades were kept going in London on low wages plus out-door relief doles,[154] one can see the origin of his fears of opening the flood gates of pauperisation: were these not the very conditions which produced it? Nor was this entirely fanciful, for not only the Majority, but even the Minority had been moved to propose—strange as it sounds to modern ears—not only voluntary re-training centres, but compulsory detention colonies of a disciplinary type for persons convicted of neglect to maintain their families or failure to apply for assistance if destitute, etc. During his stay in London in 1902, Lenin himself had spotted this problem[155] of the *lumpen proletarians*. But the conclusion Davy drew, that the degree of pauperism was regulated by administration,[156] was undermined by the Commission's special investigators, who showed that its causes lay in infirmity, under-employment, casual employment, ill-health and lack of industrial training. If the aim of the Board's officers was, as it appears to have been, to get rid of the Boards of Guardians, then they miscalculated. What would have happened if the Minister had been willing, like Winston Churchill, who had written openly in support of the Minority principles, to break new ground and to throw the departmental weight into those scales, one can only speculate.

Fourthly, there was the matter of tactics, both during the Commission's proceedings and after their Reports were issued. For the failure to produce a unanimous report some, not very fairly, blamed the chairman. Beatrice Webb, quicker and more experienced in investigation than many of her fellow-members, was a very awkward colleague,[157] even going to the length of securing private funds to conduct without their knowledge, an investigation into the Boards

[154]See his answer, qq. 2925, 2932.

[155]Krupskaya, *Memories of Lenin,* p. 50 and note.

[156]See his answers to George Lansbury, q. 346; also qq. 244, 248.

[157]See the instructive and amusing notes in her diary on her scheming and conduct. In her more restrained account in *Poor Law History,* part ii, she says it might have been better had the chairman been an experienced lawyer, though one doubts if a mere lawyer could have kept Mrs Webb in order.

of Guardians. She undoubtedly stimulated special inquiries which produced decisive evidence, but she was not in any case notably accommodating to ideas other than her own, and for all her skill in and insistence on scientific investigation, held her own conclusions with passionate conviction. It may have nettled some members that Sidney Webb, not a member of the Commission, was helping to draft the Minority Report.[158] Added to that, bringing up the Minority Reports, particularly that on Scotland, at so late a stage in the Commission's discussions that the Majority had no opportunity to reply to criticisms of the ideas contained in them, drew a protest from the chairman in a special Memorandum.[159] But Webb had done this before to the *Labour* Commission and had called forth a similar protest.[160] What would have happened if the weight of evidence had been marshalled behind an agreed report? Did the failure to do this make no difference?[161]

After the Reports were issued, the Webbs certainly made the running. They not only put out a cheap edition of the Minority Report, claiming that as it was in Sidney's handwriting the copyright belonged to him, but with the aid of a specially formed association which soon had 25,000 members and a vast amount of enthusiastic support, ran a great campaign in favour of it. Yet that campaign, though greatly stimulating opinion, failed in its immediate purpose. It was bound to emphasise the difference between the two Reports, some strong centres of opposition remained, and then controversy was pushed off the stage by the great struggles on the House of Lords' veto and on health insurance. Although, therefore, the Majority, the Minority and apparently the L.G.B. all wanted the Boards of Guardians to be abolished, they did not get it, nor did the Minority secure the break-up of the Poor Law they had demanded.

[158]It is impossible to say what parts were played by Beatrice and Sidney Webb in some of their joint projects. In this case the accounts by Pease, *History of the Fabian Society,* pp. 212–24, and by Margaret Cole in *Beatrice Webb* (1945), p. 99, do not completely tally.

[159]*Poor Law Scotland,* R. Com., pp. 283–4; 1909, Cd. 4922, xxxviii.

[160]*Labour Commission,* R. Com. Final Rep., p. 7; 1894, C. 7421, xxxv.

[161]The preface to the *New Poor Law or No Poor Law* issued from Toynbee Hall comments, 'It is impossible not to feel keen regrets that the Commission did not arrive at an unanimous report . . . having so many points of agreement, the Commission seems to have risked a good deal of popular mis-apprehension when they failed to produce any statement of conclusions signed by all their members.'

Perhaps the situation could be described by saying that while the Majority had come on a good way from deterrence, they were still ten years behind the movement of much expert, just as the Minority were in advance of much effective public opinion. At any rate, by 1917 what had seemed revolutionary and contentious in the Minority's proposals to break up the Poor Law cases and other various categories, had come to be mere common sense and without fuss the Maclean Committee on the *Transfer of Functions,* 1917, which contained two protagonists from the Majority and Beatrice Webb from the Minority, proposed a unanimous compromise to break up the Poor Law, while retaining some of the Majority's proposals. But it was not implemented until 1929. This was a long wait.

5. THEORIES IN ACTION—II

i. *The Finance of Reform: Super-Tax, Land Taxes*

When the Liberals won the election on Free Trade coupled with social reform, they set themselves a financial challenge which seemed of the first magnitude. Joseph Chamberlain had at first linked his proposals for food taxes and imperial preference with the use of the proceeds for social reforms, and even when they developed into full-scale protection it was still implied that this 'broadening of the basis of taxation' would provide the means for that end. The realisation of the social visions of the times was thus bound up with the details of finance, but the discussions about these were anything but dull. The Liberal social programme and with it the fate of the Party and Government, was dependent on the success in finding the money within the Free Trade system. Asquith[162] explicitly accepted this. But the policy was vulnerable to two influences outside their control. Their traditional party policy of economy, to which they were electorally committed at the time, meant economy in armaments. But before long the German menace meant more armaments and a bigger navy, whilst John Fisher's revolutionary mechanisation of it made it fantastically expensive. Secondly, they were very

[162]H.C. Debates, 4th ser., CLXXII (18 April 1907), cols. 1191–92.

dependent on the course of the trade cycle. For the first couple of years trade and revenue grew, but the recession of 1907-08 produced a budget deficit just as the increased social liabilities were being undertaken. What was the nature and origin of the concepts with which this problem was tackled?

By the time of Asquith's third budget it was already plain that the social programme alone precluded any substantial or permanent reduction in the level of taxation, so that the whole question of taxable capacity arose in two forms: the equity of existing taxes, particularly income tax, and the possible new sources of revenue within the Free Trade system. The outcome was, first, the incorporation of new principles into a reformed income tax, which not only increased its yield, but made it of itself an engine of social reform, and secondly, the imposition of a long-run tax which turned out to be a disappointment of cherished hopes and a complete failure.

For many years there had been discussion on the differentiation and graduation of income tax, as it came to be realised that from a tax point of view one income of £1,000 is not always the same as another income of £1,000, and that an income of £1,000 might be more than twice an income of £500. The public mind had already been prepared by Harcourt's conversion to the principle of graduation as far as death duties were concerned, by the radical view that small incomes should pay less and large incomes more on the ground that £1 in tax meant a greater sacrifice in one case than the other, a contention to which economists gave scientific sanction by conclusions drawn from diminishing marginal utility of income; and by Cannan's pointing out (1888) that capital gains were untaxed,[163] and by the economist's technical discussions, e.g. on whether it was possible to devise a simple formula for a progressive tax which would be reasonable for modest incomes without ending in confiscation of very large ones.[164] Although on both sides of the House there had been a growing realisation that a uniform tax at the 'high' rate of one shilling could not be justified in a permanent peace-time tax, there was some confusion between graduation according to size of income and differentiation between incomes of different character—

[163]E Cannan, *Elementary Political Economy* (1888), p. 41.
[164]G Cassel in *Econ. Jn.*, XI (1901).

earned and unearned, permanent and precarious. And in popular debate 'earned' and 'unearned' became mixed up with questions of moral merit, of which the contemporary satirical cartoons of bloated cigar-smoking capitalists sitting on sacks of 'unearned' money are evidence. But graduation meant the abandonment of the efficient system of deduction at the source by which two-thirds of the proceeds were collected, and its replacement by personal declaration of total income.

The Dilke Select Committee, 1906,[165] to which these difficulties were referred, confined itself mainly to expert witnesses. It was not fully unanimous, as the draft reports, counter-reports and amendments recorded in its proceedings show, but their proposals led to decisive choices of policy. On some points, e.g. retaining a single income tax and on super-tax, they rejected the evidence tendered by the expert civil servants, Primrose, chairman, and Mallet, a member of the Board of Inland Revenue.[166] First, for 'permanent' and 'precarious' which they had been asked to investigate, they substituted 'earned' and 'unearned'. Secondly, they ignored Continental experience pressed on them by Mallet, and turned their backs on that of the Netherlands, where the economist statesman N G Pierson's reforms had resulted in two separate taxes which took care of both graduation and differentiation, one on labour incomes and the other on the value of property—a wealth tax, as we now call it—which, as revived discussions on it show, might have been useful in a country where the ownership of wealth was very concentrated. Instead, determined to maintain deduction at source, their proposals meant grafting the two principles of differentiation and graduation on to the existing tax,[167] a course to which Mallet had objected.[168]

[165]*Income Tax,* Sel. Cttee. Rep., Proc., Mins. of ev., 1906 (365) ix.

[166]Dilke's draft report in the proceedings of the Committee gives a careful statement of their views, e.g. para. 36, p. xxii, and that of other witnesses, e.g. Labour Party's evidence, para. 46.

[167]Mallet says that some of the Committee came with their minds already made up, and he regarded Asquith's decision as following the more conservative members. *British Budgets,* 1887–1913, p. 280.

[168]Mallet objected to trying to do both in one tax (ev., q. 419) and Primrose to a separate super-tax. See the latter's second day's evidence (q. 3259, Memo paras. 12–21). Seligman in 1921 concluded that the combination into one tax had succeeded in accomplishing everything really needed for progressive taxation, without its dangers. *The Income Tax* (1921), p. 217.

Asquith followed the first in 1907 by reducing the tax on earned incomes under £2,000 to 9d, and Lloyd George the second, when he declined to introduce full graduation because of its interference with deduction at source, but added a super-tax, based on personal declaration, of a uniform 6d on the amount by which incomes over £5,000 exceeded £3,000. The tax had thus become not merely a device for raising money neutral as between unequal incomes, but an instrument for the positive correction of inequalities of income.

There was also a small acknowledgement that two equal incomes do not necessarily have the same taxable capacity, if one has to meet inescapable burdens, e.g. supporting children, the other does not. When Lloyd George raised the foundation rate of tax to 1s 2d, he gave to incomes under £500 an abatement of taxable income of £10 a year for every child under sixteen. To regard this minute sum of seven shillings and sixpence a year as a primitive family allowance granted at the expense of the Treasury to income tax payers but not to those with incomes below tax level, would be nonsensical. An income tax takes money away from the taxpayer, and the concession was simply a recognition, of significance for the future, that equal sacrifice might require equal incomes to have unequal amounts taken away by taxes. Differences of taxability of persons with the same income which did not matter when the rate was ninepence, became important when the normal rate rose to five shillings as in 1916. It was a step to transforming the tax on income to what it eventually became, a personal tax closely related to individual circumstances.

There remained the question of new sources of taxation, within the Free Trade system. There were many suggestions, Chiozza Money's that the State should nationalise mines and railways to secure their profits reading a little oddly now when it has had to wipe off hundreds of millions of debts of both! The principles of graduation and differentiation having been established, when the budget crisis came Lloyd George probably could have raised income tax and death duties without too much opposition. He chose instead to introduce a new set of land taxes which aroused the fiercest controversy, led the House of Lords to reject the budget and so to a grave constitutional crisis which certainly gave the voters two exciting electoral battles to fight. He had early made it plain that he regarded the social reforms as only the beginning of 'the war on poverty' and therefore needed some tax which would not damp enterprise, but would provide a source of revenue expanding over the years. Where was it to be found? For radicals there had been an answer ever since Adam Smith had said that the landlord reaped where he did not sow, Ricardo that his interest was opposed to that of every other class in the community, and J S Mill that he grew rich in his sleep, without working, risking or economising. Henry George's campaign for the single tax on land values created by the community's general efforts and progress had caught the imagination of all classes to a degree now difficult to realise. It led A R Wallace to *Land Nationalisation* (1882), a demand repeated by T.U.C. in 1907. It led radicals, such as Hobson and Hobhouse, to declare that the socially created values should belong to the community.[169] The economists on whose views the Royal Commission on *Local Taxation* took a detailed census,[170] favoured the principle, Marshall pointing out that land, though not a true monopoly, had some of the characteristics of one.[171] The problem was how to strike at true economic rent and the landlord without penalising the improvements nearly always incorporated with land and the people who made them. Was the increase in value of a site to be taken as excess above 'prairie value' or above its value with all its buildings and services around it? There were many technical discussions amongst economists on whether and on what conditions such a tax would fall on the landlord, the leaseholder, or the occupier.[172] As we have seen, in terms of public policy a tax on betterment, the rise of values due to specific public works, was clear in theory though not easy in practice.[173] The general case had been stated by O'Connor in a

[169]For the Conservative view, see Lord Hugh Cecil, *Conservatism* (1912), pp. 132–40.

[170]*Classification and Incidence of Imperial and Local Taxes*, Memos. See answers of the various authors to qq. 9–13; 1899, C. 9528, xxxvi.

[171]Ibid., pp. 115–17.

[172]For example, Edgeworth's own articles in *Papers Relating to Political Economy*, II, 126–223; J S Nicholson, *Elements of Political Economy* (1909), pp. 461–70.

[173]See above, p. 62.

Minority Report of the Commission on *Trade Depression*[174] and in the Report of the Commission on *Local Taxation*.[175]

Urban areas saw in the rating of local site values an answer to their growing problems and many Bills to provide for this were introduced; and Minority Reports of the Commission on *Local Taxation* (signed by the Chairman, Balfour of Burleigh)[176] and of the Kempe Departmental Committee on *Local Taxation* (1914)[177] supported this form of proposal. Radical newspapers published maps of London showing how it was divided between ground landlords being enriched in their sleep and detailed the fantastic sums they charged for the reversion of leases. A kind of mirage developed of the vast sums such a tax would yield, despite early warning by Cannan[178] who commented on the 'paltry' sum of £100 million Chiozza Money had estimated as the whole total of land rents, and by the Balfour Commission Minority, who thought site rating desirable and practicable, but the estimates of yield exaggerated. There was thus reason in terms of current demand for social justice and economic argument to explain Lloyd George's determination to tax this source by his four land taxes: a duty of 20 per cent on the increment value of land, 10 per cent on the reversion values of leases, a half-penny in the one pound on the value of undeveloped land and a tax on the rental value of mineral lands. It involved an expensive initial national valuation of land and the yield was not expected immediately but, in accordance with the theory, in the future.[179] This attack on a traditional form of wealth led to the cry of 'revolutionary', used as abuse by the Budget Protest League and approval by the Budget League; and what was really serious, a determined, organised and skilfully led and finally successful opposition by landowners' bodies taking every advantage of the intricacies of the

[174]*Depression of Trade and Industry*, R. Com., sect. 10 of O'Connor's separate Report; 1886, C. 4893, xxiii.

[175]*Local Taxation*, R. Com. Final Rep., pp. 178–81; 1901, C. 638, xxiv.

[176]Ibid., pp. 151–76.

[177]*Local Taxation*, Dept. Cttee.; 1914, Cd. 7315, xl; separate Rep. on *Rating and Land Values*. For reasons against, see Majority Rep., p. 10.

[178]E Cannan, review of Money's *Riches and Poverty* in *Econ. Jn.* (1906). Arnold Toynbee had earlier given a realistic warning in *Progress and Poverty, a Criticism* (1883), pp. 37–9,

[179]In both respects following J S Mill, *Principles of Political Economy*, bk. V, chap. ii, sect. 5.

English law of property and fighting every possible case in the Courts.[180] For these reasons, contrary to the enchanting visions which had been entertained, by 1914 the actual yield was still less than three-quarters of a million, and as a result of adverse legal decisions one duty had to be completely abandoned and others partially. In 1920, the experiment, which had filled so many minds and nourished so many hopes, was brought to an end. The taxes had not succeeded in bringing in money for reform nor established justice.

ii. *Economic Organisation and Development*

(*a*) *Agriculture.* The third branch of policy concerned the improvement of economic organisation, the significance of which as a means of supporting social reforms by raising productivity was fully perceived by the radicals.[181] But not much was done, for the battles over the social reforms, the waste of Parliamentary time on Bills which the House of Lords rejected, the constitutional crisis and the two elections over the veto, the Irish troubles, etc., left little time for it. Some proposals, including those which fell by the wayside, indicate the kind of design which was emerging. The basic principle was still free enterprise, but the criticisms of the competitive order exposed areas where it was failing; there were areas of neglect of essential development, areas where competition was deemed wasteful, but equally areas where monopoly restricted output and gave powers of extortion to a few or, as in the case of land monopoly, which frustrated the principle that if every man were to be ensured the means of maintaining himself, he must have access to the means of production. The agricultural labourer, for example, could not rise to independence without it. The Liberal Party, straddled between the extreme adherents to free enterprise on the one hand and vigorous

---

[180]*Land Values*, Sel. Cttee. Rep., Proc., Mins. of ev.; 1920, Cmd. 556, xix. See notes on legal decisions in Memo. by Howell Thomas, Deputy Chief Valuer, pp. 13–15, 22–41. Note Mr Justice Scrutton's decision that, contrary to the Department's practice, full site value should not assume that the land was divested of grass and other things growing on it; it would therefore vary with the seasons.

[181]J A Hobson, *Crisis of Liberalism* (1909), pp. 159–63; Money, *Riches and Poverty*, chap. xviii.

collectivists on the other, was not fully ready theoretically to tackle many of these problems.

But in one sphere it made a start. The decline of agriculture, the agricultural worker's poor pay, his bad housing and lack of any opportunity to improve his position in the industry were 'emptying the countryside'.[182] For agriculture was a one-man business, and by its nature new sources of energy must come from within. It had been a matter of concern in the late eighties and nineties. Not economics only, but State policy had divorced the labourer from the soil. The full radical answer was not worked out until the exhaustive Report of the Liberal Land Enquiry came out in 1913,[183] when peace was nearly over. The old radical answer had been embodied in the slogan used by Jesse Collings—'three acres and a cow'—and this had envisaged the creation of an independent, land-owning peasantry.[184] But this was taken over by the conservatives, willing to see the growth of a new property-owning group. Their 1892 Small Holdings Act empowered county councils to purchase holdings, sell them to applicants who were to pay one-fifth in spot cash and the rest in instalments. The Act was a complete failure. By 1902 only 569 acres had been bought by councils, only 162 sold to occupiers, the rest having had to be let to tenants. Quite apart from the real dislike of it by the farming community and the county councils the landed interests controlled, it was obvious that after paying the one-fifth the small holder would have little left for the necessary working capital. It would pay him better to take a tenancy of a larger farm and use his capital to work it. There were thus sound economic as well as social and political reasons why the Liberals should set out to create not a peasantry, but a State tenantry. The Act of 1907 made it a duty of county councils to provide small holdings and gave them powers of compulsory purchase. But the land monopoly was not so easily broken. Large farms came on to the market as working units, with their buildings; could these be economically broken up and areas

---

[182]The facts were gathered together officially in Sir R H Rew's notable Report on *Decline in the Agricultural Population of Great Britain, 1881–1906*, 1906, Cd. 3273, xcvi.

[183]Land Enquiry Committee, *The Land* (1913), I (Rural).

[184]*Labour*, R. Com. Final Rep., Collings's observations, pp. 122–3; 1894, C. 7421, xxxv.

hived off for small holdings? And it is quite clear that there was a considerable pressure on prospective applicants by farmers unwilling to lose labour.[185] Further, a profit of £2 to £3 an acre on a farm of 30 acres yielded only £60 to £90, but on 500 acres, £1,000 to £1,500, which meant that a small holder brought up on a large farm had to turn to a different type of farming. The significance of two other major features of the Land Enquiry's proposals—a minimum wage for agricultural labourers high enough to enable him to pay a commercial rent for a cottage, security of tenure for tenant farmers and land courts to fix their rents—lay in the future.

(*b*) *Economic development.* This step was supplemented by another, imaginative in principle if not in scale, the full potentialities of which current problems are making us realise. This was the establishing of a Development Fund and Commission which, as the name implies, was to aid essential projects which private enterprise had neglected or ignored. In his 1909 Budget speech Lloyd George explained that though labour exchanges and unemployment insurance were a help, they did not solve the problem of unemployment. It was not the business of the Government to create work, but it was an essential part of its duty to see that the people were equipped to make the best use of the country's resources. With the example of Denmark much in mind, he established the fund with an annual grant of £1½ million to assist in establishing schools to train forestry officers, purchase of land for forestry experiments, land reclamation, agricultural research institutes, marketing, fisheries.[186] That a good deal was expected from it ultimately is shown by Clause 18 of the governing Act,[187] which, following Bowley's proposals to regularise the demand for labour by reverse timing of public expenditure, required the Commission, if its projects employed labour on a substantial scale, to have regard to the state and prospects of employment. Sidney Webb was one of the Commissioners. The complication of British administration,[188] limited funds, and the short span of time

[185]*The Land*, I, 217–29. *Small Holdings in Great Britain*, Minority Rep.; 1906, Cd. 3277, lv. *Breviate*, I, 72–3.
[186]*Parl. Debates*, 5th ser., IV (29 April 1909).
[187]Development and Road Improvement Funds Act, 1909.
[188]Development Commission, 1st Ann. Rep., pp. 7–9, 1911 (199) xv.

A First Solution

before the war broke out limited the scale of its operations and meant that it did not grow into the major stimulus some had hoped for; but it settled down into a useful and permanent function, exercised for fifty years, in stimulating the scientific background of agricultural and other developments.

(c) *Ambivalent attitude to trusts.* On the issue of competition and monopoly the attitude was ambivalent. The 'wastes of competition' suggested larger business units, but if larger business units became near-monopolies, how were they to be regulated? Should the State try to insist on competition and if so, how? But this was putting new questions. For the traditional English attitude amongst economic theorists and politicians had been that free competition was good for efficient producers and for consumers, and though this meant that the world was a harsh one for weak, high-cost units, to the confident and vigorous Victorians this was a necessary part of the process. The Royal Commission on *Depression of Trade and Industry* (1886) heard many complaints, from trade unionists as well as manufacturers, on the ill-effects of competition, but there was no large-scale attempt to limit it by combinations. Even in 1906 in England combinations had not grown to anything like the scale of those in the U.S.A. and in Germany. For potential monopolists were not protected from competition by a tariff, freights were low so that there was no 'natural protection of distance', we had no substantial mineral resources which could be monopolised, and in many ranges of high-grade goods in which we were pioneers competition kept prices low, and a rise could be checked by consumers reverting to lower qualities.

But the facts were beginning to change. Macrosty's studies in *The Trust Movement in British Industry* (1907) showed that the tendency to combine was at work in a number of industries where conditions made it profitable, but also made it clear that these combinations often ran into difficulties, that not all were successful, and there were large competitive areas not in the least affected. Perhaps it could be said that when they were successful they were based on concentration, i.e. the economics of large-scale production, rather than attempts to secure monopoly profits without it. In the view of the

194

time, these economics of scale were best ensured by Free Trade, which permitted their advantages while checking any monopoly. The contrast between the giant combines in protectionist U.S.A. and Germany and the relatively small amount of combination in England seemed to clinch the matter. We had no anti-trust legislation like the American Sherman Act, 1890, and until two special cases came up after 1906—the third, the railways, being perennial—there had not even been any Parliamentary inquiry into a trust or monopoly.

English opinion, therefore, lagged behind the facts, not so much perhaps as they were but as they were becoming. Although economists, e.g. Marshall (1890) and Edgeworth, had worked out the theory of monopoly, its effect on prices, output and the distribution of resources, and the consequences of taxes on monopoly profits, we had done much less thinking on the practical problems of regulation than had U.S.A. or Germany, compared with whose voluminous literature ours was relatively sparse. The penetrating work of J A Hobson, Jeans (though these two relied mainly on American and German examples), Macrosty and D H Macgregor[189] was in the main fairly recent and there had been insufficient time for their ideas to work their way into detailed techniques of regulation or into prescriptions in a form a politician might seize upon. Macrosty did indeed review the methods of control in his Fabian tract (1905), notably including counter-monopolies, but his studies also set out the contemporary limits—e.g. public opinion, lack of government skill—to the effectiveness of some of them. On the other hand, the small body of collectivist opinion, starting from the economies of scale, that is from the way in which English combinations were growing, thought that as they grew and management turned into administration, they should be taken over by the State, central and local. But they were thinking of technological monopolies, such as

---

[189] J A Hobson's *Evolution of Modern Capitalism* (1894) and J S Jeans's *Trusts, Pools and Corners* (1894) draw their examples almost solely from America, but in Hobson's revised edition, 1906, some English material is inserted. H W Macrosty, Fabian Tracts, no. 88 (1899), no. 124 (1905); *The Trust Movement in British Industry* (1907). D H Macgregor, *Industrial Combination* (1906). F W Hirst in *Monopolies, Trusts and Kartels* (1905) contended that the possibility of imports made it impossible for an English combination to raise prices above international level, and that to dictate prices an English trust would have to be international (pp. 169–70).

trams, water, gas, electricity (which in fact not only 'labour' but 'conservative' councils alike often municipalised) rather than of the kind of industries and overseas trading in which combinations were coming into being.[190] English opinion was not therefore fully equipped to meet these problems. It flared up quite unreasonably over the accusation that Lever was forming a monopolistic soap trust, which he was not, yet accepted the Imperial Tobacco Company's reservation of the home market after a struggle with the American trust over Ogdens, not as a monopolistic operation, but as a defeat of the American trust.

There was an outcry when it was feared that the American Swift-Armour meat combination had agreed to divide the country into competitive and non-competitive areas, to open retail shops to drive out competition and to operate a black list. But the Committee of Enquiry was not asked to make any recommendations.[191] A similar outcry that the Shipping Conferences had on certain routes and in certain trades created a monopoly power by 'tying' shippers through deferred rebates, led to the 1909 investigation.[192] The Majority, however, justified them as the remedy for ruinous freight wars and as a means of ensuring regular scheduled services, and decided that any attempt to make them illegal could be evaded by the use of other monopolistic practices. They were not prepared to recommend a legal prohibition of all such combinations. Any evils could be abated by encouraging the formation of counter-combinations of shippers to bargain over rates. On the other hand, the Minority felt that only anti-trust legislation on the lines of the Sherman Act

---

[190]Obvious reasons of State security as well as technological advantages had already, before 1906, led both parties to accept national telegraphs (1870) and the Conservatives in 1905 to negotiate the agreement to take over the National Telephone Company. But in 1902 an Inter-Departmental Committee on *Cable Communications,* while desiring an all-British route, wanted 'free trade in cables' and rejected a suggestion of State purchase—a concession to strong cable interests which became important in 1924–28. The notion of an imperial wireless chain which then came up involved no new principle, the inquiries being about which technical system was best and the scandals surrounding the Marconi Agreement. See *Breviate,* I, 19–20, 175–6, 177, 178, 180.

[191]*Combinations in the Meat Trade,* Dept. Cttee. Rep.; 1909, Cd. 4643, xv. *Breviate,* I, 82–3.

[192]*Shipping Rings and Deferred Rebates,* R. Com. Rep.; 1909, Cd. 4668, xlvii. *Breviate,* I, 159–62.

would really suffice, but for the time being wanted the encouragement of shippers' associations and supervision by the Board of
Trade. One member argued that the legal prohibition of deferred
rebates would end in rings. The evidence of R D Holt, ship-owning
Liberal M.P., illustrates the owner's point of view. To the Chairman's question (q. 16,970) 'Then the shipping trade illustrates the
Marxian theory that competition kills competition?' he replied,
'Yes'. But deferred rebates he regarded as essential if regular services
were to be run, and it was impossible to fix rates by arbitration:
owners and shippers were buyers and sellers and there was no reason
to interfere with them.[193]

The railways presented a similar dilemma. On the State regulation
of them we had a longer experience, but they were now in difficulties,
for while there were limits on their charges, their wage bills and
other costs were rising. One has to carry one's mind back to pre-
motor-car days to realise how much their monopoly powers were
still feared. They were denounced for giving undue preferential
treatment to foreign produce, for using their powers to ruin coastal
shipping, for entering into working agreements over charges, services and traffic allocation at the expense of the public, for buying
up and sterilising canals,[194] for high charges and inefficiency compared with certain Continental railways.[195] The problem was put to
the 1911 Committee on *Railway Agreements and Amalgamations* by
Marwood, of the Board of Trade. Railways could not be compelled
to compete (qq. 653–4), and legislation could aim either at regulating
the power to make agreements or at preventing the possible bad
effects of agreements (q. 528). The Committee itself concluded (para.
185) that the more complete elimination of competition which the
improvement of railways required was inevitable, and would benefit
both the companies and the public if properly safeguarded. This
protection could not be given by regulating agreements, but by

[193]Ibid., Mins. of ev., qq. 16,765, Statement 4, 17,070–71; 1909, Cd. 4685, xlviii.

[194]For these allegations see *Railway Rates (Preferential) Treatment,* Dept. Cttee. Rep.;
1906, Cd. 2959, lv. *Railway Conference,* 1909, Cd. 4677, lxxvii. *Railway Agreements and
Amalgamations,* Dept. Cttee. Rep.; 1911, Cd. 5631, xxix, pt. ii. *Canals and Waterways,* R.
Com. Final Rep.; 1910, Cd. 4979, xii. *Breviate,* I, 145–7, 150–2.

[195]Money, *Riches and Poverty,* chap. xviii.

O

legislation dealing with any injurious consequences. On neither
shipping nor railways, therefore, was prohibition of agreements
deemed feasible. For the latter alternative of nationalisation drew
nearer, two Ministers, Lloyd George and Churchill, giving it support,
while the Royal Economic Society was moved to arrange a special
congress on the problem.[196] Acworth, then our leading expert in
railway economics, the grounds of whose opposition to it then
seemed conservative but now have something of the air of prophecy,
declared that in democratic countries nationalisation corrupted railways, was a financial failure, that comparing like with like private
lines offered the lowest fares and cheapest rates, and that the public
would suffer. We had relied upon competition, which was now
being withdrawn, and since no one had really tried to work out
what the new form of State regulation should be, how and to what
extent it was to be applied and made flexible, nationalisation appeared
to be inevitable.[197] But this was not a conclusion likely to commend
itself to the very influential group of railway M.P.s; especially as
they had been coerced by Lloyd George over their dealings with
trade unions. On the other hand the fantastically exhaustive inquiry
into Canals and Inland Waterways,[198] set up partly because of the
charge that railways had bought up separate stretches of canals to
stifle competition, to make through routes impossible and through
rates difficult to quote, came to a different conclusion. Noting the
success of the German canals, the Commission recommended that
the differences of gauge, locks and multiplicity of authorities not
financially strong enough to undertake extensive improvements
should now be dealt with by concentrating on the four main traffic
routes of the 'Cross'. These, including the railway-owned canals,
should be taken over by a central waterway board, amalgamated
and widened to take 100-ton barges. But this overlooked the fact
that whereas on the Continent there were huge inland areas with a

[196]*State in Relation to Railways* (Royal Economic Society, 1912).

[197]A M Acworth in *State in Relation to Railways,* chap. i. The Labour Party's Bill,
Nationalisation of Canals and Railways (Bill 326, 1908) was simply a means of securing
a debate in the House, but its proposals that the L.G.B. should take over and appoint
a board of control of not less than 50 nor more than 100 persons showed that they had
not got very far in thinking.

[198]*Canals and Waterways,* see *Breviate,* I, 145-7.

relatively small mileage of coastline, in Britain there was a small inland area with many miles of coastline and few large producing or consuming centres very distant from a port; and the seaways were naturally provided and the cost of traction low. One project, however, did come to fruition. The Port of London was in danger of losing its relative position both in U.K. trade and as compared with the Continental ports then being extended and modernised. The several dock companies were unable to finance the necessary substantial improvements, and after long and many bickerings over a number of years between the dock companies, the shippers, the warehouses, the L.C.C. and the Government,[199] armed with the new political majority Lloyd George was able at last to create a new Port of London Authority in the form of a public trust representative of payers of dues, wharfingers and public bodies which took over some of these tasks and was financed by the issue of fixed interest securities.[200]

Neither on the railways, canals, trusts nor shipping rings was anything done: problems and proposals went into cold storage till after the war. These industries were powerfully represented in the Party, so that there were conflicts of interests as well as ideas. It is idle to speculate on whether and how, if war had not come, it would have been able to resolve them. But apart from that, it does not seem clear that with so many storms and cross-currents, the political and administrative machine would have been able to manage more major battles simultaneously. But together with the legal decision in the case of the *Mogul Steamship Company* v. *McGregor,* that a shipping ring's acts to damage and drive an independent rival out of the trade was not unlawful, this meant that in the interim, in practice if not intent, *laissez-faire* meant *laissez-faire* for organised trading groups as well as for individuals.

CONCLUSION

The examples already examined in detail, some of which were associated with two Ministers particularly, do not complete the tale, for the effort extended to a number of other fields for which differ-

---

[199]Memo to the Bill, 1908 (109) xciii. This gives the history of some of the bills.
[200]Port of London Act, 1908.

ent Ministers, e.g. Herbert Gladstone and Samuel, were responsible. And these measures also were based on wider conceptions of social concern. The 'accidents' for which a workman might claim compensation were enlarged to include not only accidents in the ordinary sense, but injuries due to slowly developing industrial diseases; the limitation of the hours of work which applied in factories could be extended to shop assistants only if working owners were themselves prevented from serving by enforcing early closing hours. The *Probation of Offenders Act,* 1907, made it possible for Courts to develop the voluntary work of the Police Court Missionary into a salaried service of professional probation officers.[201] Herbert Samuel, who as an undergraduate had had contact with the dockers, gathered up much current reform thinking into the *Children Act,* 1908, which provided for separate places of detention for child offenders, for juvenile courts, abolished some and modified other primitive punishments, protected infants put out to nurse with foster-parents against the grosser forms of neglect and cruelty and established the State as a kind of over-parent able to remove ill-treated children from vicious parents or guardians. The selection of Justices of the Peace was made more businesslike and placed on a more democratic footing to ensure greater political impartiality and a wider representation of the classes.[202] Indeed, the number of points at which the old order was being broken into is surprising. 'It is remarkable,' wrote Keynes, in a just tribute to Asquith's generalship, 'looking back on the Liberal legislation of the eight years before the war, to see how abundant it was, yet how well chosen, and how completely on the whole it has stood the test of events.'[203]

While it was not to be expected that many changes necessary to bring English society into greater accord with the new ideals could be made in eight stormy pre-war years of the Liberal regime, there were some significant omissions. The demand for the equality and emancipation of women had long been a permanent element in some radical and socialist thought, e.g. Thompson's *Appeal of one Half*

[201]*Probation of Offenders Act,* 1907, Dept. Cttee. Rep.; 1910, Cd. 5001, xlv. *Breviate,* I.
[202]*Selection of the Justices of the Peace,* R. Com. Rep.; 1910, Cd. 5250, xxxvii. *Breviate,* I, 357–8.
[203]John M Keynes, *Essays in Biography* (1933), p. 51.

of the Human Race, Women, against the Pretensions of the Other Half, Men
(1825), and surged up again in the vigorous writings of Galsworthy,
Shaw and Wells, and in the performances of Ibsen's plays. It is a
nice comment on the extent to which this propaganda, so popular
and believed in with such conviction in some circles had *not* penetrated, that despite the violent agitation no substantial concession
was made by the Liberal Government to 'Votes for Women', that
for a time even the I.L.P. was divided and Beatrice Webb disapproved,[204] and that many solid trade unionists expected wives to
be true and subordinate. After three years' work, the Gorell Commission on *Divorce*[205] found that there was no general consensus
of religious opinion on the matter, most witnesses arguing from
general Christian principles and experience of life. The Majority
were able not only to recommend cheaper procedures in order to
reduce the increasing number of *de facto* separations amongst the
working classes unable to pay for divorce proceedings, but also to
propose to widen the grounds for divorce to include those generally
recognised as putting an end to married life, and that in this respect
women should be placed on equal footing with men. One does not
know what the fate of the report, not issued until the end of 1912,
would have been had the problems of Ireland and war not crowded
it out, but that there were strong centres of resistance is shown by
the fact that little was done about it for a couple of decades and that
by a private member's Bill. There were still bastions to be stormed.

What of the process viewed as a whole? Some doubts were expressed whether by 1912 or 1913 the urge to reform was already
exhausting itself. Two comments illustrate the grounds for such a
view. Laski, feeling that full liberty was impossible without equality,
despite the learning and acute analysis displayed in *The Decline of
Liberalism* (1940) allowed his occasional vein of Marxism of the
more naive kind and his proneness to phrase-making to lead him to
declare that Liberalism 'was prepared to be forced to be generous
when it was not prepared to be spontaneously just'. Whatever this
may mean, it is clearly a woefully inadequate account of the ethical

[204]B Webb, *Our Partnership,* pp. 360–1.
[205]*Divorce and Matrimonial Causes,* R. Com. Rep.; 1912–13, Cd. 6478, xviii. *Breviate,* I,
379.

impulses behind these efforts at social betterment; perhaps this was because he was not out of and did not fully understand some of the intellectual and ethical traditions in which they developed. In an earlier and more penetrating political assessment in 1909, when the Government was midway in its work, J A Hobson in *The Crisis of Liberalism* pointed out that when the Liberals came into power they had not formulated any organised policy of social reform, that their thinking had become specialised into particular channels, so that they were pragmatic, dealing with problems here and there and were not working on broad principles. In consequence, the question was whether the Party had the ability to work out a new positive policy based on a fresh conception of the functions of the State and to go on to tackle the organisation of mining, transport, the control of trusts and access to land. For by the application of the advantages of science and technology an intelligent people could abolish poverty. But this would require the shedding of the extreme individualists and convincing the great centre of the Party repelled by the materialistic and fatalistic dogmas of Continental Marxism.[206]

What are we to make of this? For it was precisely because at the time the Party had no highly organised doctrine and the ideas of Ministers had some flexibility, that constructive suggestions could come forward from such varied sources. It gave the opportunity to experts and civil servants, such as Llewellyn Smith, Beveridge and Braithwaite, not faced with hardened party doctrines and plans, to make original and decisive contributions; for Newsholme to point the way to develop the health services medically and Mallet to suggest a wealth tax, even though their advice was at the time rejected, and for the medical eugenists to carry their mental deficiency proposals. But the Labour Party also, spread in ideas between the solid trade union liberals and the socialists, had no comprehensive programme and indeed no common theory either. While pressing home the condition of the working class with ability, sincerity and urgency, in constructive thinking they could not compare in dash and bellicosity with Lloyd George and Churchill. Indeed, in 1920 the Webbs remarked that it was a misfortune that

[206]Anyone doubting that this impression of continental Marxism was widespread should read Bertrand Russell's *German Social Democracy* (1896).

during these years the Labour Party had not been able to place before the country the large outlines of an alternative programme based on the conception of a new social order.[207] (Though when in 1919 it did so, in a document largely drafted by Webb, this did not save them from heavy defeat.) And the one bit of well-discussed theory, on which Lloyd George acted—the taxation of land values— proved in practice to be ineffective. The truth is that no large influential group was yet ready with a new comprehensive theory, Ideas were still fluid. In some matters, e.g. unemployment, we did not yet have all the facts and—although Hobson himself lived up to his exhortation by a valiant effort to establish the theory of underconsumption—the theories of the trade cycle were still but tentative hypotheses. And it must be admitted that once the breakthrough was made and vital initial problems solved, it has proved much easier to expand the social services than to succeed in the harder task of making an effective assault on private enterprise by, to use Webb's phrase, eliminating the capitalist profit-maker in mines and railways and of turning them into economically self-supporting industries. The examples on which the optimistic hopes had been based—municipally owned public utilities—were the easy ones, technological monopolies with stable demand. And the conferment of large legal immunities on trade unions on the one hand and on the other the reliance on Free Trade to check the operations of monopolies and the failure to find other means of doing so, combined with the legal decisions sanctioning trade rings' attacks on independent rivals, meant that it was being recognised that the old doctrine of *laissez-faire* for individuals coped but awkwardly with the new fact—the activities of highly organised economic groups. There were thus a number of unsolved problems to be carried forward.

Finally, there was an element of millennialism in radical thinking of the time. As Leonard Woolf remarks in *Beginning Again* (1964),[208] 'in the decade before the 1914 war, there were political and social movements in the world, particularly in Europe and Britain, which seemed at the time hopeful and exciting. It seemed as if human

---

[207]*History of Trade Unionism* (1920), pp. 688–9.
[208]p. 36.

beings might really be on the brink of being civilised . . . the forces of barbarism and reaction were still there, but they were in retreat . . . We were, of course, mistaken . . . It was, I believe, touch and go whether the movement towards liberty and equality—political and social—and towards civilisation which was so strong in the first decade of the twentieth century, would become so strong as to carry everything before it.' This was the confident hope which helped to sustain the assault on the old order; and it was the forces outside it which brought the experiment, undertaken with so much intelligence, to its close.

Part IV

PLANNING AND FAILURE: A POST-MORTEM ON RECONSTRUCTION 1914–1924

A man's reach should exceed his grasp,
Or what's a Heaven for?

BROWNING

In the first place the practicability of our plans will not be
believed; and in the next place, supposing them to be most com-
pletely carried out, their desirability will be questioned. . . .
That is why I feel a reluctance to grapple with the subject, lest
I should be thought to be indulging in merely visionary speculation

PLATO

1. THE IDEALS AND PROCESSES OF RECONSTRUCTION

i. *Temporary Re-adjustment and Permanent Changes*

The efforts of 1906–14 had been entered upon without a prearranged plan, but nevertheless in certain fields successfully worked themselves into an intelligible design. 'Reconstruction' after the First World War was thought over and planned on a scale and with a thoroughness then without precedent in our history. In the preparation of the plans experts and contemporary knowledge had been drawn upon, the aid of 'men of goodwill' of all classes enlisted. The uneuphonious word itself came to have an emotional content, a millennialist quality not easy to convey to anyone who had not lived through those years. It meant not only re-adjusting a distorted economy and its physical rehabilitation, but infusing it with new social purposes.

The task of putting these old and new social ideals into practice was not, as in 1906 to 1914, that of inserting new pieces of machinery and a few new social principles into a substantially free enterprise economy, but into one geared for the first time to total war and cluttered up with all-pervasive Government institutions, prohibitions, restraints and operations, with the Government running the railways, canals and shipping, purchasing the bulk of many foods and industrial raw materials, and the only buyer of a substantial fraction of industry's products. It was therefore made more difficult by practical problems which the pre-war Liberal and radical reformers did not have to face. First, the simple change back from war to peace, to 'business as usual'. All governments were, in prospect, afraid of the transition. Of one problem, grand in scale, we had no relevant experience: the troubles after the Napoleonic Wars or the Boer War did not tell us how to demobilise millions of men, and to get them back into jobs with the tools and materials they needed, without dislocation, suffering and great discontent. And this at a time when a Labour newspaper, referring to events abroad, sold in Whitehall copies headed 'Crowns three a penny'. Though the incidents did not take place until depression had set in, the turbulence and 'occupation of workshops' by the unemployed, described in the early pages of Wal Hannington's *Unemployed Struggles* 1919–1936, showed what some of the possibilities had been. As it turned out, by almost accidental circumstances, this proved the easiest problem to deal with.

Secondly, what was to be done with the vast Government apparatus of control—should it be swept aside, how much, if any, was there any point in retaining? Was it a proved instrument which could be used for new, constructive ends of peace as well as the destructive purposes of war, or was it a self-expanding bureaucratic machine designed for specific war tasks and which would be nothing but an obstruction in normal economic life? When we had begun to put the machine together, much of the public and many of the Ministers had very rudimentary ideas of the economic realities which lay behind it, or how it 'worked in' with normal economic activity;

nor had all the clouds of misunderstanding dispersed when the final decisions about its future came to be made. For we entered the war not only militarily, but intellectually unprepared, with limited ideas of what it would involve. Angell's *Great Illusion* (1910) had argued that modern war could not 'pay', but naturally was not directed to showing what must be done to wage one successfully. Some Ministers had difficulty in grasping the distinction between money costs and real costs, declaring that to produce adequate supplies they were relying on placing war contracts at good prices, superimposed on normal demand. Runciman was still opposing the appointment of a food controller a year after the war had started, and some of the campaigns waged by newspapers from time to time suggested that some journalists or the owners of their papers must have been amongst the economically worst educated of the literate population.[1] The state of public economic thinking can be seen by comparing the Reports of the Committee on *Prices,* on *Meat, Milk* and *Bacon* and that on *Coal,*[2] with Cannan's review-criticism and his amusing article on the benefits of high prices.[3] For many particular problems the relevant propositions were but simple applications of the stock-in-trade of principles set out in the ordinary text-books—opportunity costs, elasticity of demand, etc. And a glance at Marshall's supply and demand schedules would have prevented many errors.[4] The way in which the consumers' purchasing power, freed when maximum prices were fixed, was diverted to other goods, for which maximum prices then had to be fixed, and in which non-rationed goods 'disappeared' from the market when they were given maximum prices, was a common contemporary source of mocking laughter. There was, however, some point in F W Hirst's complaint in his *Political Economy of War* (1915) that no first-rate economist had provided a comprehensive exposition of the economics of modern war, and

[1]See Beveridge's comment in *British Food Control* (1928), pp. 341–2.

[2]*Increase of Prices of Commodities since the Beginning of the War,* Dept. Cttee. Inter. Rep.; 1916, Cd. 8358, xiv; reprinted in *An Economist's Protest* (1927), pp. 29–34, 91–106.

[3]E Cannan in *Contemporary Review* (Mar. 1915); reprinted in part in *An Economist's Protest,* pp. 16–26.

[4]We are not alone in this. 'Attempts to fix Maximum Corn Prices in Germany' in *Econ. Jn.* (1915), 274; 'German Potato Policy' in *Econ. Jn., XXVI,* 57.

that economists had devoted their lives to studying (quite properly said Cannan)[5] the normal unconscious processes on which the wealth of nations depended. Some of these 'real' problems were discussed by Pigou in the *Contemporary Review* (Dec. 1915) and by F W Pethick Lawrence in a series of excellent propositions in the *Economic Journal* (Dec. 1915). But one cannot expect Ministers and others busy with war tasks to turn aside to master reviews and articles. Looking back in 1939, when a new war was upon us, on the problems of a war economy and re-stating propositions set out in his earlier writings, Pigou[6] agreed that in order to understand them fully, to the political economy we had read hitherto there was needed a companion volume, the *Political Economy of War*.[7] All this throws into relief the brilliance of some of the work on international shipping control, food rationing and materials controls described in Salter, *Inter-Allied Shipping Control* (1926), Beveridge, *British Food Control* (1928) and E M H Lloyd, *Experiments in State Control* (1924), by civil servants and their associates who penetrated to economic realities and much of whose efforts represented British administrative skill at its best.

The whole system was thus improvised step by step, each particular problem being tackled as it arose, by methods which seemed appropriate to it. And it was perhaps inevitable that in the decisions about its future, class interests should weigh heavily. To many business men, brought up in an atmosphere of free bargaining and private initiative, these improvised arrangements, effective as many of them were for their war purpose, were regarded as temporary expedients. The Government might know more than the business man about its schedule of requirements for war. But he would now have a new task, on which he felt he knew more than the Government: to get back his normal output and sales as soon as possible. The question was how quickly it might be safe to dismantle the controls in the hazards and uncertainties following the war; and it is clear that while many business men saw the benefits of this in their own field, they had not really envisaged either what

[5]Cannan in *Econ. Jn.* (Dec. 1915); reprinted in part in *An Economist's Protest*, pp. 49–50.

[6]Later incorporated into his *The Economy and Finance of the War* (1916).

[7]A C Pigou, *Political Economy of War* (1939), p. 2.

the result might be if all were dismantled together or the difficulties of unplanning a war-planned economy.

This feeling of 'temporariness', though widespread, was not unanimous. There were minor technical devices, such as the pooling of railway wagons or the nationalisation of mineral rights, which many thought should be permanent. But for the Labour Party the war system, with its effective control over rail and sea transport and other industries, the replacement of competitive free enterprise by bulk State purchase, the international allocation of shipping and of materials which eliminated the international competitive strains which generated war, as well as maximum prices and limited profits, were all seen as an advance to that conscious social organisation of 'production for use and not for profit' which had been the socialist dream for generations. Handing back the railways to private capitalists and production to the wastes of free competition seemed unthinkable. Transition should not mean transition backwards to a pre-war normal, but forward to a more deliberately organised society. This emerged with increasing strength as the war went on, in Party conferences from 1915 onwards and found full expression in the famous twenty-seven reconstruction resolutions of the London Conference of 1918. Some of these concerned strictly transitional problems, such as the demobilisation of military and civilian workers, but others, e.g. on the nationalisation of railways and mines, had been the subject of Party pre-war resolutions and arose simply out of its collectivist philosophy: war experience was held to have demonstrated their soundness. The problems of transition and of permanent reconstruction thus became linked. It was not all fully consistent. For a war or planned economy required at least guidance of, if not restraint on, labour mobility. But at the 1916 conference Margaret Bondfield proposed a resolution demanding the restoration of the workers' 'right of individual contract', a demand repeated in other forms up to resolution X, 1918. One resolution, XXVI, got nearer to the main issue than is suggested by the formal way it was proposed from the Chair and accepted; that on the model of the Departments' War Book there should be a Peace Book, setting out the main lines of reconstruction policy in all its branches. Any Government decision on dismantling the controls was thus bound to affect not only the task of restoring pre-war conditions—had not some features of pre-war economy gone for good anyway?—but also any schemes for its permanent re-shaping.

Thirdly, as the war turned into total war, drawing all the country's human and material resources into it, and we had to relinquish much of our export trade, sell overseas assets and incur for the first time in our modern history large international debts, the meaning of 'reconstruction' was extended to include a re-organisation of industries to a new level of efficiency, so that they could assert themselves in the international market and earn, in novel and difficult conditions, the food and raw material we needed. These hard problems of the practical sort brought their own anxieties. But reconstructed industries, however infused with the new social purposes which the ideals of the time demanded, would thus have to meet new and exacting conditions quite different from those of 1914. Success in the task of reconstruction thus required solutions at both these different levels, and that the solutions for one should not hinder the solutions for the other.

ii. *The Ideals of Reconstruction: New Elements*

These vital though humdrum matters of re-adjustment on which much depended, were neither the substance of the visions of a new order nor the elements which gave them their emotional quality. The human slaughter engendered both a revulsion and a determination that people should have more economic opportunity, more equality, more political power, and a better life and more liberty than British democracy ever had. In part this was only an enlargement and strengthening of the ideals which had been so pervasive in 1906–14, making them both more demanding and more vivid, and a general commitment of the population to them.

To the old collectivist doctrine fresh elements were added: a demand for a change not only in the ownership of industry, but in the relation of man to his work, for 'democracy in industry'. And all this attracted support from the religious and from the secular, from the intellectual and trade unionist. Of the mass of books and pamphlets which poured out from the printing presses, two works, both of which had a wide readership and great influence, and one Party statement, stand out, Tawney, with a sympathetic religious background, prescribed for *The Sickness of the Acquisitive Society* a social organisation based on functions instead of rights, that property rights should be maintained when accompanied by the performance of service, but abolished when not, that producers should stand in direct relation to the community so that their responsibility was obvious, and that the obligation for maintenance of a service should rest on the vocational and professional organisations of those who performed it. This implied principles, a standard and habit of conduct in social relations, and that economic activity should be subordinated to the social purpose for which it is carried on.[8] Bertrand Russell, with very different preconceptions, arrived at somewhat similar views by a different route.[9] The best life is that most built on the creative impulses, in whose product there is no private property, and the worst that founded on the possessive impulses, whose chief embodiment was the State, war and private property. Liberation of the creative impulse ought to be the principle of reform in both politics and economics. Anarchism, though the ultimate ideal, was impracticable at the moment, Marxism socialism and syndicalism were likely to give a better world than the one we lived in, but the former gave too much power to the State, while the second by abolishing it would have to reconstruct an authority to restrain the rivalry of different groups. The best practical system was that of Guild socialism.

The economists also had made some substantial advances. Classical economic theory had assumed that consumers' sovereignty and free enterprise would in general lead to the most productive use of resources, though there were major and a number of minor exceptions. Jevons' demonstration in 1871[10] that to achieve maximum utility a good should be so distributed between various uses that its final degree of utility (marginal utility) is equal in all uses,

[8]See *The Sickness of the Acquisitive Society* (1920) and the enlarged final chapter in the version re-published under the title *The Acquisitive Society* (1921).

[9]*Principles of Social Reconstruction* (1916); *Roads to Freedom* (1919).

[10]William Stanley Jevons, *Theory of Political Economy* (1871), pp. 68–71; 2nd ed. (1879), p. 65.

was later generalised into the statement that maximum satisfaction would be obtained if resources were distributed between employments so that marginal net products were equal. And in the hands of Marshall and Pigou, with the addition of the analytical distinctions between private costs and social costs and between increasing and decreasing returns industries, the normative rule now became, not equality of marginal private products, but of marginal social products. Of this the sweep of Pigou's *Economics of Welfare* (1921) —a development of his earlier *Wealth and Welfare*—was a striking demonstration. Thus there emerged, instead of a random list of special exceptions, a theoretical basis for coherent, organised State interventions, including transferences from the rich to the poor.

But there was one comprehensive general plan: that embodied in the New National Labour Party's statement *Labour and the New Social Order*. This powerfully written statement (Feb. 1918), based on the resolutions of the Manchester (1917) and Nottingham (1918) conferences of the Labour Party,[11] made an immense impression not only in Britain but abroad, because it gave substance —even in its title—to 'reconstruction idealism', gathered to itself and caught the mood of radical and socialist aspirations of a quarter of a century. It looked at the problem as a whole, its proposals flowing from definite principles. Capitalism was inefficient and morally indefensible. A national minimum of health, education, subsistence, guaranteed to every citizen, should be achieved by the scientific organisation of industry based on common ownership of power and transport, and unemployment prevented by stabilising aggregate demand through timed public works. Public finance should be revolutionised by progressive taxation of all incomes in excess of that required for family maintenance, by taxes on wealth and a capital levy. The growing surplus of wealth should accrue to the community and should be used for the common good.[12] It was the more impressive because it became the programme of the

[11]See *Reports of Annual Conference*: Manchester, 1917, pp. 101–25; Nottingham and London, 1918, pp. 120–39.

[12]This was severely criticised by the extreme left. See J T Murphy, *Preparing for Power,* pp. 168–9.

newly organised Labour Party,[13] now no longer substantially confined to the most active trade unionists and manual workers, but thrown open to the non-manual workers and the intellectual—'workers by hand and brain'—with the I.L.P. and Fabians affiliated. It was the only major party document to set out principles and proposals so comprehensively. Some of these views were repeated in more belligerent terms in the Trade Union Memorandum presented to the Industrial Conference in 1919,[14] after the 'coupon' election had frustrated the hopes of a Labour Party electoral victory and when the trade unionists hoped to achieve their aim through vigorous industrial action. It declared that Labour was challenging the whole structure of capitalist industry and desired to substitute a democratic system of public ownership and production.

But there was also a new element of revolutionary militancy: a revolt aginst the feared bureaucracy of the collectivist State (shared with some non-socialist distributivists, such as Belloc), against the conservatism of the older craft unions. It assumed the class war rather than the sweet reasonableness of steady progress, favoured 'direct' rather than Parliamentary methods, and aimed at taking over industry, not at the top, but from the bottom. The Guild Socialist Movement, strictly so called, came from a group of intellectuals—Orage, S G Hobson, A J Penty, G D H Cole, M Reckitt, Bechofer—and may be said to have begun by a plea by Penty, a medievalist craftsman, for the restoration of the Guild system in industry. Wage-slavery, which not only permitted workers to be exploited by capitalists, but also deprived them daily of their industrial freedom—how much freedom was there in being able to vote once in five years if in every act of their working lives they were under subordination?[15]—would be ended only if capitalistic ownership and control were ended and replaced by workers' control. This the workers should be specifically organised to capture through industrial unions on a class, workshop basis. The capitalist ousted, the workers' unions should be turned into corporations to run the

[13]Emergency Conference in London, Nov. 1918, in *Rep. Ann. Conference* (1919), app. iv, pp. 183–6.
[14]*Industrial Conference,* 1919, app. i, pp. ii, iii; 1919, Cmd. 501, xxiv.
[15]See G D H Cole and W Mellor, *Meaning of Industrial Freedom* (1918).

P

industries, and in some versions, should demand from the State the whole conduct of industrial and economic affairs. For some this vision of the extension of democracy from politics to industry was to be realised by orderly, peaceful, political means, but for others it was based on an assumption of the irreconcilable interests of capitalists and workers and of the class war. Its dramatic quality was given to it less by the intellectual group, however alluring their visions seemed to many outsiders of good-will—the National Guild membership seems in 1918 to have been about 1,000—than by the influence of ideas derived partly from them and partly from independent sources playing on trade unionists in 'lively' industries. For these one must turn less to the formal books of the intellectuals than to the large number of pamphlets, periodicals, etc., written by and circulating amongst the rank and file. Amongst these were: *The Workers' Committee* and *Compromise or Independence* by J T Murphy,[16] published by the Sheffield Workers' Committee; *Direct Action* by W Gallacher and J R Campbell (1919) for the National Council of Scottish Workers' Committees, and a little I.W.W. pamphlet, typical of many, *The Royal Road to Emancipation, All Wage Slaves May Start Now* by E L Platt.[17] The syndicalism of the *Miner's Next Step* had receded, but Tom Mann had returned from Australia, where he had contact with the notion of the One Big Union, with plans for militant unionism on a class basis which he preached in the *Industrial Syndicalist*. It was in the Shop Stewards' Movement that its dynamic was found. At the outbreak of the war some unions already had shop stewards checking union cards and reporting difficulties. When in the interests of war production the unions agreed on an industrial truce and later some strikes were made illegal, the daily frictions in the workshops which arose from the dilution of labour, rapid changes of technique, the introduction of women and the suspension of workshop practices, increased the need and rapidly multiplied the opportunities for them. Many were now not the appointees of particular unions, but were chosen by workers of all grades in the workshops. It was not long before

[16]In his *Modern Trade Unionism* (1935), Murphy adheres to his general position.
[17]In circulation 1917–19.

left-wing leaders pointed to the significance of this: the exploiting capitalist was being fought and should be ousted at the point of production by unions organised on a class basis. By linking up the shop stewards' committees into plant, district, industrial and national committees, a new revolutionary unionism could be created to replace the many unions found in one workshop and based on apathetic, ill-attended branches. In this form the new organisations could be not only the spearhead of an attack on capitalism, but could take over full responsibility for production, discipline, etc.; at one stage a kind of collective labour contract was suggested.

All this vigorous thinking led to a good deal of drafting of the proposed industrial constitutions, for example, by Murphy and Gallacher in their pamphlets, by the National Guilds League in *National Guilds* (1915) and *Towards a Railways Guild* (1917), by the Industrial Committee of the South Wales Socialist Society in *Plan for the Democratic Control of the Mining Industry* (1919); by Frank Hodges, Secretary of the Miners' Federation, *Workers' Control in the Mining Industry* (1920). The Miners' 1912 Coal Nationalisation Bill[18] had not provided for control by mine workers, but the plan presented to the Sankey Commission, 1919, by W Straker of the Northumberland Miners' Federation, did.[19] The I.L.P. also took up the ideas and issued (1919) Cole's *Workers' Control of Industry*, a statement of the general case, and R Page Arnot's *Trade Unionism: a New Model*. This was all very different from the usual proposals for nationalisation through a bureaucratic public corporation with a few men's representatives in the management. For that meant, it was argued, that instead of becoming a classless working community, the workers would simply change bosses.

Initially, these ideas were partly at least a generalisation from what seemed to be the potentialities of workers' control, for tactics included what was later called 'encroaching control',[20] i.e. step by

[18]See comments in *Towards a Miners' Guild* (1916), pp. 8–9.
[19]*Coal Industry Commission,* Inter. Rep., Mins. of ev., p. 324, qq. 8073, 8097–123; 1919, Cmd. 359, xi.
[20]One hardened Coventry shop steward laughed at a National Guild speaker at Ruskin College, who had been urging 'encroaching control'; the results of his attempts to 'encroach' were that he had had thirty jobs and not left one voluntarily.

step interference with and taking over matters which had hitherto been regarded as the function of management—questions of dismissal, promotion, selection of foreman, classification of workers and allocation of work between them, consultation over changes of process, publicity for profits and costs and making unemployment a charge on industry. What had been obtained in these fields was summarised by Carter Goodrich in the *Frontier of Control* (1919). Naturally, as the pamphlets circulating show, these movements were much influenced by the example and experience of workers' organisations in the early stages of the Russian Revolution. They caused a storm of controversy within the trade union movement by their attacks on the older leaders and the existing forms of organisation. The discussion on whether the union organisation should be area branch or workshop[21] was much more than a point of constitutional detail. But before circumstances and the influence of left-wing leaders drew it more into politics, and the end of the war undermined its basis, the movement represented an alternative set of ideals on which many hopes were based.

The task of reconstruction was to express these broad notions in working principles which, as Hobhouse put it, 'could be applied in the railways, mine, workshop and office that we know'.[22] The fertility of invention which showed itself in the range and quality of the plans was undoubtedly in part due to the cross-fertilisation of ideas which took place. For one must not be misled by later Continental experience—especially after the issue in 1920 by the Third International of the twenty-one points of affiliation,[23] which tore European labour movements asunder—and think of highly organised blocks of ideas sponsored by highly organised groups and of the whole as simply some kind of addition sum of them. Of course there were such groups, the Social Democratic Federation, for example. But to those who lived in them, intellectual excitement of the times lay in the fluidity of ideas, the way they came at one

---

[21]See J T Murphy, 'The Unit of Organisation: Branch or Workshop' in *Trade Unions: Organisation and Action* (Ruskin College, Oxford, 1919). Note the discussion which followed.

[22]L T Hobhouse, *Liberalism* (1911), p. 169.

[23]See especially conditions 1, 2, 3, 6, 7.

from every direction. For this reason there was much borrowing and inter-penetration. Even the newly organised National Labour Party could scarcely have been born at that date except by recognition and on the basis of a fluidity of ideas, which, to the puzzlement of ideologically riven Continental Labour movements, enabled members reared on the *Christian Commonwealth* to join hands with those brought up on *Justice,* in order to embark on what seemed a crusade. Engaged in thinking on reconstruction were High Church Socialists who combined ideas of Industrial Democracy with authority, Liberals with a good deal of socialism in their make-up, socialists marked by their Liberal birth, some Conservatives tinged with Fabianism. Gore, Scott Holland, Temple, cannot be pushed aside because the Church Socialist League was small in numbers, for many were, in the social structure of the day, near the seats of power and influence, exercising not only some positive, but a negative role in eroding opposition to new ideas. The Fabians cannot be written down because some of their specific proposals were not accepted, for up to 1918 they deliberately refrained from tying themselves to a given political party but, as English radicals have characteristically done, nobbled for their ideas likely people they found in both highways and hedges—ministers, doctors, parsons, trade unionists. Their attempt was to permeate[24] and their ideas did permeate. Their attempts to sort out practical answers to the question 'How?' were a constant challenge and a stimulation to the inventive capacity of others. And in this certainly the experts, both official and unofficial, especially in health and housing, not all politically aligned, were outstanding.

In the midst of all this seeing of visions, Gilbert Murray, drawing wisdom from his store of classical learning, sounded a warning note. Speaking in 1918 of the Peloponnesian War,[25] he recalled that 'the more the cities of Greece were ruined by the havoc of war, the more the lives of men were poisoned by the fear and hate and suspicion which it engendered, the more was Athens haunted

[24]The one big failure occurred when the Webbs departed from this and, in order to bring pressure on political parties, organised the campaign to carry out the Minority proposals in the *Poor Laws.*

[25]Gilbert Murray, *Aristophanes and the War Party,* Creigthon Lecture, 1918 (1919).

by the shining dreams of the future reconstruction of human life. Not only in the speculation of philosophers like Protagoras and Plato, town planners like Hippodamus, but in comedy after comedy by Aristophanes and his compeers—the names are too many to mention—we find plans for a new life; a great dream city in which the desolate and depressed came into their own again, where rich and poor, man and woman, Athenian and Spartan were all equal and at peace.' The parallel became uncomfortable: 'This utopia began as a world city full of glory and generous hope; it ends, in Plato's *Laws*, as one hard-living asylum of the righteous on a remote Cretan hill top, from which all infection from the outer world is rigorously excluded, where no religious heretics may live, where every man is a spiritual soldier, and every woman must be ready "to fight for her young as the birds do". The great hope had dwindled to very like despair; and even in that form it was not fulfilled.' And it was after the Goths had sacked Rome that St Augustine wrote *The City of God,* a spiritual vision which contrasted with the reality which had been destroyed.

So after 1918, though the physical disaster was neither so catastrophic nor so irreparable, many of the plans were not implemented at the time, some not till after the Second World War and others not at all. The generous enthusiasm and all the planning made vivid by implication in the quality of satire by L Housman in *Mr Trimblerigg*, had little to show for them. What accounts for this gap between the hopes entertained and the actual accomplishment?

iii. *The planning process*

The multitude of plans for reconstruction which issued from various Government bodies arose out of this background of intense aspiration and spontaneous canvassing of ideas by voluntary movements and by individuals; it produced a wealth of suggestions, some of which found their way into reports and proposals, whilst others remained floating around, or were still-born, or died from neglect during infancy. What was the best way for a Government to search through these ideas and work them into plans to be brought forward officially for Parliamentary and public consideration? Government thinking, like the different task of administrative operation, requires to be appropriately organised. Yet it is not certain that the methods chosen were, though fruitful in ideas, always the best. The Board of Trade, with its eye on frightening problems ahead, was early off the mark in 1916 when it appointed a number of separate committees to consider, 'especially in relation to international competition after the war', the shipping and ship-building, textile, electrical, iron and steel, and engineering trades. Their members were drawn from the separate industries and included workers' representatives. To enable witnesses to speak freely to one another they were able to mark such parts of their evidence as they wished to be confidential and in any case this was not published. In effect, it was an interesting arrangement enabling leaders in each industry to sit down and talk over its future.

In the field of reconstruction generally, several experiments led to the conclusion that neither Ministers nor Government departments harassed with the tasks of war administration could give the problems adequate attention, and some feared that the several departments might tend to approach them too narrowly in the light of their own special sphere of duties. What was needed was a body of persons free from the distractions of war administration and even from normal departmental work, without particular executive responsibilities and able to give these questions undivided attention. This was arrived at by three stages. The first step was taken by Asquith who, in 1916, appointed a committee of the Cabinet, which in turn appointed sub-committees on particular problems then becoming evident. Within its scope, the work was well done, five important reports being that of the Selborne Committee (*Agricultural Policy*) (1917–18 Cd. 8506, xviii), the Haldane Committee on *Coal Conservation* (1918 Cd. 9084, vii) with the Merz Sub-Committee on *Electric Power* (1917–18 Cd. 8880, xviii), the famous Whitley Committee on the *Relations between Employer and Employed* (1917–18 Cd. 8606, xviii), and the Balfour of Burleigh Committee on *Commercial and Industrial Policy after the War* (1918 Cd. 9032, xiii)—whose members included the chairmen of the Board of Trade Committees on the separate industries. In the second stage an attempt was made to ensure more continuous attention in the whole field and to give the body more authority to press matters, by replacing this first Reconstruction Committee with a new one under the formal chairmanship of the Prime Minister, Lloyd George, with E S Montague as his vice-chairman and deputy, and a panel of members with special knowledge. This body, also through committees, made vital investigations into *The Acquisition and Valuation of Land for Public Purposes* (Scott; 1918 Cd. 8998, xi), *Adult Education* (A L Smith, Master of Balliol; 1918 Cd. 9107, ix), *Transfer of Functions of Poor Law Authorities* (Maclean; 1918, Cd. 8917, xviii), and the great Report on *The Machinery of Government* (Haldane; 1918 Cd. 9230, xii).

The third stage was the replacement of the Committee by a full 'Minister of Reconstruction', responsible to Parliament and having direct access to the Cabinet, with the task of co-ordinating the work of the different departments, power to initiate his own inquiries and the responsibility for presenting the schemes to Parliament. This ministry also made full use of committees, some of whose work had, for good or ill, a decisive effect on policy. For example, on *Currency and Foreign Exchanges After the War* in association with the Treasury (Cunliffe; 1918 Cd. 9182, vii), on *Financial Facilities* (Vassar-Smith; 1918 Cd. 9227, x), *Trusts* (McCurdy; 1918 Cd. 9236, xiii), *Housing in England and Wales* (Salisbury; 1918 Cd. 9087, xxvi), *Housing (Financial Assistance)* (Hobhouse; 1918 Cd. 9223, x), *The Increase of Rent and Mortgage Interest (War Restrictions)* (Hunter; 1918 Cd. 9235, xiii), *Building Industry after the War* (Carmichael; 1918 Cd. 9197, vii), and a tricky legal matter, the precise meanings to be given to the twenty-three varieties of the term 'Period of the War' used in Acts of Parliament and orders made on different subjects at different dates. As a glance at the members of the committees shows, this process did enable special outside knowledge and experience to be tapped. The gain here was not only in access to special knowledge and expertise, but in securing the participation of persons who were influenced often consciously, in other cases through unconscious absorption, by the new approach and methods of social investigation so much a feature of the times. They included J A Hobson, Seebohm Rowntree, Sydney Chapman, Pigou, Tawney, A L Smith, the

Master of Balliol, the two Webbs, Richard Reiss, John Hilton, J S
Haldane, A D Hall, Merz, Mansbridge. And not only political
labour, but union leaders were brought in: J H Thomas, Bevin,
Frank Hodges, Bob Smillie; and amongst the women, Mary
MacArthur, Susan Lawrence, Marion Phillips, Mrs Pember Reeves.

This form of organisation did not commend itself to everyone.
Whilst there was everything to be said for drawing on the expert
knowledge of outsiders (though they were occasionally thought
of genially as a bit idealistic and not very practical and one or two
were said to look like it) who might bring some refreshing breezes
of new ideas, did not this tend to transfer initiative in plan-making
from the departments already having a fund of experience and who
might be involved in carrying out plans drawn up by others which
they might regard as inadequate or unworkable? The Minister's
appointment in January 1918 of a Council of 'mature experienced
persons not being present officials of any Government department'
to give practical advice could scarcely have allayed these doubts.
With a return to peace, however, in 1919 the Ministry was brought
to an end two or three years before the maximum life laid down
in the Act which created it, and the departments concerned with
final action resumed their responsibilities.

This, however, was only the more co-ordinated part of the
planning process. For towards the end of 1918 and in the two
succeeding years, both Parliament and the departments themselves
either directly or through committees they appointed were actively
considering permanent changes in our institutions. Investigations
were commenced on the Land Values Duties, Income Tax, Taxes on
Wealth (War), on *Bank Amalgamations;* a Commons Select Committee surveyed the whole problem of inland transport, including
canals, the latter being looked at again in 1921. On health there
was Arthur Newsholme's famous Annual Report 1917, three
Reports on the *Future Provision of Medical and Allied Services in
England, Wales and Scotland.* The Ministry of Labour promoted an
Industrial Conference on Causes of Industrial Unrest and steps
necessary to promote the best interests of the employer, workpeople
and the State. That the departments and the Ministry of Reconstruction occasionally overlapped and both established committees

221

on the same subject may be regarded as no more than the sprawl and confusion which arises in the strenuous circumstances of war.

These then were the two main processes by which the machinery of government gathered information and ideas, and worked them into plans in due course brought into one or the other of the official series for Parliamentary and public consideration.

Thirdly, some proposals were worked out not by any formal planning process, but by general political agreement between or acquiescence by the political parties: the extension of the franchise and the reform of education, on the one hand, and schemes for the reform of the House of Lords (1918 Cd. 9038, x) and devolution of some of Parliament's powers to regional parliaments for England, Wales and Scotland (1920 Cmd. 692, xiii) on the other.

2. PLANS: THE NEW SOCIETY

i. *Economic Policy*

What would the new, re-vivified Britain have looked like if all the plans embodying the visions, hopes and calculations of their sponsors had been carried out? War experience led to more emphasis on the need to give freer play for scientific and technological advance; its termination had released political, economic and group pressures which had been restrained; there was often a difference of tone between pre-armistice and post-armistice plans. With this inter-play of ideas the plans were not all of a piece, and there were striking inconsistencies: occasionally two Government committees would examine the same problem and come out with different answers. Nevertheless, one can put the plans together to form a broad picture of what the economic and social scene would have been.

(*a*) *Agriculture*. An early decision on the future of agriculture was a high priority. The country had for the first time been placed on a national food rationing system, and great efforts had been required to maintain an adequate but restricted and rather monotonous diet. The specific plans and the changes in them had their origin in three sources: the great necessity to expand it speedily as the shipping losses due to the German submarine campaign reached the most terrifying, pessimistic estimates; the controversy on whether and how far agriculture should be allowed to contract once again when the war was over; and the growing desire before the war, both to re-vivify it after the contraction of arable farming and to arrest rural de-population by improving the lot of the agricultural worker. Geoffrey Drage's Report[26] showed that between 1907 and 1914 agricultural wages had risen by only two shillings and not at all in the last two of these years, that they were lowest in arable and highest in pasture districts, while the Liberal *Land Enquiry* had already calculated that real wages had actually dropped since 1907.[27] The motive behind the plans included fears about national safety, idealism over what should be done to give a better life to the rural population and, of course, the strong economic interests of the farmer. There were also difficulties. The British people had become meat eaters, farmers had replaced corn with livestock and depended on imported feeding stuffs. Just before the war the value of the two tillage crops was little more than one-fifth that of stock and its produce, and we depended on imports for two-fifths of our meat and four-fifths of our grain. Yet in the nutritional calculations of the time,[28] the food value of the produce of the 3 million acres under wheat and oats was only fractionally less than that of the 36 million acres under stock. The main problem of war-time food supply was therefore regarded as that of increasing the bread supply. There was the individualism of thousands of farmers used to cultivating their particular land in the light of market prices—and it is probably true to say that no farmer in the world had shown the adaptability of English farmers to world prices—who had to be induced or forced during the war to follow a cropping programme laid down by the

[26] *Wages and Conditions of Employment in Agriculture,* Rep.; 1919, Cmd. 24, ix.

[27] The Milner Committee's view that agricultural wages were 'rising before the war' was an unnecessarily cheerful view of the facts.

[28] The Royal Society's calculations were based on the work-producing power in terms of calories. It was estimated that the average cow's consumption worked out at 12 lbs. of dry fodder for 1 lb. of human dry food, and that a pig would consume 6 lbs. of barley in the production of 1 lb. of pork containing half its weight in water. The practical solution for war policy seemed clear. See *Food Supply of the United Kingdom,* Cttee. of the Royal Soc.; 1916, Cd. 8421, ix; T B Wood, *The National Food Supply in Peace and War* (1917).

Government. Then during the war the industry lost a third of its skilled men to the Services or to munitions industries where high earnings re-inforced the appeal of national need.

The plans were therefore mixtures of bits from pre-war designs, of expedients to get war-time expansion and—since farmers could not be expected to restore acres laid down to grass since the seventies without knowing how long this would be needed—of those for settling the post-war scale and pattern of the industry. From the pre-war *Land Enquiry* came the proposal for a minimum wage for agricultural workers, from the war-time Milner Committee on the *Production of Food in England and Wales* (1915)[29] recommendations for guaranteed prices for wheat and oats—which the Government rejected, but had to act on eighteen months later—and for local committees to stimulate greater production. These war agricultural committees were in due course armed with powers under the Defence of the Realm Acts to inspect land, issue directions for its cultivation and even to take possession of land inadequately cultivated. The Selborne Committee on *Agricultural Policy*,[30] set up in 1916 by the Committee on Reconstruction, was concerned, not with war, but with post-war policy; it nevertheless had some influence on war policy as well. Urging that we should in future be less dependent on imported supplies, it repeated the Milner Committee's proposals of guaranteed prices and recommended a statutory minimum wage for agricultural workers. Both these proposals were embodied in the Corn Production Act, 1917, which was not a reconstruction, but a war-time measure. The Act also included provisions giving the Government some powers of control over the farmer's operations, a point naturally of fierce controversy. But it is remarkable that despite the seriousness of the military and shipping situation, the lag of ideas was such that the Bill was criticised in the Commons because it seemed to commit the country to guaranteeing prices after the war, and in the Lords because of the Government's proposed powers to control farming. In the end, the urgency was such that many of the proposed powers were still exercised under D.O.R.A.

[29] 1914–16, Cd. 8048, 8095, v.
[30] 1917–18, Cd. 8506, xviii.

By the end of 1919 the plans had changed again. The Royal Commission on *Agriculture*,[31] 1919, to inquire into the economic prospects of the industry, had two views. At the time the Commission reported (Dec. 1919) the average prices of wheat and oats had risen and they went on rising in 1920. The old issue of guaranteed prices and control came up again. The Majority argued that the continuance of the guarantees would not be required by the farmers if they were left free to arrange their cultivation as they thought fit, but if the nation required more corn production guaranteed prices were necessary, and four years' notice of their withdrawal should be given. But a strong Minority felt that farming had become remunerative, so that guaranteed prices were unnecessary, and in any case gave the farmer no confidence, since no Parliament could bind its successor, and public money should not be spent to divert agriculture into uneconomic fields. Farmers should be left free to cultivate their land, subject to the rules of good husbandry. How soon some of the assumptions behind either Report were to be disastrously belied had yet to be seen.

(*b*) *Transport, railways, canals, road transport.* In the discussions on the plans for industry, two old themes recur; the need to improve efficiency by forming large units of production, yet to avoid creating monopolies which might indulge in anti-social activities, such as restricting output or manipulating prices. Radicals and socialists who, as part of their case for nationalisation, had long denounced the wastes of free competition were willing to accept large unifications provided they were run not for profit, but socially. On the other hand, to the Conservative, private enterprise was now coming to mean less the free competition of small businesses and more the freedom of action for large combines. The significance of this conflict of principle emerged in the plans both for technological monopolies and for general manufacturing business.

The former covered those industries whose effective technical operation involved either costly fixed main lines and feeders, as in railways, canals and electric power transmission, or work on large

---

[31]Inter. Rep.; 1919, Cmd. 473, viii.

areas of natural resources, such as coal beds or a group of water-sheds. They were all in private ownership. The plans meant, for railways, the abandonment of the hostile attitude which had for so long treated them as dangerous monopolies; for canals the compulsory slimming of a private industry to make it a smaller, but viable one; for coal mining the unification of 3,000 coal pits; and decision on the lines of development of two industries which were the creation of new technologies: electric power, partly publicly and partly privately owned, and motor transport, still organised on the basis of atomistic competition and not easy to envisage in a nationally integrated form. In all of them technology was clamouring for new structure which would give it full play.

First, transport. An attempt, unique up to that time, and not repeated until 1929-31, was made by the Select Committee on *Transport*, 1918, to look at inland transport as a whole. The main-line railways, the nationalisation of which the radicals had urged and some Ministers and experts had before the war come to accept as inevitable, would have to be managed as a single system, either by a process of amalgamation as a step to it, or by private ownership with commercial management, or by nationalisation.[32] Churchill declared (Dec. 1918)[33] that the Coalition Government would nationalise them. But partly as a result of political changes, there were second thoughts. Some of the gains of unification without the creation of a giant monopoly or nationalisation were to be obtained by amalgamating the companies into five or six groups so arranged as to eliminate competition between them[34] and by replacing the old maximum fares by fixed ones determined by a statutory Rates Tribunal and set at a level which would yield a defined net revenue.[35] But the State was not to subsidise nor to

[32]*Transport*, Sel. Cttee. Rep., 1819 (130, 136) iv.

[33]Sel. Cttee. Rep. in Nov. 1918; Churchill's statement was made in Dec. 1918.

[34]*Outline of Proposals as to the Future Organisation of Transport Undertakings*, 1920, Cmd. 787, xli.

[35]There were also some fresh technical principles of rate-fixing. For the theory, compare the English pre-war orthodox view in Acworth's *Railway Economics* ('charging what the traffic will bear') with the statements in the Rates Advisory Committee's Report, 1920, Cmd. 1098, xxiv, and the different view of Pigou in *Economics of Welfare*, pt. ii, chap. xv.

give a financial guarantee. In the outcome the proposal to give each group a monopoly area was replaced by one drawing the boundaries between them so that each had both a monopoly and a competitive area. The long controversies over labour relations were to be met by a permanent Central Wages Board and a National Wages Board and by giving workers and officials representation on the groups' boards of management. There remained to be settled the relation of the railways to the old system of canals and the new one of road motor transport.

For canals and inland waterways there were three schemes. That of the Commission of 1909 had come to naught, and since the unifications necessary to get rid of the multiplicity of authorities, gauges, etc., could be obtained neither by amalgamation, because the railways had taken possession of key links, nor by regional public trusts, it had recommended that they should be vested in a Central Waterways Board, to which the railway-owned canals should be transferred, and proposed a major improvement of the four main routes (the 'Cross'). But the 1918 Committee were more hesitant; the estimated cost of the 'Cross' had risen three-fold and the proposed development of large-scale electric power might reduce one of its main traffics, coal. More amalgamation and modest improvements were as far as they would go. But in 1921 came the final version;[36] amalgamate them into seven regional groups owned by public trusts, with capital derived from State and local funds. These should take over the railway-owned canals, and railways should be prevented from quoting hostile undercutting rates.

What was to be done with the newly developing road motor transport industry? It consisted of many small units and the 1918 Committee did not regard it as well adapted to organisation on a national basis. By 1921 the railways had lost a considerable amount of bulk traffic to it, but their attempts to stop further losses by themselves commencing to carry by road, revived the old fears that they would drive out independent carriers and so achieve a monopoly of both road and rail transport.[37] On this, which became a

---

[36]*Inland Waterways,* Cttee. 2nd Inter. Rep.; 1921, Cmd. 1410, xiv.
[37]*Road Conveyance of Goods by Railway Companies,* Rep.; 1921, Cmd. 1228, xvii.

critical point of policy for over forty years, there was a sharp division of interests and opinion. The new vested interests regarded the traffic diverted from the railways as merely a legitimate extension of the old road hauliers business and wanted railways to be prevented from carrying by road direct. But others rejected free competition between road and rail and thought that the railways should be allowed to carry by road on conditions which prevented monopoly, i.e. the obligation to accept all traffic, published and controlled rates and the sanctioning of all agreements on rates between road carriers and the railways. The extent to which political slogans could distort vision is shown by the trade union member's view: his organisation was committed to nationalisation and was unanimously opposed to giving the railways extended powers.

(c) *Fuel and Power: Coal, electricity, water.* In what sense were there 'reconstruction' plans for fuel and power? The 1903 Commission on *Coal Supplies*[38] had found that great as were our unused resources, a large part of them were inferior in quality and costly to mine, and that 40 per cent to 60 per cent of consumption was extravagant and wasteful and could be saved. This, and the effect of the miner's eight-hour day and the war difficulties caused by the enlistment of a quarter of the miners, made it natural enough to start a series of inquiries by the appointment of the Reconstruction Committee on *Coal Conservation*[39] (Chairman, Lord Haldane) to investigate methods of preventing loss in production, use and transformation into power. And out of this important technological approach came plans for electric power.[40] The coal mining industry on which these were to depend employed a million men, and its output was based on hand labour in no less than 3,000 pits owned by 1,500 separate companies and individuals working coal beds whose ownership was divided between 4,000 surface landlords; and though before the war it had been involved in bitter nation-wide industrial struggles, no reconstruction committee was set up to make a dispassionate study of its structure and functioning as a whole. No one Ministry was

[38]*Coal Supplies*, R. Com. Final Rep.; 1905, Cd. 2353, xvi. *Breviate*, I, 130.
[39]1918, Cd. 9084, vii.
[40]See below, p. 230-1.

responsible for it or had announced a policy or plan behind which it could put its departmental drive. The situation was brought to a crisis by the miners' demand for much higher wages and shorter hours, and for a unification by nationalisation which would make these possible. The schemes prepared by the Sankey Commission of 1919, appointed to find a solution, were thus not born of quiet forethought, but devised in an atmosphere of menacing industrial strife. Nor was the Commission itself completely dispassionate, for it was composed partly of persons already 'committed'—three representatives each of owners and miners, six persons noted for their economic knowledge, three being nominated by the miners and three by the Government. One member gave evidence in support of the principle on which he was supposed to give judgement. The immediate wage issue was got out of the way, they all agreed there should be a ministry or department of mines,[41] and that the State should acquire the ownership of coal. The issue was nationalisation of mining: a group which included the owners' representatives rejected it, while one member, Duckham,[42] in a powerful report, wanted the mines amalgamated into a number of groups managed by district boards, whose shareholders were to be guaranteed a minimum and limited to a maximum dividend. Everything thus depended on the impartial chairman. The industry was already a sick one, on which the worst of disasters had fallen: it had lost the loyalty and confidence of its men. Sankey declared that the existing scheme of ownership and working was condemned and evils could not be remedied by any scheme of unification falling short of nationalisation. On the dangers of centralised bureaucracy, he was led by Haldane's most weighty evidence, based on his experience of re-organising the army (qq. 25,559–25,643), to conclude that we could provide a class of administrative officers who combined a high sense of duty with initiative, and by the current trend of thought about industrial democracy and W Straker's

[41]Three members of the *Coal Conservation* Committee had felt that there was a danger that such a ministry could be open to political pressure. *Breviate*, II, 219.

[42]*Coal Industry Commission*, R. Com. Inter. Rep.; 1919, Cmd. 359, xi. Reps.; 1919, Cmd. 360, xii.

Q

evidence,[43] to propose some degree of representation of the miners in national and local mine committees. It was this scheme which embodied the passionate hopes of the miners and of those who sympathised with them.[44] It was opposed no less strongly by the owners, less in defence of the inadequacies revealed in the million words of oral evidence than of the principles of free enterprise as such.

The future of the electric power supply should have been a technologist's dream; the requirements were clearly seen and vigorously stated by those asked to plan for it. Yet its subsequent history could well have been expressed by a satirical cartoon based on a very popular nineteenth-century picture: technology knocking at the door of politics, with the title 'Technology Locked Out'. For four committees, the Parsons Committee (1917), the Merz Sub-Committee (of the Coal Conservation Committee 1917), the Williamson Committee (1918) and the Birchenough Ministry of Reconstruction Committee of Chairmen (1918)[45] were unanimous on one point. Power supply by 600 authorities, many very small ones, was, as the Merz Committee put it, technically wrong and commercially uneconomic, and should be organised on a national basis. The Merz Committee wanted them replaced by a comprehensive system in which the country would be divided into sixteen areas, in each of which a district board would be the sole generating and distributing authority, while a central board of commissioners would stop the extension and multiplication of uneconomic stations, arrange for the transfer of existing undertakings to the boards, standardise voltages in the area, etc. From this point on there was some watering down of this plan to give the new technology a free run. Some of the Williamson Committee's proposals were the same in substance; the district board should own all authorised and future

---

[43]W Straker; see above, p. 215 and note.

[44]See the evidence of some academic witnesses, e.g. Prof Hobhouse, to see how far the acceptance of the general principle of social ownership had gone.

[45]Parsons Cttee., *Electrical Trades,* 1918, Cd. 9072, xiii. Merz Sub-Cttee., *Electric Power Supply,* 1917–18, Cd. 8880, xviii. Williamson Cttee., *Electric Power Supply,* 1918, Cd. 9062, viii. Birchenough Cttee., *Electric Power Supply,* 1919, Cmd. 93, xxix. *Breviate,* II, 156, 237–8.

generating stations and the main transmission lines, but it conceded that the existing undertakings should retain their powers of distribution, though they should purchase in bulk from the boards. While the Birchenough Committee, perhaps more open to non-technical and other influences, acknowledged and re-affirmed the principle of unification, in fact it provided less definitely for the technologists' demands. They suggested that an Electricity Board should be set up to expedite the creation of a unified system, but left free to deal with the whole problem of generation and distribution. For this change of tone several things were responsible. There were real difficulties in providing at the time capital for so complete a replacement of the old system, there were arguments on the extent to which the new authorities and stations should take on the debts and liabilities of those superseded. But there were others, which the Parsons Committee had in mind. There were strong vested interests, private and public. Large power companies, strong politically, were in no mind to have their successful undertakings or their areas interfered with, especially to take in weaker units or less profitable districts. And the very success of the collectivist socialists' campaign for municipal ownership itself made difficulties. Some local authorities owning gas undertakings looked askance at the possible new rival. Other local authorities with successful electricity undertakings based on local government areas whose boundaries were technologically unsuitable were nevertheless proud of their own collective enterprise, and were unwilling to see them swallowed up by a large district board which might be less responsive to their own needs and might not even be popularly elected. And in the background was opposition to the principle of State ownership, clearly expressed by W L Hichens in his memorandum and alternative proposals to the Birchenough Committee's recommendations. So that the difficulties which called forth the technologists' proposals were those which rendered them unfruitful. For the Electricity Commissioners set up by the Act of 1919 had no compulsory powers, but could attempt to secure co-ordination only by persuasion. And that, as the 1926 Weir Committee showed, amounted to little.

It was an easy passage of thought from power based on coal to power based on water, and many of the considerations of policy were analogous. Further, the Snell Committee set up to consider water power resources soon found that this was part of a wider question, for there were large and sometimes competing demands for many industrial uses. Water resources depended on watersheds and geological formations which had nothing to do with the local government boundaries of urban consuming areas. This created problems which could be surmounted only by the local authorities obtaining power to draw water from places outside their areas and often undertaking obligations to supply areas contiguous to their own, or by the activity of independent water companies which could break through these limitations. The necessary legal powers could be obtained only by reconciling conflicting interests and by Parliamentary Bills promoted for each project. Water resources were thus allocated by a succession of Parliamentary Bills as they came up, on arguments which took little account of the larger problems. These difficulties had retarded the development of water power, especially in Scotland. And in detail, the results were often odd. A large authority might procure water from a distant source and conduct it in mains passing through the areas of another authority, who might not be allowed to tap them, but might be compelled to secure its own water from a nearby source by a separate undertaking. This was a situation with which neither water engineers nor radicals could be content.

The Snell Committee's reference was not, however, water resources in general, but power resources. In four Reports[46] it concluded, first, that some measure of control over the water resources of the country was necessary to secure proper and impartial allocation of resources, and although it was not called upon to arrive at the distinction between areas of surplus, areas of deficiency and areas of self-sufficiency, decided that a Water Commission should be set up to keep records, group watersheds into suitable areas and arrange for setting up of watershed boards. Secondly, in the case of Scotland the State should acquire the rights of hydroelectric development, and, generally, an inter-departmental committee should be established to reconcile conflicting interests.

[46]*Water Power Resources,* Dept. Cttee. three Inter., one Final Rep.; 1919, Cmd. 79, xxx; 1920, Cmd. 776, Cmd. 1079, xxv; 1921, non-Parl.

Thirdly, the Board of Trade and Electricity Commissioners should have funds and powers to secure the development of water power. A special technical committee should be set up to investigate the utilisation of tides for power purposes, including those in the Severn estuary.

(*d*) *Trade combination and trust policy*. In the field of general manufacturing the problem of unification and monopoly had changed in three ways. First, it had become more urgent. Whereas before the war effective trade associations were much less thick on the ground than amalgamations in the U.S.A. and cartels in Germany, their machinery was so convenient for the rationing of scarce war materials, arrangements for priorities, etc. that with Government encouragement some were strengthened and many formed for these purposes. They were now widespread. And business was not slow to perceive their permanent advantages. Secondly, the problem was seen to be more difficult, for it was clear that the motives for monopoly had their origins not simply in the special circumstances of particular industries, but were deeply embedded in the competitive process itself. Thus Henry Clay, in a book which had a wide working-class readership, pointed out that while sellers had competing interests against one another in securing the largest share of trade, they had a common interest against buyers in maintaining prices.[47] Foxwell, in a shattering article on *The Industrial Struggle* (Sept. 1917)[48] vigorously questioned the assumption that competition contributed to the common good by ensuring the steady elimination of the less by the more efficient business. In so far as business activity aimed first at efficiency, hoping for profit as the reward, this might be true; and no doubt most business activity was of this sort. But on the contrary, when it aimed at profit as the first objective, and was ready to use the most direct means to that end, whether by efficiency, adulteration or false advertising, or where competition was predatory and belligerent, singling out opponents and clubbing them by unfair practices, it did not necessarily lead to the survival of the fittest productive units or to the

[47]Henry Clay, *Economics for the General Reader* (1916), chap. vi.
[48]In *Econ. Jn.*

triumph on the market of the best product. He pointed out that in 1851–54 the *Lancet* made an inquiry into the purity of fine drugs and chemicals, investigating thousands of products from many firms. Yet when he wrote, some of those whose products had been in doubt were amongst the big firms of his day, whilst of those whose products had been found pure, none appeared to have survived. While, therefore, the economists were apprehensive of monopolies, some had joined the radicals in throwing doubts on the social efficiency of the competitive process.

Thirdly, business thinking was dominated by a fear of the keen competitive power of Germany. This, which English producers had been feeling sharply before the war, especially in electrical and some other branches of engineering and chemicals, was attributed to the existence of large, strongly organised cartels which dominated certain trades, to the laws which permitted them and to the indirect support which the German Government gave to them. It was driven home when the cessation of imports revealed that for a number of things essential to war production, e.g. tungsten, magnetos, we were wholly or partly dependent on German supplies. Closer organisation would make possible and provide resources for technical innovations and a more organised trade policy for meeting German competition in its old and expected new forms.

To meet the situation two plans and one folly were offered. The drive behind the first came from the industries themselves through committees set up by the Board of Trade to consider the post-war organisation, and composed largely of their business leaders or, as some later socialist critics said, of capitalists. Those on iron and steel, non-ferrous metals, the electrical trades, engineering, chemicals, textiles and even shipbuilding, all either urged the encouragement of or pressed for large-scale combinations and units. The Balfour of Burleigh Committee on *Commercial and Industrial Policy* endorsed these proposals in general terms. The Federation of British Industries had suggested that the law on restraint of trade should be amended to legalise associations controlling output and prices and delimiting markets, and to enable them to enforce rules on their members. This the Committee proposed to do by giving them the option of registering their agreements with the Board of

Trade, in which case they would become enforceable at law. But what limits to the powers and freedom of such associations did the Committee suggest? They should register with the Board of Trade, apart from names, only the general nature and contents of their agreements, and the Board should be empowered to call on particular combines for confidential information; but Government intervention and control of the operation of combines should be restricted to cases where these could be clearly shown to be inimical to the national interest. The 'trust-busting' and publicity provided by American law were explicitly rejected. All this would have meant, both to business, which had long given lip service to free competition, and to public policy, a complete change of front. The implementation of such plans would change the face of much of British industry; free enterprise in the older sense of competition between many producers would be replaced by the freedom of highly organised groups in a strong legal position. The Committee admitted that the creation of combines for the export trade would lead to the control of home sales also, but thought this desirable in some cases, and in modern conditions, probably inevitable. But the hostile attitudes of public opinion, local authorities and the State to trade combinations would have to be modified.[49]

The second 'plan' had its origins not in committees largely confined to business men advising on the post-war organisation of their industries, but in a Committee on *Trusts*[50] set up by the Ministry of Reconstruction and composed of a few members representative of a wider range of interests, and including Ernest Bevin and the radical and socialist economists, J A Hobson and Sidney Webb. The Committee was charged with the more specific duty of examining the extension of trade combinations to see what action we needed to safeguard the public interest. It was clear from its weighty written evidence[51] that the most common form agreement simply to maintain or raise prices, led to a loss of socially desirable output, that pool and quota systems obstructed the economists of large-scale production because they stereotyped the ground plan of industry; that the

[49]For a full list of references see *Breviate*, II, 154–9.
[50]*Trusts*, Min. of Reconstruction, Cttee. Rep.; 1918, Cd. 9236, xiii.
[51]Ibid., see memos, pp. 15–43.

cost of the projected housing programme was being raised because a large proportion of the materials required were wholly or partly price-controlled. Trade combinations, they found, might at no distant date exercise a paramount control over all important branches of British industry. Their conclusions were in marked contrast to those of the Balfour of Burleigh Committee: the fullest information on trade association activities should be available to the public, the Board of Trade should collect it and make an annual report to Parliament; an independent tribunal, with a legal chairman, if required by the Board of Trade was to investigate any combination, and if it were proved that acts inimical to the public interest had been committed, the relevant facts should be published immediately; and the Board of Trade should suggest what remedial State action should be taken.

For the labour and radical members of the Committee even these proposals did not go far enough. Following their traditional line of thought, they regarded large-scale units as inevitable and desirable, and that in any case attempts to prevent them were ineffective. The evils of monopoly should be countered by encouraging independent rivals, such as co-operative enterprises, and by the use of wartime national factories, while highly organised combines restricting output to raise prices should be taken over by the co-operative movement, municipalities or the State. Two experienced investigators, J A Hobson and Sidney Webb, argued from war experience for control of prices based on costing systems without apparently realising all the difficulties involved. (Later, Beveridge pointed out that it was at best of limited service.[52] And E M H Lloyd showed what it could and could not accomplish.)

The emphasis on price control helped to put the public on a false scent which led to the third line of policy, the folly of the futile Profiteering Acts. For prices cannot be effectively controlled in a period of rising monetary demand, of inflation. Although there had been several years of inflation when the Committee was appointed, and more before the Report was signed,[53] the Minority made no

[52]Beveridge, *British Food Control*, p. 179. E M H Lloyd, *Experiments in State Control* (1924), chaps. xxiii, xxv.

[53]Appointed Feb. 1918, Rep. signed April 1919.

reference to this. In such circumstances if the producer keeps his prices down, speculators may step in and take the profits, while if he raises his price to retain his stocks he cannot help making exceptional profits himself. An effective price control usually means that prices must be fixed at all stages, after allowing margins which, if adequate for the less efficient and more dispersed units, mean large profits for the most efficient. Moreover, the techniques suitable when the submarine campaign and tight shipping allocations made it impossible for private enterprise to bring in adequate supplies and distribute them fairly and economically could not be simply transferred to a post-war situation where supplies were adequate and one was dealing with monopolies. The Profiteering Acts, passed as we were nearing the peak of inflation, were not part of a thought-out reconstruction plan, but merely a hastily prepared tranquilliser for the public. After the Committee on *High Prices*[54] had started its work, Auckland Geddes told it that the Government had decided to make 'profiteering', i.e. making 'unreasonable profits', illegal. The Food Controller's evidence—designed Beveridge said, to discourage the Government from embarking on this course—pointed out the difficulties, including that of defining strictly 'unreasonable profits'.[55] One can only assume that either the Ministers were still pretty ignorant of the working of the economic system, or that the whole operation was conscious window dressing. For though its inquiries led to a number of reports of interest to economists,[56] the Act made no real difference to prices, and the number of successful prosecutions[57] in one year did not amount to more than two days' work of the Ministry of Food.

[54]*High Prices,* 1919 (166) v.

[55]Profiteering Act, 1919, sect. i, 'unreasonable in all the circumstances'. See Beveridge, *British Food Control,* p. 288. The difficulties had already been pointed out in the Report of the Cttee. on *Trusts,* J Hilton's Memo, p. 29. The Report was addressed to A Geddes as President of the Bd. of Trade. Geddes's statement and the evidence of G H Roberts, Food Controller, are worth comparing. Geddes's claim that the Government was following the Committee's recommendation was but partly true, for the target was restricted, instead of being the whole question of monopolistic operations.

[56]For example, Reps. on biscuits, sewing cotton (3 Reps.), electric lamps, meat. For refs. and summaries of these and other Reps. see *Breviate,* II, 198–218.

[57]They are mostly not of big concerns rather hard to get at, but of little chaps taking an opportunity to snatch a little extra.

(*e*) *Commercial policy.* It was, however, less the question of industrial organisation, than that of trade policy which revealed the
strength of the commercial interests in the committees on commercial policy and industries after the war.[58] President Wilson, in his
speeches on the famous Fourteen Points for a just and durable peace,
declared for the removal as far as possible of economic barriers and
for equality of trading conditions. But this was not at all what
Britain, France and the other allies had already decided in the Paris
Conference, 1916. This was not only to secure for territories
occupied and devastated by the enemy a prior claim on resources
needed for their restoration, and to reserve to themselves their own
resources for the whole period of reconstruction—for which some
justification could be advanced—but to prevent dumping and to
loosen the hold German efficiency and 'economic penetration' had
obtained on their economic life, by prohibitions on German trade,
and up-rooting German businesses in their territories. This nationalistic, political bitterness[59] masked the resentment and hostility of the
commercial interests which had felt the pressure of German efficiency
in competition before the war, and under this cover of 'national
interest' they did not fail to press home their advantage. Lord
Curzon openly stated that he expected a long and fierce commercial
war to follow the end of hostilities. The Final Report of the Balfour
of Burleigh Committee was largely protectionist, for not only did
it want stringent action against dumping, but special protection of
'key' and 'pivotal' industries and of those industries which should
not be weakened by foreign competition or brought under foreign
domination. This was to be carried out by a special independent
board to decide on applications for tariffs and other forms of assistance—in itself a sensible enough suggestion, if the questions were
to be taken out of politics and to be free of Parliamentary lobbying
and if precise criteria could be provided to the Board. It is true that
the Majority suggested conditions about efficiency, but a strong
Minority, without arguing the case, simply declared for a 10 per
cent tariff. In either case a complete reversal of British Free Trade

[58]For summaries see *Breviate*, II, 152–8.

[59]For a vivid example of nationalistic bitterness on the economic domination of Italy
by Germany (and ourselves) see Ezio Gray, *The Bloodless War*, trans. B Miall (1917).

policy would be involved, and this, with similar developments in other countries, including the U.S.A. itself,[60] put the commercial interests in strong, prepared positions which proved a fatal obstacle to the achievement of Wilson's aims. But there were protests from the Liberals and socialists.[61] Some of the origins of the policy were to be found further back than war-time fears about key industries and dumping, in Chamberlain's Tariff Reform campaign, broad ideas of which eventually captured the Conservative Party. Even the term 'safeguarding', presently to find its way to the Statute Book in the *Safeguarding of Industries Act*, 1921, was first used in that controversy. But the country was not ready to accept full protection —it was rejected in the election of 1923 and not raised again in that of 1924—and though they eventually became permanent, the duties to protect key industries and to prevent dumping, including exchange dumping, which that Act established for limited periods, were as far as the public would then go.

ii. *Social Policy*

(*a*) *Housing*. In social policy there were two fields in which there were major reconstruction projects—housing and health. The need for houses seemed simple and obvious enough: the war shortages of labour and materials had reduced annual house building to a fraction and the task was to make up the accumulated deficiency— 300,000, 500,000 or whatever might be the correct assessment of it. Encouraged by the slogan 'Homes for Heroes', that is how the public saw it. But no sooner was the operation embarked upon than it ran into a sea of troubles which nearly proved fatal to it. Of some of them the planners already had (or could have had) knowledge;

---

[60]The American Export Association Act, 1918 (Webb Act), which exempted export associations from some provisions of the Sherman Anti-Trust Act, was unfortunate in its international effects in that it was seen by European countries to herald the appearance of giant American export combines and to render the more necessary the defensive, protectionist measures which the Wilsonian policy aimed to prevent. It definitely hardened the attitude of European governments and producers. All the major countries were in fact preparing for a fierce competitive trade struggle. For a defence of the Act and its text, see W S Culbertson, *Commerical Policy in Wartime and After* (1919), pp. 168–71, 434–7.

[61]See *Economist* and *New Statesman*, both 4 May 1917.

others could perhaps have been 'known by foresight'; whilst others could scarcely have been anticipated. The post-war problem was thus not the old one of the housing of slum dwellers, but that of meeting the banked-up demand of the ordinary man. Working-class houses had normally been provided by private investors building or buying to let, and hitherto the assumption of State policy had been that usually they would meet that demand. But although the immediate difficulties were due to the virtual cessation of house building during the war and in some areas were acute because of the influx of munition workers,[62] the lag was not entirely due to this. Between 1901–11 the number of additional families formed annually was probably about 100,000 while the annual addition to the number of houses was only 84,000.

The Royal Commission on the *Housing of the Industrial Population of Scotland*, 1917,[63] appointed in 1912 following an inquiry by the Miners' Federation in 1909, was initially concerned with the per-manent general situation. Their report made it clear that the appalling conditions revealed arose not only from the lack of vigour of local authorities, land prices, etc., but from the fact that private enterprise had been unable to provide houses at rents which the workers could pay. The remedies they proposed meant a revolution in national policy. It would be impossible in the disturbed commercial condi-tions after the war for private enterprise to undertake speedily a task of the necessary size, and financial assistance to stimulate local authorities would alone be adequate; the State should therefore take full responsibility for fourteen years. The provision of houses by local authorities should no longer be optional, but a duty, and the scheme must be backed by a strong central organisation. For seven years the State should pay the running losses and at the end the difference between capital costs and valuation. The Commission signed its Report in September 1917, but in the meantime the Salisbury Panel[64] which had been set to work on the emergency

[62]See Monica Baldwin, *I Leaped Over the Wall* (1950), for her experiences in a mun-ition factory.

[63]R. Com. Rep.; 1917–18, Cd. 8731, xiv. *Breviate*, II, 431–2.

[64]*Housing in England and Wales*, Min. of Reconstruction Advisory Housing Panel on the Emergency Problem, Memo.; 1918, Cd. 9087, xxvi.

problem, presented its Report in October 1917 with substantially the same conclusions: the State should build and own the working-class houses necessary to make up the shortage, but they should then be transferred to the local authorities at a figure which allowed for the fall in costs by the end of the period.

A great amount of intensive work was done on the whole problem. First, the numbers required had to be determined. The planners had little more to go on than the 1911 Census, already five or six years out of date, while in the meantime there had been a great redistribution of working-class population; and help from the National Register and rationing figures was limited. The Salisbury Committee estimated the number of houses required in 1918 at 300,000. The Tudor Walters Committee[65] in 1918 said 500,000, to include the pre-war deficiency. But the surveys made by local authorities under the *Housing, Town Planning, Etc. Act,* 1919 (The Addison Act) produced a total of 800,000. And the current annual need was about 100,000. There had to be a good deal of guesswork, the Ministry taking as a crude measure the normal growth of population at four and a half persons per house.[66]

What standard of housing should be provided? Here the idealism of the time found full expression. There was general agreement that the question was not simply one of providing more 'units of accommodation', but of bringing into reality 'a wholly new and generous vision of working class housing'. The Women's Housing Sub-Committee[67] in 1918 set out the new minimum requirements—three rooms up, three rooms down, and a number of amenities, but added that these would be of little use unless the superficial area of the houses were raised above what had been common in the past. The Tudor Walters Committee recommended a minimum size of 760 feet super, and in towns a house density of not exceeding 12 to the acre. And great pains were taken to provide local authorities with suggested house designs, site layouts, etc. When the need for house room was so great and so many were 'waiting', how much of

[65]*Building Construction in Connection with the Provision of Dwellings for the Working Classes,* Cttee. Rep.; 1918, Cd. 9191, vii. *Breviate,* II, 434–5.

[66]Min. of Health, 1st Ann. Rep., 1919-20, pt. ii, p. 12; 1920, Cmd. 917, xvii.

[67]Rep.; 1918, Cd. 9166, 9232, x. *Breviate,* II, 433.

the scarce labour and materials it was justifiable to direct to improving the standards of the few likely to enjoy them—though most reformers envisaged it as a new permanent standard—was a matter of values and judgement. But most were untroubled by doubts about our ability to carry out the programme with this additional task, and it is not clear whether anyone worked out how significant was the cost of new standards in terms of the number of houses which could have been built at nearer the existing standard; that came up for consideration later.

But a crash programme of this size would put an immense strain on an industry depleted of much of its man-power and short of essential materials. The Carmichael Committee on the *Building Industry After the War*[68] felt that the supplies of materials would be inadequate for all the needs for at least two years and that a central committee should be set up to allocate supplies and operate a system of building permits. It was also clear, as the Scottish Commission had argued, that it would require a co-ordinated drive. From Addison's *Diary,* it appears that the Local Government Board was nervous about the capacity of local authorities who built about 5,000 a year in normal conditions, to undertake 300,000 in very difficult ones. Nor was it at first very forthcoming in proposals to build up a strong organisation to carry through this great programme.

There remained the major problem of costs, rents and financial aid. With costs at the end-of-war levels, to secure a minimum return private investors would have had to charge rents far above the 1914 level the Rent Restriction Acts permitted for existing houses and which the public had come to regard as 'proper'. The outcry which would have followed the erection of houses for which only the better-off workers could pay, politicians were well able to imagine. Quite apart from other considerations, reliance on private unsubsidised building was politically impossible. The only question, therefore, was how much central aid? Seventy-five per cent of costs? But this would mean that the remaining twenty-five per cent would have to be borne alike by wealthy authorities requiring few working-class houses, and by poor working-class areas needing many such

[68] 1918, Cd. 9197, vii. *Breviate,* II, 434.

houses, but having meagre resources of rateable value. And it would not have been easy to enforce the new minimum standards in such conditions. Hitherto the local authorities had borne all of any loss on building working-class houses; by the Act of 1919 the State now undertook to carry the whole of the loss over and above the produce of a penny rate. The size of the loss depended on the rents to be charged, and on this the question had been pre-judged. To meet an immediate difficulty a step had been taken which had a profound effect and later made the solution more difficult. The famous rent strike at Glasgow—the agitation spread to Sheffield and other areas where there was abnormal pressure—led to the Rent Restrictions Act, 1915—which for working-class houses pinned rents at the 1914 level. The fact that the vast majority of the working class were paying rent at that level made it impossible to charge rents on new houses much out of relation to them. Costs had to be forgotten, and in the end rents were to have regard to those obtaining in the locality, including controlled rents, though the amenities of the new houses and the class of tenants for whom they were provided might be taken into account.

Such was the generous and imaginative plan to deal with an emergency and to bring new conceptions to working-class housing.

(*b*) *Health*. At the outbreak of the war the developments in the health services had left a number of problems urgently requiring solution. The public sanitary and preventive services had been expanding, the number of full-time medical officers increasing; in some areas the Poor Law infirmaries had been transformed into public hospitals, the education authorities were inspecting and arranging for the treatment of school children, and local authorities were extending midwifery services, establishing infant welfare clinics, and some were providing nursing. Into this the National Health Insurance Scheme, while it had brought millions of manual workers under the care of the doctors, had introduced a quite different and in some ways contrary line of development and created independent and complicated administrative machinery. It covered only a part of the employed population, made no provision for wives or children, and the standard of treatment was low. The hospitals were located in a haphazard manner, admission to some of them being easy, in others, conditional on the patient collecting an adequate number of letters from individual subscribers. The general effect was in considerable degree to separate the preventive from the curative services.

In the meantime the loss of life during the war had sharpened the public consciousness of the ordinary losses of life and health,[69] and not least of a preventible part of it, infant mortality, to which Newsholme again called attention by re-issuing in 1917 his famous 1910 Report and by extending his researches to the whole field of child mortality, at ages 0—5.[70] What was to be done about it? If the problem had been purely one of science, and we could have started with completely new ground, that task would have been to assess the needs of each group of population for general and special hospitals, consultants, general practitioners, nurses, etc. at so many per thousand families. That was, in effect, what eventually the Welsh Committee on *Medical and Allied Services* (1920) did: one midwife for every 100 births, one doctor for every 400 homes, one outdoor nurse for every 3,000 population and so on. But the ground was littered with established and confused interests and institutions. No large-scale commission or other form of inquiry was appointed, but evolution of thought can be followed in a number of official and Parliamentary Papers. First, the Maclean Committee on *The Transfer of Functions of Poor Law Authorities*[71] (signed Dec. 1917, issued 1918) recommended the transfer from the Poor Law of all its health services for the infirm, sick, etc. to the local health authority, one member, Sir Robert Morant, stating two conditions: that before transfer the local services should be unified on comprehensive lines, and secondly, that the central responsibility for the different forms of service should be vested in a new authority, a Ministry of Health. To the last recommendation the Committee on the *Machinery of Government* (signed Dec. 1918) added that the responsibility for health insurance should also be transferred to it.[72] This was done—though

[69]Witness the publication (1919) of a series of books for health and social workers and general readers by Scharlieb, Savage, Robertson, Cates and others (Cassell's English Public Health Series).
[70]1910, Cd. 5263, xxxix, reprinted 1917; 1917–18, Cd. 8496, xvi.
[71]1917–18, Cd. 8917, xviii.
[72]Rep., pp. 58–63; 1918, Cd. 9230, xii.

not without some doubts on the part of friendly societies who, as always, feared for their independence—when the Ministry was created in 1919. It was widely welcomed as initiating a new era in public health. But in September 1918 Newsholme, writing his last Report, that for 1917-18, as Chief Medical Officer,[73] pointed out that the creation of the Ministry of Health would not of itself save a single life,[74] but could effect good only if it were able to improve and unify the confused machinery and give it drive. Medical services should be available to all who needed them and not only to insured persons and poor law applicants; and in essentials should be as efficient as those available to richer persons. The provision of institutions should be systematised, every doctor should be able to call on nursing services, if necessary at public expense. And to ensure the most economical distribution of doctors many of the facilities would have to be arranged at centres. The progress of medical science would require an extension of communal provision and some scrapping of old administrative machinery. It was a powerful, honest and far-sighted statement. The next official shot came from his successor, Sir George Newman, in his *Outline of the Practice of Preventive Medicine* (1919),[75] who repeated Newsholme's plea for the unification of local health machinery, but added two new ones: for a new unit of local health administration which would make full co-ordination possible and—no doubt bearing in mind the attitude of the medical profession and the necessity of bringing in those engaged in the new health insurance service—for a structural and co-ordinated body of medical men (including general practitioners) to be charged with its administration.[76] While endorsing the need for medical services to be available to all who needed them, he went on to say that this did not mean that they should be free.[77] But in one respect the climate of opinion was already beginning to change.

[73]Op. cit., p. xiv; 1918, Cd. 9169, xi, esp. pp. x-xx, 'The Needs of the Future'.

[74]This phrase—together with his references to communal provision—came in for some stupid and ignorant criticism. It was, however, quoted in a footnote in Newman's *Outline of the Practice of Preventive Medicine,* 1919, Cmd. 363, xxxix.

[75]1919, Cmd, 363, xxxix.

[76]Op. cit., p. 121.

[77]Op. cit., rev. ed., p. 134.

R

Newsholme's generous vision that all should have facilities equal in essentials to those accessible to the rich was modified to 'a standard which constitutes something in the nature of a *national minimum* of what is both necessary and practicable in all areas rather than what might be desirable if carried out by the most enlightened and competent authorities'.[78]

These ideas were developed in more detail in the Interim Reports of the Consultative Council on the *Future Provision of Medical and Allied Services for England, Wales and Scotland*.[79] These were entirely medical men's reports setting out schemes which, starting from the domiciliary services of general practitioners, linked them with the institutions: primary health centres, staffed by general practitioners, secondary health centres with full-time staffs and with a teaching hospital and medical school as the hub. The English Report, in a diagram, gave the scheme for Gloucestershire. But this involved two new principles. In order to co-ordinate these activities each area would have a single health authority to supervise all services, preventive and curative, either a statutory committee of existing local authorities or an entirely new *ad hoc* authority dealing with health services only—an idea which some authorities did not find palatable. In either case the elected representatives were to have three-fifths of the membership, the majority of the remainder being representatives of the medical profession. Secondly, while some members wanted the new institutional services to be free for all, the majority preferred standard charges which could be covered by insurance. The Reports for Wales and Scotland apply similar principles to their special conditions, but, as we have seen, the Welsh Report worked out in detail the staffs and institutional beds required per thousand population.

The effect of the scientific approach for which Newsholme and others had argued was thus to produce plans for co-ordinated and organically connected services; but they threw up questions of principle on which discussion was to rage for a quarter of a century: whether unification should involve a new *ad hoc* administrative unit,

[78]Op. cit., para. 142, pp. 112–13; 1926 ed., para. 176, p. 146.
[79]English Rep., 1920, Cmd. 693, xvii. Welsh Rep., 1920, Cmd. 703, xvii; 1921, Cmd. 1448, xiii. Scottish Rep., 1920, Cmd. 1039, xvii.

as the English and Welsh Reports suggested; whether the services though available to all should be free, or in the case of institutional treatment, provided at standard charges, or as the Scottish Report proposed, there should be public provision for all in the National Health Insurance grade, including women and children, with some help for those above it for special services they could not pay for; whether the doctor should be a salaried officer—as the Irish Vice-Regal Commission had proposed and the Royal Commission on the Poor Law rejected—or whether salaried service should be restricted to those not in contact with the individual patient, as the English Report proposed; and finally, what was to be the standard treatment, the best (Newsholme) or an attainable minimum (Newman). And Newsholme wanted medical care to be separated and put in a position to develop free from the limits of insurance against loss of earnings.

iii. *Industrial Unrest and Disputes*

The search for a new machinery and a code of practice. What means had the State for dealing with the problem of industrial relations and unrest during the war and reconstruction after it? As we have seen, the new problems presented by nation-wide strikes and lock-outs in basic industries—coal mining, railways, port work—damaging output and employment in the whole economy had not, by the outbreak of war, called forth a comprehensive theory or machinery for handling them. The great disputes had been dealt with by improvised expedients: the political skill of two Ministers, a royal commission of inquiry into one, a special Act providing a statutory minimum wage in another, House of Commons resolutions of exhortation to employers, partly accepted in one case (railways), and ignored in the other (London docks). Nor was there a strong central trade union organisation which could bring a collective point of view to bear. Unions had rejected a compulsory 'cooling off period' of inquiry before strikes. Some unions wanted collective contracts to be legally enforceable, but not others, and unions in industries half-organised wanted their agreements made binding on other employers or workers not partners to them. The limitations of this collection of expedients were revealed in the three phases through which the labour problem passed: the war, with its primary necessity of mobilising the efforts of the whole population; the immediate post-war, when unions were at the peak of membership and demanding a new status and a new social purpose in industry; and in the disastrous phase of deflation. The changing moods of labour and the new ideas which bubbled up in the industrial turbulence, and the passions behind them are most vividly conveyed, not by the formal accounts of the disputes, but by the pamphlets and leaflets which poured out from the unions and labour groups.

In the conditions in which war broke out there was no question of planning beforehand and policy had to be built up as we went along. Some of the expedients—the 'industrial Truce', leaving certificates and embargoes to prevent workers from chasing round from one munition works to another to find the highest bidder, restraint on employers' powers of sacking, the suspension of workshop practices etc.—were merely temporary, passing into disuse as the war ended. We are not here concerned with the techniques of industrial guerilla warfare, but with permanent State policy and the atmosphere in which it was formulated. There were four matters on which war-time events contributed to the situation which had to be dealt with when the war ended.

First, the most striking break from pre-war doctrines was that the State now took the powers of coercion which it had hitherto lacked:[80] in defined circumstances strikes and lock-outs in munition works were prohibited and the Minister could refer industrial differences to the Committee on Production, a single arbitrator or a tribunal including representatives of both sides, whose awards could be legally binding on both parties. The prohibition could be applied by proclamation to any other industry where a dispute was directly or indirectly prejudicial to the supply of munitions, a power which was applied in July 1915, to the South Wales Coal Industry and in December 1916, to the card room workers. In July 1918, the Government threatened to conscript into the army the Coventry engineers on strike.

[80]Munitions of War Act, 1915.

Secondly, the friction which arose in temporary war-time conditions was most intense over the labour dilution agreements accepted by the national union, for these meant tricky adjustments in the individual workshops where the shoe pinched, and gave the shop stewards' movement both a task and an opportunity. The criticisms and unrest developed into an attack on capitalism, the Clyde Workers Committee even trying to make it a condition of their co-operation that all industries should be taken over by the Government and workers vested with the right to take part in management in every department equally with the managers. In certain industrial centres some workers were not only anti-capitalist, but anti-war as well, either on pacifist grounds, as many members of the Independent Labour Party, and the British Socialist Party were apt to be, or on class grounds as the Socialist Labour Party was overtly. The war was a capitalist war in which the workers of all belligerent countries would lose, and they should endeavour, as had been urged by the Second International, to use every means to bring it to an end and use the crisis to overthrow capitalism. These ideas, found wherever these bodies had members, were less widespread than the propaganda suggested, but were strong enough to cause difficulties and unofficial strikes in some areas—the Clyde, South Wales, Sheffield, Coventry. In the Clyde area a number of shop stewards were arrested and deported from it, their journals occasionally suppressed.

Thirdly, the formation of the Triple Industrial Alliance between miners, railwaymen and transport workers, mooted before the war and ratified in 1915, was a new portent both to unions and to the Government. The pre-war strikes in each of these industries had affected employment in the others and the gains from mutual consultation seemed obvious. Its purpose was not sympathetic strikes or even sympathetic mutual support, but that each should arrange for its wage agreements to terminate on the same date.[81] Each would put forward its own demands simultaneously and were not to accept settlement unless the other two also settled. If a strike came each would thus be striking for its own programme and incidentally

---

[81]This is not formally stated in the published agreed conditions (*Labour Year Book,* p. 23) but see Miners' Federation Annual Conference *Report,* 17 Aug. 1921, pp. 12–13, 20–1, esp. 3rd para. on p. 21.

assisting the others, and the influence of the massive power of these three great bodies of 800,000 miners, some 300,000 railwaymen and 250,000 transport workers should force the employers in their industries, some of whom had been very obstinate on 'recognition', into conceding satisfactory settlements. Great hopes were entertained by labour of the advances which could be secured peacefully by its means.[82] To the Government, which had difficulties enough before the war in handling nation-wide strikes in these industries separately, the prospect of being faced with three simultaneously was indeed something to think about.[83]

Fourthly, the first Russian Revolution of 1917 was hailed with delight by all sections of the British working class, for it meant the fall of an oppressive autocracy they had always hated and the release from real, inward shame they had felt in fighting alongside it as an ally. The Albert Hall demonstration of welcome for the Revolution was followed by a Leeds conference which accepted, with support from MacDonald and Snowden, W C Anderson's resolution in favour of forming, following the example of Russia, a Workers and Soldiers Council.[84] There is no doubt of the great sense of liberation and the stimulus it gave to general thinking of the place of labour in society.

Finally, there was one penetrating study modern in approach—perhaps the first of its kind in this country—of the more deep-seated causes of industrial unrest—that by the Commissioners on *Industrial Unrest* for the South Wales area.[85] In other districts the Commissioners limited their field of inquiry to matters peculiar to the war period, but those for Wales argued that unrest had become a permanent condition in the Welsh coalfields. For years the Welsh miners had manifested a disposition to 'down tools' on very slight grounds and the temporary causes during the war period were aggravated by more deep-seated ones. The Report describes the

[82]For example see G R Carter, *The Triple Industrial Alliance* (1917), author's foreword to 2nd ed.; and an article by W B Reckitt in *Labour Year Book* (1919), pp. 23–5.

[83]It received reminders of the existence of the Alliance in 1916 when it sent a deputation on demobilisation, and in 1917 when a Triple Alliance Conference demanded the conscription of wealth.

[84]The vast mass of the British working class were not anti-war; it was this and not the defection of leaders which meant that this resolution came to nothing in practice.

[85]*Industrial Unrest, Area No. 7*, 1917–18, Cd. 8668, xv.

rapid expansion of the Welsh coal industry and its development in the valleys, which led to unsatisfactory and congested housing, absence of amenities, and the domination of the lives and thoughts of the inhabitants by the apparatus of one industry. The building up of great colliery amalgamations had raised in the minds of colliery workers the fear of a monopoly directed to their industrial subjugation, so that they had come to regard a single trade union ('The Federation') as a means of securing industrial emancipation. The traditional political and religious outlook of the old Welsh collier had been slowly giving way to advanced political and social views based on the conviction that capital and labour were necessarily hostile. This analysis had already been expressed in dramatic form by a Welsh playwright, J O Francis, who in *Change* (1913) illumined the local and family tensions these changes of political ideas and loyalties produced.[86] The Welsh Commissioners' recommendations included proposals directed not only to temporary, but to the more permanent causes. There must be a new spirit of partnership in industry; the existing system must be modified so as to identify the worker more closely with the control of industry and to give him security, i.e. he should not be dismissed except with the consent of his fellow workmen. Membership of a recognised trade union should be a condition of employment; conciliation boards and industrial councils should be established, wage disparities removed and hours of work reduced.

But after the end of hostilities there was no single overriding objective on which workers could be compelled to follow one employment rather than another or providing a criterion on which industrial stoppages could be banned. The restraints would not then be tolerated, nor were they of a kind which expressed the ideals of a new status for labour which had been so prominent an element in war-time thinking. Pre-war policies had been inadequate, few of the war-time devices seemed likely to be applicable to the conditions of peace. What was the new policy to be? The question was put to the Ministry of Reconstruction Whitley Committee, appointed 1916, to consider the permanent *Relations between Employers and Employed.*

[86]Welsh version, 1929. For some of the atmosphere in recollection, see R Williams, *Border Country* (1960).

Its Final Report was signed in July 1918. This Committee, like its famous predecessor, the Labour Commission, did not go into the wider causes of industrial unrest, but stuck fairly closely to its last, the relations of employers and their workmen. But the welcome its proposals received from many was enthusiastic because they seemed to give practical expression to the ideals of a new status for labour and of industrial democracy without which, indeed, its reports could scarcely have been written. Starting from the proposition that a permanent improvement in industrial relations depended not only on the existence of representative organisations on both sides, but involved the active co-operation of the workers, for well-organised industries it suggested joint industrial councils confined to representatives of unions and employers, district councils and, important to the whole structure, works committees representative equally of management and workers.[87] Trades with little in the way of representative organisation, either of workers or employers, should be provided for by the extension of the trade board system, hitherto confined to industries where wages were unduly low.[88] In improving machinery for handling industrial disputes, the Committee adhered to the traditional approach that in general industries should make their own agreements and settle their own differences. Compulsory arbitration was again rejected on the ground that since it was not desired either by employers or workers, its imposition would cause unrest. But their contention that during the war compulsory arbitration had not been successful in preventing strikes would seem to have stretched the evidence a bit. For although the rank and file tried to get round the industrial truce by unofficial strikes, there were many successful arbitrations under the Munitions of War Act. They equally rejected the compulsory 'cooling off' period, as the unions had done earlier.[89] The Committee proposed that the voluntary practices should be supplemented by a permanent body for arbitration to which both parties could resort if their normal machinery broke down, and by empowering the Minister of Labour to hold

[87]*Relations between Employers and Employed,* Cttee. Inter. Rep.; 1917–18, Cd. 8606, xviii; 1918, Cd. 9001, xiv.
[88]Ibid., 1918, Cd. 9002, x.
[89]Ibid., 1918, Cd. 9099, vii.

inquiries into disputes. The Government accepted broadly the Committee's proposals on all three lines of policy,[90] so that in this respect the Committee must be counted a successful one. Such was the machinery by which the labour problems in the period of reconstruction were to be handled.

The plans for the trades boards proved generally acceptable, and did result in some millions of workers being brought within the scope of this form of collective bargaining.[91] And the Ministry of Labour made special efforts to promote the formation of Joint Industrial Councils.[92] But it was the proposals for workshop committees which seemed to offer the greatest hope for a new era of permanent industrial relations based on democratic arrangements. Indeed, one American commentator, thinking of the part played by workshop organisation in the Russian Revolution, complimented the British on the political genius which enabled them to light the fires of revolution in the domestic grate! But this is not how many saw it. For the labour and radical members of the committee—Clynes, J A Hobson, Susan Lawrence, Mallon, Mona Wilson—whilst supporting the proposals for representation, stated that these could not be expected to settle the more serious disputes arising in an economic system governed by private profit.[93] The National Guilds League[94] and the Shop Stewards movement[95] declared that they did not provide 'self-government in industry' at all, but aimed at killing the independent workshop movement by retaining its form but changing its principles from class warfare to class collaboration. They had envisaged the workshop committee not as 'joint', but as consisting of workers only and based on the opposition of and not on a community of interest with management, and as instruments

[90]Trade Boards Act, 1918; Industrial Courts Acts, 1919. The Ministry of Labour made a special effort to promote the formation of workshop committees and J.I.C.s.

[91]For a list of trades boards, including earlier ones, in the order in which they were established see *Industrial Negotiations and Agreements* (T.U.C. and Labour Party, 1923), p. 11.

[92]Ibid., app. i, pp. 51–2, for a list of industries covered in 1921.

[93]1918, Cd. 9153, viii.

[94]National Guilds League, *National Guilds or Whitley Councils* (1918).

[95]J T Murphy, *Compromise or Independence* (1918) and *Preparing for Power*, pp. 142–3. Also *Labour Year Book* (1919), pp. 251–6.

with which to advance the control of industry entirely by the workers. In Gallacher's scheme the committees were to undertake bulk labour contracts for the entire business of production and were themselves to distribute the proceeds amongst the workers. The only industries in which the 'Whitley' committees could be organised were those where there was no private profit (as in State concerns) or where the unions were strong. Certainly they would be unsafe in industries where there were a large number of competing unions. Nor were the unions always favourable, for they feared the committees might take over some of the authority of the unions and their branch officers. The men feared that their representatives would be 'nobbled' by employers or put into an ambiguous position of dual allegiance, and possible representatives wondered whether if they said anything which differed from the men's policy, they would be suspect. Employers were naturally sensitive, for it was not in the joint national councils, but in the workshops where the function and disciplines of management they did not wish to share were exercised. And some unions declined to co-operate partly out of suspicion, partly because they already had strong union organisation. The Committee had suggested nothing, it was declared, which changed the fundamental relationship of capitalist and worker.

The real test came from industrial turbulence which had begun to show itself before the fighting had ended and the pent-up claims of labour could assert themselves, e.g. the C.W.S. strike (proclaimed under the Munitions of War Act); a startling strike of the Metropolitan Police (later followed by an unsuccessful provincial strike); the miners' demand not only for higher wages and shorter hours, but for the nationalisation of the mines and democratic control of the industry which would make the better standards possible,—something new; a threatened rail strike, a number of successful demands for shorter hours, and an unsuccessful forty-hour week strike on the Clyde. The discontents were influenced by the great war-time inflation which had made the rise in the cost of living new in magnitude and significance. The Sumner Committee's[96] endeavours to measure it on a limited statistical basis showed that up to

[96]*Working Classes and the Cost of Living,* Cttee. Rep.; 1918, Cd. 8980, vii. The sharp controversy on whether the rise in the index accurately measures the rise in the workers'

July 1918, it was 67 per cent, 75 per cent, and 81 per cent for skilled, semi-skilled and unskilled respectively—and led to the first fumbling efforts to ensure that real wages did not fall, by linking them to the cost-of-living index. This began in December 1917, when the N.U.R. agreed that any fresh claim should depend on a given rise in the index. But behind these disputes were the passionate demands of organised labour for a recognition of its new status in society.

New tensions were introduced because the political expression of these emotions and grievances was frustrated by the 'coupon' election of December 1918, when Lloyd George's appeal induced the electorate to send to Parliament a majority, including many 'hard-faced men who looked as though they had done well out of the war', as Keynes unkindly put it, unsympathetic to the new ideals. There were some 400 Conservative and Liberal followers of Lloyd George, the independent Liberals were crushed and Labour taking second place with only some 72 seats obtained by 320 candidates.

Deprived of effective political expression, Labour had therefore to rely on its industrial arm, and by contrast here everything seemed favourable. For the inflationary boom created great opportunities for aggressive union policies. The number of trade unionists which by 1914 had risen to 4 million, was 6,500,000 in 1918 and reached the startling peak of 8,300,000 in 1920. Added to this was the looming but untested strength of the Triple Alliance, regarded as a weapon of hope with which to break through the established, to the new social order.

This seething unrest went far beyond the 'normal' disputes in particular industries for which the Whitley Committee had devised its machinery, and the Government had to try again. It took three steps, one—perhaps an echo with a difference of the 1911 Industrial Council—was to call a National Industrial Conference of employers and trade unionists to survey the whole ground, the second to resort to one of the pre-war tools and set up a Commission (Sankey) on

---

cost of living, now perennial, really began at this time. On the special difficulties of measuring changes when war or other circumstances had caused a change in the items consumed, see A L Bowley, 'Measurement of Change in the Cost of Living' in R. *Stat. Soc. Jn.* (May 1919); Pigou, *Economics of Welfare*, pt. i, chap. v sects. 3–8.

the Coal Industry, whilst the third was to use its powers under the new Industrial Courts Act to appoint an independent inquiry into the Dock Dispute. Each of these had a dramatic quality of its own.

Starting from the view, certainly widely held, that with the fighting only just ended any preventible strike or lock-out might have a shattering effect on the war-weakened economy, the Conference was asked to consider the causes of unrest, including specifically the questions of recognition, minimum wages and maximum hours which were running through all industry at the time, and unemployment and its prevention. Its career was a chequered one. First, the miners, railwaymen, transport workers and engineers declined to join it. In accordance with the unions' apparently mounting industrial power, the trade union representatives compensated for Labour's weakness in Parliament by presenting to the Conference a vigorous statement which in aggressiveness went far beyond *Labour and the New Social Order.* The fundamental cause of unrest, it declared, was not the smaller and special grievances which came to the surface at any particular time, but the increasing vehemence with which Labour was challenging the whole structure of capitalist industry. It was not willing to acquiesce in a system in which industry was conducted for the benefit of a few, or in which labour was bought and sold as a commodity; it had a right to equal democratic partnership, and demanded the substitution of a democratic system of public ownership with an increasing element of control by the organised workers themselves. Mines, railways, docks, the supply of electric power, ocean-going shipping and key industries should be nationalised at once and this should be accompanied by giving organised workers the greatest practical control over conditions and their management.[97] Two minor points indicate the nature of some of its thinking. It was striking that in the final up-swing of inflation, which was to bring its own penalties, the memorandum argued that a general increase of wages by improving the worker's purchasing power would have the general and permanent effect of limiting continuous unemployment by bringing consumption into something like equilibrium with

[97]*Industrial Conference,* Rep.; 1919, Cmd. 501, xxiv. Rep. only, Cmd. 139, app. i, pp. ii-iii, vii, xi.

256

production (p. viii, para. 5a). It also proposed non-contributory unemployment benefit at flat rates and revived the Webbs' suggestion in 1909 (the difficulties of which led to its omission from the insurance scheme) that this should be administered by trade unions, which should also receive 50 per cent of any additional benefits paid. In much of this Memorandum, if the hands were the hands of the chairman, Arthur Henderson, the voice was remarkably like that of the secretary, G D H Cole.

The full Joint Committee avoided these larger issues. But amongst its specific recommendations were a legal eight-hour day, with powers of variation to fit the special circumstances of different industries, a legal minimum wage with a commission to determine what it should be; full recognition of trade unions and employers' associations as negotiating bodies; the regulation of Government contracts to stabilise employment, wider arrangements for maintaining the unemployed and the under-employed.

The second expedient was the appointment of the Sankey Commission, whose conclusions on the structure of the mining industry have already been referred to. Its place in the story here is that the miners having linked their claim for a rise of pay and shorter hours with the re-organisation of the industry through nationalisation, for the first time a great privately owned industry was publicly and mercilessly scrutinised, with an array of experts of all kinds on either side, every defect in organisation and deficiency in management being dragged to light. Neither mine nor royalty owners were spared. When at the end of the first stage of the inquiry three members, including the chairman, concluded that the existing system of ownership and working stood condemned and that some other system, either nationalisation or a method of unification by national purchase and/or joint control be substituted, and that whatever system was put in its place the colliery workers should be given an effective voice in the operation of the mines, the miners' battle of ideas seemed half-won.[98] It appeared a resounding proof of the

[98]It is illustrative of the mood of the times that the miners wanted to choose half the members of the central body, that two should be representative of consumers, the Government appointing the remainder, and of the development of opinion that their own nationalisation Bill of 1912 did not include these provisions. *Coal Industry Commission,* vol. I, 1st Stage Rep., Mins. of ev.; 1919, Cmd. 359, xi; see W Straker's ev., p. 324 and q. 8688.

whole radical and socialist case for a fundamental change in industry generally which had been canvassed for so long. Similarly, the third event (later, in 1920), the new Court of Enquiry into the dock workers' claim for 16 shillings a day, was highlighted both by a dramatic confrontation of an independent statistical witness on the costs of a docker's minimum standard[99]—the difference between the parties was between £3 17s 6d and £6—and also by the declaration of the Court that the time had passed for assessing the value of human labour on the poverty line, that the system of casual labour must be torn up by its roots through the registration of all workers in the docks and the maintenance of unemployed casual men.[100] Although this was of necessity a statement of aims and principles of reform and did not deal with the practical difficulties, it was hailed as the 'Dockers' Charter'. It was in principle a victory in a long struggle going back to Booth and the Webbs.

Such were the schemes produced by the methods, new and old, which the Government had decided to use. The Sankey Plan, the Shaw Award and even the Industrial Conference seemed to indicate that the ideas which had been so long germinating were at last producing fruit, and that we were on the threshold of a new stage in industrial organisation.

iv. *The machinery of Government*

The range of reforms proposed made it certain that an attempt would be made to get out of the way the constitutional difficulties which had obstructed projects before 1914 and to tune up the whole machinery for the new tasks. Four major changes were proposed. The first, carried out, was to widen the basis of the franchise. Having recruited the armed forces by conscription and replaced men on war work by women, it was impossible not to extend the franchise to substantially manhood suffrage, or to women over thirty—an age limit designed to prevent the creation of an electorate dominantly female. Two proposals sprang from a desire to settle

[99]*Transport Workers: Wages and Conditions,* Mins. of ev., pp. 185–91; 1920, Cmd. 936, xxiv.

[100]Ibid., Ct. of Enq., paras. 16–20; 1920, Cmd. 936, xxiv.

problems left over from the fierce political struggles which the war had suspended. The ending of the Lords' veto by the Parliament Act, 1911, still left remaining the reform in its powers and membership which the radicals had demanded, with all this implied for the relationship of political power to class structure. The situation created by the passing of the Government of Ireland Act, its temporary suspension, the vigorous opposition of Ulster and the Easter Rising was, as later events were to show, highly dangerous. But neither of these could be dealt with by planning. The decisions to be made were political, only the political parties could enforce them and the machinery set up in the hope of arriving at them was political: small conferences representative of the parties to work out compromises. Neither had easy going, but some progress was made. Yet each was clearly influenced by the canvassing of ideas and volume of writing, academic and otherwise, which had been going on for some time. That the chairman of the first should be Bryce, scholar and statesman, the author of the *Holy Roman Empire*, the *American Commonwealth, Studies in the History of Jurisprudence*, and later *Modern Democracies*, was a guarantee that these would not be overlooked: so it proved. A statement, noteworthy for its significant title, *The Reform of the Second Chamber*,[101] set out very clearly the limited functions proposed for a House in which the hereditary element was to be reduced to a quarter, and later one-ninth of the membership, the main body of which was to be elected, not directly, for fear of creating a popularly elected rival to the Commons, nor nominated, nor chosen by local authorities, but indirectly elected by M.P.s organised into thirteen areas. The second endeavoured to set the problem of Ireland in the context of 'Home Rule all round' and to relieve legislative congestion in Parliament by *Devolution*[102] of some of its powers to local legislatures for England, Wales and Scotland. In this also progress was made, but sharp divisions remained about the basis on which the local chambers should be elected.

In the fourth field, however, there was an attempt to study and

[101]1918, Cd. 9038, x.

[102]1920, Cmd. 962, xiii.

plan ahead irrespective of party claims. The creation of a small, inner War Cabinet and of a number of new war-time ministers itself raised a query: was the existing organisation of departments, grown up over time in response to varying needs and not always with logically delimited functions, likely to be the best one for dealing with the manifold peace-time tasks? The famous scheme of departments drawn up by Bentham was the product of one mind with a highly organised political theory. The Haldane Committee's Report on the *Machinery of Government*[103] was the work mainly of four of its members,[104] who held no common political theory but possessed a high level of administrative experience and acquaintance-ship with the study of it in the modern mode. It was this common scientific approach which gave this first official review of our machinery that power and consistency which led to its enduring influence on thought. A smaller Cabinet, a first-class research organisation, standing Parliamentary Committees to consider the activities of the main departments, distribution of work between departments on the basis of the kind of service rather than the class of persons to be dealt with, Treasury control to be aided by the appointment in each department of a Finance Officer and an Establishment Officer, and the creation of a Ministry of Health, were amongst its specific suggestions.

3. THE FAILURE OF RECONSTRUCTION

The disastrous events after 1918, which wrecked so many plans for a more intelligently guided economy and in the end landed us with a million unemployed for whom it seemed no work could be found, were the outcome of a combination of inexperience, inadequate theory, correct theory, erroneous theory, the pressures of vested economic interests and of confusion between short-run problems whose urgency led us to snatch at imperfect diagnosis and

[103]1918, Cd. 9230, xii.
[104]See the notes at the end of the Report by members unable to take full part in its proceedings. Beatrice Webb gives an interesting description of its methods of work in *Methods of Social Study* (1932), pp. 149–51.

vital long-term ones. Thinking was hampered by harking back to the past, by the presumption that getting back to normal meant to the pre-war balance of industries, that restoring the relationship of various countries' currencies meant to pre-war ratios which had in fact gone for good. To avoid getting lost in the story of the bewildering attempts to find solutions for the great international war debts, reparations, wild depreciations and devaluations of currencies, attempts to prevent adverse trade balances, and remedies which made the diseases worse, one needs to pick out only certain events which indicate the terms on which the problems of implementing the plans were thought about.

i. *Three adverse decisions*

(a) *The election of 1918.* The perils which put the plans in jeopardy were three in number: it was the combination of them which proved fatal. One followed from the vote of the electorate, the other two from decisions of policy. One had nothing to do with the planning processes, but was political; to meet the second there was no ordered plan, for the third there was. The first was the ambiguous election of 1918: it has a good deal to answer for and does not stand up to questions well. For democracy spoke with two voices. One through the ballot, in exceptionally emotional circumstances exploited by slogans which one could wish could be expunged from the British record, and aided by internecine disputes of the Liberal party, resulted in more votes for the Conservatives than for either the Liberals or the Labour Party separately, but more for these two together than for the Conservatives. But the new House was dominated by the Conservative Members. What did this mean? There is no doubt that many voted for Lloyd George in the confidence that the successful war-time Prime Minister would also manage the tasks of reconstruction. There was no modern public opinion poll to tell us what the wishes of the electorate were in detail. The other voice, through the trade unions at the Industrial Conference of 1919, proclaimed not only *Labour and the New Social Order,* but aggressive versions of it. The Labour Party obtained only seventy-two seats, so that large numbers of trade unionists at this

261

time must simply have 'voted for Lloyd George', and though not with intent, against policies which their unions supported politically. Though radicals, liberals and labourites had exercised considerable, but not exclusive, influence on the principles and details of the plans, it was now a mainly Conservative House which was to preside over reconstruction and to decide if and when to act. The Conservatives, though not without social sympathies, were concerned less to restrain than to promote the vigour of private enterprise and often reverted to crude versions of economic theory inherited from previous generations. In policy, therefore, the legislature turned its back on many new social ideas and on the approach to problems of the Cambridge school of economists, and followed a trade policy which failed in its immediate object.

It is not being sentimental over the decline of an historic democratic party to feel that it was a misfortune that the Liberal Party was split and reduced in numbers at this time. With its internal tensions arising from an unusually wide spread of ideas between free enterprise on the right and the new radicalism on the left, this was always a possibility in conditions of stress. But by the influence of its left it had proved a useful medium through which radical and some collectivist ideas could pass to the Statute Book to give society a new direction. There was now no single party vehicle for them and for a whole generation this healthy traffic of ideas was stopped. The voters, now presented with two sharply opposed groups whose confrontation seemed to harden the doctrines of both and with a third trying to assert its independence of either, so chose that but for two not very effective interludes, most of the ideas on which so much imaginative effort had been spent were put aside for twenty years.

(*b*) *Premature abolition of war-time controls.* Secondly, the future of controls was not settled as a planning decision. Despite the mistakes, overlapping, omissions and confusions incidental to their creation in conditions of emergency and stress, by the end of the fighting its parts had been drawn together into a reasonably orderly working system. Taking it to pieces in conditions of great economic uncertainty could not be a simple operation. To leave the restoration of the normal economic system to the unco-ordinated activities of individuals was full of dangers. It was perhaps natural to think of scrapping the controls one by one, promptly or tardily as the scarcities which occasioned them were relieved. In various stages, this is what some departments tried to do: each considered its own problem. But it was not in selective terms that the decision was made.

In many belligerent countries with strong trade union and socialist movements, there were demands for new social objectives and, to prevent future economic wars, that all countries should be free to share in the markets of the world and have access to necessary raw materials. These ends required, said the Labour Party, that much of the apparatus of control be retained.[105] That is not how business interests saw it. Overwhelmingly—not only in Britain, but in most of the belligerent countries—business men rebelled against the continuance of war-time restrictions and were determined to be free of them, not only to restore their own businesses in their own way and to be able to seize the utmost advantage from the acute shortage of peace-time products, but to be unhampered in that international commercial struggle which Curzon had prophesied. They objected to controls established for temporary war purposes being used for quite different permanent ones and were determined that they should be got rid of before they could be used for socialistic experiments of which they disapproved. This, with the spectacle of the Russian Revolution in front of them and in the phase in which union strength and industrial unrest were rising to a peak, must have seemed to them only too likely. The strength of this obsession —even making every allowance for propaganda rhetoric—it is not easy to realise without re-reading the declarations of prominent business men. In their view the replenishment of overseas assets and the restoration of exports in the great branches of manufacturing industry, even if aided by the anti-dumping legislation and freedom to create large-scale monopolies able to carry on belligerent overseas commercial warfare, still depended on the vigour and effort of private business. They therefore insisted, not only that proposals

---

[105]See above, p. 206 et seq.

for continuing useful devices should be set aside, but that the Acts which set up the Ministry of Munitions, Food, Shipping and some coal control should be allowed to lapse in March 1921. By the middle of the year nearly all the machinery had vanished. Radicals and socialists saw many hopes disappear with them, and whatever may have been the gain for a few months, many business men were in little better case. For the over-hasty removal of the controls contributed to the many difficulties which were to follow later.

(*c*) *Monetary policy, the Cunliffe Report, monetary theory.* By contrast, for the third and worst peril there were carefully thought-out plans which had nothing directly to do with the creation of a new social order, but were devised simply to restore and safeguard the conditions of trade and employment on which the success of all other projects depended; they concerned monetary policy. Yet it was in the handling of inflation and deflation that the most grievous failures occurred—grievous because of the unforeseen part they played in wrecking the other plans. Was this because some of the plans were not carried out or carried out too late because they became muddled up with individualism in business policy? Or was there something wrong with the theory of them? The term 'inflation' as applied to currencies did not come into common use until the war, 'deflation' until 1919. Nor was it until the wild disorders of the world's currencies demanded thought and action that anything like precise technical meanings were given to them, and even so they had a variety of meanings. Cannan names J S Nicholson as being first off the mark in detecting the existence of the war-time inflation in England and confesses that he himself did not begin to be suspicious till 1916 or 1917.[106] It was in December 1917 that Pigou set out the various contemporary meanings of 'inflation',[107] and their number increased. Was it merely a rise in general prices? Was it too much money? Did this include credit? Did it mean a fall of the value of paper money in terms of the standard metal? Should its use be limited to the increase of money

[106]Cannan, *An Economist's Protest*, p. x.

[107]'Inflation' in *Econ. Jn.* (Dec. 1917), 486 et seq.

(and credit) connected with violent price movements? Or was its most important feature—as it often seemed then—their relationship to the violent fluctuations of the foreign exchanges? Was the essential point that the expansion of bank money was made greater than it would otherwise be by some action of Government? Was a rise in prices due to an influx of gold and the currency expansion based on it, inflation? These differences of definition were not just 'logic-chopping', but the result of a search for a fuller understanding of the phenomena and were of practical importance; for the different features they emphasised would call for differences in remedial policy.

We did not by the end of the war always know what answers to the questions were most appropriate for public policy; indeed, it was not till after the consideration of the great disturbances of national currencies in the early twenties that we arrived for a time at something like a standard doctrine on some of them. Some of the current propositions were but derivations from or amplifications of the received version of the quantity theory of money. This, and the later theory of purchasing power parity derived from it, were in due course criticised as mere words, as over-simplified, or as just obvious. But an understanding of and concentrated drive to apply the simplest lessons to be derived from them were the first need of the Governments and peoples of the time; the later scientific, theoretical refinements might then well have added to the confusions of public policy. For attempts to restore the various currencies to order would affect different groups of the population differently, favouring some, harming others, sometimes creating injustices. In steering through such difficulties it is invaluable to have simple, explainable and fundamental rules to hold on to. If, therefore, these concepts were erroneous, we have to say that their relevance at the time made them an outstanding example of the practical usefulness of economic error.

During the war all belligerent Governments, including our own, were in a hurry to obtain munitions of war or materials for making them, food for their troops and civilian populations etc. Raising money by taxation or loan was far too slow a process, and in one way or another they issued extra means of payment, of which the increase of paper currency notes was evidence, to enable them to bid for the goods and services they wanted against the competition of the public. Thus the great inflation commenced. What was to be done about it when the war ended? The Cunliffe Committee, appointed in January 1918, to consider this, was, in terms of the experience it represented, an extremely strong one; its Report,[108] presented in August, was unanimous and on the major point, apparently the witnesses who came before it were also. The unlimited issue of currency notes in exchange for credits at the Bank of England was at once a consequence and an essential condition of the methods which the Government adopted to meet its war expenditure (p. 5, para. 11). In the normal working of the gold standard, the great rise of prices would have led to a drain of gold, a rise of the discount rate, a restriction of credit and a fall of prices until the situation was restored. But although the Treasury notes were theoretically convertible into gold, there was a legal prohibition on gold coinage and the industrial uses of gold, and although its export was not illegal, the submarine campaign, insurance, etc., made it impracticable for anyone except the Government. The exchanges, which would otherwise have been unfavourable, had been pegged by a costly process of using borrowed American dollars, and that clearly could not be continued after the war. The conditions for an effective gold standard therefore no longer existed, and unless they were re-introduced there would be a danger of credit expansion and a drain of gold which might jeopardise the convertibility of the notes and the country's international trade position. It was imperative that 'the conditions of an effective gold standard should be restored without delay' (p. 5, para. 15). To achieve this, Government borrowing should cease at the earliest possible moment, the capital for re-stocking, plant, etc. should come from genuine savings and not from the creation of fresh purchasing power. Caution should be exercised in undertaking far-reaching reconstruction capital programmes, such as housing. Secondly, a legal limit should be placed on uncovered note issue, which should be appropriate to a gold reserve concentrated in the Bank, of £150

[108]*Currency and Foreign Exchanges after the War*, Treasury Cttee. Inter. Rep.; 1918, Cd. 9182, vii. *Breviate*, II, 81–2.

millions. And the actual issue should be slowly reduced, the amount issued in one year to be the maximum for the next. The Committee on *Financial Facilities*, 1918,[109] similarly composed of men of financial experience, also said that State borrowing should cease, that no attempt be made to reconstruct industry through a further expansion of credit, that the gold standard should be restored and credit expansion checked. On the major issues, therefore, the judgement of the country's financial experts was clear and unequivocal.

What was done about this? For fifteen months or so, nothing. On the contrary, from May 1919 to April 1920 some of the main recommendations were ignored, inflation proceeding faster than ever. The wholesale price index which in 1918 had stood at 192, in 1919 at 206, by April 1920 was 265. Prices were rising at $2\frac{1}{4}$ to 4 per cent per month. Government borrowing did not cease, for though their war expenses were ended, all belligerent Governments, British included, were now faced with new liabilities—cost of demobilisation, liquidation of war-time liabilities, repair of damage, subsidies to food-stuffs, etc. At the end of the strain of war the peoples wanted, to use the phrase current after the next war, less austerity. New demands for capital expenditure, e.g. for a great housing programme, were politically impossible to resist. These could not be met without firm, even drastic priority arrangements, but opinion of the dominant Party in the House and of business was insisting on the end of controls. If, therefore, the Treasury administrators had been asked why they had not carried out the recommendations, they would have had some excuse for replying 'We couldn't'. As the dollar pegging of foreign exchanges could not be continued and free gold export would drain away the basis of the currency, the export of gold was prohibited. The way was then open for further inflation and the conditions for an effective gold standard were even less favourable. But it was remarkable that the inflationary Government borrowing was exceeded by trade inflationary borrowing, which rose to £400 million in the year following the armistice. This boom was partly due to re-stocking and re-equipping activities: business men were in a great hurry—as the Government had been to get munitions.

[109] 1918, Cd. 9227, x.

But since it required means of payment, it could have been checked by the banks which supplied them.[110] Pigou had given a warning early in 1916. 'It is practically certain that to make good the havoc and waste of war, there will be a strong industrial boom. This boom, if history is any guide, will generate in many minds an unreasoning sense of optimism leading to much wild investment. The results some years after will be failures, crisis and depression. If this danger is to be obviated or mitigated, it is imperative that the Government and the banks should so act as to restrain and keep within reasonable limits the initial peace boom.'[111]

Some of the unprecedented total of new capital issues was used in an orgy of speculative take-over bids and mergers at fantastic prices. The *Financial Facilities* Committee had expressly said that there should be some control over capital issues and the export of capital. Yet in March 1919, it was decided to allow companies to market securities with the restriction that the proceeds were to be used inside the country, and in November 1919, all securities were freed. A misguided business and political world, sometimes without much intelligence, and sometimes not without a good deal of greed, had insisted on unfettered *laissez-faire* (so long as that did not prevent monopolies, or hinder the erection of tariffs against 'enemy' imports) and on a bonfire of controls and priorities. All this could have only one end. In the meantime there were immediate casualties. The inflation was a major cause of the wreckage of the much-needed housing programme. Much time and effort were wasted in futile campaigns and legislation against profiteering, which was so obviously a consequence and not a cause of rising prices that one wonders whether many supporting it could have been so stupid or were simply disingenuous. Most important of all, during this period progress towards the stable money and exchanges which two authoritative committees had declared essential was nil.

The second phase, deflation, has to be looked at separately. The caning of dull pupils—both at home and abroad—for not learning

[110]See R G Hawtrey, *Currency and Credit* (1930), p. 407–8.

[111]Pigou, *The Economy and Finance of the War* (1916), p. 88. Note his later comment in *Industrial Fluctuation* (1927), 'But will anybody seriously contend that, if we had insisted on controlling bank credits and currency so as to keep the average level of prices steady, there would have been no industrial expansion?' (p. 197).

their lessons was soon to become more severe, and like other severe beatings, often drove the harassed victim into further errors. For the whole scene of rising prices, rising profits, rising wages, rising trade union membership, and a trade union unemployment percentage of nearly nil—the basis on which many hopeful plans had been made—changed dramatically in a year. In December 1919, the Cunliffe Committee re-affirmed its general proposals, the Government accepted the principle of the 'Cunliffe Limit' and it became our settled policy to restore the pound to its pre-war parity. This decision and the circumstances—the price inflation had become dangerous—therefore implied a restriction on credit expansion. The bank rate was raised from 6 per cent (Nov. 1919), then to 7 per cent (April 1921). Prices, which in the second quarter of 1921 were 30 per cent above the figure at the beginning of 1919, a year later were 25 per cent below; wages, 25 per cent above, began to fall in the spring of 1920 and at the end of the year were below their initial figure. Unemployment amongst trade unionists, only 1 per cent in the spring of 1920, shot up to 20.9 per cent in the second quarter of 1921 and remained at 10 per cent for another $2\frac{3}{4}$ years. Trade union membership, which increased from $4\frac{1}{2}$ million in 1918 to $6\frac{1}{2}$ million in 1920, fell back to $4\frac{1}{2}$ million in 1923. The industrial threat of organised labour, the power of the trade unions, thus dwindled to little more than a capacity to delay. These disasters led to the abandonment of many reconstruction plans and sent others into indefinite cold storage.

For Britain, so largely dependent on international trading, these internal difficulties could not be detached from external ones. Other belligerent countries were worse off. Unable to meet their day-to-day liabilities, to reduce their floating debt and in urgent need of various outside supplies, their currencies depreciated to unprecedented levels. In the spring of 1921 the values of German, Hungarian and Polish currencies had fallen to 1/5, 1/40 and 1/200 of their gold parities and some other currencies became so worthless that forms of barter began to appear. It was at this point that Cassel's theory of purchasing power parity—a simplified approximation, as he himself pointed out—became important. A country's currency was bought for the internal purchasing power it possessed, so that the amount of another currency given for it depended on its purchasing power and the internal purchasing power of the currency offered: that is, the valuation of one currency in terms of another depended on the relative purchasing power of the two currencies. Given normal freedom of trade, which would check any deviations, the exchange rate would be established on that basis. If one country decreased the internal purchasing power of its currency by inflation, or the two countries inflated their currencies at different speeds and so altered their relative internal purchasing power, an appropriate new parity would be established. This theory, criticised on scientific grounds, e.g. it assumed that export prices moved in the same degree as the general price index, or as being just obvious, might nevertheless have given politicians a broad and useful guide to action in the bewildering trade and currency difficulties, had they been willing to recognise it. The world's currencies were now independent paper currencies no longer tied to gold. In Great Britain, Holland, Switzerland and Scandinavia the inflation had not gone as far as in France and Belgium, while in Germany, Austria and Poland depreciation had gone much beyond the hope of restoring the old parities. The old norms, the old parities had gone. There was thus no prospect of any early achievement of the aim Britain had given herself, the restoration of the gold standard at the old parity.

To depreciation were added the troubles of under-valuation, which drove countries into policies which made matters worse. Some tried to get round their difficulties by imposing hindrances to trade, various restrictions on imports, export licences, selling to the foreigner at higher prices than to home buyers, all restrictions on the use of the currencies which made them less attractive and reduced their value below their purchasing power parity. Those whose currencies were under-valued had to offer more for their essential imports, while the countries whose currencies had become over-valued were exposed to a new kind of dumping, 'exchange dumping', the competition of imports from countries with under-valued currencies whose goods could be obtained cheaply. It added yet another to the arguments for protection put forward in succession by Chamberlain's Tariff Reform movement, by three of the reports by the Balfour of Burleigh Committee,[112] all signed by December 1917, before the Cunliffe Committee had been appointed. The result was a growth of tariffs designed to counter exchange-dumping which, although they may have eased the need for adjustment in the threatened country, did not go to the root of the difficulty and were yet another obstacle, in a world going protectionist, to the realisation of the ideals of freer trade which had been set forth by President Wilson.

We have to look at these events and the Cunliffe plan with an understanding of the state of knowledge in 1918. The Committee desired to avoid that post-war inflation against which Pigou had warned. As M J Bonn put it later,[113] inflation as a thought-out or not thought-out policy is temporary; if pursued long enough, it topples over into economic dislocation. The Committee's advice covered much more ground than the 'Cunliffe limit', which in a sense was just a method of implementing it. The later criticism that the 'limit' was unnecessary, because credit control would be adequate, or that it was undesirable because it might restrain business, or at a later stage still, that a little inflation might be desirable, were not relevant to the problem as it was when the reports were written in 1918. At that date, even the Cunliffe Committee could not 'judge to what extent legal currency may be depreciated in terms of bullion' but thought it practically certain that there was 'some depreciation' (para. 14). Pigou had made a guess in December 1917,[114] but the extent of it was not revealed until the dollar support of the exchange was withdrawn, when the rate fell from 2.76 to 3.378 in February 1920, and showed that the pound's external value had moved with the relation of its purchasing power to the internal purchasing power of other currencies. In any case, their advice was not acted upon at the time, and when a year later they re-affirmed it, there would have been no sense in chasing other currencies downhill.

The Cunliffe Committee had declared the restoration of the gold

[112]*Commercial and Industrial Policy,* Cttee., two Inter. and Final Reps.; 1918, Cd. 9032, 9033, 9035, xiii.

[113]*Is Unemployment Inevitable?,* ed. W T Layton (1924), pp. 148–9.

[114]*Econ. Jn.* (Dec. 1917).

standard to be the only effective remedy for an adverse balance of trade and undue credit expansion (p. 5, para. 15). Though a paper currency should theoretically be capable of management so that it is the most stable form of money, in fact few countries had used it with discretion, the temptations to lapse being too strong. With the example of Europe, even at that date, in front of them, there was a case for returning to a gold standard which, if it did not remove, at least limited the opportunities for Governmental indiscretions. Writing in 1919, Keynes commented that 'Lenin is said to have observed that the best way to destroy capitalism is to debauch the currency. In the latter stage of the war all belligerent Governments practised from necessity or from incompetence what a Bolshevist might have done from design. Even now when the war is over, most of them continue out of weakness the same malpractices.'[115] Keynes' view of the circumspection of European Governments at this time can be judged from his declaration that if he had influence with the United States Treasury, he would not lend a penny to a single one of them.[116]

Did the Cunliffe Committee under-estimate the practical difficulties of the policy, at home and abroad? As to the first, the Report did not go into the rigidities and resistances in the British economy which were to make deflation painful. In a flexible system such as that implied in the theory of free competition, a shock of this kind would be absorbed by re-adjustment all round, but rigidity at some points would deflect its force to parts less fenced-round, and create unemployment of both physical and human resources. In fact, all groups, capitalists and workers alike, seemed determined not to recognise that the boom was over and put up strong resistances. The general level of understanding was low. But though some of this was doubtless expected, it would have required the knowledge given only by later experience to foresee what became apparent only later, how strongly these rigidities were built into

[115] J M Keynes, reprinted in *Essays in Persuasion* (1931), pp. 77–8. See also a short vivid description of inflation in Germany in 'The Effects of Currency Inflation', written by Prof M J Bonn whilst the events were in progress, in *Is Unemployment Inevitable?* pp. 148–64. There is a later useful account in the introduction to F G Graham, *Exchange, Prices and Production in Hyper-inflation: Germany, 1920–23.*

[116] J M Keynes, *Economic Consequences of the Peace* (1919), pp. 266–7.

the economy. To bring order into the world's currencies an immense effort was needed from all countries, and as a leader in trade and finance we had both an interest and a responsibility in trying to establish and enlarge an area of stability. And the determination to persist in it despite the difficulties was not devoid of virtue. In the light of knowledge then available, were they not right to try? The extent to which those whose decisions and pressures contributed to the wild monetary policies of some other countries had been afflicted by the gods with madness, could scarcely have been anticipated. In the whole complex of international problems, which included reparations and inter-ally debts and the political difficulties associated with them, despite our leadership our monetary policy was but one, though an essential component. The doubts as to whether we had over-estimated our strength, whether a subtle change had not come over our whole economic position and in that of London as a financial centre, did not come until later.

But the Committee's recommendations were made before the cessation of the fighting, before the post-war inflation, before the subsequent collapse. In the next few years there was much to learn; indeed, there are few periods in which such theoretical advances were made in such a short time. First, the quantity theory of money was put into an improved form, the 'Cambridge equations', which gradually replaced the older 'Fisher equations', though the latter were easier for ordinary people to grasp (and it would have been well for Europe had their significance even in this version been more fully understood and applied). Next, it was not until the Genoa Conference of 1922 that the public began to understand the differences between the policies of devaluation and deflation. In fact, most European countries, after wading through the losses, miseries and injustices of prolonged depreciation, had eventually, by devaluation, let in the gold standard by the back door. Thirdly, there was for us the problem of the alternative of stable prices or stable exchanges. The accepted doctrine, which the Committee expressed, was that if you could not have both, the gold standard gave the best compromise, and in the case of a country so dependent on international trading, if a choice had to be made, priority should be given to stable exchanges. The new ideas, which later Keynes brilliantly expounded,[117] were that the gold standard was unlikely to give both, and that it was vital for us to have stable prices. For deflation re-distributed wealth in the opposite direction to inflation; it discouraged industrial activity because it increased the burden in commodities of business men's debts, manufacturers faced a fall in prices and in the value of their stocks; it favoured the rentier against the active classes of society, increased the real burden of the expanded national debts at the expense of the taxpayer and meant lower money wages and unemployment for the workers. It has to be added that Keynes's views had, even in 1923, by no means won general acceptance; in fact the authorities still kept the restoration of the gold standard in view.

If we move from the work of experts down to more modest levels, how undeveloped were the views of the public on monetary policy is shown, for example, by the statements which came from the Labour movements.[118] Although the interests of the workers were so closely involved and there was the usual crop of currency cranks and some individuals with ideas, it was perhaps not to be expected that they would have much fresh to say on it as official doctrine. Monetary policy as such was not dealt with in the Fabian Essays, in any Fabian tracts in this period up to 1929, nor in *Labour and the New Social Order*. In September 1920, a joint committee of the Labour and Co-operative movements in a memo on the *Cost of Living* said simply that every country should be required to take all possible steps to rehabilitate their currencies, and that in countries where a return to the gold standard was impracticable, a new parity of exchange should be established,[119] which thus accepted the emphasis which the Cunliffe Committee had placed on the exchange problem. Chiozza Money, in the *Triumph of Nationalisation* (1920),[120] was concerned chiefly with bank amalgamations and the dangers of monopoly, and thought of a nationalised banking system as a

---

[117] J M Keynes, *A Tract on Monetary Reform* (1923), chap. vi.

[118] The radical J A Hobson's *Gold, Prices and Wages* (1913) was not one of his most successful or influential efforts. Keynes wrote a highly critical review in *Econ. Jn.*, XXIII (1913), 393–8.

[119] *Unemployment: A Labour Policy* (T.U.C. and Labour Party, Jan. 1921), p. 14.

[120] pp. 223–6.

means of securing cheap credit for housing and other public projects. Even in 1927, *Labour and the Nation* (drawn up on the instruction of the Blackpool Conference) takes but a few lines to declare
that the provision of capital, its direction to channels of the greatest
utility, and the banking system are vital to the whole community,
which should determine the principles on which it should be
administered; and a searching inquiry into financial methods and
credit was promised.[121] For the rest, a vision of society whose main
economic activities were socially owned and controlled led some
groups into the grand irrelevancies of nationalising banks, the
profits of bank shareholders, currency experiments in an island, etc.
and away from the real issue, which was the monetary policy to be
followed. This infertility in monetary theory was no doubt due
partly and was a tribute to the immense prestige of the Bank and the
confidence in its strength and capacity, so that it never occurred to
many to question its policies fundamentally. Over a long period
changes in the general price level and therefore in the relationship
of rentiers, business men and workmen had taken place by slow
degrees. The changes of fortune which the scale and speed of the
inflation and deflation of 1918 to 1923 bestowed or inflicted on the
various classes thus presented the Labour Party and unions with a
new aspect of the conflicts of interests. And monetary policy
involved not only balancing the claims of the various groups, but a
technical knowledge and experience of business operations of which
they had little close personal acquaintance, and for that reason they
did not find it easy to contribute much. As a result, the developments in monetary theory were to come from professional economists, and not from socialists or socialist doctrine.

ii. *Scrapping the Plans*

The steps taken to deal with the disastrous situation created by
the collapse were a compound of panic, of confusion between reasoned attempts at economy in the sense of cutting out work and
activities no longer necessary or being performed by an extravagant

---

[121]*Labour and the Nation* (1927), p. 20.

use of labour and resources, economy in the sense of reducing money expenditure (even if it meant stopping useful work without ensuring that labour and resources were turned over to other useful purposes instead of lying idle) and of fundamental hostility to the reforming ideals and programme, to anything savouring of State ownership, and of ignorant disregard of the results of scientific social research of half a century. Indeed, Government policy showed little of that open, experimental quality which had so distinguished the thinking on reconstruction.

Two major policies—those relating to housing and agriculture—soon succumbed. The troubles of the housing programme came partly from the plans themselves, partly from the inflationary rise of prices general to the whole body politic. The Carmichael Committee had found that since the resources of the industry were for a time limited and there were many rival demands, a system of building licences was needed to give the scheme priority. This was not provided. There was much leeway to be made up in repair work and lack of control over this and much building work of other kinds gave builders easy alternatives. Then the man-power of the industry, particularly of skilled men, had to be enlarged, and that took time. Nor were the unions, with memories of unemployment behind them, always helpful. The total number of men in the industry in 1918, 590,000, was still only 675,000 in 1919. The Committee also urged that a rise in productivity was vital; in fact it dropped. For according to C T Jones, one firm's records showed that the number of bricks laid per man-hour fell from sixty-six in 1895 to forty-four in 1920. The character of the State guarantee—all loss exceeding the penny rate—gave neither the local authorities nor contractors nor unions any incentive to be economical;[122] this meant that all plans had to be closely scrutinised by the Ministry, and at times there was bound to be a jam of plans awaiting approval. The combination of great drive from the centre with financial terms which, whatever their merits, permitted inefficiencies, and gave the participants in the operations opportunities for getting a good deal out of them, and, particularly, the failure to restrict rival

[122]Sometimes what happened amounted to recklessness. See E D Simon, *The Anti-Slum Campaign* (1933), pp. 13–14.

276

demands drastically, helped to produce the delays and the rises in costs. This was superimposed on a building industry caught up both in war-time and post-war inflation. Between 1914 and 1918 bricklayer's and carpenter's wage rates rose by about 80 per cent, and after the inflation movement began speeding up following the end of hostilities, the increase reached 130 per cent. The house which cost £300 or so before the war rose to £800 and by 1920 to as much as £1,000.[123] The Government took fright, and when in the middle of the year world inflation came to an end and prices crashed, it stopped the programme. Of the proposed 300,000 needed in 1918 only 96,000 had been completed under the programme by the middle of 1922, plus about 66,000 subsidised and unsubsidised houses erected by private enterprise, and the rate of house building did not reach 70,000 until 1921. Since 1909 the argument had been that public works schemes were instruments to be used in depression, and some now learned that it was a risky business to launch one, unprotected by other measures, on the top of a boom. But people were scrambling for houses and the drive was in full accord with public insistence, and any Minister who did not show some would not have held office for long. The public has now learned more about the use of priorities, but the new Parliament, committed as many of its Members were to free enterprise and energetic competition, was unlikely to be persuaded of it. Full success was therefore impossible. In such circumstances the political machine commonly sets an unfortunate Minister the task, and sacrifices him when the inevitable failure becomes obvious: as happened on this occasion. But from the point of view of the housing programme alone, it is arguable that once the rate of building had been raised, when the depression came there was a case for continuing rather than stopping it.

The quickest *volte-face* was in agricultural policy. In this case fall of prices was the enemy. The war-time system of guaranteed prices and minimum agricultural wages was, on the recommenda-

[123]It is sometimes said that the Ministry should have used its powers of approval to keep down costs and to prevent local authorities from competing with one another. But the target had been set high and loudly proclaimed, and this would have led to more negotiation and bargaining and probably more delays. It is doubtful whether this course was politically possible.

T

tion of the Royal Commission on *Agriculture*, 1919[124]—the Labour
members dissenting on guaranteed prices—continued by the Agriculture Act, 1920, with a written-in proviso that four years' notice
of its termination was to be given. Eight months afterwards the
Act was repealed, both guaranteed prices and the statutory general
minimum wage disappearing.

The plans for re-organising industry fared little better. By
contrast with the Benthamites who, while creating institutions to
alleviate ill-consequences of mechanisation and urbanisation, were
nevertheless on the side of the new techniques of their day, after
the election of 1918 political power rested with those whose wealth
and established position derived from technique as it had developed
rather than as it was developing. There was no drive to make
room for the technical urgencies of the fuel and power industries.
The Sankey proposals for mine nationalisation were not accepted,
the Duckham Report not pressed because the owners opposed it,
and mining royalties were not nationalised. The schemes for electric
power were not proceeded with, there was no national water plan.
The one breakthrough was in the *Railways Act*, 1921, by which
the companies themselves, given some initiative in amalgamation,
secured some of the gains for which they had long pressed in spite
of Parliamentary opposition. The control of trusts and monopolies
was turned into bogus anti-profiteering measures. For many
branches of manufacturing, on the contrary, the emphasis was
defensive—'safeguarding', assured markets, freedom to create
monopolies. The policy of protection for some of the manufacturing
trades recommended by the various committees was, after some
hostile voting on the part of the electorate, implemented step by
step, but not always with the results hoped for. Many of them,
after a screening process, were provided with tariffs giving them
the 'assured home market' demanded as the means of up-rooting
German trade here and as the basis of aggressive selling overseas;
and, moreover, they were left unhampered in building up large-scale
or monopolistic combines without the checks and restraints regarded
as desirable by the Committee on *Trusts*. In this case we should
probably look a little further ahead, for the unhappy story of British

[124]1919, Cmd. 473, viii. *Breviate*, II, 96–7.

industry and exports after 1924 shows how inadequate the diagnosis and ineffective the prescriptions were. By that date the Balfour Committee on *Industry and Trade* was appointed to go over the whole ground again and to find out what the early committees had missed, its massive and much more expert investigations being published in seven volumes.[125] By the time it had finished its work in 1929, the deficiencies of the 1916–18 analysis had become more obvious. Our exports of machinery had grown less both absolutely and proportionately than those of other leading countries; we were not securing our share of the new growing industries. We failed to get trade in regions little affected by the war, and though the return to gold in 1925 made many difficulties, some obstacles it revealed rather than created. Many of our troubles were due to causes affecting ourselves rather than our competitors. Thus it was left to the Committee to conclude (1929) that the first step to improving the competitive power of British industry was to subject its organisation and equipment to a thorough process of reconditioning.[126]

It was on general social and Labour policy that the coolness to the results of investigation, reaction and hostility were most manifest. Two cases show the risks which even 'non-contentious' proposals ran. The deadlock between the 'Majority' and 'Minority' schools of thought on Poor Law reform had been broken by the compromise at last worked out by the Committee on the *Transfer of Functions,* 1918, but the agreement between these two powerful bodies of opinion did not result in action. War wages and full employment had reduced pauperism and it was not until the machinery began breaking down badly after the economic collapse of 1920 that a move was made, first by the Government's taking power to suspend defaulting Boards of Guardians (1926) and finally, in 1929, by putting the compromise into operation. The Haldane Report on the *Machinery of Government* had an enduring general influence on thinking about the subject, yet there was more excuse for its being ignored. Prepared by a committee of the

[125]*Industry and Trade,* Cttee. Reps., vols. 1–6; 1925–29, non-Parl.
[126]Ibid., vol. 7, Final Rep., p. 297; 1928–29, Cmd. 3282, vii.

Ministry of Reconstruction, when that Department came to an end it was a waif for whom no friendly doorstep could be found; its virtue—dispensing with formal hearings of oral evidence[127] in favour of close and fertile conversation—meant that it did not attract public interest nor reveal the practical difficulties which constituted part of the problem; two of its seven members took little part in its proceedings,[128] and Haldane himself was under a cloud. It thus became rather a hole-in-the-corner affair. Most important of all, despite difficulties and mistakes, the administrative machinery had come through its great war tasks in reasonably good order, and no great breakdown occurred demanding action.

Social policy is closely related to State spending. There was, of course, a real problem. The Treasury difficulty was how to finance old and new activities without more taxes and more borrowing. Having asked the departments to save £175 millions and received from them proposals for £75 millions, it directed the Geddes Committee to suggest the remainder. Without any clear idea of the effect of their proposals on the general level of economic activity, the Committee laid about it vigorously and indiscriminately wherever it saw 'reducible expenditure', whether this saved real resources or not, or damaged the social policies which had been part of the idealism associated with the war, or cast aside improvements in economic organisation, such as Labour Exchanges, arrived at after painful experience and years of scientific inquiry. Not only should the use of Labour Exchanges not be made compulsory (Barnes Committee),[129] but consideration should be given to abolishing them (Geddes Committee).[130] As many council houses as possible should be sold, the school entry age should be raised to six years, secondary education should be confined to those capable of profiting by it, local authorities should be told how much they could spend on education, and the Minister's estimates reduced by

[127]B Webb, *Methods of Social Study,* chap. vii, esp. pp. 149–51.

[128]E S Montague was in India for much of the time; another member was added only after a good deal had been done and he had been too involved in other duties to examine the proposals of Part II in detail.

[129]*Work of the Employment Exchanges,* Cttee. Rep.; 1920, Cmd. 1054, xix.

[130]*National Expenditure* Cttee. 1st Inter. Rep.; 1922, Cmd. 1581, ix.

£16 millions. It is difficult not to conclude there was more than one motive behind these measures, that in addition to searching for economies, those opposed to the new social ideals were taking every advantage of the situation to secure the modification or abandonment of the plans for realising them.

In labour policy the reaction and hostility were no less obvious. Three of the plans—the Sankey Report, the Industrial Conference and the 'Dockers' Charter', were in difficulties before the depression engulfed them. Were the first two just politically dishonest, delaying actions designed to enable the Government to evade or defeat them one by one? It has to be granted that a Government of any political colour, faced with perilous industrial disputes whilst engaged in the task of re-adjusting the economy on a grand scale, might properly have played for time to enable it to sort the problems out under less pressure. Whatever the correct interpretation of the pledges and assurances by Bonar Law and other members of the Government, the miners—and many others—read them as an undertaking to nationalise if the Commission recommended it and would not have accepted the procedure otherwise. The Government does not come well out of the subsequent manoeuvres. When later, under pressure from strongly organised opposition from mine-owners, business and its own supporters in Parliament, the realities of business power politics led it to reject nationalisation, not to persist with the Duckham Plan, and not to nationalise mining royalties, and the belated introduction of the excuse that no Government could delegate to a Commission its responsibility for decisions on high policy, though formally correct, does not let it out of the charge of some political dishonesty.[131] But these manoeuvres and the obtuse, unyielding opposition of the owners were later to bear bitter fruit for both owners and the country. The National

---

[131]The miners themselves were not free from mistakes in tactics. Their insistence, in order to obtain a good hearing, on equal representation on the Commission led, in the form in which it was granted, to the appointment on their side of members all of whom were in agreement with and some committed to nationalisation before the inquiry began. When, therefore, it was later stated that the 'Majority' of the Commission agreed with it, it was obvious that the opposition had a means of decrying the authority of the Report of the six 'labour' members and to say that they could not be bound by the conclusions of one independent member, the chairman.

Industrial Conference's proposals mostly had a similar fate. The Government did draft eight-hours Bills, but its dilatoriness and the hostility of some industrialists under the plea of flexibility produced so many exceptions that labour ceased to regard them as worth very much, lost interest, and the proposed national industrial council was not set up. The Shaw Award, the 'Dockers' Charter' also ran into difficulties. The pay award was implemented, but schemes of decasualisation by limiting numbers and registration did not get far. The difficulties in this case were not political but the obstinate nature of the problem, including the attitude of the men, and were still unsolved for another forty years.[132] Dock and ship-owners wanted a margin to meet contingencies, but if that margin was to be given maintenance by a levy on the volume of goods handled, it had to be kept down to a manageable size. For the union, which had started a recruiting campaign, it meant telling some of its own men that they must leave the industry permanently. In 1914 there were 54,000 men in the London Docks, the number rising to 61,000 after the war, as against a probable dock requirement of some 40,000. But three years after the Report there was little tangible result save the setting up of national and local joint councils and much of the pay increase was lost. Trade Boards, extended in 1918 as recommended by the Whitley Committee, from the sweated trades where wages were 'unduly low' to those where there were 'no effective arrangements for wage negotiations,' had, according to the Cave Committee,[133] become machinery for the 'public regulation of wages', and this extension beyond the original purpose of preventing sweating should be stopped—the Government accepted this[134]—and minimum wages should be based on the lowest grade of labour.

At the same time the collapse of prices, and the sapping of the unions' strength and bargaining power meant reduction of wages

[132]The two employers' representatives accepted the principle of registration, subject to the condition that the men should work regularly, be mobile in the district within which they worked and should accept other than their usual employment when ordinary work was not available. Rep., p. 18.

[133]*Trade Boards Acts,* Cttee.; 1922, Cmd. 1645, x. *Breviate,* II, 322.

[134]*Administration of the Trade Boards Acts,* Statement of Government Policy; 1922, Cmd. 1712, xvii. *Breviate,* II, 323.

and the end of dreams of industrial democracy. One by one the unions—miners, railwaymen, port workers, iron moulders, builders, seamen and engineers in succession—had thrust upon them strikes or lock-outs in market conditions which made success impossible. The miners lost their national wage and returned to district rates. The Triple Alliance, looked upon as the spearhead of the movement, after some signs that it was going to be aggressive, on 'Black Friday' broke when the other two members were called upon to strike, not simultaneously for their own programmes, but in support of the miners' demands, at a point when the miners themselves were not completely united on their next step.[135] The whole basis of the aggressive, confident challenge of the workers' side in their declaration of aims to the National Industrial Conference, made when inflation and union membership were at their peak, was destroyed. Could it be wondered that these successive wage reductions and defeats, accompanied by the abandonment of the plans for social amelioration, would build up in the minds of the workers a conviction that there was a deliberate and organised attempt of the employing classes to break down the workers' standards which one day might have to be finally resisted by united effort? It was this conviction, rather than syndicalist theory, which eventually helped to make the General Strike of 1926. Nor did the defence that these were unavoidable consequences of a necessary monetary policy convince them; for they had had no hand in formulating it, and for some that also was 'bosses' policy'.

Of course, the hopes of 'workshop control' went as well. The shop stewards' movement had already dwindled as war contracts came to an end. Cole had argued (1917) that the guild idea was not that of joint control by employers and employed, which could not even be a stage to the evolution of the guild. The development of trade unionism towards guilds must take the form not of acceptance of joint *responsibility* for the conduct of industry, but of increasing *interference* with it. Only where a whole province of industrial management could be taken bodily out of the hands of the employers and transferred to the workers did he regard it as

[135]See Miners' Federation, Ann. Conference *Report* (Llandudno, 1921), pp. 12, 13, 20–1.

well and good.[136] But with unemployment at 10 per cent and firms fighting for contracts and sales in depression, it was not possible for unions or unofficial movements to 'encroach' on managerial functions. The programme for workers' control was thus made impossible, and the rejection by many unions of the more limited Whitley works committees—one had only to look at the meagre list of functions the Ministry of Labour suggested for it in 1920[137] to see why—thus brought a notable and idealist movement to an effective end. And it also meant that the opportunities for the rank and file to learn about management slipped away, at the same time as the German unions, 'preparing for control', were beginning to take an interest in it and some of their members were going to America to become acquainted with it.

iii. *Consequential problems*

(a) *Unemployment: old practices and defective theory.* The great changes in the level of prices and economic prospects brought in their train two further problems, for which we had no effective plans, but only old ideas and practices—unemployment and the increased real burden of war debt. So emerged the post-war unemployment running up to a million, new in volume and character, sometimes increasing, sometimes decreasing, sometimes stable, but always heavy beyond previous experience, which in changing forms lasted until 1939, and for which we were quite unprepared. A considered judgement in 1924[138] was that while normal unemployment in years neither particularly good nor particularly bad was about 500,000, the surplus above this in 1921 was 1,600,000, falling to 500,000–600,000 in 1924. This was a new experience. Clearly it exceeded and some of it was different from that underemployment not cyclical which filled the minds of the Poor Law Commissioners. How much could be guessed, at that date, as

[136]G D H Cole, *Self-Government in Industry* (1917), p. 281. The italics are Cole's.

[137]Reprinted in *Industrial Relations Handbook,* app. ii, pp. 237–8; 1944, non-Parl., Min. of Labour.

[138]*Is Unemployment Inevitable?* p. 82.

cyclical? Was part of it due to 'delayed depression'? The earlier advances in trade cycle theory already referred to[139] had been gathered into what may be regarded as the standard doctrine of the time, in Pigou's *Economics and Welfare, 1921* (Pt. VI). However, misled perhaps by pre-war experience, the authorities seemed at first to have regarded it as 'unemployment of the old type'.[140] Slowly there began to be questions whether, obscured by these circumstances, there might be some fundamental and permanent change in our economic position. We were thus looking at the problems in uncertain half-light, groping our way forward. Efforts during the war by officials responsible for the 1911 Act to get a general insurance scheme started to cope with post-war unemployment were opposed by employers and workers, and were only partly successful.[141] The immediate main question was the provision of work.

One line of thinking about it proved to be a non-starter. The Labour side's contention to the National Industrial Conference that a general rise of wages would limit continuous unemployment by bringing consumption more in equilibrium with production was aimed at permanent social inequalities rather than depression.[142] Theories that under-consumption was the cause of unemployment and trade cycles had had a long and, to the orthodox, a not very respectable history, but the scale of unemployment brought a revival of them. The most organised one had common features: depressions came from periodic over-production, which led to a greater out-turn of consumption goods than the purchasing power in the hands of the public could absorb at current prices. The consequence was collapse and unemployment. But their origin lay in the unequal distribution of wealth, for since the arts of consumption lagged behind the arts of production, the rich saved virtually automatically.

---

[139]See p. 158 above.

[140]*Unemployment Insurance*, R. Com. Mins. of ev., ev. by Price, qq. 18, 22, 122–5, 128–9; 1931, non-Parl.

[141]Beveridge, *Unemployment*, p. 373. *Civil War Workers*, Cttee. 2nd Inter. Rep.; 1918, Cd. 9192, xiv. *Breviate*, II, 444.

[142]*National Industrial Conference*, Rep., pp. vii, v. The whole question became a subject of theoretical controversy, the position of which up to 1930 is surveyed by Beveridge in *Unemployment*, pp. 360–72.

Saving and consumption thus got out of gear. It was this, not the aberrations of the monetary system—these were but the reflections of the real facts—which caused industrial fluctuations. This radical and at times heretical view, was set out fully by J A Hobson, who had championed it consistently in the *Industrial System* (1909) and *Economics of Unemployment* (1922). The former had a very large circulation amongst workers' classes, to whom it offered a rational explanation at a point where they were touched and could understand it. For the less sophisticated workers who did not go into classes it seemed an obvious fact that the more wages men had the more they could buy and thus help to keep the wheels of industry turning; that cutting wages reduced their purchasing power and sent things into reverse.[143]

Neither this view nor the bald statement—which Hobson did not make—that a general rise of wages would limit unemployment, had any chance of acceptance by employers facing falling prices and demanding wage cuts.[144] And writing in 1922 with post-war depression in mind, Hobson agreed that for Great Britain no purely national solution was feasible, that international action by credits to raise the purchasing power of the devastated and stricken parts of the Continent would be necessary. At home it would be folly to try to set men at work in their own trades where plant was idle; public works, particularly those using large amounts of labour in proportion to capital, should be undertaken.

These theories ruled out, to handle the problem there were available old practices—public works—and a new ten-year-old theory. This was Bowley's suggestion to the *Poor Law* Commission, made with the trade cycle in mind, that the total demand for labour could be made relatively stable by holding back postponable public works from good years and transferring them to the bad ones.[145] This proposal attracted widespread notice and in a

[143]For a cautious orthodox statement, see Bowley's 'Effect on Unemployment of Adjusting Wage Rates' in *Is Unemployment Inevitable?*, pp. 378–82.

[144]One variety of these theories, the Douglas Scheme, secured a wide and enthusiastic following and gave rise to discussions even among economists, but had no influence on policy whatever.

[145]See Bowley's later statement of it in *Is Unemployment Inevitable?*, pp 366–7. 'An essential condition of success is that plans should be prepared' (p. 876). They had not been.

hardened form became official Labour Party doctrine. 'The Government can, if it chooses, arrange the public works and orders of the national departments and local authorities in such a way as to maintain the aggregate demand for labour at an approximately uniform level from year to year' (L.P. Conference, 1917). 'It is known that the aggregate demand for labour can be maintained year in and year out at an approximately even level' (L.P. Conference, 1918). The doctrine was stated generally in their *Prevention of Unemployment Bill*, 1920, Clause 4.[146] To it was added the notion that such measures would stimulate business generally, but at the time this development did not get much further. For the theory that the injection of public works expenditure would generate employment and the incomes of those concerned, whose subsequent expenditure would also, with leakages, generate further incomes and employment until the final result was some multiplier of the initial expenditure and of initial employment, was not precisely formulated until 1931, by Kahn.[147]

On balance, the discussion helped to create a favourable background for the public works programme aided by the State through the Unemployment Grants Committee, 1920–30. But the programme soon ran into some of the old difficulties. There was a difference between local public works to relieve long-term unemployment in specially hard-hit areas and those which aimed at maintaining employment and spending power over the whole country. There was some confusion whether they were to be works of social utility, using men of normal skill for the job, or whether they were relief works to be shared out amongst the unemployed, each getting a 'turn on', as in Stepney. The Government itself wavered and was not always consistent, at one time treating them as relief works which should employ as much labour as possible, whilst at the same time discouraging ordinary capital expenditure. And works were started whilst bank credits were being restrained. Added up, the direct additional employment, though useful, does not seem to have been more than about 130,000 at any one time,

---

[146]See *Unemployment: A Labour Policy*, pp. 10, 11, 18, 37.

[147]R F Kahn, 'The Relation of Home Investment to Full Employment' in *Econ. Jn.*, XLI (June 1931).

which was not very significant compared with unemployed of one million. Although the Unemployment Grants Committee ventured a guess, it is difficult to say how much secondary employment was stimulated. But harassed Ministers yielded to the temptation to change their reports of the amount of employment created from so many man-months to so many man-weeks and even man-days!

The theory itself was not agreed nor completely water-tight. It was objected that any resources taken by the State to provide extra employment at one point would only reduce the power to purchase labour at another, that private employment would contract as public employment expanded, and that this clearly would be the result if the works were paid for out of taxation or genuine savings. Pigou defended the theory[148] on the ground that the funds for the works could come from the reduction in the amount otherwise needed for insurance benefits, and from bank credits. Hawtrey, on the other hand, while agreeing that public works could give more employment if accompanied by more bank credits, said that the employment would be due to the bank credits and not specifically to the works themselves. These were therefore an unnecessary ritual which could be dispensed with.[149] Perhaps the conclusion to be drawn from practice was that if public works were to be used for this purpose, the amount spent must be big enough to make a difference, it must be concentrated, and done at the right time; from theory, that we had not yet gone far enough to see our way out of the difficulties.

(*b*) *War debt and capital levy: reputable theory, a failure of practice.* The second problem was the increased money and real burden of war debts, amounting to about £7,000 to £8,000 million, the issue of policy being proposals to reduce them by some form of tax or levy on capital. These were canvassed politically with great enthusiasm, discussed by economists with exceptional vigour, and they roused contradictory ethical claims and conflicting class interests. They were put forward during inflation as an alternative to war

[148]Pigou, *Economics of Welfare*, pp. 886–8, and in *Is Unemployment Inevitable?*, pp. 128–30.

[149]R G Hawtrey in *Economica* (March 1925), 28–44.

borrowing, and during deflation to diminish the burden in real terms of borrowing which should never have taken place. The target varied from the dubious gains of war profiteers to all gains of war-made wealth, then to increases of wealth (except possibly that due to genuine exceptional effort), to holdings which had not changed in substance but merely risen in price, and to total accumulated wealth. They drew from Inland Revenue memoranda which exhibited the experience and ability of that Department at its best.[150] The proposals were a central feature of two elections. Yet although much opinion, including that of most economists, had consolidated in their favour, between 1919 when they were first examined by a Committee,[151] and 1927 when the Colwyn Committee reported on them,[152] opinion turned adverse, not only because of successful pressure by hostile interests, but because of an alteration of fundamental circumstances, which led some prominent economists to change sides. The proposals which had stirred up so much came to nothing. It was a most remarkable example of the hazards which even well-attested ideas have to run when launched into public life.

What accounts for the failure of so promising a proposal, which had strong support from many professional economists and appealed to the popular sense of justice, to have any influence on policy? One has to think not only of the merits and demerits of the tax as such, but of the kind of thinking about it which influenced the final judgement: The main question was: would it be better for the national finances and our future competitive power to pay off a substantial part of the immense debt by a once-for-all tax, than to discourage effort and enterprise with heavy annual interest etc. payments raised by taxes on incomes and profits for many years to come? Should the price level fall substantially, the debt holders would be paid in pounds having a greater real purchasing power than those they had lent. Considerations of this kind led many

---

[150]*Increase of Wealth (War)*, Sel. Cttee., Memos. by Bd. of Inland Revenue; 1920, Cmd. 594, xxvii. Also in Sel. Cttee. Apps., pp. 225–97.

[151]*Increase of Wealth (War)*, Sel. Cttee. Rep., Procs., Mins. of ev.; 1920 (102) vii.

[152]*National Debt and Taxation*, Cttee. Rep., pp. 246–96; Minority view, pp. 297–413; 1927, Cmd. 2800, xi. This Report proved to be a post-mortem on the proposals.

economists to support the principle vigorously, Keynes, for example, saying at the end of 1919 that 'a capital levy for the extinction of debt is an absolute pre-requisite for sound finance in every one of the European belligerent countries'.[153] Politically, the tax was early annexed by, and became the treasured possession of the Labour Party. In successive annual conferences from 1916 onwards[154] it persistently criticised the Government's policy of meeting so large a proportion of war expenditure out of loans[155] which would involve heavy annual interest charges on debts and would get in the way of social reforms. But the necessary war taxes should be borne by those most able to pay, the wealthy classes, and this meant amongst other things, taxes on accumulated wealth. After military conscription had been introduced other claims of equity were expressed by the use of the phrase 'conscription of wealth'. But the popular campaign in support of the tax, which, though simple in principle, was admittedly not easy to explain to public audiences (as the speeches of politicians showed), laid more stress on its use as a means of getting at war profiteers than on those who, though in no way acting anti-socially, were nevertheless so placed that exceptional war profits just came their way. For the latter group the gains were windfalls, and as such were not only ethically, but economically of high taxability. But this moved the discussion from the general taxation of total wealth to taxes on the increases of wealth during the war. To the popular mind this was easier to understand, since it was in principle clear who were and who were not to pay, whereas

[153] J M Keynes, *Economic Consequences of the Peace,* p. 263. Pigou, *Economics of Welfare,* pp. 678–88.

[154] Labour Party Annual Conference *Reports:* Bristol, 1916, p. 155; Manchester, 1917, p. 199; Nottingham, 1918, p. 133; London, 1918, p. 79. See also F W Pethick Lawrence, *A Levy on Capital* (1918) and his evidence to the Sel. Cttee. on *Increase of Wealth (War).* He also wrote a Labour Party pamphlet (see q. 3114). Also J A Hobson, *Taxation in the New State,* pp. 162–229, and E Hugh Dalton, *The Capital Levy Explained* (1923).

[155] They were not alone in this view. Pigou in 1916 had written: 'The main argument which deters economists from proposing to throw nearly the whole cost of government upon the shoulders of those best able to bear it, is not relevant to the problem of financing a world war. . . . The ratio in which the war is financed by money borrowed from people with large incomes should be much diminished; and the ratio in which it is financed with money collected from them under some form of progressive taxation should be much increased.' *The Economy and Finance of the War,* pp. 82–3.

with a general wealth tax there was only the word of some politician on who should be exempted. Inland Revenue regarded it as impracticable for them to distinguish between these various forms of gains, and following J A Hobson, thought that those due to genuine extra effort and saving could be let out by exempting small fortunes, and by graduating the tax above this limit on the assumption that the larger the increase of the wealth the greater was the probability that part of it was due to fortuitous war gains. But taxes on increases of wealth would mean two valuations on an individual's property, which given certain conditions it thought was possible, while tax on total wealth had the advantage, that only one would be required.

There were a number of practical conditions of success, only some of which were eventually fulfilled. First, the levy should be imposed at once. Stamp and some officials were alarmed at the weight of the debt and regarded the reduction of it as urgent[156] in order to avoid both the increase of real burden which a fall of prices would mean, and the great difficulties of valuing securities if a levy were imposed during a period of falling prices. 'If 'twere done, 'tis well 'twere done quickly'. In part of the campaign for the tax (1922–24) the increase of the real debt burden became the main argument, though the force of this depended a little on dates. If those who had put money into war loan early in the war, had been repaid at the end of the inflation, e.g. in 1919–20, or even up to 1921, they would have been given back in real terms less than they had given up.[157] But by 1925–26 the great fall of prices had raised the real burden of the debt by 61 per cent; and in 1927 the Colwyn Committee reported that over two-thirds of the debts had been incurred at prices above the level of those years.

Secondly, Stamp and others asserted that a tax of this scale and complication could be successful only if the persons affected gave the kind of co-operation which had made the war-time excess profits duties workable, and that anything like the organised opposition which destroyed the land values duties would make the work of

[156]*Increase of Wealth (War)*, Sel. Cttee., Mins. of ev., Stamp's ev., qq. 3119–120, 3171; 1920 (102) vii.

[157]*National Debt and Taxation*, Cttee. Rep., p. 66, para. 200; 1927, Cmd. 2800, xi. J Stamp, *Wealth and Taxation Capacity* (1922), p. 177.

administration impossible.[158] There were some who genuinely preferred the known pains of heavy taxes to the unknown ones of a levy, others feared that there would be no guarantee that the once-for-all tax would not be repeated, especially as it was being pressed as part of the programme of the socialist party. But there was a strong and vigorous opposition from entrenched business and financial interests determined not to concede the principle— a 'raid on property'—or to lose their gains. Banks which had early invested substantially in war loans were not eager to have their holdings thus reduced, with all this implied. For below the discussion of the pros and cons there was a struggle on how the real costs of the war should be distributed between the various classes, and in that tussle a good deal of ethical and economic argument was little more than rationalised defence of personal and group interests. One cannot say how far this opposition would have dissolved if confronted by a resolute Government determined to embark upon it, but it did succeed in delaying decisions until what Stamp had regarded as the time for the tax had passed, and therefore a vital condition was broken.

Thirdly, during the delays we plunged into depression and both expert and popular opinion shifted. Pethick Lawrence in arguing the case for the levy in 1918 had said that it would bring about deflation.[159] Many who had vigorously supported it at first, e.g. Keynes, Pigou,[160] agreed that the time for it had now passed and for the same reason the professional economists who at first had been mostly of one mind, now became divided on its expediency. Nor in the new conditions could the rank and file of the Labour Party be roused to its old passionate interest in a proposal now gone stale. For two other reasons support weakened. If the Government chose to take a share of the taxpayer's property in the present, it would each year lose the income tax and super-tax on its proceeds and eventually death duties as well. It was Inland Revenue's estimate (1927) that for a levy on any scale which had been seriously discussed

[158]*Increase of Wealth (War)*, Sel. Cttee. Rep., Mins. of ev., q. 3118 (col. 2).
[159]*A Levy on Capital*, pp. 73–4.
[160]*National Debt and Taxation*, Cttee. Mins. of ev., Pigou (para. 5, p. 436; para. 10, p. 437), Keynes (p. 534, qq. 7552, 7557–87), Pethick Lawrence (qq. 6252–53, 6310); 1927, non-Parl.

these deductions would reduce the net annual savings to something of the order of £50 million, which finally caused Keynes
and Pigou to change their minds,[161] and shook even Dalton. It
became doubtful whether so disturbing a tax was worth the probable proceeds. As time passed and people settled down to live with
the great national debt, the fear that the high level of annual taxes
would discourage enterprise and effort began to lose a little of its
force, for a young generation was growing up which had not known
taxes at the old pre-war level and was accepting the new high rates
as normal.[162]

Looking back on these events, timing was vital. The levy was a
tax which should be imposed at the right time: our post-war difficulties would have been that much less.[163] Secondly, it presumed
reasonable co-operation by the taxpayer, but there was a strong,
organised opposition, partly genuine, partly a defence of class interests, partly confused and ignorant.[164] The economic argument was
nearly all on one side. Once again the conservative elements had
shown an obtuseness in understanding economic analysis to which
the radical and labour groups, if less experienced, were nevertheless
more open. And it was a weakness that they were to display in
much of their post-war policy from which the country and some
of their own interests were to suffer.

CONCLUSION

This had been our greatest and most promising effort not only
to give society new objectives, but to devise the means whereby
some of them could be attained. Unlike the reformers of 1906–14,
who had to press through the party machine on a limited range of
problems then politically urgent—the sweated trades, unemployment, labour mobility and health—those of 1914–16 were presented with unique opportunity to put theories into concrete plans

[161]Ibid., Rep., p. 254–5, para. 732.
[162]Colwyn Cttee., Mins. of ev., Coates' Memo. of ev., paras. 26, 28, qq. 9362, 9405–
15, 9467–70.
[163]Ibid., Mins. of ev., Pethick Lawrence, para. 12, pp. 449; Pigou, Memo. of ev.,
pp. 5, 436.
[164]Ibid. See comments of the Minority on the various arguments of Majority Rep.,
paras. 202, 208, 222–3, 231–2.

U

covering a large part of the economy, through officially provided machinery for working them out and putting them forward for legislative consideration. And the arrangements were fluid enough to make room for the experts and social investigators outside the ring of M.P.s and civil servants. The contrast between the success with which some of the aspirations of 1906–14 were realised and the failure to make good the more vividly felt hopes and more intense intellectual efforts of 1918–30 thus becomes more striking. When so many things had promised success, it was a melancholy end of the endeavours to plant Jerusalem in England's green and pleasant land.

Was there anything in this wreckage of positive value worth salvaging for the future, anything which, if absorbed into experience, would make for a success in a future effort? Were there any general weaknesses in the general body of ideas which transmitted flaws to the plans they sponsored, so that they were unacceptable or unfitted to survive in the turmoil of the time? No doubt a social philosopher could ask some critical questions about the basis of the theories, just as at a lower, political level Conservatives, such as Lord Hugh Cecil,[165] could find some assumptions objectionable and defects in many of the conclusions drawn from them, and would have expressed no surprise if they failed in practice. But the whole body of ideas was near enough in time to be broadly similar to those which before the war had stimulated the successful forays into the capitalist order, though they were strengthened, extended and with new elements added. All the old colours of the spectrum were there, but some were rather stronger in tone and in a broader band. Though these ideas did not succeed in changing the face of things at the time, and in the coming years seemed to have diminished in effective force, they had a life of their own, were tough and, educated by the long depression, many survived to take charge of another spell of reconstruction a quarter of a century later. Though not embodied in Acts, they helped to keep alive the soul of Britain in difficult and dark days to come.

Secondly, did the defects in the individual plans themselves contribute to failure? In the main and with the exception of two vital

[165]Hugh Cecil, *Conservatism*.

areas, commercial and monetary policy, no. They were not escapist visions produced in the strains of war, but very practical affairs, many of which have in substance since been carried out. Nor can we say that the plans were 'born before their time'. For in many of these fields—in coal mining, railways, electric power, hospital organisation, police organisation, new techniques were, if one may personify, struggling to break out of the institutional bonds obstructing their logical development. If some of the proposals were collectivist in character, this was one way of accommodating them.

Thirdly, the machinery for collecting ideas and preparing plans was productive enough, and the array of reports sponsored by the Ministry of Reconstruction must have gratified its creators. Indeed, the fertility of inventions and plethora of plans might have proved an embarrassment had there been a drive to put many of them through the House. For in their claims on Parliamentary time there would have been some danger of their getting in one another's way unless there were firm decisions of priorities, considerable changes in procedure and a readier acceptance of delegated legislation. But there was no plan for the plans. Nor was the House apparently then ready to accept changes which would diminish its powers of scrutiny of Bills containing novel principles. It made heavy weather of the Railway Bill promoting amalgamation, taking the unusual step of setting up two committees to deal with it. And the place of the Departments in implementing schemes was not fully allowed for. When they began to turn to peace-time tasks there were bound to be difficulties in working on the principle that the Minister of Reconstruction was responsible to the House for the plans and the Departments for executing them. They would often be not the true parents, but only foster-parents to be entrusted with the task of giving the children the build and appearance likely to ensure their successful life. They would have to fill in the framework of the proposals with the machinery for making them work, to adapt them both to the available means and the political views of their own Ministers and in the light of what their experience suggested as practicable. The decision not to continue the Ministry of Reconstruction, on whose work so many hopes had centred, was received by many with great dismay as heralding the abandonment of the reconstruction drive.

Yet whatever the political motives behind it, it was not in itself completely devoid of sense.

On some of the problems presented to us for action we just did not know enough—about monetary theory, to enable us to understand fully the choice between stable exchanges and stable internal prices, about the functional relationship between saving, investment, consumption and total output, or the conditions in which banks could increase the supply of money and decrease interest rates or the State increase its spending during general depression, to enable us to handle unemployment in any but a fumbling way. The one point on which the Labour group insisted was that a policy which meant that for any length of time large numbers of men were idle and not producing must be wrong, though they were not then able to provide any convincing analysis of how in the circumstances full employment could be achieved. The solutions depended on the economists' progress in their technical analysis; great efforts were needed and in the next few years did lead to vital advances.

At the time the gap between the theory of the expert and the economic opinion of the market place and policy-makers was very wide. The economists' warnings against financing so much of the war expenditure by borrowing and of the need to restrain post-war inflation were unheeded because these were the easiest courses; the fraud of the Profiteering Acts betokened either astonishing ignorance or cynical window-dressing; workers getting high war wages were reluctant to envisage a preventive extension of unemployment insurance; the capital levy, supported by most economists, was delayed by the pressure of propertied interests until it was too late. What the economists meant by competition was that no business should be able to dominate the market, that no unnecessary restrictions should be imposed on the movement of persons and resources from areas of low to areas of higher productivity. But this was not the idea of competition on which Government policies rested; in the main this was a reversion to crude notions of *laissez-faire* in which private enterprise was apt to mean just freedom from State interventions. Instead of being regulated, the activities of great monopolies were left unrestrained, instead of mobility being promoted, rigidities were introduced by the imposition of tariffs; transference from the rich to the poor by services provided out of taxation was to be limited or reduced. And by an illegitimate transfer of ideas relevant to private concerns, in which cutting expenditure might be an appropriate way of dealing with difficulties, we embarked on an 'economy' policy for reducing public spending even where this was likely to reduce employment and output. Economists as diverse in approach as Cannan and Pigou agreed that economic progress involved 'a great extension of conscious social organisation'.[166] Success in any future effort would thus depend not only on economists' solutions of the technical problems of monetary and employment policy, but also on narrowing the gap between their theories and those of the policy-makers and the public through a wider understanding of broad principles. To have that influence the theories had not only to be abstractly true, but apt for the occasion, and this included, to use Morley's words, 'the long tale of consummating circumstances'.[167]

Carrying through a comprehensive social reconstruction which involves transfer of property and power, imposes new duties and creates new rights, requires public co-operation and support. How much was forthcoming? Were the bright and warning visions only wish fulfilments of a vigorous intellectual minority? One cannot survey the voluminous literature on reconstruction, noting the wide variety of its sources, and that the reconstruction committees were very mixed politically or call to mind how widespread were the hopes, without rejecting this conclusion. How widely held outside the circles of business and economic power were the opposed beliefs, rooted in history, of the value of private enterprise and free competition, even though their meanings were confused and changing, we have no precise means of knowing. Beneath the contest of ideas was the struggle of class interests; there had to be some change in the balance of their political strength. Support for such a programme would have to wait until experience had eroded confidence in the one set of beliefs and circumstances had given power and opportunity to implement the other.

[166]Cannan, *Economic Outlook* (1912), p. 281.

[167]J Morley, *Notes on Politics and History* (1913), p. 30.

Part V

EPILOGUE AND PROLOGUE

What large questions you are raising, as if we were beginning anew on the subject of the commonwealth . . . you little know what a swarm of questions you are raising

PLATO

To sum up is out of fashion . . . the longer we remain with any period or person the more impertinent it seems to generalise

J PALMER

It was twenty years before these social ideals were able to emerge again in strength, before the economists had success in grappling with the theory of employment or their ideas had penetrated to the policy-making groups or the public, and the advances in social knowledge could be gathered up for an effort comparable to that of the years following 1906. One may well ask why it took so long for such a favourable conjunction of circumstances to occur. Only slowly did it come home to us how deep-seated some of our difficulties were: certainly the economic facts to be grappled with were hard enough. For the whole period there persisted a deadweight of unemployment which never fell below a million and seemed irreducible whatever we did: and this was added to by the world depression after 1929. Of course we made progress in many ways—witness the great municipal housing estates, the new schools,[1] some extension

---

[1]For the variations in consumption, see *Britain in Recovery* (British Association, 1938), pp. 25–36.

298

of the social services. But the concentration of so much of the unemployment in the basic staple export industries which had hitherto
been our pride and joy, and in the areas dependent on them—
'structural unemployment', as it now came to be called—whilst
other parts of the country were prosperous and expanding, divided
the community both economically and emotionally. The waste of
productive power was bad enough, but worse was the poverty,
destruction of family standards and morale in distressed areas, the
cruelties which were so vividly expressed in *The Road to Wigan Pier,*
Love on the Dole and *Memoirs of the Unemployed*. The bewilderment
and bitterness were the greater because the reformers had launched
their attack on unemployment with the high hopes that at last we
were within reach of the means of reducing it to a minimum. None
of their remedies seemed appropriate to the new form and volume
of it. Yet so much depended economically and spiritually on liberation from this incubus. There were many turns of events, twists of
policy, changes of expedient, misunderstandings and errors, a vast
output of scientific, statistical and polemical literature about them.
If often the devices were inconsistent and self-defeating, this was
due not only to pressures of interests and groups trying to avoid or
shift the pains of adjustment to others, though these played their
part, but to confused, or more accurately, unsuccessful thinking. We
did not know the answers. The advances of 1906–14 were possible
because there was a confluence of reforming ideas; in the inter-war
years, by contrast, there were the sharpest possible conflicts in
approach, analysis and prescription. It was on a resolution of these
that progress depended.

First in this tangle of theories and policies was the attempt to
regain the advantages we had enjoyed from London's strength as a
financial centre and to contribute to international stability by leading
the way back to the gold standard. This we did in 1925, but at the
old parity, which added to our difficulties. Later to be denounced
as rash, ill-considered policy unfortunate in its consequences, this
had been a steady objective of British policy since the Cunliffe and
Vassar-Smith Reports. It was most carefully considered, the experts
being given full opportunity to advise; and it was at first welcomed
by the authoritative press. So far from being a step which nailed

the unemployed to a cross of gold in the interests of the City financiers it was, as Professor Sayers has pointed out,[2] part of an unemployment policy set forth by implication in an official document printed in the First Report of the Balfour Committee on *Industry and Trade*, and signed before the decision was made.[3] Though world trade had declined, by 1925 our proportion of world exports was beginning to rise. If the international currency disorganisation could be put right (and our return to gold would help), exports could revive and our unemployment figures fall. It was realised that there would have to be difficult reduction in costs, though both the resistance to these and our rigidities were under-estimated. Most of all, perhaps, as Sayers pointed out, London's weakened position as a financial centre—still not fully recognised—had made the pre-war weapon of credit restriction inappropriate for the purpose. But the new form of the gold standard was vulnerable and finally impossible to maintain: a concentration in London of other countries' reserves not only in gold but in foreign exchange—some of it acquired not by export surpluses, but by short-term loans—all of which could be withdrawn if there were a crisis in confidence. The crisis came to a head in 1931 when foreigners saw with amazement two main pillars of British strength threatened, the pound sterling by our inability to re-adjust our economy or reduce costs, and the Navy, our prop in peace and war for a century, by a 'mutiny'.[4] So for the first time we entered an era in which, when planning our home policy, we found ourselves continually looking over our shoulders at the behaviour of the pound and the balance of payments, whose soundness we had been accepting as if it were, like air, a free economic good which need not be thought about.

The second line of policy, implied by the first, was to reduce the level of internal costs. The high post-war level of taxation on

[2] R S Sayers, 'The Return to Gold' in *Studies of the Industrial Revolution: Essays presented to T S Ashton* (1960), pp. 317–19.

[3] *Survey of Overseas Markets*, Cttee. on *Industry and Trade*, intro., pp. 1–26, esp. p. 25; 1925, non-Parl.

[4] The mutiny was greatly exaggerated and was a mere incident in the series of strains caused by our underlying disequilibrium. But a foreign banker, when assured that there was nothing to worry about and that we had our own way of doing things, replied, 'Perhaps there isn't and perhaps you have, but you are going to pay for it.'

incomes was attacked on the ground that it discouraged effort, enterprise and risk-taking, but after a detailed examination of the witness from Inland Revenue, W H Coates, the Colwyn Committee on *National Debt and Taxation* gave it a relatively clean bill of health by concluding that it did not raise costs and prices.[5] To relieve the burden the May Committee, 1930–31, proposed wholesale reductions of social expenditure on education, health, etc., on arguments which would not convince an economist today.[6] The main brunt of the attack fell on wages. The reductions after the collapse of 1920 let to bitter industrial struggles which culminated in the national strike of 1926 and the prolonged coal dispute which occasioned it, and left for a quarter of a century a bitter legacy of hostility and distrust which has still not entirely disappeared. The case for reductions was simply stated: the amount of labour purchased is a function of its price and the fact of unemployment indicated that the price was too high. Demand for it in certain industries had fallen, but wages had been maintained, not necessarily by aggressive wage movements, but because, shielded by unemployment insurance, the unions were not now so pressed to consider reductions.[7] Pigou made a guess to the Macmillan Committee that some 5 per cent of the abnormal unemployment could be attributed to the high level of money wages.[8] Professor Gregory, a member of the Committee, argued that if there were no rise in world prices temporary reductions were inevitable, though they need not mean a proportionate reduction of standards or be permanent.[9]

But did this mean that all money wages should be reduced, on the ground that they caused unemployment diffused throughout the

[5]*National Debt and Taxation*, Cttee. Rep. app. xi, pp. 66–114; 1927, Cmd. 2800, xi. Also Mins. of ev., vol. II, pp. 636–56; 1927, non-Parl. The economic theory on which the conclusion was based (though not the conclusion itself) was later criticised. See D H Robertson, *Economic Journal* (1927), 566–81; D Black, *Incidence of Income Taxes* (1939), pt. i.

[6]*National Expenditure*, Cttee. Rep.; 1930–31, Cmd. 3920, xvi.

[7]For one statement of it see L Robbins, *The Great Depression* (1934), pp. 83–4.

[8]*Finance and Industry*, Rep. See his evidence before the Cttee., Mins. of ev., vol. II, 32nd and 33rd days, pp. 46–8. Note also his examination by Keynes and Gregory, pp. 78–93; 1931, non-Parl.

[9]Rep., Addendum iii, pp. 234–6; 1930–31, Cmd. 3897, xiii.

system? Or that they were too high in the export trades where the bulk of unemployment was? But they were lowest in the export trades and highest in the sheltered trades providing services and goods for home consumption—a differential gap which caused concern and bitterness. But no tolerable cut could have kept in operation those redundant shipyards bought up and dismantled by a corporation set up for the purpose. And as Clay[10] argued, it might have been possible to employ many of the unemployed miners if wages were reduced to £1 a week, but could one impose wages so absolutely low, so out of relation to wages paid in other trades? Were the wages paid in the sheltered industries too high, not because they gave rise to unemployment in those trades, but because they involved high charges to the industries dependent on them? The May Committee[11] indeed recommended the reduction of the pay of police and teachers, a cut of unemployment benefit by 20 per cent along with increased contributions, and that those who had exhausted their benefit rights should be subject to a means test. That the workers should object was obvious. But so did Keynes and other members of the Macmillan Committee who signed the addendum.[12] They were not convinced that wage reductions would bring a proportionate increase in employment, felt that it would be unwise to start an international race in wage-cutting, and that if reductions were necessary they should be applied not only to wages, but by taxation and other ways to rentiers who had gained by the great fall in prices. And since the volume of employment depended on effective demand, wage cuts would reduce the purchasing power of the victims, and therefore have repercussions on the demand for the services of other trades.

A further line of policy can be described as 'getting out of the rain'. A number of industries had made it plain to the Committees on trades after the war not only that they wished to have large combinations with pretty free powers of price and output control—a demand strengthened by the call for 'rationalisation' of industry—

[10]Henry Clay, *The Problem of Industrial Relations* (1929), p. 180.

[11]*National Expenditure*, Rep.; 1930–31, Cmd. 3920, xvi.

[12]*Finance and Industry*, Rep., pp. 194–200. See also Addendum by T E Gregory, pp. 234–6.

but they wanted an assured home market as well. And when it became clear that there were great obstacles in the way of increasing exports, this grew more insistent and developed into a wholesale encouragement of large units, buttressing of monopolies with their restrictive practices, levies, quantitative regulation of imports, subsidies to shipping lines to scrap and build, arrangements to buy and scrap redundant shipyards, paying some hop producers not to produce hops, buying up redundant cotton spindles, and promoting a semi-monopolistic steel organisation with great powers of price control and discrimination, and so on.[13] Obviously there were gains to some of the producers so protected, but whatever their particular defensive merits, taking them together as a general employment policy, some of the arguments in their favour were muddled. The contention that the great fall of prices reduced profitability, discouraged output and restricted employment was stood on its head by Neville Chamberlain, who seemed to think that the situation would be cured by a rise of prices obtained by a restriction of output. This brought a tart comment from Pigou, who in a letter to *The Times* said that 'The Chancellor has pinned his faith to a rise of prices so firmly that he sees no difference between a rise brought about *via* more money and one brought about *via* less production. But the only reason why "most people" desire a rise in prices is that, in the present conditions, they regard this as the most powerful method by which an increase in production, and so in employment, may be brought about. They want prices to rise so that more people will be employed: they do not want less people to be employed in order that prices may rise. By restricting production to nothing at all we could make prices infinite, just as we could make the interest rate nil.'[14]

Much of this was contrary to what our problem needed when viewed from the outside or in the light of economic theory. Another phase of the debate began when A Loveday published *Britain and World Trade* (1930) and Professor Robbins *The Great Depression*

---

[13]For details of many of these arrangements see *Britain in Depression* (1934) and *Britain in Recovery* (1938), pub. by the British Association for the Advancement of Science.

[14]*The Times,* 11 Nov. 1932, p. 10b.

(1934). Loveday's book, issued before the critical year of 1931 and written from his outside position at the League of Nations, reminded us of something of which we had not been sufficiently observant, that in 1926–28 Britain was lagging miserably behind in a world which was, on the whole, abundantly prosperous, and that the crisis was not the whole story. With an array of damaging statistics he made it clear how little there was in the illusory explanations with which we had comforted ourselves. The argument that slackened demand in war-impoverished Europe was responsible, he destroyed by showing that our loss of trade was greatest in the countries least affected by the war. Nor was it the competition with countries enjoying the alleged benefits of inflation, for we lost trade both to the financially pure and the financially reprobate. It was not merely or simply the fact of our monetary policy, for other countries following a policy like our own had progressed more than we had done. Though bad organisation in our staple trades added to our difficulties, we had made relatively small progress in the new industries for which we would seem to have been as well adapted as our more successful competitors. He therefore blamed our lack of flexibility, including in this term unimaginative and shortsighted business leadership and over-rigid wage rates.

Robbins also cleared the air of various illusory explanations of the depression after 1929. It was not due to a fall in the general price level, for this was a consequence rather than a cause; nor to deflation, since immediately preceding the crash the banks were creating easy money conditions. He severely attacked the rigidities introduced into the competitive system by inflexible wage rates, trade union restrictions, monopoly prices, output restriction schemes, tariffs, subsidies, quotas, etc. These he regarded as important causes of our relative economic decline and a main reason for the high level of unemployment. There was nothing one sided in his strictures, for bolstering up financial houses, protecting businesses against losses due to their own follies, miscalculations or misfortunes, were condemned as severely as rigid trade union policy. If he demanded reduction of wages, he also prescribed reductions of capital and liquidations for unsound businesses. These two pieces of work definitely established the charge of rigidity brought against our post-war system, and it was no loss to have the principles of free enterprise so clearly set forth.

But there was another side to this, which stirred up other controversies. Amongst economists there had been a movement in which Robbins himself was a leader, to make economic theory more logically consistent and to free it from ethical and value judgements which, whatever their validity and practical usefulness, could not be properly deduced from its fundamental premises. It was strengthened by a revived interest in such works as Wicksteed's *Commonsense of Political Economy* (1910, reprint 1933) and most of all by the stimulus of renewed contact with the work of the older and younger representatives of the Vienna school of economists. There were some theoretical consequences; for example, it had been argued that the law of diminishing marginal utility of income gave support to the view that there would be a gain of satisfaction if incomes were more evenly distributed between rich and poor. This was now rejected by economists of this school on the ground that there were no means of testing or comparing one man's satisfaction with that of another, and therefore that a number of pseudo-scientific generalisations based on the assumption that there were, e.g. that transfers from the rich to the poor would increase total welfare, that a graduated income tax was less injurious than a poll tax, had no *scientific* foundation.[15] Though they might be desirable on ethical or political grounds, many of the prescriptions on economic welfare, which exerted so much influence in 1906–21, were thus thought to be logically undermined.

As thinking along this line developed, the radical and trade unionist felt that not only were the blessings which the welfare economists had given to his policies being withdrawn and the May Committee pressing for reductions in State spending on the social services, but that his traditional means of defending and raising his standard of life were also threatened. Hutt, in his *Theory of Collective Bargaining*,[16] argued that trade union action might be disadvantageous to workers as a whole and lead to an exploitation of both consumers

[15]L Robbins, *Nature and Significance of Economic Science* (1932), pp. 122–5.
[16]W H Hutt, *Theory of Collective Bargaining* (1930).

and non-unionised workers. Hicks, in *The Theory of Wages,* criticised minimum wage legislation and trade union rules on the ground that employers are able to evade and defeat them, that they must lead to a great waste of capital and encourage men to cherish illusions which will be shattered disastrously.[17] Means of preventing temporary exploitation of labour might sometimes be desirable,[18] though exploiting capital was a breach of faith with investors.[19] But certain policies which seemed adverse to capital might cause it to be 'wasted', 'destroyed', 'consumed'—all phrases which, though they had a scientific content, had also, at least to socialists, strong emotional associations. In rejecting the socialist alternative, Hicks argued that it was useless to expect more security than the system could give, and that indeed, the workmen had been relieved of some insecurity because with the division of labour there proceeds a concentration of risks on a small class of entrepreneurs.[20]

The ball was thus back in the trade unionists' and socialists' court. Their first response was the standard socialist case, set out in speech, pamphlet and book. The cogency of these economists' propositions, they argued, depended on whether they were being applied to a society in which property was so widely distributed that it allowed many to have access to entrepreneurship, or to one like the British, which denied it to most. Were workers to accept pleas for flexibility of wages or for 'consumer's sovereignty', if consumers' incomes were based partly on inherited opportunities for attaining better-paid work and partly on inherited investments? 'The price system is perverted by inequality of incomes.'[21] Nor could the great capitalist organisations desist in the search for profitable monopolistic practices without frustrating their whole *raison d'être,* and the financial gains and economic advantages which such group could win by successful political manipulation were too great to prevent them from exercising it. These practices were deeply embedded in the capitalist system and could be removed only by taking over great

---

[17]J Hicks, *Theory of Wages* (1932), pp. 229–32.
[18]J Hicks in *Econ. Jn.* (1931), 146.
[19]Hutt, p. 90.
[20]Hicks, *Theory of Wages,* pp. 198–9, 200, 202, 206, 231–2.
[21]D Jay, *The Socialist Case* (1937), chaps. xxix, xxxii.

areas of industrial property. But here the professional economist had something new to say.[22] For a close examination of the contemporary world of business showed that it was not one of pure competition between many sellers and many buyers, as the early economists had envisaged it, nor of a few big monopolists, as radicals and socialists feared, but rather that these were the two extremes, the outer edges of the wide field of business which lay in between; in this, competitive elements were mixed up with endeavours to create little monopolistic areas by branding products, advertising and other selling costs. The economic disadvantages which arose from this situation called for remedies different from a mere 'take-over'.

The third part of the answer was 'planning'. The capitalistic combinations had justified their monopolistic policies and Ministers their support of them by attacking the 'chaos of competition', the 'waste of competition' and 'ruinous price-cutting'—phrases which occur in numerous reports, evidence, speeches, etc. These charges had always been part of the socialist case, but their remedy was different, and at this date (after the Russian Revolution), they proposed to bring order out of chaos by socialist planning. With their gaze fixed on a million unemployed this, they declared, together with measures designed to equalise incomes (which itself would mitigate the swings of booms and depressions) would enable them to stabilise output and therefore employment.

But planning would involve the State in deciding what must be produced, how much of each class of goods, how much should be saved, what numbers of workers should go into each occupation, etc. On the conditions in which this would be practicable there was a vigorous technical controversy. In a purely competitive society this is not accomplished by conscious social decision, but is the effect of individuals making their own choice of consumption and occupation, taking into account the prices and wages prevailing in the market. How could the State control and give unified direction to the use of all major economic resources on pre-determined economic

---

[22]For example, E Chamberlin, *The Theory of Monopolistic Competition* (1933). Also F Zeuthen, *Problems of Monopoly and Economic Warfare* (1930) and J Robinson, *The Economics of Imperfect Competition* (1933).

and social principles and yet permit what seemed to be the *sine qua non* in a western democracy, free choice of consumption and occupation? The important matter was not what the administrative machinery should be, but the criteria on which multitudinous economic decisions were to be based and how to ensure their mutual consistency. But the Marxist had thought singularly little about this: the inherent forces of capitalism would bring it through the class struggle to the triumph of proletarian revolution. Speculative thinking about what would happen after the 'take over' must be subordinated to the task of understanding and furthering the revolutionary process, and the tasks after victory need not be worried about until it came. There was thus a certain closing of the eyes to these problems. There had been one notable exception. Karl Kautsky, in Part II of his *The Social Revolution* entitled *The Day After the Revolution,* hints at these questions (e.g. pp. 150–6), adding that areas of small industry and production of articles of taste could be left to private business (pp. 158–67). 'Just as little as the needle and thimble, will brush and palette, or ink and pen belong to those means of production which must under all conditions be socialised' (pp. 172).[23] War experience had shown the possibilities and difficulties of extensive State direction, but that problem was relatively easy, in that the Government's criteria were based not on individuals' choices but on the schedule of war requirements decided by itself. The early Russian experiments after 1917 in war, civil war and economic breakdown were at first painful, confused, and involved a degree of coercion not acceptable in the West in peace-time.

But Professor Mises of Vienna brought the discussion to the real economic issues.[24] If there were to be free choice of consumption and occupation, the amount and price of each good produced and the numbers and wages in each trade would thus be derived from individuals' demands; the materials and labour used in the many intermediate stages of their production would have to be moved

[23]The lecture was given in 1902. The references are to the translation published by Kerr (1922 ed.). Another translation, published by *Justice,* I have not seen.

[24]L von Mises, *Economic Calculation in the Socialist Commonwealth* (1920). Reprinted in *Collectivist Economic Planning,* ed. F A Hayek (1935).

into each use in accordance with those demands expressed in prices. How could the central authority plan the use of economic resources without reference to the prices indicated by the sum of these individual demands? If it did, on what basis would the prices of all the intermediate stages be fixed? His conclusion was that an attempt to do it would mean a great waste and mis-direction of effort and that rational economic calculation would be impossible. This was a challenge which could not be ignored. Its importance was shown by the great volume of writing, socialist and other, in an endeavour to meet it, e.g. M Dobb, R H Hall, Barbara Wootton, Douglas Jay. Various solutions were proposed: there might be waste and inefficiency, but this would be a small price to pay for a more just distribution of wealth; consumer's choice could be restricted, e.g. two or three standard types of wireless sets offered at fixed prices instead of a multitude of types; the prices of the basic factors of production could be fixed with or without fixing prices of the final goods and the intermediate prices either estimated or left to sort themselves out. Or one could start with existing prices and work out from them (Kautsky, pp. 151-2). But a sudden drastic redistribution of income might, as in Russia after the second revolution, lead to a collapse in e.g. the price of fine china and other luxuries and a fantastic rise in the price of common necessities, such as boots, because there was no production to meet the demand. Hence, as Jay put it, one could move to more equalitarian society in which most producers would still be working for profit according to the price index, and although consumers would be buying in a free market, powerful economic forces under the control of a central authority would be operating to mitigate inequality.[25]

These technical discussions, serious and engaging to economists if not to the general public, were not trivial dry-as-dust academic pedantry, and though they had little immediate direct bearing on policy, were significant for the future of planning in two ways. First, they turned the attention of socialists and economists to the ideas and problems not of a communist or free enterprise State but of a 'mixed' economy; and this did become a centre of policy.

[25] Jay, *The Socialist Case*, pp. 302-3.

W

Secondly, it was a weakness of the Marxists that, more concerned with the dynamic aspects of society, they had not added to their armoury more of the techniques of the orthodox economists. They may have been good Marxists, but they were not good economists. But this discussion helped to foster a new generation of young economists, such as Durbin and Gaitskell who, though sympathetic to the questions Marx had raised, were also expert in contemporary economic theory as well. These were to become powerful in socialist thinking and in due course to participate in political power. In that phase the old term 'reconstruction' faded out and was replaced by 'planning'.

All this looked like a conflict of irreconcilables, left the public mind in confusion and uncertainty, and was no base from which an effective and widely supported policy could grow. But Keynes's theories brought the issue to new ground. They eventually changed the whole intellectual scene and enabled us to break out of the grim entanglement into new and confidently hopeful possibilities of policy. His work aroused immense discussion amongst economists, some hostile, some sympathetic, some constructive, and it was out of all this that the theory finally emerged. It is easiest to leave aside the specific and often notable contributions of the various economists, e.g. by D H Robertson in *Banking Policy and the Price Level* (1926), and the technical theoretical details, and to trace its growth through Keynes's own work, to note what its implications for policy were and why it became acceptable. Like another great influential theory, that of Bentham, it was thoroughly discussed and worked out within a small expert group, who both developed its implications and spread the doctrine vigorously in books, articles and pamphlets. New theories, if they are to overcome obstacles and survive, often have to be 'put across'. And both at the beginnings of its formulation and its fully developed statement seventeen years later, it tallied with the aspirations of many, including sophisticated intellectuals and the intelligent workmen who might not understand the difficult argument, but sensed from popular versions of it what its implications were.

The story begins with his *Economic Consequences of the Peace*, 1919, a brilliantly written analysis of the state of Europe after the war.

Europe was in grave peril, he felt, and not merely through temporary dislocations. Under *laissez-faire* the capitalist system had been driven forward by the great growth of population, the immense opportunities of investment created by technical improvements and the discovery of new natural resources. The rich grew even richer, though only on the condition that they did not consume their riches, but saved and invested the major portion of them. But the war had brought these favourable conditions to an end and economic stagnation was a real possibility. The book received an immense welcome from the radicals, pacifists and socialists who hated the war settlement and the 'old men' who had failed to lead Europe to a better life. In terms of economic theory its analysis was simple and the details straightforward. But by 1923 he turned to the English problem, dominated as it was by the apparently irreducible level of mass unemployment, by rigid costs and rigid institutions. This presented a crucial theoretical problem, for classical theory had assumed that the economic system had an in-built tendency to move towards full employment. If employment were at a lower level, various adjustments of wages and interest rates would occur to restore it. Some held that theoretically, completely plastic wages would, in the absence of monopolies, eliminate unemployment. But the current facts were in plain contradiction to this; the system seemed to have come to rest at some kind of equilibrium with unemployment at a high, mass level. Why was this? It could not be explained by mere economic frictions.

Keynes tried to answer. In 1923 in the *Tract on Monetary Reform* he now added some more elaborate theory. If rigidities cannot be reduced, then we must turn to monetary management and choose, not as we had done traditionally, stable foreign exchanges, which might require difficult internal adjustments, but stable internal prices. A return to gold would put a great strain on our inflexible economy. This reversed the Cunliffe and Vassar-Smith prescriptions. But it still left the fundamental questions unanswered. The classical economists had concentrated their attention on the principles governing the allocation of resources to alternative uses: what they had not considered was the theory of output as a whole and its relation to the theory of money. This Keynes now attempted in *Treatise*

311

on Money, 1930, a work full of vital technical matters, but still short of the answer. But he did make one important move essential to it. The classical economists had assumed that if voluntary savings exceeded voluntary 'investment' (i.e. outlay on capital equipment, stocks, etc.), the rate of interest would fall and investment would be stimulated to fill the gap. He now argued that this need not happen, for the decision to save and the decision to invest were made by different people.

These themes were pursued in his comments on Lloyd George's plan in *We Can Conquer Unemployment* for a large loan expenditure of £250 millions for public works; in the famous Memo issued by the Treasury opposing it,[26] which declared that if inflation were to be avoided, the capital could be raised only by diverting it from other uses and raising the rate of interest; in Kahn's explanation of the multiplier;[27] in Keynes's part in the Macmillan Committee on *Finance and Industry,*[28] 1931, and addendum to the Report; and in the *Means of Prosperity,* 1933, where, pointing out the absurdity of the shortage of houses whilst there were 250,000 building operatives out of work, he explained how by the mechanism of the multiplier loan expenditure would generate an increase in the national income and employment.

In 1936 came the final statement in *The General Theory of Employment, Interest and Money.* This was not a popular book, but one addressed to economists, though its sales were fantastic. By the aid of the new concepts of 'propensity to consume', 'marginal efficiency of capital' and 'liquidity preference' he put his contentions into rigorous form. Briefly, employment depends on effective demand, on spending; and spending may be on consumption goods or via saving on 'investment', i.e. outlay on capital equipment, stocks of material, etc. The former gave employment, but because the decision to save and the decision to invest were made by different people, saving might, but need not. The amount the community

---

[26]*Certain Proposals Relating to Unemployment,* Memo. 1929; 1928–29, Cmd. 3331, xvi.
[27]See above, p. 287.
[28]*Finance and Industry,* Cttee. Mins. of ev., vol. II; 1931, non-Parl. See also evidence of Hopkins, qq. 5565–689.

as a whole decides to save depends on total income and its distribution and on people's propensity to consume, while the amount business men decide to invest depends not on savings but on their expectations of profits and their preference for liquidity, their view of the balance of advantage between holding money and capital outlay. The rate of interest is settled, not by the rate of saving, but by business men's preference for liquidity. This means that when people's desire to save exceeds the amount business people decide to invest, the rate of interest does not do what classical economic theory had assumed it would, automatically fall so that expansion is encouraged and employment restored. On the contrary, there will be redundant stocks, profits will fall and orders will be reduced until the level of output and incomes falls to a new level on which savings at that level equal investment. The rate of interest can thus just remain stuck at a level inconsistent with full employment, and the actual volume of employment also remain stuck at some level below it. Once it is at such a level, only an increase in investment or an increase in the propensity to consume can raise the level of output and employment. The variable which brings savings into equilibrium with investment is thus not the rate of interest, but the level of employment.

From this analysis it would be possible to draw many new prescriptions for remedying mass unemployment. This would not be done by reducing money wages or by the widely indiscriminate reduction of State spending proposed by the May Committee; and in some circumstances it might be best not to raise, but to lower the rate of interest to a figure which would stimulate capital investment; the Treasury objection to public works by loan expenditure was unsound. To prevent mass unemployment total outlay must be maintained; if it fell, Government action to raise it by increasing investment or increasing the propensity to consume through a redistribution of income might be required.

There was no parallel in the history of economics for the attention which, after some hesitation, the work was given; economists all over the world examined it paragraph by paragraph, discussed it, poured out articles and books about it. In its development it had encountered sharp criticisms—in England, especially by those who had been influenced by the Vienna school represented by Hayek. Some eminent economists were still sceptical for some time after its publication: it was based on a short-run analysis and argued on rigid assumptions; they found gaps in the chain of reasoning, and it involved a new way of looking at things. It was published in 1936 and three years later the trials and distractions of the Second World War were upon us. Yet out of the discussions, by 1944 Keynes's ideas had found their way into official policy, in Britain in the White Paper on *Employment Policy*[29] and by 1945 in similar official Canadian and Australian White Papers. For a technical economic book to have been so decisive in the formation of major State policy in so short a time there was no previous example. It was apt for the British problem, was developed and pushed by a closely-knit group, and helped on its way by the attention of critics as well as supporters.

It was potent in two other ways. Several basic concepts—income, saving, investment, consumption, employment, the foreign balance, etc. were quantitative, and economists and statisticians had been slowly and spasmodically trying to collect and improve statistics about them. But these had now a new functional relationship and the statistics therefore a new meaning. They became a powerful aid to analysis and vital guide lines to policy, soon found their way into the Chancellor's budget speeches, and by 1941 into the material printed for Members to show the numerical basis of his policy.[30] There was a new sense of possessing what could be made an effective means of social control. Then the theories brought a great sense of intellectual release, and seemed to lead to the Delectable Mountains from which a new world could be glimpsed. For if the major problem of unemployment could be got out of the way, the limits it had imposed on other lines of social advance also disappeared. Theory had suggested that the problem of the difference between low wages in the export trades and the higher wages in the sheltered trade should be remedied by a transfer of labour from one to the

[29]Statement; 1943–44, Cmd. 6527, viii.

[30]*Sources of War Finance, an Estimate of the National Income*, 1938, 1940, 1941; 1941–42, Cmd. 6347, ix.

other,[31] and that provided the surplus workers in the over-stocked trades were spread over the country and in other occupations, they could be absorbed without throwing others out of work. A large voluntary transfer did take place, but it left derelict areas with large, permanent unemployment. The fact is that we did not know how to contract great localised staple industries. The organised transfer of labour brought but modest relief.[32] How could one, without opposition, push labour to areas of lower unemployment, if in fact their own unemployment were still above their 'normal'? So there were inquiries into the exact size of the labour surplus in the derelict areas.[33] Public works in these districts which created 'a temporary, artificial and substitute employment market' were rejected.[34] Transfer other new industries to these areas? Not easy in a background of unemployment: compulsion was rejected, spontaneous growth of viable new industries being the only solution. At least the growth of new industries round London could be stopped, so that these sought other locations.[35] In conditions of full employment controlled location of new industrial development now seemed possible. This also found its way into official policy. What were we to do with a man when he had exhausted his statutory unemployment benefit? Try to determine if he were genuinely seeking work, as the Blanesburgh Committee suggested?[36] Subject him to a household means test, as the Royal Commission on *Unemployment Insurance* proposed?[37] Yet the only real test was to offer him a job—and that could not be done if there were no jobs to offer. There now seemed hope of securing something like full employment and that all this,

[31]Clay, *The Problem of Industrial Relations,* chap. v. *Finance and Industry,* Cttee. Mins. of ev. (Pigou), qq. 5949, 5978; 1931, non-Parl.

[32]*Industrial Transference,* Bd. Rep.; 1928, Cmd. 3156, x. *Special Areas in Scotland,* 4th Rep.; 1937-38, Cmd. 5604, xiii.

[33]*Industrial Surveys,* S.W. Scotland, Merseyside, Lancashire, S. Wales, all 1932, non-Parl.

[34]*Industrial Transference,* 1928, Cmd. 3156, x. *Investigations . . . into Certain Depressed Areas,* Rep. iii, S. Wales; 1933-34, Cmd. 4728, xiii.

[35]*Investigations . . . into Certain Depressed Areas,* Rep. iv, Scotland; 1933-34, Cmd. 4728, xiii. *Special Areas (England and Wales),* 3rd Rep.; 1936, Cmd. 5303, xii.

[36]*Unemployment Insurance,* Dept. Cttee.; 1927, non-Parl.

[37]*Unemployment Insurance,* R. Com. 1st Rep. See also Minority Rep.; 1931-32, Cmd. 4185, xiii. *Breviate,* II, pp. 377-80.

on which so much sincere effort and thought had been expended, with the heart-breaking difficulties, distress and bitterness, could be swept away.

The change of atmosphere also helped indirectly to ease the path for advances in the social services which had hitherto been blocked. The plans for the scientific organisation of the hospital services which had been outlined by the Consultative Council,[38] the severance of insurance medical benefits from cash benefits so that they could be expanded, as proposed by Newsholme and supported by the Minority Report of the Royal Commission on *Health Insurance*,[39] had their own powerful, expert and popular support not related to the problem of unemployment. Many other ideas and pressures led to the Beveridge Plan for the social insurances (1942) in which another master in his field gathered up proposals for change and expansion urged by social workers and investigators.[40] These projects faced the opposition of strong groups interested in the *status quo* in ideas and institutions and political courage was needed. But behind the resistance had been the fear of adding fresh burdens to Government spending; and this was now seen in a new light. For though the Statutory Committee on *Unemployment Insurance* of which Beveridge was the chairman, had in their Reports for 1935–40 been compelled to rest their various recommendations on unemployment levels of 16 per cent, 15 per cent, 13 per cent and so on, by the date of the plan he was able to base his scheme on the assumption of an unemployment level of $8\frac{1}{2}$ per cent.[41]

Of course it was not as easy as all that. Theories of this kind rarely, if ever, cover all the possibilities; and the unceasing changes in society create new problems and demand new criteria for adequate policy. The Keynesian doctrine had to be filled in; he himself did this for its international aspects in his work on the Bretton Woods agreement. He indicated the way out of the depression; what we later

[38]See above, p. 246.

[39]See above, p. 173. *National Health Insurance*, R. Com. Rep.; 1926, Cmd. 2596, xiv.

[40]See Beveridge's early booklet, *Insurance for All and Everything* (1924). P Ford, 'The Beveridge Report—A Commentary' in *Social Welfare* (Jan. 1943).

[41]*Financial Condition of the Unemployment Fund*, Reps. Breviate, II, 383–5.

failed to do was to find the way out of the inflationary booms which arise in over-full employment. Beveridge, who had followed up his public report on social security with a private one on *Full Employment in a Free Society* (1944), now aimed at a 3 per cent only of unemployment, but emphasised that the accomplishment of this was dependent on the willingness of strongly organised business groups not to meet the increased demand by raising prices instead of by more production, and of trade unions to refrain from competitive sectional wage bargaining which set up a spiral of rising prices, and to develop some kind of unified wage policy which took account of the situation as a whole. The difficulties of forecasting, let alone controlling, the behaviour of the major economic quantities proved greater than was anticipated.[42] And the task required a new administrative organisation and some changes in the outlook and training in the civil servants involved. But these troubles lay in the future.

Data, theory and the shaping of policy were at last being drawn together, and there was wanting only the idealism stimulated by revulsion from the calamity of war and by favourable political circumstances to provide the drive for an endeavour to put it into practice. Liberal, radical and socialist reformers now saw the opportunity of making substantial social changes by democratic means, instead of by a long social struggle doubtful in outcome. They could be achieved by intelligence. The epilogue to a failure thus became the prologue to a success.

[42]See, e.g., E Devons, 'Planning by Economic Survey' in *Economica* (Aug. 1952), and R Tress, 'The Contribution of Economic Theory to Economic Prognostication' in *Economica* (Aug. 1959).

INDEX

Index

Beales, H L, 49-50
Bechofer, C E, 213
Becker, C, 16
Bell, Lady Florence E E, 105
Belloc, H, 111, 125, 179, 213
Benbow, W, 26
Bentham, J, 13, 16, 79, 278
  central administration and, 28-32, 55-7,
  260
Bentinck, Lord William, 27n.
betterment, 62, 65, 189
Beveridge, W H, 1st Baron, 21, 45, 80, 94,
  98, 122n., 123, 136, 158, 159, 160, 161,
  163, 202, 207n., 208, 236, 237, 285n.,
  316
Bevin, Ernest, 221, 235
Birchenough, H, 231
Black, Clementina, 137
Black, D, 301n.
Black Book, The, 13, 20n., 27
Blackley, William, 87
Blackstone, William, 17
Blanesburgh, R Y, Baron, 315
Blatchford, Robert, 109
Blockley, C, 27n.
Boards of Guardians, 31, 95, 99, 167, 168,
  175, 180-5, *passim* 279
Boards of Health, 29, 31
Boer War, 86, 96, 101, 124, 206
Bonar Law, A, 281
Bondfield, Margaret, 209
Bonn, M J, 271
Booth, Charles, 34, 48, 70, 79-86, 89, 94,
  97, 99, 105, 123, 130, 139, 181, 258
  assessment of, 83-6
Booth, F W, 178n.
Booth, W, 44
Bosanquet, H, 48n.
Bowden, W, 4
Bowley, A L, 85, 106n., 107, 107n., 158,
  193, 255n., 286
Bowley, M, 26n.
Bowring, J, 11
Brace, W, 143n.
Bradbury, J., 122
Braithwaite, W J, 122, 169, 202
Brassey, T, 89
Bray, J F, 33
Brend, W A, 107n., 172n., 173
Brentano, L, 21n., 22n.
Bretton Woods, 316
British Association, 52, 158, 164n.

British Socialist Party, 109n., 249
Broadhurst, Henry, 46, 47, 49n., 89, 127n.
Brodrick, G, 99n.
Brougham, H P, Baron, 29
Brown, E H, Phelps, 54, 66n.
Bryce, James, 1st Viscount, 259
Buccleuch, 5th Duke of, 55
Budget League, 190
Budget Protest League, 190
Buer, M C, 10n.
*Building Construction . . . Dwellings for the
  Working Classes,* Cttee., 241
Building Industry after the War, Cttee., 220,
  242, 277
building societies, 79
Bulkley, M E, 176n.
Buller, C, 29
Bunbury, Henry, 122
Burdett, Sir Francis, 9
Burke, E, 30
Burns, E, 140n., 141n.
Burns, John, 94, 126, 170n.
Burt, Thomas, 47, 69, 73, 75, 78, 104n.
Bussell, F W, 112

Cabinet:
  Committees of, 219
  inner, 260
Cable Communications, Inter-Dept. Cttee.,
  196n.
Cairnes, J E, 52, 73
Campbell, J R, 214
Campbell-Bannerman, Sir Henry, 127n.,
  147
canals, 197, 198, 199, 225, 227
Canals and Waterways, R.Com., 197n., 198,
  227
Cannan, E, 18n., 116, 186, 190, 207, 208,
  264, 297
Canning, George, 27n.
capital, lack of, 8, 26, 55
capital issues, 268
capital levy, 288-93, 296
Care and Control of the Feebleminded,
  R.Com., 177, 178, 179
Carlile, R, 9
Carlyle, A J, 114
Carlyle, T, 43, 109
Carmichael, J, 220, 242, 276
Carpenter, E, 45

Index

Index

Index

Index

Squire, Miss R E, 158
Stamp, J, 291
standard of living, 110-1 *see also* cost-of-living; poverty
Stanley, E L, 64
state, role of, 42-3, 47, 70, 85, 118, 132, 182, 196n., 202, 206-8
  see also under separate headings, e.g. economic planning; health insurance; nationalisation; pensions; public works; wages, legal minimum; unemployment insurance, etc.
State of Large Towns and Populous Districts, R.Com., 55, 102, 106
Statistical Abstract, 11-12
statistics, collection of, 11-12, 50, 51, 54, 70, 92-3, 105-6, 314
Statute of Artificers, 15
Steel-Maitland, A D, 158
Stevenson, R L, 112
Stigler, G J, 15, 18
Straker, W, 215, 229-30, 257n.
strikes, 34, 68, 73, 138, 144, 150-1, 153-4, 155-6, 214, 252, 254, 283
  blacklegging and, 151-2, 155, 162
  general, 23, 26, 283, 301
  public utility services, 153, 154, 155, 249, 254
  state intervention, 151, 155, 248
  see also disputes, industrial; *Labour,* R.Com., disputes and
subnormality *see* mental deficiency
Sumner, 1st Viscount, 254
super-tax, 187-8
surveys, social *see* social surveys
sweated trades, 137-41, 282
Sweating System, Sel. Cttee., 55, 66-7, 73, 74, 77, 85, 103, 105, 137

Taff Vale judgement, 144, 151
Tariff Reform League, 125
tariffs, 125, 238, 268, 271, 278
Tawney, R H, 45, 113, 139n., 211, 220
taxation 132, 187-91, 300-1
  income tax, 132, 186-8
  land values, 189-91
  local, 189-91
  new sources of, 188-91
  super-tax, 187, 187n., 188
  war debt and, 288-93

Taylor, A J P, 34n.
Taylor, Helen, 110n.
telegraphs, national ownership of, 196n.
Temple, William, archbishop, 112, 113, 217
theological criticism and social conditions, 112-16
Thomas, C J Howell, 191n.
Thomas, J H, 155n., 221
Thompson, E P, 48n.
Thompson, H M, 73
Thompson, W, 23, 33, 200
Thomson, C E Poulett, 11, 12n.
Thorne, W, 149n.
Thornton, W T, 73
Tillett, Ben, 46n., 47, 56n., 74, 149n.
Times, The, 68, 71, 138n., 303
Torrens, R, 16, 19, 63
Town Holdings, Sel.Cttee., 65n.
Town Improvements (Betterment,) Sel.Cttee. 63n.
town planning, 22, 131
towns:
  growth of, 5,7
  see also health; housing; sanitation, town planning
Toynbee, A, 4, 46, 190n.
Toynbee Hall 123, 123n., 160n., 184n
Tozer, W, 97n., 162
Trade, Board of, 92, 139, 152, 197, 219, 233, 234, 234-5, 236
trade boards, 139-40, 252, 253, 282
Trade Boards Act, 1909, 139, 140, 141
Trade Boards Act, 1918, 253n., 282
Trade Boards Acts, Cttee., 282
trade combinations *see* monopolies
trade cycles, theory of, 11, 51-2, 53, 54, 77, 93-4, 99, 159, 203, 285
Trade Disputes Act, 1906, 144, 147
Trade Disputes and Trade Combinations, R.Com., 144-7, 151n., 153n.
Trade Union Act, 1871, 145
trade unions, 16, 18, 39, 42, 44, 45, 66, 172
  autonomy of branches, 48
  blacklegging and, 149, 151, 155, 162
  collective bargaining and, 75, 150, 152
  constitutional problems, 150
  in other countries, 153
  industrial relations and, 99
  industrial safety and, 91-2

333

Index